Mosdos Press Literature

CORAL

Mosdos Press
CLEVELAND, OHIO

EDITOR-IN-CHIEF
Judith Factor

EXECUTIVE EDITOR
Libby Spero

CREATIVE/ART DIRECTOR
Carla Martin

CURRICULUM
Jill Brotman

SENIOR EDITOR
Abigail Rozen

COPY EDITOR
Laya Dewick

LESSONS IN LITERATURE
Tim Tibbits

TEXT AND CURRICULUM ADVISOR
Rabbi Ahron Dovid Goldberg

ISBN # 0-9742160-4-6
ISBN # 978-0-9742160-4-1 Student Edition

ANTHOLOGY SERIES

RUBY

CORAL

PEARL

JADE

GOLD

JOURNEYS

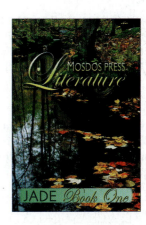

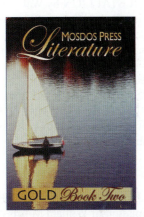

acknowledgments

ILLUSTRATORS

Tsippora Degani: *The Black Stallion, The Whimbrel*

Aviva Gross: *Afternoon on a Hill, The Birds' Peace, The Eagle, Figures in the Field Against the Sky, My House, Waking*

George Kocar: *The Greatest Snowball Fight in History, A Niche in the Kitchen, The Quangle Wangle's Hat, The Speckled Hen's Egg, The Street Boy, The Streets are Free*

Eva Martin: *Kate Shelley*

Lydia Martin: *The Day of the Turtle*

Sue McDonald: *74th Street, Hattie's Birthday Box, Kate Shelley, The Memory Box, Truth, The Whippoorwill Calls*

Leah Neustadter: *The Butterfly and the Caterpillar*

UNIT ONE

Samuel's Choice
SAMUEL'S CHOICE by Richard Berleth. Text copyright © 1990 by Richard J. Berleth. Reprinted by permission of Albert Whitman & Company. All rights reserved.

Slower Than the Rest
Reprinted with the permission of Simon & Schuster Books for Young Readers, an imprint of Simon & Schuster Children's Publishing Division from EVERY LIVING THING by Cynthia Rylant. Copyright © 1985 Cynthia Rylant.

Kate Shelley
KATE SHELLY written by Robert San Souci and illustrated by Max Ginsburg. Text copyright © 1995. Published by arrangement with Dial Books for Young Readers, a member of Penguin Group (USA) Inc.

New Providence
NEW PROVIDENCE: A CHANGING CITYSCAPE copyright © 1987 by Renata von Tscharner and Ronald Lee Fleming and The Townscape Institute, Inc., illustrations copyright © 1987 by The Townscape Institute, Inc. and Denis Orloff, reprinted by permission of Harcourt, Inc.

The Silent Lobby
"The Silent Lobby" by Mildred Pitts Walter; reprinted by permission of the author.

To a Daughter Leaving Home
"To a Daughter Leaving Home", from THE IMPERFECT PARADISE by Linda Pastan. Copyright © 1988 by Linda Pastan. Used by permission of W. W. Norton & Company, Inc.

Whatif
From A LIGHT IN THE ATTIC by SHEL SILVERSTEIN. COPYRIGHT © 1981 BY EVIL EYE MUSIC, INC. Used by permission of HarperCollins Publishers.

The Whippoorwill Calls
"The Whippoorwill Calls" first appeared in *Cobblestone*, February, 1981. Reprinted by permission of the author.

UNIT TWO

Gold-Mounted Guns
Copyright © 1922 by F. R. Buckley. Reprinted by permission of Curtis Brown, Ltd.

The Disappearing Man
"The Disappearing Man" by Isaac Asimov, from Boys' Life, June 1978; copyright © 1978, Boy Scouts of America, published by permission of The Estate of Isaac Asimov c/o Ralph M. Vicinanza, Ltd.

The Speckled Hen's Egg
From THE TALKING CAT AND OTHER STORIES OF FRENCH CANADA by NATALIE SAVAGE CARLSON. COPYRIGHT © 1952 BY NATALIE SAVAGE CARLSON. Used by permission of HarperCollins Publishers.

The Black Stallion
From THE BLACK STALLION by Walter Farley, copyright 1941 by Walter Farley. Copyright renewed 1969 by Walter Farley. Used by permission of Random House Children's Books, a division of Random House, Inc.

By the Shores of Silver Lake
BY THE SHORES OF SILVER LAKE BY LAURA INGALLS WILDER. TEXT COPYRIGHT 1939, 1967 Little House Heritage Trust. Used by permission of HarperCollins Publishers.

UNIT THREE

One Throw
Copyright © 1950, renewed 1978 by W. C. Heinz Reprinted by permission of William Morris Agency, Inc. on behalf of the Author.

The Birds' Peace
"The Birds' Peace" from *The Big Book for Peace* © 1990, reprinted by permission of Mr. Ted Rand.

Hattie's Birthday Box
From BIRTHDAY SURPRISES: TEN GREAT STORIES
EDITED by JOHANNA HURWITZ. BIRTHDAY SUR-
PRISES COPYRIGHT © 1995 BY JOHANNA HUR-
WITZ. Used by permission of HarperCollins Publishers.

I Am Winding Through a Maze
From IT'S RAINING PIGS AND NOODLES. TEXT
COPYRIGHT © 2000 BY JACK PRELUTSKY. Used by
permission of HarperCollins Publishers.

74th Street
From THE MALIBU AND OTHER POEMS by Myra
Cohn Livingston. Copyright © 1972 by Myra Cohn
Livingston. Used by permission of Marian Reiner.

Unit Four

The Day of the Turtle
From THE WRECK OF THE ZANZIBAR by Michael
Morpurgo, illustrated by Francois Place, copyright ©
1995 by Michael Morpurgo, text. Used by permission of
Viking Penguin, A Division of Penguin Young Readers
Group, A Member of Penguin Group (USA) Inc., 345
Hudson Street, New York, NY 10014. All rights reserved.

Prairie Fire
TEXT COPYRIGHT 1935, 1963 Little House Heritage
Trust. Used by permission of HarperCollins Publishers.

The Streets are Free
© First printed in Spanish by Ediciones EkarÈ, Caracas,
Venezuela, Original Title: La calle es libre

One Day in the Desert
ONE DAY IN THE DESERT by JEAN CRAIGHEAD
GEORGE. TEXT COPYRIGHT © 1983 BY JEAN
CRAIGHEAD GEORGE. Used by permission of
HarperCollins Publishers.

Choose a Color
© 1993, 1994 by Jacqueline Sweeney. All rights reserved.
Reprinted by permission of Marian Reiner for the author.

For Crows and Jays
"For Crows and Jays" first appeared in *Cricket*,
November, 2000. Reprinted by permission of the author.

One Day
"One Day" first appeared in *Cricket*, November, 2002.
Reprinted by permission of the author.

A City Ditty
From A POEM FOR A PICKLE by Eve Merriam.
Copyright © 1989 Eve Merriam. Used by permission of
Marian Reiner.

Unit Five

The Memory Box
THE MEMORY BOX by Mary Bahr. Text copyright
©1992 by Mary Bahr. Reprinted by permission of Albert
Whitman & Company. All rights reserved.

Founders of the Children's Rain Forest
"The Founders of the Children's Rain Forest" from IT'S
OUR WORLD, TOO! by Phillip Hoose. Copyright ©
2002 by Phillip Hoose. Reprinted by permission of Farrar,
Straus and Giroux, LLC.

Jessica Govea
"Jessica Govea: Education of a Union Organizer" from
WE WERE THERE, TOO! by Phillip Hoose. Copyright
© 2001 by Phillip Hoose. Reprinted by permission of
Farrar, Straus, and Giroux, LLC.

The Street Boy
*From MIRROR, MIRROR: TWISTED TALES by Norman
Silver. Published by The Chicken House/Scholastic Inc.
Copyright © by Silverman. Reprinted by permission of
Scholastic Inc.*

Waking
From I FEEL THE SAME WAY by Lilian Moore.
Copyright © 1967 Lilian Moore. Copyright renewed and
reserved. Reprinted by permission of Marian Reiner for
the author.

Unit Six

Small Steps
SMALL STEPS: THE YEAR I GOT POLIO by Peg
Kehret. Text copyright © 1996 by Peg Kehret. Excerpt
reprinted by permission of Albert Whitman & Company.
All rights reserved.

What a Wild Idea
With permission of Louis Sabin (text) and Christine
Mortensen (illustrations) and *Boys' Life*, September 1990,
published by the Boy Scouts of America.

Flight Into Danger
"Flight Into Danger" by Arthur Hailey; reprinted by permission of the author.

Passage to Freedom
Passage to Freedom: The Sugihara Story Text copyright ©
1997 by Ken Mochizuki. Permission arranged with LEE
& LOW BOOKS Inc., New York, NY 10016.

unit 1

COURAGE

unit 2

GROWING

CONTENTS

unit 3

AIMING HIGH

unit 4

THE WORLD AROUND US

CONTENTS

unit 5

FINDING OUT WHAT'S INSIDE

unit 6

THE GRAND FINALÉ

CONTENTS

unit 1

COURAGE

WHAT IS A STORY?

- A story has four elements: plot, character, setting, and theme.

- The **plot** is the action of the story. It is what happens to the characters from the beginning to the end of the story.

- The **characters** are the people, animals, or even objects (for example, robots) that the story is about. The action happens to, or is caused by, the characters in the story.

- The **setting** is the time and place in which the story's events occur. The setting may be described in great detail or hardly at all. When you remember a story, you almost always remember its setting.

- The **theme** is the main idea presented in the story. It is the idea that the author wishes to present through the plot, characters, and setting.

THINK ABOUT IT!

1. Can you summarize the story's plot in one sentence? Try it!

2. The story is really about three characters. Who are they?

3. Where does the main character live? What time of day is it? What is the weather like? Does the action take place indoors or outside? Together, these details make up the setting of the story.

4. In your opinion, who is the most important person in this story? What is his connection to the main idea, or theme, of the story?

To Know Freedom

Robert stood on what looked like a narrow stone path, only the path didn't go anywhere. Instead, it made a hexagon on the ground.

Robert reread the directions Grandpa had scrawled from memory.

Follow picket fence out back to white gazebo with wrought iron trim.

"Gazebo." That was a word he'd had to look up. "A free-standing, roofed, usually open-sided structure providing a shady resting place."*

Where was that gazebo? Except for the abandoned farmhouse and the rickety picket fence, Robert didn't see any structure of any sort.

Not being certain where he was made Robert uneasy. How much more frightening his great-great grandfather's journey must have been to this same spot, heading north from Virginia to this Pennsylvania town.

Frustrated and hot from the late afternoon sun, Robert plopped down on the grass in the center of the hexagon. No shade here.

Shade! That was it!

Suddenly Robert realized that he was in the exact right spot. He had found the gazebo—or where it used to be. Someone must've torn down the gazebo's structure. The stone hexagon was the foundation.

He leaped to his feet.

From the center of the gazebo, head due north 150 paces.

Grandpa had told him countless times the way his own grandfather had used the moss on the trees, the wind, and the North Star to keep his course on his journey to freedom.

Robert looked up at the sun. At 4 p.m. the sun would be to the west. Robert turned north and started counting steps.

At 120 Robert noticed a small cluster of simple stone grave markers peeking out amid tall weeds up ahead. He broke into a trot.

Pushing aside the weeds, Robert found the headstone he was looking for. Tearing a sheet of paper from his notebook, he held the paper up to the stone and began rubbing with the edge of his pencil. Slowly, the inscription came into view:

"Here lies Nathan R. Smith,

Who by the Grace of the Almighty

Lived to Know Freedom."

Grandpa was going to be very proud!

---

* Definition from *The American Heritage Dictionary.* Second College Edition. Boston: Houghton Mifflin, 1982.

INTO . . . *Samuel's Choice*

Samuel is 14 years old. He is a slave in Brooklyn, New York, at the time of the American Revolution. He sees American soldiers losing in a battle with the British. Samuel has his master's boat; he could help rescue wounded soldiers. But Americans have made his people slaves. Freedom from the British will not mean freedom for slaves. Samuel must decide whether to risk his life to save George Washington's soldiers, or simply stand and watch the fight.

When you have finished the story, think about whether Samuel has made the right choice. What would have become of him had he remained loyal to Isaac van Ditmas? What would he have thought of himself if he had remained "neutral," refusing or afraid to help either side?

EYES ON . . . *Historical Fiction*

This is a story that *might* have occurred in Brooklyn, New York in 1776. The background and some of the details are true. The Revolutionary War, fought between the American colonies and England did, of course, take place. It is a fact, too, that in 1776, one-third of the people in Brooklyn were slaves. However, the characters and the plot of *Samuel's Choice* are **fictional**, that is to say, made up by the author. Stories whose backgrounds are true but whose plot and characters are made up, are called **historical fiction**. *Samuel's Choice* is a good story with interesting characters. The time and place are clearly described. Samuel makes a difficult choice. This is a story of hope.

Samuel's Choice

Richard Berleth

My master, Isaac van Ditmas, was a very rich farmer. In my fourteenth year, he bought me from his old aunt in Flushing and took me from my parents to work as a slave in his flour mill on Gowanus' Creek in Brooklyn. That same time he bought Sana Williams, Toby, and others to keep the gardens and kitchen of his big house on New York Harbor.

At the end of Long Island, the Heights of Brooklyn overlook the East River and Manhattan Island. To the south lay the town of Brooklyn; it was only a small one in those days. The long South Road ran across Long Island's hills, through fields of wheat and rye, connecting Brooklyn town with the Narrows at the entrance to New York Harbor.

Gowanus Creek, where the flour mill stood, wound out of this harbor into the green fields and lost itself in ponds and marshes. On a summer evening, the mosquitoes rose like clouds from still waters and settled, stinging, on our bare arms and necks.

---

1. Gowanus (guh WAH nuss)

The Grist Mill

Farmer Isaac was a strict man. Our day began at sunrise and ended when the light faded. Round and round the great stone wheel[2] rolled and rumbled all day long, driven by tides flowing in and out of the creek. We ground wheat to make bread at the mill. We shoveled the flour into bags, and loaded the bags into boats, to be brought to bakers in Manhattan. But little bread we ever saw. Van Ditmas was a stingy man. Many nights I went to bed with my stomach growling and only the taste of the raw flour on my lips.

When Farmer Isaac saw that I had grown strong and could row a boat well, he taught me about the currents that flow between Brooklyn and Manhattan, about setting a sail and holding a course. I was to row Mrs. van Ditmas and her daughters over to Manhattan, or down the Brooklyn shore to Staten Island across the harbor. Isaac shook me by the collar and warned me never to row or sail except where he sent me. I was his property, according to the laws of the Crown Colony,[3] and he could do what he wanted with me.

Work you do not choose to do is always tiring. And even the house slaves, who labored in Farmer Isaac's kitchen, got little sleep and less food. Whenever I felt the fresh sea breeze on my face, I would look up at the gulls flying where they pleased and I would dream. I wondered how it was to be free like them, to go where I wanted.

---

2. *The great stone wheel* was part of the mill that milled or ground the wheat into flour. The mill was built next to a stream; the force of the water caused the millwheel to turn. The millwheel was attached to a pair of heavy round stones. The wheat was placed between the stones and, when the stones turned, the wheat was crushed and ground into flour.

3. A colony is a country that is governed by another country. Before the Revolutionary War, America was a colony of England. Since the government of England was often referred to as *the Crown*, America is called here, a *Crown Colony*.

America, being ruled by the king of England, was not a separate colony. And these were troubled times in all the colonies. The night came when Manhattan Island[4] was lit up like daytime with a hundred bonfires. We gathered on the steps of the great house and heard the cheers and shouts echo over the water. Then came the sound of drums and fifes,[5] songs and cannon firing.

"What's all that racket over there?" Sana asked.

"That's the sound of people going free," old Toby answered. "Free from the king of England. Free from the likes of van Ditmas."

"How they get free, Toby?"

"Why they up and said they was free, girl, and wrote those words down on paper."

Sana laughed. "You gotta do more than say you're free. That king and Isaac, do they care what anybody say?"

What was it, I wondered, that made people think they could change their lives? They called their freedom "liberty," and they marched through Brooklyn town cheering for that liberty.

When the Sons of Liberty[6] finally came, waving their flags, Isaac locked us in the house.

In the kitchen, the servants argued. "Liberty ain't for Africans," one said. "And it got nothin' to do with us," another said.

But Sana just shook her head. She was fifteen and had been to school. She could write her name and could read. "Nobody here's gonna be free unless they take the risk. Open your eyes! War is coming to Brooklyn 'tween that English king and those Sons of Liberty. We can't say who'll win. We can't say how many black slaves are ever gonna get free. But one thing is sure—it's never gonna happen under Isaac van Ditmas."

---

4. Although most people think of Manhattan as simply one section (or borough) of New York City, actually, Manhattan is cut off from the rest of New York City by water. That is why it is referred to here as *Manhattan Island*.
5. Up until modern times, most armies had a small band that played lively music for the soldiers as they marched into battle. The two instruments most often played were *drums and fifes*. A fife is a high-pitched flute.
6. The *Sons of Liberty* were the American patriots who fought the British during the Revolutionary War.

The talk made my head spin. One moment it seemed to offer hope, and then the arguments turned and I didn't feel hope anymore. One day Liberty men nailed a proclamation to a tree by the South Road. But before anyone could tell me what it said, Isaac came and tore it down and stamped on it in the dust. That was the day Sana promised she would teach me to read. "That writing, Samuel," she said later, "was the Declaration of Independence, made by Thomas Jefferson in the Congress at Philadelphia."

So the summer of 1776, my fourteenth one, passed on. Day by day, my back and arms grew stronger with hard work. More than once I looked up from filling flour sacks to find a cool jar of buttermilk left by Sana. Then I'd drink the milk and fill the empty jar with flour. When she fetched the jar back, she would hide it. One day I asked what she wanted with so much flour. She just smiled and said, "That flour will be bread for our freedom day."

While I sailed on Farmer Isaac's errands or loaded sacks of flour, the war crept towards Brooklyn. On a fine morning we woke in the slave quarters to the thunder of great guns out in the harbor. I ran up to the house. Sana just kept on calmly with her work. "Washington's come to New York," she said, grinning. "Those are guns out of Governors Island practicing to scare off the British."

Well, the guns sure scared off Farmer Isaac. After Washington arrived, he and Mrs. van Ditmas never crossed to Manhattan again. I hoisted the sail of my boat to carry the farmer's wife and daughters, with all their trunks, to an old uncle's house on Staten Island.

And there on Staten Island, I saw them. The king's army had come from across the sea and on the hillside meadows had pitched its tents by the thousands. The sun glinted on rows of

WORD BANK
proclamation (PRAHK luh MAY shun) *n.:* an official announcement

brass cannon and bayonets. Redcoats came down from the hills. They spread over the green grass like streams of blood, and they sat in barges and were rowed across to the Brooklyn shore. A barge passed nearby. We saw the smiling, sunburned faces of the soldiers. "Hurrah!" they cheered, and the van Ditmas girls waved and giggled.

The Wharf

Back in the kitchen of the big house, I told what I had seen. "Those great ships have hundreds of cannon," Toby said.

"There's got to be thousands of Redcoats," somebody else said, "and they gonna whip these Liberty Boys but good."

"General Washington will find a way," Sana said, but her eyes held back tears. "It can't just end like this!"

Old Toby put an arm around her. "Trouble is, dear, it can. These Americans are settin' up to fight their king, and that means all the king's ships, and men, and cannon."

"No business for us black slaves, I'm tellin' you," said Joseph Martin.

"Not with Isaac down so hard on the Liberty Boys," Loretta added.

It seemed to me the slaves were right. I could not think how the ordinary Americans I had seen, fresh from their farms and shops, could ever drive away an army of real soldiers.

The next day, while I loaded sacks into a wagon, I heard the sound of fifes and drums. Southwards, along the road past the

WORD BANK

bayonets (BAY uh NETS) *n.:* a long-pointed steel weapon attached to the open end of a gun

barges (BAR juz) *n.:* flat-bottomed vessels, usually pushed or towed through the water, for carrying freight or passengers

mill, came a hundred of Washington's recruits, their feet shuffling in the dust. An American officer rode beside them on a gray farmhorse.

"Captain!" Sana called to him. "Thousands of them are landing down the shore!"

"We know that, girl," he called back. "Don't worry, we'll handle them lobster backs.⁷ General Washington himself is coming over to Brooklyn." But the men marching past us didn't look so sure. Many seemed frightened. Some were barefoot. Some looked hungry and sick. Their flags drooped. As they passed, Sana read the names of the colonies embroidered on their banners: Pennsylvania, Delaware, Maryland, Rhode Island. They had come from far away to a strange place.

Farmer Isaac stood by the fence, puffing on his pipe. "You be quiet, girl. This isn't no fight of yours. If them fools want to break the king's law, they can get themselves killed with no help from my slaves."

Sana shook her head. I knew she felt sorry for the ragged men and boys marching past. Maybe they were not fighting for her liberty. Not yet. But freedom had to start somewhere. That summer it was starting in Brooklyn.

When the officer was gone, and Isaac, too, one of his men stopped by the wagon. He just stood there and stared at me. "You thirsty?" I asked him. He nodded and held his empty canteen upside down. I snatched my jug of buttermilk out of the wagon and poured it into the canteen. The boy took a long drink.

7. The British soldiers were called "redcoats" because they wore red jackets with white breeches. Here, they are nicknamed *lobster backs* because a lobster's back is red.

WORD BANK **recruits** (rih KROOTS) *n.*: new members of the army

"Thanks," he said. "My name's Nathaniel. Joined up at Boston on my fourteenth birthday."

"You know how to shoot that thing?" I asked, pointing at his musket.

"Think so," he muttered. "Shot it yesterday in camp."

"You scared?" I asked him.

"No, I ain't," he said.

"Well, you oughta be," I told him.

All day long the guns crashed and boomed on the Long Island hills. While the mill wheel rumbled and ground, soldiers rushed down the South Road.

Suddenly there was shouting. A soldier appeared in the doorway. "The British are coming!" he cried. "The Americans are running!"

The road filled with crowds of American soldiers, now running north along the road, back toward Washington's lines. Tired, frightened people. Most were sopping wet. Where they stopped to rest, the dust turned to mud under their feet.

Cannonballs were whizzing through the air. One crashed through the roof of the mill. Farmer Isaac was nowhere to be seen. Sana knelt by someone who had fallen beside the road. She tied a strip of petticoat around a bloody gash in his leg. He was soaked and shaking. When I looked at his face, I saw that he was Nathaniel, the boy with the empty canteen.

"Stop staring," Sana shouted at me. "He's trembling. Wrap him in them empty sacks." Nathaniel told us how he swam across Gowanus Creek to escape from the British. But the tide was running fast. Dozens of Americans were wounded and many couldn't swim. The army was trapped without boats in the swamps around the creek. Some were still fighting, but lots of soldiers were being shot like ducks in the marshes. Washington's men needed help badly.

WORD BANK

musket (MUSS kit) *n.*: an old-fashioned gun used by foot soldiers (later replaced by the rifle)

wounded (WOON ded) *adj.*: injured

Sana's eyes pleaded with me. She knew I tied my boat in the reeds along the creek. Her look said, "It's up to you, Samuel."

Nathaniel groaned. The small red spot on his bandage had begun to spread. Toby had come and was kneeling beside Sana. He shrugged. "You got the boat, Samuel. It's your choice."

Sana and Toby got set to carry Nathaniel up the road into the American lines. Sana caught me looking at the bag on her shoulder.

"That's my freedom flour," she said. "I'm going where I can bake my freedom loaf." A moment later, more soldiers ran between us. When they had passed, Sana, Toby, and Nathaniel were gone.

All at once the road was empty. From away in the distance came the roar of muskets. Isaac van Ditmas was gone. Sana was gone and the soldiers were, too. I was alone.

Was this freedom? I thought about that boy Nathaniel from far away. How a lot more people just like him were trapped in the marshes along the creek. And how Isaac sneered at them, and how the British king from across the waters sent his soldiers to shoot and imprison them. I looked at my hands, grown strong from pulling ropes and oars and sacks. Then I knew my choice. Those hands now were going to pull people, pull them to freedom.

I ran to the creek, pushed the boat out into the rushing tide, and slid the oars into their locks. On the opposite bank Americans were wading in the muddy water up to their waists, shouting for help. In the distance others were holding the British back from the water's edge. Great clouds of gunsmoke rolled over these brave soldiers. When the air cleared, I could see fewer and fewer of them.

As I pulled near, wet and weary men flopped into the boat. Others clung to the sides. "Row, row!" they shouted. I pulled on the oars with all my might.

Out we shot into the current. Bullets splashed in the water near us. When we reached the far bank, the men cheered. I turned again into the creek and rowed back for more.

Six times I crossed the creek. Each time the battle grew closer, the fleeing Americans fewer. By now muddy water slopped around my ankles. My back ached from pulling on the oars.

Major Mordecai Gist

Just as I was raising the sail to race out of the creek, I glimpsed a big man in a blue coat and three-cornered hat alone in the bullreeds. He threw himself into the boat and ordered me to sail for Washington's camp. The British were close behind him. As we fled down the creek into New York Harbor, they fired at us from the banks. When the big man had caught his breath, he pointed up at the sail. Black holes gaped in the canvas.

"Musket balls," he said and winked. "Compliments of General Cornwallis."[8]

As the boat carried us out into the harbor, I steered northward along the Brooklyn shore toward Brooklyn Heights and Washington's camp. I wondered what Farmer Isaac would say about his torn sail. But most of all, I wondered what had happened to Sana and Toby.

My passenger's name was Major Mordecai Gist. He commanded the Maryland soldiers who had held back the British while other Americans escaped. "Oh, what brave boys I lost

---

8. Charles Cornwallis was a major general in the British army. The expression "compliments of" is used to identify the giver of a gift or donation. For example, flowers donated by Mr. Smith might be accompanied by a card saying, "Flowers compliments of Mr. Smith." The speaker here is implying that the musket balls are "gifts" being sent to the Colonists, *compliments of General Cornwallis.*

WORD BANK
glimpsed (GLIMPST) *v.:* saw for a brief moment
gaped (GAYPT) *v.:* were open wide

today," said Major Gist, "and this war has only begun." He asked how I came to be fishing men out of the creek. I told him about Farmer Isaac, Sana, and Nathaniel.

When I tied the boat to the dock below the Heights, Major Gist clapped his hands on my shoulders and looked me in the eyes. "Samuel," he said, "out in that creek you did more than many a free man for your country. I'd take it as a privilege if you'd consent to be my orderly and march beside me. And General Washington may need handy boatmen like you soon enough."

The next day it rained and rained. A thick sea fog covered the land. I looked everywhere for Sana. Many soldiers crowded into the camp, but they could tell me nothing. Alone and frightened, I mended the holes in my sail, pushing the big needle through the canvas, drawing it back again. Then, I heard voices nearby. Major Gist stood there with an officer in a fine blue uniform. They asked me how deep the water was at this point between Brooklyn and Manhattan. They wanted to know if a British ship could sail between the two places. I told them that most ships could. Only the fog was keeping the British men-of-war[9] from trapping Washington's army on Long Island.

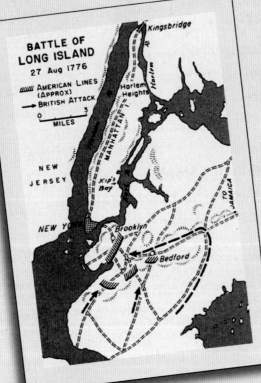

The officer in the blue uniform thanked me. He and Major Gist walked away, looking thoughtful.

The next day the heavy rains continued. I spread the sail over the boat and slept

_____
9. A *man-of-war* is a warship.

snug and dry. Then I heard the voice I missed more than any in the world calling, "Samuel, Samuel Abraham!" Sana had found me! It was not a dream. "You chose, Samuel," she said. "You did it right. You chose our new country." From under her cloak she took a hot, steaming loaf wrapped in a napkin—her freedom bread, the sweetest I ever tasted. While we ate, she told me that Toby and Nathaniel were safe.

But this new country was in danger. Major Gist came to me again and explained that every boat was needed to carry Washington's army from Brooklyn to Manhattan. The army had to retreat that night. I was going to help save the army with Farmer Isaac's boat. Wouldn't he be surprised?

On the night that General Washington's army left Brooklyn, the worst storm I'd ever seen blew in from the Northeast. The wind howled. It drove the rain, stinging, into our eyes. It shook buildings and knocked down chimneys. And it whipped the water at Brooklyn Ferry into a sea of foam.

Down from the Heights in file marched Washington's army. The men entered the boats Major Gist and others had gathered at the ferry landing.

"What we need is a rope to cling to," someone said in the dark. "A rope stretching from here to Manhattan to guide us against the wind and current."

"There's rope here in the shipyard," a soldier remembered. "Buoys to float the rope across, too. But who can cross this flood in the dark?"

"Can you do it, Samuel?" Major Gist asked. "Can you get across with the rope?"

"I can do it, Major," I shouted, the wind tearing the words out of my mouth. But I wasn't sure. Even if the rope were fed out

WORD BANK

retreat (rih TREET) *v.*: move back, away from the enemy
buoys (BOYS) *n.*: a floating object, fastened or anchored so that it remains in one place, used as a marker for sailors

from shore slowly, the sail might split or the rope might tear down the mast.[10] But the British ships were sure to force their way between Brooklyn and Manhattan. I had to try.

When the rope was ready, I tied it to the foot of the mast. Sana jumped into the boat. I shouted at her to stay behind, but she wouldn't move. There was no time to lose. I shoved off into the swirling current.

My only hope was to let the shore current carry me out into midstream, and then, as the wind and tide thrust the boat toward the other shore, raise the sail and race for the Manhattan landing.

Fighting the rudder,[11] I heard Sana's voice in my ear. "Will we make it, Samuel?" Water crashed over the side. Sana was bailing as fast as she could. "I can't swim, Samuel!" she cried into the wind. We were halfway across to Manhattan, and the boat was filling with sea. The gale was spinning up around. The rope was pulling us backward. I heaved at the sail, praying the mending wouldn't tear.

Then, as the sail filled, the boom[12] swung around with a crack, and we were darting forward at last. On the Manhattan landing, by lantern light, we could see people waiting. Over the roar of the storm, we heard them cheering us on. But Isaac's boat was sinking. The rope was tearing the mast out of the bottom. With a terrible crash, the mast broke and was carried

---

10. A *mast* is a large, strong pole on a ship, to which the ship's sails are attached.
11. A *rudder* is a long flat blade attached to the bottom of the ship's stern (back end). The pilot steers the ship by turning a wheel attached to the rudder. As the rudder is turned one way or another in the water, the boat's direction changes.
12. A *boom* is a large pole attached to the mast.

WORD BANK — **gale** (GAYL) *n.*: a strong wind

over the side. A second later the bow[13] smashed into the side of a wharf, and I found myself in the water swimming with one arm, clinging to Sana with the other.

We stumbled ashore on Manhattan Island, where kind people wrapped us in blankets. They were smiling—the rope was across! The boats full of Washington's soldiers would follow. We had done it, together.

All through the night Washington's men followed that rope, boat after boat, across the water. In the stormy darkness, every soldier escaped from Long Island.

And so the fight for freedom would go on. It would take many long years before we would beat the British king, but never again did I wonder what freedom was, or what it cost. It was people pulling together. It was strong hands helping. It was one person caring about another.

And where was Washington? Many times that night Sana and I hoped to see him.

"Why, Samuel," Major Gist told us later, "he was that officer in the blue coat who asked you how deep the water was between Brooklyn and Manhattan. Last night the general arrested a farmer in Brooklyn for helping the British. That farmer, Isaac van Ditmas, turned all of his property over to the Army of the Continental Congress[14] in exchange for his freedom. It seems now that you and Sana have no master."

From that day forward, we and Isaac's other slaves were to be citizens of a new nation.

---

12. The *bow* is the forward end of a ship.

13. Representatives of the Colonies met in 1774, 1775, and 1776. The group of representatives, who gathered to plan and discuss the American Revolution, was called *the Continental Congress*. The army formed to fight the British was called *the Army of the Continental Congress*.

WORD BANK **wharf** (HWARF) *n.:* a pier; a wooden walkway built next to or jutting into the water so that boats can come alongside it to load or unload

Historical Note

The Battle of Long Island was George Washington's first battle in the American War for Independence. It was a defeat. From Brooklyn, General Washington retreated to Manhattan, then to New Jersey, and in the last month of 1776, he crossed the Delaware River into Pennsylvania. Thus ended one of the longer and more bitter retreats in American history. On December 26, Washington crossed the icy Delaware once more into New Jersey. There, at Trenton and again at Princeton, his soldiers (many of whom had escaped from Brooklyn) defeated their enemy. In 1781, General Cornwallis finally surrendered at Yorktown. The British troops who fired on Samuel at Gowanus Creek on August 27, 1776, were commanded by General Cornwallis.

Major Mordecai Gist led the Maryland state troops in the Battle of Long Island. He and Isaac van Ditmas are historical figures (although the arrest of van Ditmas did not actually occur). Samuel Abraham and Sana Williams are fictional, but modeled on the many nameless people of Brooklyn, slave and free, who made Washington's escape possible.

About the Author

Richard Berleth was born in Huntington, Long Island. He holds degrees from Colgate and Rutgers Universities, and is presently Chair of the Communications Department at St. Francis College in Brooklyn Heights, New York. He is the author of several children's books, and happens to live on the site of the Battle of Long Island that figures prominently in *Samuel's Choice*. Currently, he is at work on a history of the American Revolution in upstate New York.

Studying the Selection

FIRST IMPRESSIONS

In the story, Sana says that "Nobody here's gonna be free unless they take the risk." Why does being free require taking a risk? Do you think this is still true today?

QUICK REVIEW

1. Write down two words or phrases that describe Isaac van Ditmas.

2. Why was Samuel hungry all of the time?

3. Why did Isaac teach Samuel about "the currents that flow between Brooklyn and Manhattan" and "setting a sail and holding a course"?

4. What does Samuel say about doing work you "do not choose to do"?

FOCUS

5. On page 24, Samuel finds himself alone. Everyone has gone. He asks himself, Is this freedom? Reread several paragraphs before this line in the story, and the paragraph that follows it. What do you think Samuel's question means?

6. In a short paragraph, explain why you think that *Samuel's Choice* is a good story.

CREATING & WRITING

7. Imagine that you are Samuel. Why do you decide to help the wounded soldiers?

8. You are Samuel. You have just met a soldier who wants to give up. He is tired, hungry, and discouraged. He does not believe the Colonists can win against the mighty British. How do you persuade him to stay and fight?

9. You are a slave. You are going to join a group of slaves in the center of Brooklyn to protest being kept in slavery. Each of you has made a sign with a message on it. Make your sign for the gathering.

LESSON IN LITERATURE . . .

WHAT IS PLOT?

- The events that take place in a story make up the plot. Some of the events happen to the story's characters, and some are caused by the story's characters.

- The plot starts early in the story. As events unfold, a conflict arises for the main character. A conflict is a struggle to overcome some problem or challenge. If the plot is to hold our interest, there must be a conflict.

- At one point in the story, everything changes. The main character either overcomes the problem presented in the plot, or is defeated by it. This point in the story is called the story's climax.

- After the climax, the story comes to a conclusion. This is the part of the story where the reader feels that all has been explained, and the story is complete.

THINK ABOUT IT!

1. As the story opens, Rusty is unhappy. Why?

2. In one or two sentences, describe the story's conflict.

3. What action does Rusty take to solve his problem?

4. What happens to Rusty that almost prevents him from achieving his goal?

5. What do you think is the climax of the story?

6. How is Rusty's problem solved at the conclusion of the story?

New Kid

All alone in the fenced-in backyard, Rusty hurled the baseball as hard as he could into the air. When a gust of wind caught the ball, Rusty ran after it.

Just over the fence he could see the kite the kids next door had been trying all morning to keep in the air. Back home, if somebody had a kite, everybody had a kite. And the new kid wouldn't be left playing catch by himself for a whole week without somebody comin' over to say "Hey."

Suddenly, the wind slammed the kite right into a tree near the fence.

The neighbor, a redhead, appeared at the top of Rusty's fence. Rusty watched as the kid reached for the lowest hanging branch.

Rusty stepped closer. "Why don't you let me try?"

"You?"

"Lots of trees back home. Used to climb all the time."

The kid shrugged. Rusty climbed up the fence. On the other side a bunch of kids stared up at him.

"Give me a boost," Rusty ordered.

Pulling himself up on the lowest branch, Rusty climbed the next several branches as easily as he would a ladder, but he couldn't quite reach the kite.

"You guys got a broom?" he shouted down.

One of the younger boys raced off. An instant later he returned with a broom.

The moment Rusty nudged the kite free, the wind slammed it into a branch a little further out.

With his left hand he inched as far out along the branch as he could. With his right he reached out with the broom. The delicate material of the kite was caught in some twigs. One false move and there would be no kite to rescue. Using the stick end of the broom, he gently lifted the edge of the kite. It fell free.

When Rusty got down there were high fives all around.

The red-haired kid handed him the string. "You fly it first."

Rusty took off running. Behind him, climbing higher with each step, was the kite. On all sides, panting and shouting their delight, ran Rusty's new friends.

Blueprint for Reading

INTO . . . *Slower Than the Rest*

At the beginning of *Slower Than the Rest,* Leo finds a turtle. He keeps it. He loves it. He names it Charlie. Everybody knows that turtles move more slowly than other animals. In this story, Leo thinks more slowly than other children, so Leo does not care if his turtle is slow. In fact, in Leo's eyes, Charlie runs "as if no one had ever told him how slow he was supposed to be."

This story shows us that speed is not what is really important. We also see that a person doesn't have to be smart to be courageous.

EYES ON . . . Plot

Plot is a word for story. The plot is the unfolding of connected events in a story. The events weave a tale that makes us want to read on. We want to know what is going to happen and how it will all end.

After you have read this story, pick several important facts from the first two paragraphs. Write them down. These are part of the **plot.** Write down the **characters'** names. Remember: An animal can be a character!

What is the turning point in the story? This is the moment when Leo's being slower suddenly doesn't matter. This moment is the **climax.** Write down the sentences in which the climax occurs.

Slower Than the Rest

from *EVERY LIVING THING* by Cynthia Rylant

Leo was the first one to spot the turtle, so he was the one who got to keep it. They had all been in the car, driving up Tyler Mountain, when Leo shouted, "There's a turtle!" and everyone's head jerked with the stop.

Leo's father grumbled something about turtle soup, but Leo's mother was sympathetic toward turtles, so Leo was allowed to pick it up off the highway and bring it home.

WORD BANK

sympathetic (SIM puh THEH tik)
adj.: to have a positive or favorable feeling about something

Leo loved Charlie from the very start.

Both his little sisters squealed when the animal stuck its ugly head out to look at them, and they thought its claws horrifying, but Leo loved it from the start. He named it Charlie.

The dogs at Leo's house had always belonged more to Leo's father than to anyone else, and the cat thought she belonged to no one but herself, so Leo was grateful for a pet of his own. He settled Charlie in a cardboard box, threw in some lettuce and radishes, and declared himself a happy boy.

Leo adored Charlie, and the turtle was hugged and kissed as if he were a baby. Leo liked to fit Charlie's shell on his shoulder under his left ear, just as one might carry a cat, and Charlie would poke his head into Leo's neck now and then to keep them both entertained.

Leo was ten years old the year he found Charlie. He hadn't many friends because he was slower than the rest. That was the

Charlie took care of Leo's happiness.

way his father said it: "Slower than the rest." Leo was slow in reading, slow in numbers, slow in understanding nearly everything that passed before him in a classroom. As a result, in fourth grade Leo had been separated from the rest of his classmates and placed in a room with other children who were as slow as he. Leo thought he would never get over it. He saw no way to be happy after that.

But Charlie took care of Leo's happiness, and he did it by being congenial. Charlie was the friendliest turtle anyone had ever seen. The turtle's head was always stretched out, moving left to right, trying to see what was in the world. His front and back legs moved as though he were swimming frantically in a deep sea to save himself, when all that was happening was that someone was holding him in midair. Put Charlie down and he would sniff at the air a moment, then take off as if no one had ever told him how slow he was supposed to be.

Every day, Leo came home from school, took Charlie to the backyard to let him explore and told him about the things that had happened in fifth grade. Leo wasn't sure how old Charlie was, and, though he guessed Charlie was probably a young turtle, the lines around Charlie's forehead and eyes and the clamp of his mouth made Leo think Charlie was wise the way old people are wise. So Leo talked to him privately every day.

Then one day Leo decided to take Charlie to school. It was Prevent Forest Fires week and the whole school was making posters, watching nature films, imitating Smokey the

WORD BANK

congenial (kuhn JEE nee uhl) *adj.*: agreeable; pleasant
frantically (FRAN tik lee) *adv.*: wildly and desperately

Slower Than the Rest ~ 37

Bear. Each member of Leo's class was assigned to give a report on Friday dealing with forests. So Leo brought Charlie.

Leo was quiet about it on the bus to school. He held the covered box tightly on his lap, secretly relieved that turtles are quiet except for an occasional hiss. Charlie rarely hissed in the morning; he was a turtle who liked to sleep in.

Leo carried the box to his classroom and placed it on the wide windowsill near the radiator and beside the geraniums. His teacher called attendance and the day began.

In the middle of the morning, the forest reports began. One girl held up a poster board pasted with pictures of raccoons and squirrels, rabbits and deer, and she explained that animals died in forest fires. The pictures were too small for anyone to see from his desk. Leo was bored.

One boy stood up and mumbled something about burnt-up trees. Then another got up and said that if there were no forests, then his dad couldn't go hunting, and Leo couldn't see the connection in that at all.

Finally it was his turn. He quietly walked over to the windowsill and picked up the box. He set it on the teacher's desk.

"When somebody throws a match into a forest," Leo began, "he is a murderer. He kills trees and birds and animals. Some animals, like deer, are fast runners and they might escape. But other animals"—he lifted the cover off the box—"have no hope. They are too slow. They will die." He lifted Charlie out of the box. "It isn't fair," he said, as the class gasped and giggled at what they saw. "It isn't fair for the slow ones."

WORD BANK

occasional (uh KAY zhun ul) *adj.*: occurring once in a while
rarely (RAIR lee) *adv.*: hardly ever

Charlie is a turtle who likes to sleep in.

Fire endangers all woodland animals.

Leo said much more. Mostly he talked about Charlie, explained what turtles were like, the things they enjoyed, what talents they possessed. He talked about Charlie the turtle and Charlie the friend, and what he said and how he said it made everyone in the class love turtles and hate forest fires. Leo's teacher had tears in her eyes.

That afternoon, the whole school assembled in the gymnasium to bring the special week to a close. A ranger in uniform made a speech, then someone dressed up like Smokey the Bear danced with two others dressed up like squirrels. Leo sat with his box and wondered if he should laugh at the dancers with everyone else. He didn't feel like it.

Finally, the school principal stood up and began a long talk. Leo's thoughts drifted off. He thought about being home, lying in his bed and drawing pictures, while Charlie hobbled all around the room.

He did not hear when someone whispered his name. Then he jumped when he heard, "Leo! It's you!" in his ear. The boy next to him was pushing him, making him get up.

WORD BANK   **drifted** (DRIFF ted) *v.*: slowly moved away

"What?" Leo asked, looking around in confusion.

"You won!" they were all saying. "Go on!"

Leo was pushed onto the floor. He saw the principal smiling at him, beckoning to him across the room. Leo's legs moved like Charlie's—quickly and forward.

Leo carried the box tightly against his chest. He shook the principal's hand. He put down the box to accept the award plaque being handed to him. It was for his presentation with Charlie. Leo had won an award for the first time in his life, and as he shook the principal's hand and blushed and said his thank-you's, he thought his heart would explode with happiness.

That night, alone in his room, holding Charlie on his shoulder, Leo felt proud. And for the first time in a long time, Leo felt *fast.*

WORD BANK

beckoning (BEK uh ning) *v.*: motioning to someone to come closer
plaque (PLACK) *n.*: a metal plate engraved with the name of a person being honored

About the Author

Cynthia Rylant was born in 1954 in Hopewell, Virginia. She spent the early years of her childhood with her grandparents, in a mountain town that had neither electricity nor running water. Her first picture book, *When I was Young in the Mountains*, told the story of her happy and secure life in those poor surroundings. Rylant went on to write many picture books, poems, short stories, and novels. She prefers to write about "people who don't get any attention," like Leo in *Slower Than the Rest*, and to make them "absolutely shine." Cynthia Rylant lives in Washington.

Studying the Selection

FIRST IMPRESSIONS
What do you love, in the same way that Leo loves Charlie?

QUICK REVIEW

1. Where were Leo and his family, when he spotted the turtle?

2. What does Leo call the turtle?

3. Why doesn't Leo have many friends?

4. Where did the expression, "slower than the rest," come from?

FOCUS

5. How does Leo show that he has courage?

6. What is the climax of the story? Why is that moment so important?

CREATING & WRITING

7. It took courage for Leo to speak to his class about the suffering of animals that move slowly. He may have feared they would laugh at him and call *him* slow. But he did speak, and the class listened with great interest. Think about a time when you wanted to step forward and speak about something that you felt was wrong—but you just couldn't. It was too scary. Perhaps you waited too long and the moment had passed. Write about the experience in two paragraphs. In the first paragraph, explain what happened or what was said that you felt was wrong. In the next paragraph, write down what you wish you had said.

8. Leo and his family noticed the turtle on the highway. Then they rescued it and took it home to take care of it. Why do you think Leo's family did this? Think about it and write your answer in one or two paragraphs.

9. Create a turtle either by drawing one or making one from clay.

WHAT IS CHARACTER?

- The people or animals in a story are its characters.

- Stories include main characters and secondary characters. The secondary characters are those who have a smaller part in the story.

- In some stories, the author talks mainly about what the characters *do*. In others, the focus is on what the characters *think* or *feel.*

- In some stories, the author describes a character's thoughts and actions in a positive or negative way. We understand that this is a "good" character or a "bad" character.

- Sometimes the author is careful not to express an opinion about a character. The author wishes the reader to form an opinion without help from the author.

THINK ABOUT IT!

1. Use three adjectives to describe Marie.

2. Although we are told only about Marie's actions, we can imagine what Marie was thinking and feeling as she took those actions. Describe Marie's thoughts and feelings as she packed Brady's lunch each day.

3. Do you prefer stories that tell you what to think about each character, or stories that force you to make up your own mind?

Just Like Mom

Before Mom died, Brady hardly paid any attention to his sister, Marie. Five years older than Brady, she seemed to live in an entirely separate world. After Mom died, Marie became the most important person in Brady's life.

Dad had a good job; he took good care of them. But it was Marie who got Brady up every morning and got him ready for school. She always packed his lunch for school, just like Mom had. And just like Mom, she never let him take "junk food" for lunch.

Every afternoon, Marie picked him up after school and walked him home, just like Mom had. And just like Mom, she never accepted "I don't know" or "Nothing" in response to the question "What did you do in school today?" She really wanted to know.

Every evening, Marie made dinner for Brady and Dad, just like Mom had. And just like Mom, she made everyone help clear the table while she did the dishes.

It wasn't until years later, when Brady was in high school and would microwave pizza for himself and Dad after football practice, that Brady realized something. He finally understood that in order for her to get him up and ready for school on time, Marie had had to get up that much earlier herself. And that in order to walk him home from school every day, Marie had had to give up the after-school sports and activities he took for granted. And that because she made dinner, cleaned up, helped him with his homework and helped him get ready for bed, Marie didn't get to start on her homework until after she was through taking care of him.

Marie was just like Mom, and now that Marie was off to college, he missed them both very much.

INTO . . . Kate Shelley

Kate Shelley: Bound for Legend is about a girl who actually lived from 1866 to 1912 on an Iowa farm. As a child, she had heavy responsibilities. Farm families worked very hard and had little money. When Kate was nine, her father was killed in a railroad accident. Shortly afterwards, her oldest brother, Michael, drowned in the Des Moines River. (In the story, he is called James.)

Kate's mother was "broken in health and spirit." Kate's responsibilities at home grew and she could not go to school. *Kate Shelley* shows how this young girl, only fifteen years old, behaved with extraordinary courage in a great crisis. Why are such stories retold again and again?

EYES ON . . . *the Character*

Characters are the people in a story. The word *character* is usually used for the people in fictional stories, but it may also be used for a nonfiction account such as *Kate Shelley.*

In a short piece like a short story, we learn mostly about the main character. The author describes what the character does, says, and thinks. The author also teaches us about this person from the way other people in the story—the secondary characters—respond to the main character. Describing a character in these and other ways is called **characterization.**

The word *character* has other uses that are important to understand. Sometimes we ask about a person's *character,* meaning how that person usually behaves and thinks. Or we may state, "Kate Shelley is a person of strong character." What do we mean when we use the word this way?

KATE SHELLEY:
BOUND FOR LEGEND

Robert D. San Souci

A railroad bridge crossed Honey Creek not far from Kate Shelley's little Iowa farmhouse. Every day trains sped back and forth over the trestle,[1] heading east toward Chicago or west toward the long Des Moines River Bridge on the way to Salt Lake City. As they roared past, the trains brought a touch of excitement to fifteen-year-old Kate's life.

---

1. A *trestle* (TRESS uhl) is a framework of wood or steel beams that resembles a large sawhorse. This framework can support a *trestle bridge* on which railway tracks may be laid. In the story, the word trestle is used to mean trestle bridge.

Once the railroad had been the Shelley family's main source of income. Kate's father, who had died three years earlier, had been a section foreman on the Chicago & North Western Railway. Now, in 1881, the farm—a patch of pasture and timber set amid rugged hills in the heart of Iowa—supported the family.

Good-natured, sturdy Kate had taken charge of the family because of her mother's poor health. She helped with the plowing and planting. With her nine-year-old sister Mayme she gathered firewood and tended the vegetable garden. She even taught herself to shoot to keep hawks away from the chickens.

Kate saw the younger children, Margaret, Mayme, and John, off to school in the morning and helped tuck them in at night. She kept them away from the dangerous banks of Honey Creek, because none of them could swim. One brother, James, had drowned shortly after his father's death. Kate was the one who discovered his riderless horse beside the Des Moines River, where the boy had been swept away while wading.

WORD BANK

foreman (FOR mun) *n.:* a person in charge of a department or group of workers, as in a factory

timber (TIM ber) *n.:* trees; an area of woodland or forest

rugged (RUG ged) *adj.:* rough; rocky and hilly

In moments between chores Kate read every book she could lay her hands on, to make up for her lack of schooling. She loved to ride bareback through the forests in autumn or row a skiff along the broad, smooth surface of the river in high summer.

But the railroad was her real love. When errands took her to the little coal mining village of Moingona, a mile away, she would stop by the train station. She would linger in the waiting room with its potbellied stove and high-backed bench. Sometimes she would hear urgent tapping from behind the ticket window as news came over the telegraph wire, or as the stationmaster sent word to distant stations to alert approaching trains of hazards.

Adventure appealed to Kate. "She was absolutely without fear," her sister Mayme would recall later in life. But her adventures were confined to farm and family for the first fifteen years of her life—until one July day in 1881.

When the eastbound freight from Moingona neared the Shelley farm on the afternoon of Wednesday, July 6, 1881, Kate and her mother were taking the wash off the clothesline. It had

WORD BANK

linger (LING er) *v.*: stay longer than usual
hazards (HAZZ erds) *n.*: dangers

rained for most of a week, and now black clouds were heaping up on the horizon, threatening another storm. But Kate stopped pulling sheets, shifts, and stockings from the line long enough to watch Engine 230 help a freight train climb the grade up to Honey Creek Bridge on its way to Boone, a town five miles distant.

The freight train was late. Kate knew the schedules by heart, and she could recognize each of the local "pushers" (Number 230 was one) by its whistle. These four locomotives sat on sidetracks until they were needed to help push or pull heavy trains up the steep slope.

As Mrs. Shelley and Kate lifted the full laundry basket, the sky went dark as if a black curtain had been flung across the sun. They barely reached the back door of their two-story clapboard[2] house before the first heavy raindrops began to fall.

Soon the deadly storm broke. "You can only imagine what a fearful thing it is to see the heavens grow black and blacker until the light of day is all shut out," Kate later said, "to see the clouds torn into fragments by the fierce lightnings, and the torrents fall and swallow up the earth."

Thunder rattled loose glass in the window frame, while fierce wind hurled sheets of rain against the house. Kate watched anxiously as Honey Creek's waters rose higher than she had ever seen them.

She soon began to fear for the safety of the animals in the barn on the slope below the house. Putting on an old coat and hat, she hurried to the barn through the ankle-deep water gushing down the hillside.

The water was just as deep inside. The plow horses, cattle, and hogs were splashing nervously in their stalls and pens. Kate led each of them to higher ground in an oat field, then turned them loose.

By the time she returned to the barn for a last look around, the water had grown knee-deep. Hearing a terrified squealing, Kate discovered several piglets that had climbed onto an island of hay. She carried them to the safety of the oat field and tucked them under the sow. Then, drenched and chilled, she ran back to the house.

---

2. A *clapboard* is a long, thin board, thicker along one edge than another. A *clapboard house,* often called "a frame house," is covered with these overlapping boards.

WORD BANK **fragments** (FRAG ments) *n.:* bits and pieces of something

As she dried off by the kitchen stove, Kate heard the frightening noise of trees being uprooted by the gale. The younger children were fed and put to bed, but the effort didn't take Kate's mind off raging Honey Creek. With every lull in the downpour, Kate saw picket fences, parts of walls, even small trees pile up against the straining supports of the trestle over the brimming stream.

As Kate noted the passing hours, she began to worry about the midnight express. "Surely no trains will be dispatched in this storm," Margaret Shelley said to soothe her daughter.

It was well past eleven o'clock when Kate clearly heard the rumble of a pusher engine climbing the grade to Honey Creek Bridge. She heard its bell clang twice. Then there was a dreadful crash, followed by an awful hiss of steam as hot metal hit cold water.

"Oh, Mother!" cried Kate, clutching Margaret's hand. "It's Number Eleven. They've gone down Honey Creek Bridge!"

For a moment the two stared at each other in horror, while Mayme, awakened by the sound, huddled in the kitchen door. Then Kate reached for her damp coat and soggy straw hat hanging beside the stove. "I must go to help the men," Kate said.

Mrs. Shelley begged her not to go, but Kate insisted. "If that were Father down there," she said, "we'd expect

WORD BANK **lull** *n.:* a temporary calm or quiet

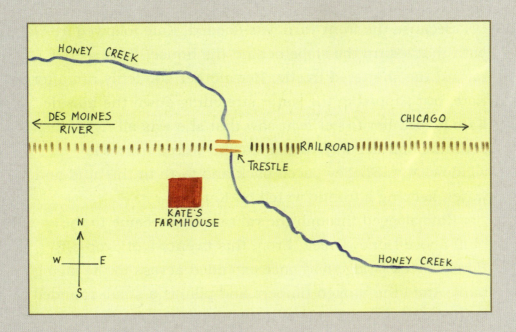

someone to help him." Then, mindful of a grave danger, she added, "And I must stop the midnight train from the west."

Hundreds of passengers bound for Chicago would be aboard the express train headed for the ruined Honey Creek Bridge. Kate told her mother that she would go to Moingona Station and have the stationmaster telegraph a warning down the line. If she couldn't reach the station in time, she would flag down the train herself.

Quickly she took her father's old railroad lantern and filled it with oil. There was no wick, so Kate grabbed an old flannel skirt and tore off a strip. In a moment she had lit the lamp.

"Kate, if you go out there, you'll be lost or hurt," her mother said in a last effort to make her stay.

"I could never forgive myself if I didn't," she replied.

Her mother sighed, "Go, then, in the name of G-d, and do what you can."

Because the front yard was flooded, Kate followed a path that led up the slope behind the house, then veered toward the shattered trestle. Her mother suddenly ran after Kate, but slipped in the water streaming down the hillside. Kate helped her to her feet, saw that she was all right, then continued on her way. While Mayme stared from the window, Mrs. Shelley paced back and forth in the mud and water, keeping a frantic watch on Kate.

Kate slogged through the rain until she came to the bluff above Honey Creek. From this twenty-foot drop-off, Honey Creek Bridge had once extended across to the facing bluff. Amid the broken timbers and pilings a small rounded section of the steam engine jutted out of the churning black water. Only a bit of railing marked the sunken "tender," the special car that carried water and coal for the engine. The unfortunate crew had been sent out to check for storm-damaged tracks. Kate would later learn that two men aboard the locomotive had been killed.

Moving along the cliff, Kate waved her lantern. In response two men shouted up to her. She could barely see them as they clung to some willow branches above the raging water. She called back to them, and they yelled something up to her. But the storm was so fierce that she couldn't make out what they said.

Kate realized that she could do nothing for them by herself, and time was running out for the midnight express.

She turned and headed for the Des Moines River Bridge. Moingona Station and its telegraph were on the other side.

Kate struggled on against the pelting rain as bushes and brambles snagged her clothes. The lightning seemed a hundred times more frightening in the open, but it lit the long bridge that was her goal.

Inch by inch, Kate fought her way up the steep approach to the bridge. Though the span was normally a full fifty feet above the water, the angry river seemed only a short distance below her. Before she reached the bridge, the wind extinguished her feeble lamp, and she had no way to relight it.

Fearfully she peered into the dark, afraid that the midnight express might be speeding across the bridge. But

WORD BANK **extinguished** (ex TING wishd) *v.*: put out (a light or a fire)

no whistle knifed through the howling wind; no engine's headlamp hurtled toward her.

Nearly seven hundred feet long, the Des Moines River Bridge was a ladder of cross ties, each nearly two feet apart. Though Kate had crossed the bridge in good weather, its splintery ties were studded with twisted spikes and nails to discourage such foot traffic.

"Those who cross a railroad bridge on a swiftly moving train can form no conception of the sensation a traveler experiences who attempts to cross on foot," Kate later said. "A misstep would send me down below the ties into the flood that was boiling below. I got down on my hands and knees, carrying yet my useless lantern and guiding myself by the stretch of rail."

Shivering from the wet and cold, Kate crept along, avoiding the worst buffeting of the wind. She would reach her fingers out to locate the next tie, then cross to it with the help of the iron track. Again and again, her skirt or coat sleeve caught on a nail or spike or splinter. Her hands and knees were cut and bleeding. Several times she nearly lost her hold on the rain-slick ties. The hungry river was terrifying to Kate, who was near the spot where her brother James had drowned.

"Halfway over, a piercing flash of lightning showed me the angry flood more closely than ever," Kate would remember, "and swept along upon it a great tree—the earth still hanging to its roots—was racing for the bridge, and, it

WORD BANK **buffeting** (BUFF ih ting) *n.:* repeated hitting and pushing

seemed, for the very spot I stood upon. Fear brought me upright on my knees, and I clasped my hands in terror, and in prayer, I hope, lest the shock should carry out the bridge."

Kate braced for the crash. But the huge tree swept between the pilings, its branches grabbing and slapping at her through the ties. She was spattered with water and foam from the snapping limbs before the raging waters swept the tree into the darkness downriver.

Without her lantern Kate knew she had no hope of flagging down the midnight express. She had to reach Moingona Station so that a warning could be sent.

So tired that she could only think of reaching the next tie, and then the next, Kate began to crawl the rest of the way across the bridge. The cold numbed the stinging in her hands and knees. Raising her head, she took heart when she saw the lights of the railway station in the distance.

At last she reached solid ground. She paused just long enough to catch her breath. Then, forcing herself to her feet, she ran the half mile remaining to Moingona Station.

She burst into the waiting room, where several men were talking, and blurted out her warning. Kate later admitted that she had no memory of how, exactly, she told her tale. She only remembered someone saying, "The girl is crazy."

But the station agent cried, "That's Kate Shelley! She would know if the bridge was out!"

Then Kate, exhausted by her ordeal, collapsed on the spot.

When she came to a few moments later, she was lying on the hard, cold wooden bench. To her relief she found that the midnight express had not yet come through.

Much later she would learn that the train had been halted forty miles to the west, at the edge of the storm. The passengers were safe, but other lives were still in danger.

"The crew from Number Eleven still need help," Kate said. She quickly agreed to guide the rescue mission to save the men. Though others tried to get her to rest, Kate would not be put off.

Engine 230, sidetracked in the Moingona Station yard, was quickly filled with volunteers carrying ropes and shovels. As it headed for the fallen trestle, the engineer kept sounding the whistle to let the stranded men know that help was on the way.

Riding in the cab, Kate must have held her breath as the train eased across the Des Moines Bridge. But the structure proved solid, and the storm was quieting at last.

Exhausted yet determined, Kate guided the others to where she had seen the two crewmen in Honey Creek. The men, Number Eleven's engineer and brakeman, still clung to branches above the receding water, but there was no way for the rescuers to get down to the stream. Kate had to lead them into the hills behind her home—reversing the path she had traced earlier that evening—to an undamaged railroad bridge beyond the house.

WORD BANK **receding** (ree SEE ding) *adj.*: returning to a lower level; moving back and further away

Only now could they follow the track back west to reach the stranded men. By the time they were brought to safety, the rain had almost ceased, and chilly gray dawn had begun to lighten the sky.

Shaking from cold and weariness, Kate was brought home. Her mother hugged her, then put her to bed, mounding the blankets above the shivering girl.

The story of Kate's bravery was telegraphed all over the state and across the nation. She was celebrated in countless newspapers as "the Iowa heroine."

But Kate was too sick to care. Over and over she repeated to Mayme, "I can still feel the cold rain on my face."

At one point her teeth began to chatter so loudly that Mrs. Shelley was forced to send for the doctor; but all he could do was whittle a peg from soft wood. He told Kate's mother, "Put this between her teeth to keep her from breaking them."

Strangers gathered in the yard to look at "Our Kate," as they called her. Some even asked for a bit of her skirt or a lock of her hair. Mrs. Shelley shooed them away.

It was nearly three months before Kate's strength came back. During this time as she lay in bed, she was greeted by the trains that blew their whistles when they passed the Shelley farmhouse.

Finally, one afternoon she announced that she felt well enough to go outside. Escorted by her mother, sisters, and brother, Kate stepped out on the porch, hoping to catch a glimpse of the westbound train. To her surprise, the train stopped in front of the house, and crew and passengers leaned out to cheer her. Red-faced but delighted, she waved back to them.

Later, when she was able to go into town, the trains would stop and carry her to Moingona.

Many honors came to Kate in the days that followed. She received a medal from the state of Iowa, inscribed:

Presented by the State of Iowa, to Kate Shelley, with the thanks of the General Assembly in recognition of the Courage and Devotion of a child of fifteen years whom neither the fury of the elements, nor the fear of death could appall in her effort to save human life during the terrible storm and flood in the Des Moines Valley on the night of July 6th, 1881.

There were other gifts and awards, but perhaps the most wonderful for Kate was a lifetime pass on the railroad. In the years that followed she attended Simpson College, and in 1903 became station agent at Moingona. She held this job until illness forced her to retire in 1911. She died the following year at the age of forty-six.

Always modest when asked about her heroic deed, Kate would say, "I believe that G-d makes strong the weakest and makes the poorest of us able to do much for His merciful purposes."

Kate's final train ride came on the day of her funeral. A special train stopped at the Shelley home to pick up her coffin and carry her to the Boone depot. Her resting place was in the peaceful cemetery on the edge of Boone.

ABOUT THE AUTHOR

Robert D. San Souci (SOO see) was born in San Francisco in 1946. He is best known for his use of folktales, stories, and legends in his stories. Although the majority of his books and stories are written for children, he has also written several books for adults. Many of his books are illustrated by his younger brother Dan, with whom he shares ideas, work, and a birthday— October 10! San Souci likes to work on several projects at once, and hopes to continue writing as long as there is "an audience…willing to listen." He lives in California.

Studying the Selection

FIRST IMPRESSIONS
What would it take for you to crawl across a 700-foot bridge hanging over a raging river in the dark?

QUICK REVIEW

1. What is the name of the main character in the story?

2. How old was Kate when the incident of the train occurred?

3. At what place and time do the events occur?

4. What had happened to Mr. Shelley?

FOCUS

5. Why did this 15-year-old girl become a national heroine? Your answer should be no more than two or three sentences.

6. Who is the most important character in this story? Who do you think is the next most important character? Why?

CREATING & WRITING

7. In two or three paragraphs, describe the courageous actions of someone you know. If you don't know of any such actions, write about the courageous actions of a character in a book you have read, or a story you have heard.

8. It is 1881. You are the chairperson of an organization. Tonight you are having a dinner to honor Kate Shelley. She is attending the dinner. Write out the speech in which you introduce her to the members of the organization. Don't forget to give your organization a name!

9. With two to four other students, act out one of the scenes in the story. Remember to use dialogue. Rehearse your scene and practice, before presenting your drama to the class. Your presentation should last about five minutes.

SETTING

- The setting of a story has three parts: place, time, and mood.

- The place is where the story unfolds.

- The time includes the period of history, the season, and the time of day in which the events take place.

- The mood is the feeling the author creates as a background to the story. The mood may be joyful, gloomy, or frightening. There are so many moods a writer can create.

- The setting may be described in detail or hardly at all. When you try to remember a story, you will find that you have stored away a picture of the setting along with the plot and characters.

THINK ABOUT IT!

1. In what time period would you place "Morning Search"? Reread the story and find three clues to the time period in which it is set.

2. What details of Nicole's house are given in the story? What time of day is it? What time of year is it?

3. The mood of the story is especially important to conceal the surprise ending. How would you describe the story's mood—and how does it help hide the surprise?

Morning Search

"Nicole, you'd better hurry up!" Mom called from downstairs.

Nicole was angry with herself. She couldn't find her textbook anywhere. She left her book in exactly the same place—on her bedside table—every night, so that she wouldn't have this problem in the morning. Last night, though, she'd been enjoying *Little House on the Prairie* so much, that she had read it instead of her textbook, and now she had no idea where her school book was.

Nicole reached around the back of the bedside table and under the bed. She ran her hands over the clean surfaces of her dresser and her bookshelf. With her feet, she gently felt the floor around her dresser and in front of her closet. Nothing.

"Nicole! Joey's already finished his breakfast." At the sound of the word "breakfast" she was suddenly aware of the smell of buttered rye toast. She grabbed her backpack and placing her left hand on her door frame, turned a sharp left out into the hallway. As she zipped toward the stairs, she almost stepped on a small object on the carpet. Her foot automatically pulled back before she stepped down onto what she was certain was one of Joey's matchbox cars. She gently kicked the toy in the direction of Joey's room.

As she reached the top step, she felt for the railing. About seven steps down, the sound of the stairwell opening to her right told Nicole she was at the landing, and she turned and headed down the remaining stairs to the kitchen.

Nicole walked straight to her seat and pounced on her toast.

Halfway through her breakfast, she turned suddenly toward the sound of Mom unzipping her book bag.

"My textbook?" she asked.

"You left it by the fireplace last night," Mom said. "I'm putting it in your book bag now."

"By the front door, please?"

"With your cane."

Nicole was relieved. "Thanks, Mom," she said.

Taking a final bite, she headed for the door.

INTO . . . New Providence

This is the story of a city. It is written as though it were true. But the city of New Providence is imaginary. A group of historians and city designers created it from old designs and plans of actual cities.

This is a story of how a city changes over time. The story has no characters. There are many settings, but no action. We see the city change over time, because we are given snapshots: from 1910, 1935, 1955, 1970, 1980, and 1992.

The theme of the story can be expressed in a word: change. The detailed pictures show the changes and the text explains them. No opinion is offered as to whether the changes are good or bad. The story just presents the facts. It is left to the reader to form an opinion.

EYES ON . . . Setting

The **setting** is the physical background of a story. The setting tells the reader *when* the story takes place and *where* it takes place. Setting can also include the weather, the clothing people wear, the furniture and design of a house, the region—whether city or country, and other details that help the reader enter into the story. All the things we need when we are planning a play—props, costume, scenery, and makeup—are the setting.

New Providence: A Changing Cityscape is nearly all setting and theme. Notice that the descriptions are very clear and exact. None of the poetic language that we see in *Kate Shelley* is used to describe *New Providence*.

See if you can keep track of the changes to the cityscape as you read the selection.

NEW PROVIDENCE
A CHANGING CITYSCAPE

CONCEIVED BY RENATA VON TSCHARNER AND RONALD LEE FLEMING ❧ THE TOWNSCAPE INSTITUTE ❧ ILLUSTRATIONS BY DENIS ORLOFF

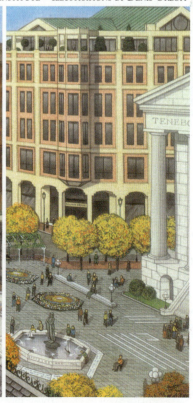

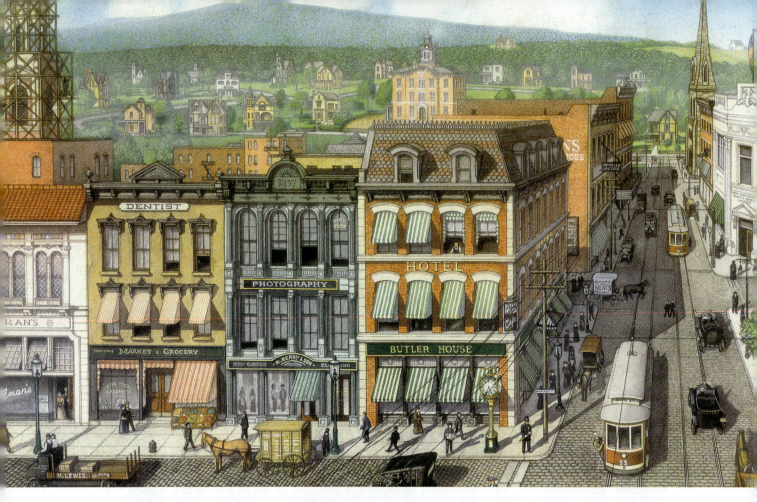

Put the city up; tear the city down; put it up again; let us find a city…. —CARL SANDBURG

1910

New Providence is thriving. Cobblestone[1] streets bustle with activity—Model T Fords, streetcars, and horse-drawn carts carrying meat, milk, and ice. There is no concert in the bandstand today, but a crowd has gathered in the square in front of the Town Hall and the Tenebo County Courthouse. A fountain has been built in commemoration of Chief Tenebo, a Native American from a local tribe. The statue is about to be unveiled. Around the base of the fountain is an inscription: GOOD CITIZENS ARE THE RICHES OF A CITY.

---

1. *Cobblestones* are naturally rounded stones that were used to pave streets before asphalt came into use.

WORD BANK
thriving (THRY ving) *adj.:* doing very well; prospering
commemoration (kuh MEM uh RAY shun) *n.:* in memory of some person or event
inscription (in SKRIP shun) *n.:* a word or words carved on stone or other hard surface; a brief dedication or note written by hand in a book, on a photograph, or on a similar item

New Providence's good citizens—women in long skirts and men in hats—buy fruit at the sidewalk stand in front of the grocery and most of their clothing and household items at Getz & McClure's, the largest store in town. They shop for shoes and jewelry and office supplies and have supper at Gilman's or at the Butler House Café.

The rural hillsides surrounding the city are lush, with comfortable Victorian homes dotting the landscape and the Bloom mill and worker housing in the distance. The large red brick schoolhouse is attended by all school-age children in the region. A flock of birds flies peacefully overhead.

New Providence is filled with a typical jumble of late-nineteenth-century architectural styles: Gothic, Classical, and Romanesque revivals, Queen Anne and Italianate Victorians. Pictured here is the Colonel Fleming House, which was built in the late eighteenth century and is the last single-family home left on the square.

WORD BANK **rural** (RUH rul) *adj.*: characteristic of or having to do with the country (compare to *urban*: characteristic of or having to do with the city)

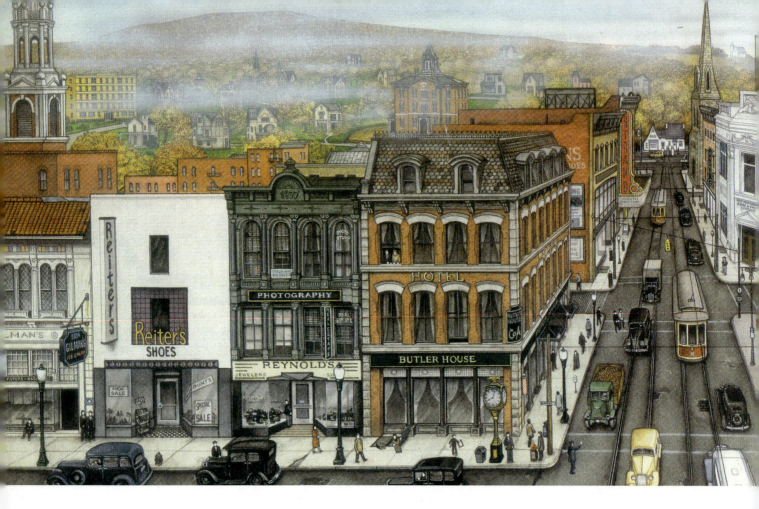

1935

As a mist rolls into New Providence, effects of the Great Depression are visible; the city has fallen on hard times. Gone is the bandstand from the courthouse square, where homeless men now huddle over trash can fires for warmth. A WPA sign publicizes the Works Progress Administration, a jobs program funded by the government. A line of jobless men waits for free bread outside the post office, and hoboes[2] are taking a free ride out of the city on trains. Many buildings are in need of repair.

But even in times such as these, life goes on. There is a concert playing at the Strand Theater. A huge Coca-Cola advertisement goes up on the side of a building. A streetlight now controls automobile traffic. The Bloom mill—expanded before the stock market crash—is still in operation, the grocery has become a shoe store, and the dry goods store, a jeweler's. The Colonel Fleming House now accommodates

---

2. *Hobo* is an old-fashioned word for a tramp or a jobless person who wanders from place to place.

three small businesses. Art Deco chrome and glass streamline some of the storefronts, contrasting with the older styles of the upper stories. A modern yellow apartment building squats on the hillside, while a biplane and a blimp cruise the skies.

The house at the end of Main Street has been replaced by a cottage-style gas station.

A neoclassical granite post office has been constructed, revealing the train station in the distance.

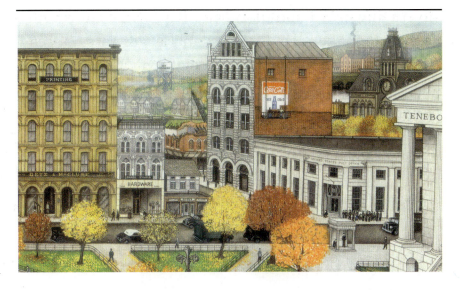

1955

A postwar prosperity settles over New Providence, although there are signs that downtown is deteriorating.

The night sky glows with neon, holiday lights, and lighted billboards advertising bread and used cars. Part of the courthouse square is now paved with asphalt to make room for more and larger cars. Buses have replaced streetcars. Franchises[3] like Rexall's and Woolworth's have moved into town, and the Alpine Motel attracts traveling businessmen. The New Providence Symphony Orchestra is performing at the Strand.

---

3. Sometimes companies, instead of doing their own marketing, sell the right to market their products or services to private individuals or groups. This right is called a *franchise* (FRAN chyz). The people who have bought the franchise use the name, advertisements, and products of the company, but privately own and run their own stores.

WORD BANK   **deteriorating** (dee TEER ee uh RAYT ing) *v.*: becoming worse in some or many ways

The elegant Butler House is now a liquor store and a boarding house for transients.[4] Next to it, a Victorian cast-iron building is being covered with prefabricated siding. Getz & McClure's has already been sheathed with stark metal grillwork and a currently popular style of lettering. Two of the small businesses in the Colonel Fleming House are boarded up. Behind it, a bland new building has been erected to house Monarch Insurance. The old slate roof of the Town Hall has been replaced by asphalt shingles. A fire is raging at the train station, while the citizens of New Providence go about their holiday shopping.

4. *Transients* (tran ZEE ints) are people, usually workers or salesmen, who stay in a city for a short time.

The nuclear age arrives: An air-raid siren has replaced the decorative ornament atop Town Hall, and the courthouse bears a fallout shelter sign.

The baby boom following World War II explains the new addition to the schoolhouse. The surrounding hills are gradually filling up with the ranch-style and split-level houses of suburbia.

1970

By 1970, downtown New Providence is an uninspired jumble of old and new. To attract people from thriving suburbia, part of Main Street has been converted into a pedestrian[5] mall, dominated by a harsh concrete fountain. But there is less traffic than ever in the city center, and fewer people actually live there.

A number of people in town today are gathered outside the courthouse, taking part in a protest march against the Vietnam War. Across the newly sunken and cemented square, a mugging is in progress. Graffiti mars the area, as do more and more billboards, and an Army/Navy surplus[6] store. The post office and several other buildings have been demolished and turned into parking lots, the Bloom mill is for rent, and the train station tower remains burnt out.

5. A *pedestrian* (puh DESS tree un) *mall* is a large area closed to traffic, used by people walking on foot.
6. *Surplus* is something extra or left over. *Army/navy surplus stores* sell leftover army and navy supplies.

WORD BANK   **graffiti** (gruh FEE tee) *n.:* words or pictures painted illegally on public property

The Alpine Motel is now a Holiday Inn, a Fotomat has opened, and a famous musician is playing at the Strand. A day school has opened, complete with colorful murals and giant toadstools. The Colonel Fleming House seems about to be rescued by a preservation group.[7] Victorian homes in the hills are disappearing to make room for highways, look-alike suburban housing, and another addition to the school. In the afternoon sky, a jet flies over the increasing number of powerlines strung across the horizon.

7. A *preservation group* is an organization that has been formed to save old buildings or sculptures that have historical value from being destroyed or changed.

An ordinary digital clock now hangs where there was once a quaint shoe sign, and the bank's classical architecture has recently been covered with mirrored glass.

The Butler House features trendy boutiques, a Day-Glo mural, and resident hippies. Space-age pavilions line the sidewalk.

1980

Ten years later, there are signs that downtown New Providence is sadly in need of recovery—and also signs that help is on the way.

Chief Tenebo's statue has been vandalized; debris blows around its dry base and across the square. Graffiti is everywhere, street lamps are smashed, and a police box has appeared. The Colonel Fleming House has been moved across the street, but its placement does not look permanent. In its old location are a Cor-Ten steel sculpture and Monarch Insurance's new highrise, which bears no architectural relationship to the buildings around it.

But the streets seem more populated, and people are again living—even barbecuing—downtown in the new red brick infill structure[8] next to McDonald's.

| WORD BANK | **vandalized** (VAN duh LYZD) *v.*: deliberately destroyed or damaged |
| | **debris** (duh BREE) *n.*: the remains of anything destroyed; bits of old waste matter lying about |

The only billboard in town advertises health food and a cultural event. The old Strand Theater is being expanded into a Cultural Center. And although the Butler House has been all but abandoned, a sign shows that rehabilitation is being planned. A superhighway now cuts through the hillside, making downtown more accessible to summer holiday travelers. A large parking structure has been built, and well-tended plantings soften the mall.

8. An *infill structure* is a building placed so as to fill up the gap between two other buildings.

Graffiti and rusted steel girders indicate that citizens' groups have so far been able to prevent further construction of a highrise office tower on the old post office site.

A Health Center has replaced the Medical Offices, and New Providence has its first McDonald's.

It is wisdom to think the people are the city.... —CARL SANDBURG

1992

In the sunny afternoon sky a flock of birds heads back to its winter home. Below, people have returned to the city—living, shopping, working, playing. New Providence has never looked better. Sidewalk vendors sell their produce once more, and traffic again flows through handsomely paved streets. Buses are made to look like old-fashioned trolleys. Chief Tenebo has been restored, and the bandstand is back, a concert in full swing. Gone are graffiti, billboards, and harsh sculptures. Plants and fall flowers are everywhere—even the parking structure has been elegantly camouflaged.

All of the old building facades have been renovated, and the condition of most buildings is strikingly similar to what it was in 1910. The Town Hall's slate roof has been restored, and the air-raid siren is gone. Street furniture is comfortable and

| WORD BANK | **facade** (fuh SOD) *n.:* the front of a building, especially a decorative one |
| | **renovated** (REN uh VAY tuhd) *v.:* restored to good condition as by repairing or remodeling |

compatible with[9] the architecture. The circular clock is back in front of the Butler House, now beautifully refurbished. An arcaded building where people live and work occupies the site of the controversial tower, serving as an entry into the restored train station, and an atrium full of plants softens the Monarch Insurance skyscraper. A Fitness Center has replaced the Health Center, and an arts festival is in progress at the Strand Cultural Center.

The good citizens of New Providence have worked hard to make the city livable again—and true to its heritage.

9. *Compatible with* means that something fits in with the people, objects, or ideas around it.

The Colonel Fleming House has been carefully restored—not as a historical museum but as an outdoor restaurant.

New buildings and additions to existing structures have been designed to complement the medley of architectural styles in downtown New Providence.

New Providence, a small American city, will not be found on any map. It is the creation of a team of architectural historians and designers, and yet its fictional cityscape is truly authentic. The buildings, the signs, even the street furniture can be found somewhere in urban America. Almost every detail was discovered in old photographs and assembled by the design team at The Townscape Institute.

Baltimore, Maryland (McDonald's building and H_2O fountain); Binghamton, New York (courthouse lights); Boston, Massachusetts (church in center and 1970 concrete plaza); Brookline, Massachusetts (church); Cambridge, Massachusetts (signs); Chelsea, Massachusetts (storefront); Chicago, Illinois (metal awning on the Butler House); Cincinnati, Ohio (1987 City Identity System booth); Denver, Colorado (building across the street from courthouse in 1910); Eugene, Oregon (1970 modern concrete fountain); Flint, Michigan (1910 shoe sign and street awnings); Fresno, California (1970-1980 sculptural clock tower); Garland, Utah (Bloom mill); Grand Rapids, Michigan (City Hall); Heber City, Utah (water tower); Junction City, Kansas (corner bank); Knoxville, Tennessee (billboard); Los Angeles, California (Getz & McClure building); Milwaukee, Wisconsin (suburban villas); Montclair, New Jersey (Colonel Fleming House); Montgomery, Alabama (Victorian cast-iron building); New York, New York (Butler House and train station); Portland, Oregon (fountain base); Richmond, Virginia (signs on Reiter's shoe store); Salem, Ohio (cornice on Main Street); San Diego, California (circular clock); Scottsdale, Arizona (parking structure with plantings); Staunton, Virginia (stained glass in McDonald's building); Syracuse, New York (layout of courthouse square); Topeka, Kansas (Alpine Motel sign); Townsend, Massachusetts (bandstand); Traverse City, Michigan (mansard roof on Butler House); Upper Sandusky, Ohio (horse fountain and pavilion); Waltham, Massachusetts (bench); Washington, D.C. (Masonic building); Westerville, Ohio (gas station); Wilkes-Barre, Pennsylvania (park outline); Wilmington, Delaware (1970 metal Main Street shelters); Winooski, Vermont (Main Street building).

QUICK REVIEW

1. What is the name of the city?

2. Which years of the city's existence are described?

3. What is the Butler House?

4. Whom does the fountain commemorate?

FOCUS

5. Select one change that stands out for you. Do you think it is a change for the better or for the worse? Why?

6. Choose a year and describe how New Providence looked that year. You may even choose a year in the future.

CREATING & WRITING

7. Choose one of the cityscapes described in the story, and write about what New Providence was like that year and why.

8. Choose a subject from 1910: cobblestone streets, Model T Fords, streetcars, horse-drawn carts, bandstand concerts, food shopping before there were supermarkets, or Victorian homes. Do you wish we had some of those things today, or are you thankful that we don't? Perhaps you have mixed feelings— you like the idea of, say, horse-drawn carts, but you know they would be slower and bumpier than a car. Write a paragraph about what life would be like if we still had the item you chose.

9. Draw a picture of one or several of the buildings in New Providence. In the caption, name the buildings and the year.

THEME

- The theme of a story is the idea that runs through the entire story.

- The idea that the author chooses for a theme is one that he thinks is true for all people, not just for the characters in the story.

- The plot, characters, and setting all help express the theme.

- Stories, poems, plays, and songs may express the same theme in different ways.

THINK ABOUT IT!

1. What idea is expressed in Sarah's words, "I can't spend one more day of my life as a slave"?

2. How does the river contribute to the theme of the story?

3. Can you list three ideas in the story that are true for everyone, not just for the characters in the story?

4. Name a story, poem, or song whose theme is "freedom."

No Turning Back

"Sarah, you can't swim across. You'll freeze."

The fear on Aunty's face didn't stop Sarah from taking the next step into the cold water of the river. "I can't spend one more day of my life as a slave, Aunty."

"We can try again tomorrow night," Aunty said.

Sarah turned her head around to face Aunty, but she kept her feet planted firmly in the direction of freedom. "Aunty, what is it you been saying to me these last two weeks when I get scared? When we hidin' in a swamp and feel the snakes swimmin' by our feet? When we hear those hounds baying in the distance?"

Aunty looked down. "'G-d will provide.'"

"'G-d will provide.' All my whole life, Aunty. When they sold Mama down to Alabama, you tell me G-d gonna provide. G-d got us this far. Why ain't He gonna provide right now?"

Aaaaaaaooooooo! The baying of the dogs was getting closer.

"No turning back now, Aunty," Sarah whispered fiercely. "C'mon."

Suddenly Aunty pointed downriver. A flat boat was being poled upriver by a white man in dark clothing. He was struggling against the current of the river, but he was headed straight for them.

"Tracker didn't say it was going to be a white man," said Aunty.

Sarah stood tall and proud. These weeks in the woods—this taste of freedom—had changed her. Either this white man was their ride to freedom, or she would dive in and outswim him to the other side.

About twenty feet from Sarah the man cupped a hand over his mouth.

"You folks sure ain't quiet," he shouted. "I heard you half a mile away."

Sarah held her breath.

The man drew to within fifteen feet. "Good thing, I guess. Rucker said you was *supposed* to cross down that way."

Sarah breathed a huge sigh of relief. "You Mr. Rucker's man?"

The man nodded. "Rucker will meet you at the barn," he said. "C'mon, get on before you freeze."

Barely aware of the chilly air, Sarah turned her eyes heavenward and mouthed the words, "Thank You."

INTO . . . The Silent Lobby

A group of people travel to Washington, D.C. in an old bus. These are poor people dressed in old clothes. They have come to insist on their right to vote—a right that is guaranteed by the Constitution. It takes courage and determination to stand up to people who are more powerful than you, who look down on you, and who make you feel poor and shabby.

EYES ON . . . Theme

A famous person said, *Never doubt that a small group of committed citizens can change the world.* This is a powerful idea. This is what *The Silent Lobby,* which is based on events of the 1960s, is about. (*Committed citizens* are people who have made a firm decision to bring about some change.) This idea is the theme of this story.

The theme is the message of a story. It is what the author wants us to know, the reason the author wrote the story. The author uses plot, setting, and characters to express the theme. Themes are about ideas like the struggle for freedom, courage, personal responsibility, and justice.

THE
SILENT LOBBY
MILDRED PITTS WALTER

THE OLD BUS CHUGGED ALONG the Mississippi highway toward Washington, D.C. I shivered from icy winds and from excitement and fear. Excitement about going to Washington and fear that the old bus would stall again on the dark, lonely, icy road and we'd never make it.

Oh, just to sleep. The chug-chug-chugging of the old motor was not smooth enough to make soothing sounds, and I could not forget the words Mama and Papa had said just before me and Papa left to pick up twenty other people who filled the bus.

"It's too dangerous," Mama had said. "They just might bomb that bus."

"They could bomb this house for that matter," Papa said.

"I know," Mama went on. "That's why I don't want you to go. Why can't you just forget about this voting business and let us live in peace?"

"There can be no peace without freedom," Papa said.

CONSTITUTIONAL AMENDMENT XV

Passed by Congress February 26, 1869.
Ratified February 3, 1870.

Section 1.
The right of citizens of the United States to vote shall not be denied or abridged by the United States or by any State on account of race, color, or previous condition of servitude—

Section 2.
The Congress shall have the power to enforce this article by appropriate legislation.

"And you think someone is going to give you freedom?" Mama asked with heat in her voice. "Instead of going to Washington, you should be getting a gun to protect us."

"There are ways to win a struggle without bombs and guns. I'm going to Washington and Craig is going with me."

"Craig is too young."

"He's eleven. That's old enough to know what this is all about," Papa insisted.

I KNEW. IT HAD ALL STARTED TWO YEARS AGO, IN 1963.

Papa was getting ready to go into town to register[1] to vote. Just as he was leaving, Mr. Clem, Papa's boss, came and warned Papa that he should not try to register.

"I intend to register," Papa said.

"If you do, I'll have to fire you." Mr. Clem drove away in a cloud of dust.

"You ought not go," Mama said, alarmed. "You know that people have been arrested and beaten for going down there."

"I'm going," Papa insisted.

"Let me go with you, Papa," I was scared, too, and wanted to be with him if he needed help.

"No, you stay and look after your mama and the house till I get back."

Day turned to night, and Papa had not returned. Mama paced the floor. Was Papa in jail? Had he been beaten? We waited, afraid. Finally, I said, "Mama, I'll go find him."

"Oh, no!" she cried. Her fear scared me more, and I felt angry because I couldn't do anything.

At last we heard Papa's footsteps. The look on his face let us know right away that something was mighty wrong.

"What happened, Sylvester?" Mama asked.

"I paid the poll tax, passed the literacy test, but I didn't interpret the state constitution the way they wanted. So they wouldn't register me."

Feeling a sense of sad relief, I said, "Now you won't lose your job."

"Oh, but I will. I tried to register."

---

1. Before someone can vote in an election for the first time, the person must complete a form and send it into the local board of elections. The person's name will then be placed on the list of *registered voters* and, on election day, that person can vote.

WORD BANK	**struggle** (STRUH gul) *n.:* a fight
	alarmed (uh LARMD) *adj.:* suddenly frightened or worried

Even losing his job didn't stop Papa from wanting to vote. One day he heard about Mrs. Fannie Lou Hamer and the Mississippi Freedom Democratic Party. The Freedom Party registered people without charging a poll tax, without a literacy test, and without people having to tell what the Mississippi Constitution was about.

On election day in 1964, Papa proudly voted for Mrs. Hamer, Mrs. Victoria Grey, and Mrs. Annie Devine to represent the people of the Second Congressional District of Mississippi. Eighty-three thousand other black men and women voted that day, too. Great victory celebrations were held in homes and community centers. But the Governor of Mississippi, Paul B. Johnson, declared all of those eighty-three thousand votes of black people illegal. He gave certificates of election to three white men—William Colmer, John Williams, and a Mr. Whittier—to represent the mostly black Second Congressional District.

Members of the Freedom Party were like Papa—they didn't give up. They got busy when the governor threw out their votes. Lawyers from all over the country came to help. People signed affidavits saying that when they tried to register they lost their jobs, they were beaten, and their homes were burned and businesses bombed. More than ten thousand people signed petitions to the governor asking him to count their votes. There was never a word from the governor.

MY MIND RETURNED TO THE SOUND OF THE OLD BUS

slowly grinding along. Suddenly the bus stopped. Not again! We'd never make it now. Papa got out in the cold wind and icy drizzling rain and raised the hood. While he worked, we sang and clapped our hands to keep warm. I could hear Sister Phyllis praying with all her might for our safety. After a while we were moving along again.

I must have finally fallen asleep, for a policeman's voice woke me. "You can't stop here near the Capitol," he shouted.

"Our bus won't go," Papa said.

"If you made it from Mississippi all the way to D.C., you'll make it from here," the policeman barked.

WORD BANK

affidavit (AH fih DAY vit) *n.:* a written statement made with the promise to tell the truth

petition (puh TIH shun) *n.:* a written request signed by a large number of people

At first the loud voice frightened me. Then, wide awake, sensing the policeman's impatience, I wondered why Papa didn't let him know that we would go as soon as the motor started. But Papa, knowing that old bus, said nothing. He stepped on the starter. The old motor growled and died. Again the policeman shouted, "I said get out of here."

"We'll have to push it," Papa said.

Everyone got off the bus and pushed. Passersby stopped and stared. Finally we were safe on a side street, away from the Capitol with a crowd gathered around us.

"You mean they came all the way from Mississippi in that?" someone in the crowd asked.

Suddenly the old bus looked shabby. I lowered my head and became aware of my clothes: my faded coat too small; my cotton pants too thin. With a feeling of shame, I wished those people would go away.

"What brings you all to the District?" a man called to us.

"We've come to see about seating the people we voted for and elected," Papa answered. "Down home they say our votes don't count, and up here they've gone ahead and seated men who don't represent us. We've come to talk about that."

"So you've come to lobby," a woman shouted. The crowd laughed.

Why were they laughing? I knew that to lobby meant to try to get someone to decide for or against something. Yes, that was why we had

| WORD BANK | **lobby** (LAH bee) *v.*: to work at influencing lawmakers to vote a certain way |

CONSTITUTIONAL AMENDMENT XXIV

Passed by Congress August 27, 1962. Ratified January 23, 1964.

Section 1.
The right of citizens of the United States to vote in any primary or other election for President or Vice President, for electors for President or Vice President, or for Senator or Representative in Congress, shall not be denied or abridged by the United States or any State by reason of failure to pay poll tax or other tax.

Section 2.
The Congress shall have power to enforce this article by appropriate legislation.

come. I wished I could have said to those people who stood gawking at us that the suffering that brought us here was surely nothing to laugh about.

The laughter from the crowd quieted when another woman shouted, "You're too late to lobby. The House of Representatives will vote on that issue this morning."

Too late. That's what had worried me when the old bus kept breaking down. Had we come so far in this cold for nothing? Was it really too late to talk to members of the House of Representatives to persuade them to seat our representatives elected by the Freedom Party, not the ones chosen by the governor?

JUST THEN RAIN BEGAN TO FALL. THE CROWD QUICKLY LEFT, and we climbed onto our bus. Papa and the others started to talk. What would we do now? Finally, Papa said, "We can't turn back now. We've done too much and come too far."

After more talk we all agreed that we must try to do what we had come to do. Icy rain pelted us as we rushed against cold wind back to the Capitol.

A doorman stopped us on the steps. "May I have your passes?"

"We don't have any," Papa replied.

"Sorry, you have to have passes for seats in the gallery." The doorman blocked the way.

"We're cold in this rain. Let us in," Sister Phyllis cried.

"Maybe we should just go on back home," someone suggested.

"Yes. We can't talk to the legislators now, anyway," another woman said impatiently.

"No," Papa said. "We must stay if we do no more than let them see that we have come all this way."

"But we're getting soaking wet. We can't stand out here much longer," another protested.

"Can't you just let us in out of this cold?" Papa pleaded with the doorman.

"Not without passes." The doorman still blocked the way. Then he said, "There's a tunnel underneath this building. You can go there to get out of the rain."

WORD BANK	**legislators** (LEH jiss LAY torz) *n.:* lawmakers

WE CROWDED INTO THE TUNNEL AND LINED UP ALONG
the sides. My chilled body and hands came to life pressed against the warm
walls. Then footsteps and voices echoed through the tunnel. Police. This
tunnel...a trap! Would they do something to us for trying to get in without
passes? I wanted to cry out to Papa, but I could not speak.

The footsteps came closer. Then many people began to walk by. When they
came upon us, they suddenly stopped talking. Only the sound of their feet
echoed in the tunnel. Where had they come from? What did they do? "Who are
they, Papa?" I whispered.

"Congressmen and women." Papa spoke so softly, I hardly heard him, even
in the silence.

They wore warm coats, some trimmed with fur. Their shoes gleamed. Some
of them frowned at us. Others glared. Some sighed quickly as they walked by.
Others looked at us, then turned their eyes to their shoes. I could tell by a
sudden lift of the head and a certain look that some were surprised and scared.
And there were a few whose friendly smiles seemed to say, Right on!

I glanced at Papa. How poor he and our friends looked beside those well-
dressed people. Their clothes were damp, threadbare, and wrinkled; their shoes
were worn and mud stained. But they all stood straight and tall.

My heart pounded. I wanted to call out to those men and women, "Count
my Papa's vote! Let my people help make laws, too." But I didn't dare speak in
that silence.

Could they hear my heart beating? Did they know what was on my mind?
"L-rd," I prayed, "let them hear us in this silence."

Then two congressmen stopped in front of Papa. I was frightened until I
saw smiles on their faces.

"I'm Congressman Ryan from New York," one of them said. Then he
introduced a black man: "This is Congressman Hawkins from California."

"I'm Sylvester Saunders. We are here from Mississippi," Papa said.

"We expected you much earlier," Congressman Ryan said.

"Our old bus and bad weather delayed us," Papa explained.

"That's unfortunate. You could've helped us a lot. We worked late into the
night lobbying to get votes on your side. But maybe I should say on our side."
Mr. Ryan smiled.

"And we didn't do very well," Congressman Hawkins said.

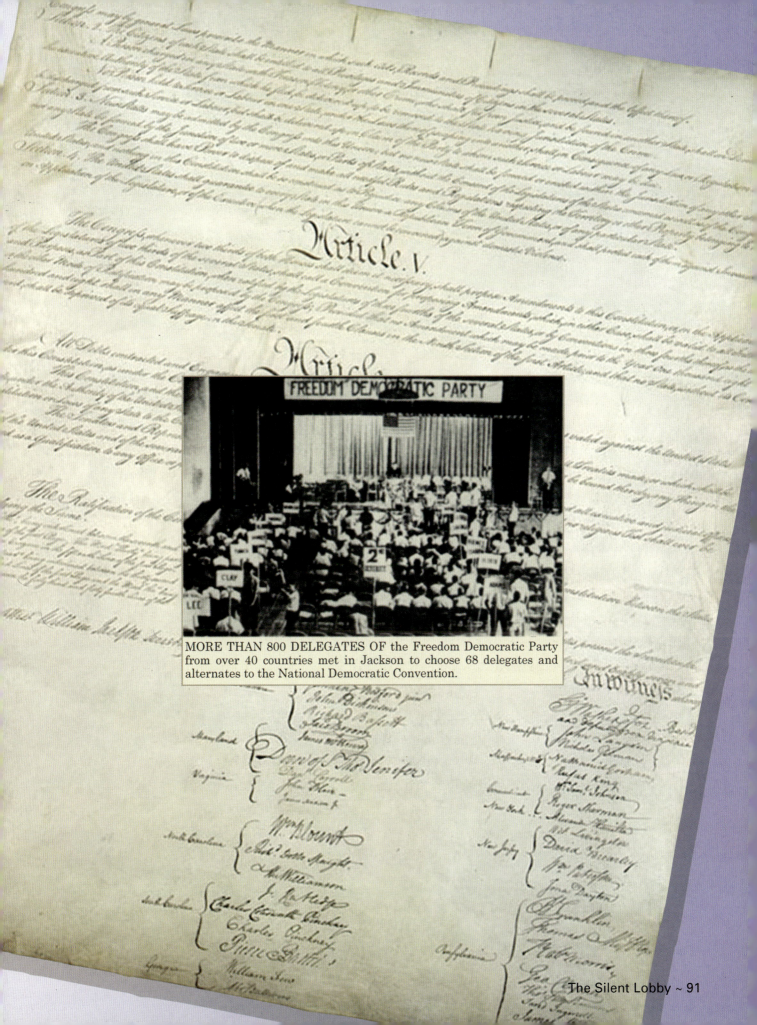

MORE THAN 800 DELEGATES OF the Freedom Democratic Party from over 40 countries met in Jackson to choose 68 delegates and alternates to the National Democratic Convention.

CONSTITUTIONAL AMENDMENT XXVI

Passed by Congress March 23, 1971.
Ratified July 1, 1971.

Note: Amendment 14, section 2, of the Constitution was modified by section 1 of the 26th amendment.

Section 1.
The right of citizens of the United States, who are eighteen years of age or older, to vote shall not be denied or abridged by the United States or by any State on account of age.

Section 2.
The Congress shall have power to enforce this article by appropriate legislation.

"We'll be lucky if we get fifty votes on our side today," Congressman Ryan informed us. "Maybe you would like to come in and see us at work."

"We don't have passes," I said, surprised at my voice.

"We'll see about getting all of you in," Congressman Hawkins promised.

A LITTLE LATER, AS WE FOUND SEATS IN THE GALLERY, Congressman Gerald Ford[2] from the state of Michigan was speaking. He did not want Mrs. Hamer and other fairly elected members of the Freedom Party seated in the House. He asked his fellow congressmen to stick to the rule of letting only those with credentials from their states be seated in Congress. The new civil rights act would, in time, undo wrongs done to black Americans. But for now, Congress should let the men chosen by Governor Johnson keep their seats and get on with other business.

Then Congressman Ryan rose to speak. How could Congress stick to rules that denied blacks their right to vote in the state of Mississippi? The rule of letting only those with credentials from a segregated[3] state have seats in the House could not justly apply here.

I looked down on those men and few women and wondered if they were listening. Did they know about the petitions? I remembered what Congressman Ryan had said: "We'll be lucky if we get fifty...." Only 50 out of 435 elected to the House.

Finally the time came for Congress to vote. Those who wanted to seat Mrs. Hamer and members of the Freedom Democratic Party were to say, yes. Those who didn't want to seat Mrs. Hamer were to say, no.

At every yes vote I could hardly keep from clapping my hands and shouting, "Yea! Yea!" But I kept quiet, counting: thirty, then forty, forty-eight...only two more. We would lose badly.

Then something strange happened. Congressmen and congresswomen kept saying "Yes. Yes. Yes." On and on, "Yes." My heart pounded. Could we win? I sat

---

2. *Congressman Gerald Ford* later became the 38th president of the United States.
3. Prior to the Civil Rights Act of 1964, in some states, black Americans were kept separate from white Americans in many situations. For example, white children and black children were sent to separate schools. States where blacks and whites were kept separate by law were called *segregated* (SEG rih GAY tid) *states.*

WORD BANK | **credentials** (kruh DENN shulz) *n.:* documents showing that a person has privileges

on my hands to keep from clapping. I looked at Papa and the others who had come with us. They all sat on the edge of their seats. They looked as if they could hardly keep from shouting out, too, as more yes votes rang from the floor.

When the voting was over, 148 votes had been cast in our favor. What had happened? Why had so many changed their minds?

Later, Papa introduced me to Congressman Hawkins. The congressman asked me, "How did you all know that some of us walk through that tunnel from our offices?"

"We didn't know," I answered. "We were sent there out of the rain."

"That's strange," the congressman said. "Your standing there silently made a difference in the vote. Even though we lost this time, some of them now know that we'll keep on lobbying until we win."

I felt proud. Papa had been right when he said to Mama, "There are ways to win a struggle without bombs and guns." We had lobbied in silence and we had been heard.

ABOUT THE AUTHOR

Mildred Pitts Walter was born in 1922. The seventh child of an African-American family in Louisiana, young Mildred experienced poverty and racial prejudice. However, her parents gave her a strong sense of pride and strength. After graduating from college, she moved to Los Angeles, where she taught elementary school and worked with her husband in the civil rights movement. When Walter asked a book publisher for children's books about black people, he suggested she write one herself. The result was one book, and then many more fiction and nonfiction works about people of color. Mildred Walter lives in Denver, Colorado.

Studying the Selection

FIRST IMPRESSIONS

How would you have felt, standing in the tunnel, as the congressmen and women walked by?

QUICK REVIEW

1. Where is the old bus coming from and where is it going?

2. Who were the three people who had been elected by the people of the Second Congressional District?

3. What organization registered people without charging a poll tax, without a literacy test, and without people having to tell what the Mississippi Constitution was about?

4. What had Papa's boss said he would do, if Papa registered to vote?

FOCUS

5. Why does Papa insist that Craig go on the bus ride to Washington?

6. One of the themes of *The Silent Lobby* is the struggle for equality—black Americans are supposed to have the same rights as white Americans and they are struggling to get those rights. Why don't people want them to vote?

CREATING & WRITING

7. You are a member of Congress. You changed your vote, after seeing the people from Mississippi standing in the tunnel. Write a letter home to one of your grandparents, explaining why you did so.

8. Read through the story once again, and list some examples of actions that show that people from Mississippi don't give up. Make sure you give the page numbers in parentheses.

9. Study the stanza from the *I Have a Dream* speech that your teacher has provided. You and the rest of your classmates will recite the part assigned to you. Notice how some of the lines are repeated, making the speech almost like a song or a poem.

To a Daughter Leaving Home

Linda Pastan

When I taught you
at eight to ride
a bicycle, loping along
beside you
5   as you wobbled away
on two round wheels,
my own mouth rounding
in surprise when you pulled
ahead down the curved
10   path of the park,
I kept waiting
for the thud
of your crash as I
sprinted to catch up,
15   while you grew
smaller, more breakable
with distance,
pumping, pumping
for your life, screaming
20   with laughter,
the hair flapping
behind you like a
handkerchief waving
goodbye.

Whatif

Shel Silverstein

Last night, while I lay thinking here,
Some whatifs crawled inside my ear
And pranced and partied all night long
And sang their same old Whatif song:
5   Whatif I'm dumb in school?
Whatif they've closed the swimming-pool?
Whatif I get beat up?
Whatif there's poison in my cup?
Whatif I start to cry?
10   Whatif I get sick and die?
Whatif I flunk that test?
Whatif green hair grows on my chest?
Whatif nobody likes me?
Whatif a bolt of lightning strikes me?
15   Whatif I don't grow taller?
Whatif my head starts getting smaller?
Whatif the fish won't bite?
Whatif the wind tears up my kite?
Whatif they start a war?
20   Whatif my bed falls through the floor?
Whatif the bus is late?
Whatif my teeth don't grow in straight?
Whatif I tear my pants?
Whatif I never learn to dance?
25   Everything seems swell, and then
The night-time Whatifs strike again!

The Whippoorwill Calls
(for Harriet Tubman)

No one hears her
Coming
Through the woods
At night
5   For she is like
A whippoorwill
Moving through the trees
On silent wings.

No one sees her
10   Hiding
In the woods
By day
For she is like
A whippoorwill
15   Blending into leaves
On the forest floor.

And one night
The whippoorwill calls
And the warm air
20   Carries the haunting sound
Across the fields
And into the small dark cabins.

And only the slaves know
It is Harriet.

Beverly McLoughland

Figures in the Field Against the Sky!

Antonio Machado

Figures in the field against the sky!

Two slow oxen plowing

a knoll in early autumn:

between the black heads

5 bent below the heavy yoke

hangs a basket made of broom and reed—

a child's cradle.

Behind the team

a man plows, leaning toward the earth;

10 a woman

throws seed in open furrows.

Under a cloud of flame and crimson

in the green fluid gold of sunset,

these shadows grow gigantic.

ABOUT THE AUTHORS

Linda Pastan, born in New York City in 1932, was already on her way to a promising career as a poet, when she dropped everything to marry and start a family. Once her children were in school, however, she resumed writing poetry. As we see in *To a Daughter Leaving Home,* she often drew upon her life as a wife and mother for subject matter. Pastan has written more than fifteen volumes of poetry. The Pastans live in Potomac, Maryland.

Shel Silverstein, born in 1930 in Chicago, Illinois, started drawing and writing in his early teens. After his service with the U.S. armed forces, he worked as a cartoonist until a well-known editor convinced him to write for children. He wrote and illustrated sixteen books for children, among them *A Light in the Attic.* He also wrote numerous songs. Shel Silverstein died in 1999 in Key West, Florida.

Beverly McLoughland, born in 1946 in New Jersey, was an elementary school teacher before deciding to pursue a career as a writer. Her poems have appeared in magazines and anthologies for young people. She has also published a collection of her own poems. Her wonder at human creativity and the natural world are the inspiration for many of her poems. She currently lives in Virginia.

Antonio Machado, born in 1875, was one of Spain's greatest 20th century poets. By the early 1900s he had begun writing poetry, taken a teaching position, and married. In 1912, one year following his wife's death, Machado published a volume of poems in her memory. After graduating from a Madrid university, he and his brother wrote several plays together. During his lifetime, Machado wrote more than twenty volumes of poetry, and nine plays.

Studying the Selection   POETRY

To a Daughter Leaving Home

1. What is this poem about? Give a short, simple answer in two or three sentences.

2. In how many sentences is the poem written?

3. Describe one kind of repetition the poet uses. Give examples from the poem.

4. Give an example of onomatopoeia from the poem.

5. What is the strongest picture you have in your mind from the poem? (There is no single correct answer to this question.)

Whatif

1. What is a "whatif"?

2. This poem is different from the other three in several ways. In two sentences, describe two of the ways *Whatif* is different from *To a Daughter Leaving Home, The Whippoorwill Calls,* and *Figures in the Field Against the Sky!*

3. Pick one of the Whatifs and think about how a person could deal with such an event if it actually happened. After all, difficult events occur in all of our lives. Most of us, at some time, don't feel smart enough, brave enough, or liked enough by other children in school. How do we find courage? How do we get through embarrassing situations? Write one or two paragraphs. You may write something humorous if you wish.

The Whippoorwill Calls

1. How is the second stanza like the first stanza?

2. In this poem, Harriet Tubman is compared to a whippoorwill. Write a three stanza poem, similar to this one, about another hero you know of. In the first two stanzas of your poem, compare the hero to a bird, animal, or insect. In the third stanza, let the reader know who the hero really is.

3. Choose one of the stanzas to memorize. Your teacher will organize groups for performance before the class.

Figures in a Field Against the Sky!

1. Why does the poet use an exclamation point?

2. Where does the poet repeat the letter *f?*
Where does the poet repeat the letters *b, h,* and *k,*

Where does the poet repeat the long *o* sound (don't forget to include –*ow*—where it sounds like *oh*)?

Where does the poet repeat the letter *g?*

3. This poem has three sentences. Pick one and rewrite it in prose (regular sentences, not poetry). Use a dictionary if there are any words you don't understand.

EXTRA! EXTRA! READ ALL ABOUT IT!

Create a Newspaper

1. You have read five selections in this unit: *Samuel's Choice, Slower Than the Rest, Kate Shelley, New Providence,* and *The Silent Lobby.* Pick one of the selections and make a table for your selection, using the column categories below. For *New Providence,* your **Who** will be The City. For *Slower Than the Rest,* you will have to make up your **When**—but it could just be the day before the date the newspaper is published.

Selection	Who	What	When	Where
Samuel's Choice				

2. Now, on a large sheet of paper, create your newspaper: its name, its motto, the date of publication. If you are not familiar with newspaper formats, ask your parents or teacher for a newspaper, so that you have an example to follow. A newspaper motto is something like, "All the News That's Fit to Print," "The Journal That Helps You Judge," or "More News Than You Need."

3. Now you are ready to create the headlines and write the copy (words) for your news story—the big story of the day, for example, **Samuel Makes Big Decision** or **Boy Brings Turtle to School** or **New Providence: Down in the Dumps.**

4. Make sure your news article includes the who, what, when, and where. Try to conclude your article with **Why**—why did the event occur.

THE MYSTERIOUS STORYTELLER

You Are a Stranger Who Has Come to Town to Tell a Story

1. Once more, pick one of the selections. Now, you are going to be one of the characters in the story you have selected. You may be a major character or one of the minor characters. You can even be one of the buildings in New Providence. Make or find some piece of clothing or a prop (such as a cane if you were an old person or a chimney if you were a building that had a chimney) that helps you look like the character. You can also—with help from a grownup or a sibling—put on makeup to help you get into character, when the time comes for your presentation.

2. Your presentation will be very simple. You will give your audience some biographical information about yourself. You will conclude by asking your class, "Who am I?" Biographical information could be something like, "I am a woman. I was born in Brooklyn, New York and lived from 1725 to 1810. During my life I have made a lot of buttermilk." And so forth. Give several facts about your life, so that your class can make a good guess. Don't be afraid to be funny.

3. Make notes on index cards for that moment when you are to be the mysterious stranger. Practice your presentation in front of your family to make sure it works smoothly. Good luck!

THE PLAY'S THE THING!

Acting and Teamwork

1. Your teacher will help you and your class form small groups.

2. You and your group are going to act out a scene from one of the five stories in which a small group of people is involved in the action. Will you be American soldiers fighting the British in a creek? Will you be the students listening to the turtle presentation? Will you be a group of homeless men standing over trash can fires during the Great Depression in New Providence? There are many possibilities.

3. You and your team will get together to work out a short script and rehearse your big scene.

4. Good luck with your presentation!

IT TAKES COURAGE TO WRITE

Your Favorite Courageous Character

1. What is courage? Look up the word in the dictionary and write down the definition(s). Now look up the word in a good thesaurus and write down some of the synonyms given for courage.

2. Think about the characters in each of the selections, including those in the poems. All of them have courage. But which one impressed you the most? Who did you think was most brave?

3. Now it's time to write several paragraphs. In your first paragraph, you are going to say what courage is. You are going to tell your reader what some of the synonyms are for courage, too. For the final sentence of your first paragraph you will write something like, "These words remind me of _____ *the hero or heroine* _____ in _____ *the name of the story or poem* _____, and I am going to write about (him or her)." Use your second paragraph to give examples of your hero's good qualities and actions. Use your third paragraph to conclude. Here is an example of a conclusion: "For all of these reasons, I picked this character as my favorite. I hope that I can be as brave if I ever have to face the situation my character faced."

unit 2

GROWING

CONFLICT

- Conflict means a struggle.

- A conflict can be *external* or *internal*.

- An *external* conflict is a struggle between a person and another person, a group of people, or a force of nature.

- An *internal* conflict is a conflict of ideas or feelings *within* a person.

THINK ABOUT IT!

1. What is the external conflict at the center of the story?

2. What did Ryan do to Ernie the last time they raced?

3. What do you think are Ryan's two internal conflicts in this race?

4. What is the outcome of Ryan's internal conflict?

The Race

Ernie's stomach was tight as he waited for the starter's pistol. He looked over at Ryan Douglas, the boy he had to beat. Ryan refused to make eye contact.

Bang!

Ernie lurched forward with the other runners, keeping a close eye on Ryan.

By the end of the first mile, the pack of runners had started to spread out. Ten or fifteen steps behind Ryan, Ernie didn't want to get any closer as they entered the woods. The last time he tried to pass Ryan in the woods, the other boy had stepped on his foot, sending him plunging to the ground and costing him the race.

Ryan left the woods for the final half-mile less than ten seconds ahead of Ernie, but when Ernie came out into the late summer sun, it seemed like Ryan had doubled the distance between them. He couldn't afford to start sprinting. Not yet. Picking up his pace slightly, he began slowly to whittle away the distance between them. Ryan never looked back, but each time Ernie got within a few steps, his opponent surged ahead.

Ernie refused to panic. He had time. Turning up his pace one more notch, he closed the gap between them to a single step and allowed himself to cruise at Ryan's pace.

A lump formed in Ernie's throat as he spotted the crowd at the finish line.

His legs felt strong. His wind was good.

Ernie threw himself into high gear.

Breaking first gave him the edge he needed. Though he could feel the other boy's footsteps pounding the grass behind him, Ernie concentrated only on the finish line. The crowd, the coaches, the other racers all disappeared. From somewhere deep inside himself, Ernie drew an extra surge of energy and bolted across the finish line a full five strides ahead of Ryan.

Afterward, when Ernie was stretching, he heard a voice behind him say, "Great race."

Ernie turned around. It was Ryan.

"Thanks," Ernie said.

Ryan smiled. "I'll get you next time."

Ernie smiled back. "I'll be there."

INTO . . . Gold-Mounted Guns

At some point in your life, you may find yourself copying the not-so-nice behavior of a friend or acquaintance. When we do this, it is usually because we want to be part of "the group," or accepted as a friend by the person whose behavior we are copying. At times, being bad or mean makes us feel as though we are strong or brave, or as though our lives are very exciting. If you have ever done this, was anyone hurt by your behavior? You'll see what happens in this story full of surprises.

EYES ON . . . Conflict

When we are mean, we may feel bad inside. That means that our behavior is *in conflict* with what we think is right. This is **internal conflict**. It's as if our actions are having an argument with our ideas.

Being mean isn't necessarily robbing a person of his money—which is what happens in *Gold-Mounted Guns.* Being mean can be choosing not to talk to someone, because your friends make fun of, or ignore, that person. Most of us are taught not to hurt other people's feelings, but most of us also want to be accepted and popular. That can sometimes create a conflict within us.

Sometimes, a person's conflict is with an outside force, such as the weather, a fire, or a disease. This is called **external conflict**. After you read this story once, see if you can find both kinds of conflict in it.

Gold-Mounted Guns

F. R. Buckley

Evening had fallen on Longhorn City. To the south a lone star twinkled in the velvet sky. Soon a hard-faced man ambled down the main street and chose a pony from the dozen hitched beside Tim Geogehan's[1] general store. The town was lit only by weak lights from the one store and one saloon,[2] so it was from the dark shadows that a voice came. It was calling to the hard-faced man.

"Tommy!" the voice softly called.

---

1. Geogehan's (GAY gunz)
2. A *saloon* is a bar.

WORD BANK	**ambled** (AM buld) *v.*: walked slowly and casually
	hitched *v.*: fastened, tied

The hard-faced man made a slight movement—a bare flick of the hand at the gun belt, but it was a movement perfectly understood by the figure in the shadows.

"Wait a minute!" the voice pleaded.

A moment later, his hands upraised, the figure of a young man moved into the zone of light that shone bravely out through Tim Geogehan's back window.

"Don't shoot," he said, trying to control the nervousness caused by the weapon pointing steadily at him. "I'm—a friend."

For perhaps fifteen seconds the newcomer and the hard-faced man studied each other with the steady eyes of those who take chances of life and death. The young man noted the sinister droop of a gray mustache over a hidden mouth, and shivered a little as his gaze met that of a pair of steel-blue eyes. The lean man with the gun saw before him a boyish yet rather handsome face marked now by a certain desperation.

"What do you want?" he asked, sharply.

"Can I put my hands down?" countered the boy.

The lean man considered.

"All things bein' equal," he

WORD BANK	**sinister** (SIN iss ter) *adj.:* looking a bit frightening or threatening
	desperation (DESS puh RAY shun) *n.:* a feeling of hopelessness
	countered (KOWN terd) *v.:* answered a question with a question

said, "I think I'd rather you'd first tell me how you got round to callin' me Tommy. Been askin' people in the street?"

"No," said the boy. "I only got into town this afternoon, an' I ain't a fool anyway. I seen you ride in this afternoon, and the way folks backed away from you made me wonder who you was. Then I seen them gold-mounted guns of yourn, an' of course I knew. Nobody ever had guns like them but Pecos Tommy. I could ha' shot you while you was gettin' your horse, if I'd been that way inclined."

The lean man bit his mustache.

"Put 'em down. What do you want?"

"I want to join you."

"You want to *what?*"

"Yeah, I know it sounds foolish to you, mebbe," said the young man. "But, listen—your side-kicker's in jail down in Rosewell. I figured I could take his place—anyway, till he got out. I know I ain't got any record, but I can ride, an' I can shoot the pips out of a ten-spot at ten paces.[3] I also got a little job to bring into the firm,[4] to start with."

---

3. A *spot* is a playing card and *pips* are dots. A ten spot is a playing card with ten pips, or dots. Ten paces is the distance a man covers when he takes ten normal steps. The speaker can shoot the dots off a card while standing ten steps away from it.

4. A *firm* is a company. Here, the word is used humorously; the crook is calling his gang of outlaws a "firm."

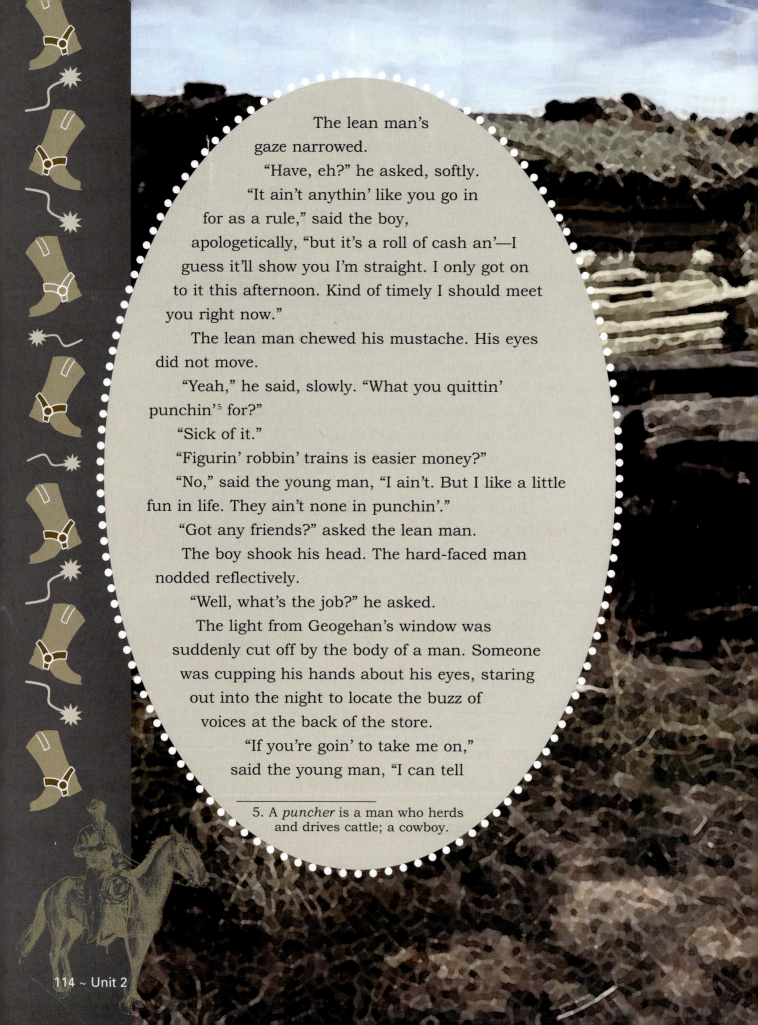

The lean man's gaze narrowed.

"Have, eh?" he asked, softly.

"It ain't anythin' like you go in for as a rule," said the boy, apologetically, "but it's a roll of cash an'—I guess it'll show you I'm straight. I only got on to it this afternoon. Kind of timely I should meet you right now."

The lean man chewed his mustache. His eyes did not move.

"Yeah," he said, slowly. "What you quittin' punchin'[5] for?"

"Sick of it."

"Figurin' robbin' trains is easier money?"

"No," said the young man, "I ain't. But I like a little fun in life. They ain't none in punchin'."

"Got any friends?" asked the lean man.

The boy shook his head. The hard-faced man nodded reflectively.

"Well, what's the job?" he asked.

The light from Geogehan's window was suddenly cut off by the body of a man. Someone was cupping his hands about his eyes, staring out into the night to locate the buzz of voices at the back of the store.

"If you're goin' to take me on," said the young man, "I can tell

_____

5. A *puncher* is a man who herds and drives cattle; a cowboy.

you while we're ridin' toward it. If you ain't—why, there's no need to go no further."

The lean man slipped back into its holster the gold-mounted gun he had drawn. He glanced once at the figure in the window and again, piercingly, at the boy whose face now showed white in the light of the rising moon. Then he turned his pony and mounted.

"Come on," he commanded.

Five minutes later the two had passed the limits of the town.[6] They were heading for the low range of hills to the south. By this time, Will Arblaster had given the details of his job to the unemotional man at his side.

"How do you know the old guy's got the money?" came a level question.

"I saw him come out of the bank this afternoon, grinnin' all over his face an' stuffin' it into his pants-pocket," said the boy. "An' when he was gone, I kind of inquired who he was. His name's Sanderson. He lives in this yer cabin right ahead a mile. Looked kind of a soft old geezer—kind that'd give up without any trouble. Must ha' been quite some cash there, judgin' by the size of the roll. But I guess when *you* ask him for it, he won't mind lettin' it go."

---

6. The borders of a town are called the *town limits*.

WORD BANK	**piercingly** (PEER sing lee) *adv.*: sharply and knowingly
	level (LEH vul) *adj.*: sensible; spoken in a calm, even voice

"I ain't goin' to ask him," said the lean man. "This is your job."

The boy hesitated.

"Well, if I do it right," he asked, with a trace of tremor in his voice, "will you take me along with you sure?"

"Yeah—I'll take you along."

The two riders rounded a shoulder of the hill. There, in the moonlight, they saw the dark shape of a cabin, its windows unlighted. The lean man chuckled.

"He's out."

Will Arblaster swung off his horse.

"Maybe," he said, "but likely the money ain't. He started off home. If he's had to go out again, likely he's hid the money someplace. Folks know *you're* about. I'm goin' to see."

Stealthily he crept toward the house. The moon went behind a cloud-bank, and the darkness swallowed him. The lean man, motionless on his horse, heard the rap of knuckles on the door— then a pause, and the rattle of the latch. A moment later came the heavy thud of a shoulder against wood—a cracking sound, and a crash as the door went down. The lean man's lips tightened. From within the cabin came the noise of the boy stumbling over furniture. Then the

WORD BANK

stealthily (STELL thuh lee) *adv.*: quietly, carefully, and secretly so as not to be discovered

fitful fire of a match
lit the windows. The man
on the horse, twenty yards away,
could hear the clumping of the
other's boots on the rough board floor,
and every rustle of the papers that he
fumbled in his search. Another match scratched
and sputtered, and then came a sudden cry of
triumph. Running feet padded across the short
grass and Will Arblaster drew up, panting.

"Got it!" he gasped. "The old fool! Put it in a tea
canister[7] right on the mantelshelf.[8] Enough to choke a
horse! Feel it!"

The lean man, unemotional as ever, reached down
and took the roll of money.

"Got another match?" he asked.

Willie struck one, and watched, panting, while his
companion flipped through the bills.

"Fifty tens," said the lean man. "Five hundred
dollars. Guess I'll carry it."

His cold blue eyes turned downward, and focused
again on the younger man's upturned face. The
bills were stowed in a pocket of the belt beside
one of those gold-mounted guns. For a moment,
the lean man's hand seemed to hesitate over
its butt; then, as Willie smiled and nodded,

---

7. A *tea canister* is a small box or jar, often
part of a set, used for holding tea.
8. A shelf built above the opening of
a fireplace is called a *mantelshelf*
or mantelpiece.

WORD
BANK

fitful (FIT full) *adj.:* stopping and
starting

it moved away. The match burned out.

"Let's get out of here," Willie urged. The hand which had hovered over the gun-butt grasped the boy's shoulder.

"No, not yet," the man said quietly. "Not just yet. Get on your hawss, an' set still awhile."

The young man mounted. "What's the idea?"

"Why!" said the level voice. "This is a kind of novelty to me. Robbin' trains, you ain't got any chance to see results, but this here's different. Figure this old guy'll be back pretty soon. I'd like to see what he does when he finds his roll's gone. Ought to be amusin'!"

The boy tried to laugh. "Ain't he liable to—"

"He can't see us," said the lean man with a certain new cheerfulness in his voice. "An' besides, he'll think we'd naturally be miles away. An' besides that, we're mounted, all ready."

"What's that?" whispered the boy, laying a hand on the man's arm.

They listened.

"Probably him," the lean man said. "Now stay still."

There were two riders—by their voices, a man and a girl. They were laughing as they rode up to a broken-down old stable at the rear of the house.

WORD BANK   **novelty** (NAH vul tee) *n.:* new experience

They put up the horses, then came round to the front. Walking to the door, their words came clearer to the ears of the listeners.

"I feel mean[9] about it, anyhow," said the girl's voice. "You going on living here, Daddy, while—"

"Tut-tut-tut!" said the old man. "What's five hundred to me? I ain't never had that much in a lump, an' shouldn't know what to do with it if I had. 'Sides, your Aunt Elviry didn't give it to you for nothin'. 'If she wants to go to college,' says she, 'let her prove it by workin'. I'll pay half, but she's got to pay t'other half.' Well, you worked, an'—Where on earth did I put that key?"

There was a silence, broken by the grunts of the old man as he searched his pockets. Then the girl spoke, and the tone of her voice was the more terrible for the restraint she was putting on it.

"Daddy—the—the—did you leave the money in the house?"

"Yes. What is it?" cried the old man.

"Daddy—the door's broken down, and—"

There was a hoarse cry. Boot-heels stumbled across the boards, and again a match flared. Its pale light showed a

_____
9. An old-fashioned definition of the word *mean* is selfish or stingy. That is how the word is used here.

WORD BANK   **restraint** (ree STRAINT) *n.:* control, holding back

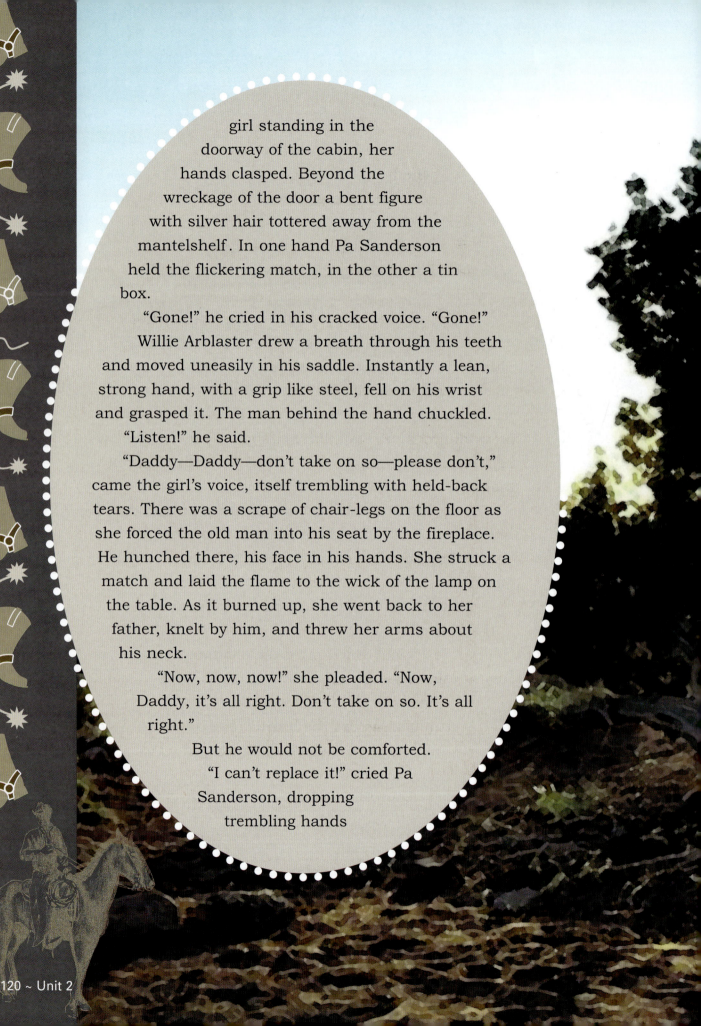

girl standing in the
doorway of the cabin, her
hands clasped. Beyond the
wreckage of the door a bent figure
with silver hair tottered away from the
mantelshelf. In one hand Pa Sanderson
held the flickering match, in the other a tin
box.

"Gone!" he cried in his cracked voice. "Gone!"
Willie Arblaster drew a breath through his teeth
and moved uneasily in his saddle. Instantly a lean,
strong hand, with a grip like steel, fell on his wrist
and grasped it. The man behind the hand chuckled.

"Listen!" he said.

"Daddy—Daddy—don't take on so—please don't,"
came the girl's voice, itself trembling with held-back
tears. There was a scrape of chair-legs on the floor as
she forced the old man into his seat by the fireplace.
He hunched there, his face in his hands. She struck a
match and laid the flame to the wick of the lamp on
the table. As it burned up, she went back to her
father, knelt by him, and threw her arms about
his neck.

"Now, now, now!" she pleaded. "Now,
Daddy, it's all right. Don't take on so. It's all
right."

But he would not be comforted.

"I can't replace it!" cried Pa
Sanderson, dropping
trembling hands

from his face. "It's gone! Two years you've been away from me. Two years you've slaved in a store. And now I've—"

"Hush, hush!" the girl begged. "Now, Daddy—it's all right. I can go on working, and—"

With great effort, the old man got to his feet. "Two years more slavery, while some skunk drinks your money, gambles it—throws it away!" he cried. "Curse him! Whoever it is, curse him! What's a man goin' to believe when years of scrapin' like your aunt done, an' years of slavin' like yours, an' all our happiness today can be wiped out by a low sneakin' thief in a minute?"

The girl put her hand over her father's mouth. "Don't, Daddy," she choked. "It only makes it worse. Come and lie down on your bed. I'll make you some coffee. Don't cry, Daddy darling. Please."

Gently, like a mother with a little child, she led the heartbroken old man out of the watchers' line of vision, out of the circle of lamplight. More faintly, but still with heartbreaking distinctness, the listeners could hear the sounds of weeping.

The lean man chuckled, and pulled his bridle.

"Some circus!" he said appreciatively.

"C'mon, boy."

His horse moved a few paces, but Will Arblaster's did not. The lean man turned in his saddle.

"Ain't you comin'?" he asked.

For ten seconds, perhaps, the boy made no answer. Then he urged his pony forward until it stood side by side with the man's.

"No," he said. "An'—an' I ain't goin' to take that money, neither."

"Huh?"

The voice was slow and meditative.

"Don't know as ever I figured what this game meant," he said. "Always seemed to me that all the hardships was on the stick-up man's side—gettin' shot at an' chased and so on. Kind of fun, at that. Never thought 'bout—old men cryin'."

"That ain't my fault," said the lean man.

"No," said Will Arblaster, still very slowly. "But I'm goin' to take that money back. You didn't have no trouble gettin' it, so you don't lose nothin'."

"Suppose I say I won't let go of it?" suggested the lean man with a sneer.

"Then," snarled Arblaster, "I'll blow your head off an' take it! Don't you move, you! I've got you covered. I'll take the money out myself."

His revolver muzzle under the man's

WORD BANK

meditative (MEH dih TAY tiv) *adj.:* thoughtful

nose, he snapped open the pocket of the belt and pulled out the roll of bills.

Then, regardless of a possible shot in the back, he swung off his horse and with steady, determined steps, walked to the lighted doorway of the cabin.

The lean man, unemotional as ever, sat perfectly still, listening. Soon there came a burst of voices from the cabin, sounded their surprise, their joy.

It was a full ten minutes before Will Arblaster reappeared in the doorway, alone. His figure outlined against the light, he made a quick movement of his hand across his eyes, then stumbled forward through the darkness toward his horse. Still the lean man did not move.

"I'm sorry," said the boy as he mounted. "But—"

"I ain't," said the lean man quietly. "What do you think I made you stay an' watch for, you young fool?"

The boy made no reply. Suddenly the hair prickled on the back of his neck and his jaw fell.

"Say," he demanded hoarsely at last. "Ain't you Pecos Tommy?"

The lean man's answer was a short laugh.

"But you got his guns, an' the people in Longhorn all kind of fell back!" the boy cried. "If you ain't him, who are you?"

The moon had
drifted from behind a cloud
and flung a ray of light across
the face of the lean man as he
turned it, narrow-eyed, toward Arblaster.
The pale light picked out the grim lines of
that face, emphasizing the cluster of sun-
wrinkles about the deep eyes and underscoring
with black lines the long sweep of the fighting jaw.
"Why," said the lean man dryly, "I'm the sheriff
that killed him yesterday. Let's be ridin' back."

ABOUT THE AUTHOR

Frederick Robert Buckley's story *Gold-Mounted Guns*
was printed in Redbook magazine in 1922. As a matter
of fact, he won the famous O' Henry Award for this
story! Buckley and his wife wrote and sold many
plays for the theater. The West was the setting for
many of his works and portraying cowboy
characters was a favorite for him. His son carried
on his father's legacy as a writer, also using
the Western theme in much of his work.

Studying the Selection

QUICK REVIEW

1. When the story opens, in which city do we find the characters?

2. What time of day is it?

3. How long has "the boy" lived in town? What is his name?

4. Do we ever learn the name of the "hard-faced man"?

FOCUS

5. Look up the word *conscience* in the dictionary. Write down the definition. How do we know that Will Arblaster has a conscience?

6. After Will takes the money, he tells the "hard-faced man" that they should "'get out of here.'" But the man says, "'Not just yet. Get on your hawss, an' set still awhile.'" Why does the hard-faced man say this?

CREATING & WRITING

7. In one or two paragraphs, describe what you think is the story's lesson.

8. In *Gold-Mounted Guns,* we see that Will Arblaster has an inner conflict after he robs Mr. Sanderson. In one paragraph, tell how the story lets us know that he feels bad. In a second paragraph, describe what he does about it.

9. Create a collage of images and words that paint a picture of what life was like in Longhorn City.

LESSON IN LITERATURE . . .

SEQUENCE

- Sequence means the order in which events occur.

- In a nonfiction story, the sequence of events is part of the true reporting of the facts. A change in sequence means the story is, in part, untrue.

- In a mystery, the solution will often depend on the order, or sequence, of events.

- Some stories are purposely written out of sequence. An author may use flashbacks, mixing present and past events, or may hide some past event only to reveal it later on in the story.

THINK ABOUT IT!

1. When Angela was little, how did she and her grandfather spend Sunday afternoons?

2. How does Papa behave after his stroke?

3. In this story, some events take place in the present, some, in the recent past, and some, in the more distant past. When did the stroke take place? When did Angela's grandfather make spaghetti and meatballs? When did Angela make pizzelles by herself? Are the story's events told in sequence?

4. List in sequence the six steps of pizzelle making that are mentioned in the story.

Angela and Papa

Sunday afternoons meant Papa's famous homemade spaghetti and meatballs. It also meant cousins. The best part, though, was making pizzelles—the flat, Italian cookies Papa made on a special waffle iron. Ever since Angela was little, she'd been her grandfather's "official stacker," going over early on Sundays to help Papa mix the batter and stack the cookies on the metal cooling racks.

Then came Papa's stroke. Papa was not the same. He could not move his left arm or leg, and he seemed very sad, staring blankly from his armchair.

One day, while visiting Papa, Angela got an idea.

In eleven years of making pizzelles, Angela and Papa had discussed many things—school, friends, her parents, missing Nana—but they'd never discussed the recipe. It was time to put all that watching and helping to use.

"Eggs!" she shouted as she cracked four eggs into the glass bowl they'd always used.

She thought she saw Papa turn his head when she shouted "Vanilla!" He always said vanilla was the secret to good pizzelles.

When the batter was mixed, she plugged in the griddle and went to get Papa. Helping him to take very slow steps, Angela got Papa seated at the table just as the light indicated the griddle was hot.

Opening the lid, she placed a drop of batter on each of two flower-shaped griddles and pressed down gently.

"Very hot," she said as she placed the first two steaming pizzelles on the cooling rack. "No tasting yet." Papa's exact words.

In a short while, Angela spread a clean dish towel in front of Papa. "Ready, stacker?" she asked, mimicking Papa's ship-captain tone. "Commence stacking."

Gently taking Papa's right hand in hers, she helped him to pick up one cookie and move it to the towel. Then another.

"You seem to have a knack for this," she said. "I'd say you should be moving up to chief cook in no time."

Slowly, a smile appeared on Papa's face. It wasn't a big smile, but it was the first she'd seen in a long time.

INTO . . . The Disappearing Man

Here's a new word: *ratiocination* (RAT ee oh sih NAY shun). See if you can say it ten times! Ratiocination means the process of exact thinking, or reasoning. Ratiocination was the word used by Edgar Allan Poe, who wrote the first detective story in 1841. The word, ratiocination, leads us to the theme of *The Disappearing Man:* problems are best solved through careful thought. Physical activity, running here and there searching for clues and evidence, is not the best way to find a criminal. The detective's mind is the best instrument for detection!

EYES ON . . . *Sequence*

A **sequence** is a connected series of events. When we describe events in sequence, we are reporting them in order. Notice that word—*order.* Have you ever attended a school graduation? On such occasions, the students do not run in a mob onto the stage. They file onto the stage in an orderly sequence, one after the other.

Sequence of events is especially important in a mystery or detective story. When there's a problem to solve, we must figure out what happened first, what happened next, and so forth—to make sure nothing is missed. A clear understanding of the sequence of events will give the detective a better idea of *why* they occurred and *who* or *what* caused them.

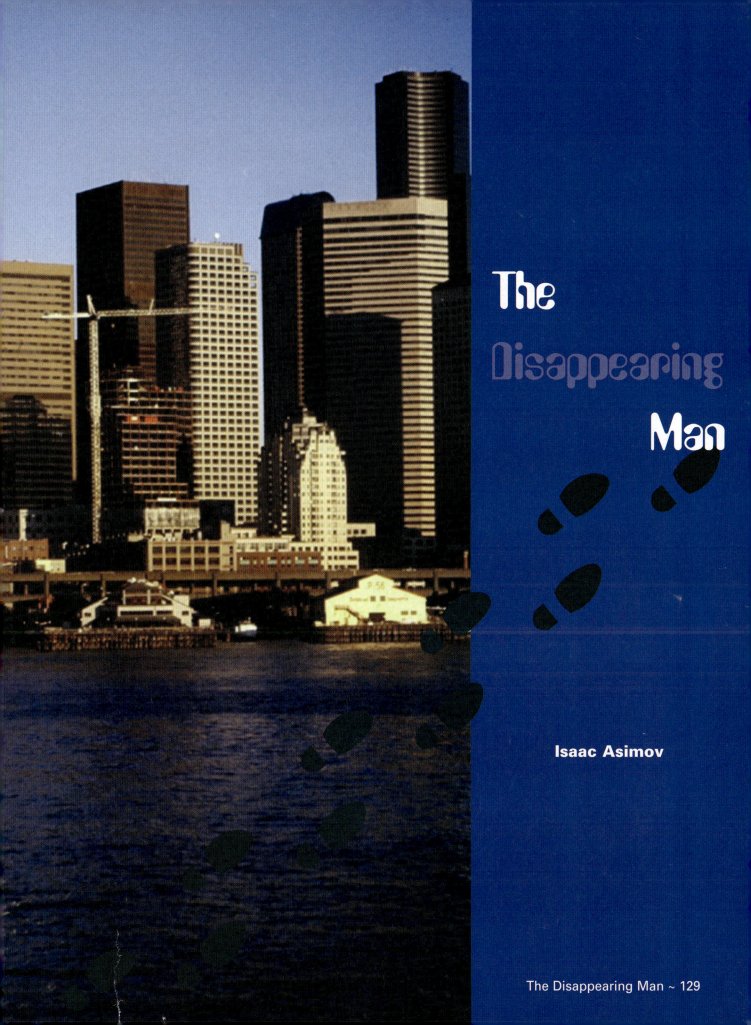

The

Disappearing

Man

Isaac Asimov

I'm not often on the spot when Dad's on one of his cases, but I couldn't help it this time.

I was coming home from the library that afternoon, when a man dashed by me and ran full speed into an alley between two buildings. It was rather late, and I figured the best thing to do was to keep on moving toward home. Dad says a nosy fourteen-year-old isn't likely to make it to fifteen.

But in less than a minute, two police officers came running. I didn't wait for them to ask. "He went in there," I said.

One of them rushed in, came out, and shouted, "There's a door open. He went inside. Go 'round to the front."

They must have given the alarm, because in a few minutes three police cars drove up, there were plainclothesmen on the scene, and the building was surrounded.

I knew I shouldn't be hanging around. Innocent bystanders get in the way of the police. Just the same, I was there when it started and, from what I heard the police saying, I knew they were after this man, Stockton. He was a loner who'd pulled off some pretty spectacular jewel robberies over the last few months. I knew about it because Dad is a detective on the force, and he was on the case.

"Slippery fellow," he said, "but when you work alone, there's no one to double-cross you."

I said, "Doesn't he have to work with someone, Dad? He's got to have a fence[1]—someone to peddle the jewels."

"If he has," said Dad, "we haven't located him. And why don't you get on with your homework?" (He always says that when he thinks I'm getting too interested in his cases.)

Well, they had him now. Some jeweler must have pushed the alarm button.

The alley he ran into was closed on all sides but the street, and he hadn't come out. There was a door there that was open, so he must have gone in. The police had the possible

---

1. A *fence* is a person who receives stolen goods from a thief and finds a buyer for them.

WORD BANK	**loner** (LO ner) *n.*: a person who has little to do with other people **peddle** (PED dl) *v.*: sell

exits guarded. They even had a couple of officers on the roof.

I was just beginning to wonder if Dad would be involved, when another car came up, and he got out. First thing he saw me and stopped dead. "Larry! What are you doing here?"

"I was on the spot, Dad. Stockton ran past me into the alley."

"Well, get out of here. There's liable to be shooting."

I backed away, but I didn't back off all the way. Once my father went into the building, I got into his car. The driver knew me, and he said, "You better go home, Larry. I'm going to have to help with the search, so I can't stay here to keep an eye on you."

"Sure, you go on," I said. "I'll be leaving in a minute." But I didn't. I wanted to do some thinking first.

Nobody leaves doors open in New York City. If that door into the alley was open, Stockton must have opened it. That meant he had to have a key; there wasn't time to pick the lock. That must mean he worked out of that building.

I looked at the building. It was an old one, four stories high. It had small businesses in it, and you could still see the painted signs in the windows in the fading light.

On the second-floor window, it said, "Klein and Levy, Tailors." Above that was a theatrical costumer, and on the top floor was a jeweler's. That jeweler's made sense out of it.

If Stockton had a key to the building, he probably worked with that jeweler. Dad would figure all that out.

I waited for the sound of shots, pretty scared that Dad might get hurt. But nothing happened. Maybe Stockton would see he was cornered and just give in. I hoped so. At least they didn't have to evacuate the building. Late on Saturday, I supposed, it would be deserted.

After a while, I got tired of waiting. I chose a moment when no police officers were looking and moved quickly to the building entrance. Dad would be hopping mad when he saw me, but I was curious. I figured they had Stockton, and I wanted to see him.

They didn't have him.

There was a fat man in a vest in the lobby. He looked scared, and I guess he was the watchman. He kept saying, "I didn't see *any*body."

| WORD BANK | **evacuate** (ee VAK yoo AYT) *v.*: leave |

Police officers were coming down the stairs and out of the old elevator, all shaking their heads.

My father was pretty angry. He said, "No one has anything?"

A police sergeant said, "Donovan said no one got out on the roof. All the doors and windows are covered."

"If he didn't get out," said my father, in a low voice that carried, "then he's in the building."

"We can't find him," said the sergeant. "He's nowhere inside."

My father said, "It isn't a big building—"

"We had the watchman's keys. We've looked everywhere."

"Then how do we know he went into the building in the first place? Who saw him go in?"

There was a silence. A lot of police officers were milling about the lobby now, but no one said anything. So I spoke up. "I did, Dad."

Dad whirled around and looked at me and made a funny sound in the back of his throat

WORD BANK	**milling** (MILL ing) *v.*: moving aimlessly

that meant I was in for it for still being there. "You said you saw him run into the alley," he said. "That's not the same thing."

"He didn't come out, Dad. There was no place else for him to go."

"But you didn't actually see him go in, did you?"

"He couldn't go up the side of the building. There wouldn't have been time for him to reach the roof before the police—"

But Dad wasn't listening. "Did *anyone* actually see him go in?"

Of course no one said anything, and I could see my father was going to call the whole thing off, and then when he got me home I was going to get the talking-to of my life.

The thought of that talking-to must have stimulated my brain, I guess. I looked about the lobby desperately and said, "But, Dad, he *did* go into the building, and he didn't disappear. There he is right now. That man there." I pointed, and then I dropped down and rolled out of the way.

There wasn't any shooting. The man I pointed to was close to the door—he must have been edging toward it—and now he made a dash for it. He almost made it, but a police officer who had been knocked down grabbed his leg and then everyone piled on him. Later they had the jeweler, too.

WORD BANK	**edging** (EDJ ing) *v.:* moving slowly and cautiously

I went home after Stockton was caught, and when my father got home much later, he did have some things to say about my risking my life. But he also said, "You got onto that theatrical costume bit very nicely, Larry."

I said, "Well, I was sure he went into the building and was familiar with it. He could get into the costumer's if he had to, and they would be bound to have police uniforms. I figured if he could dump his jacket and pants and get into a uniform quickly, he could just walk out of the building."

Dad said, "You're right. Even after he got outside, he could pretend he was dealing with the crowd and then just walk away."

Mom said, "But how did you know which police officer it was, Larry? Don't tell me you know everyone by sight."

"I didn't have to, Mom," I said. "I figured if he got a police uniform at the costumer's, he had to work fast and grab any one he saw. And they wouldn't have much of an assortment of sizes anyway. So I just looked around for a police officer whose uniform didn't fit, and, when I saw one with trouser legs stopping above his ankles, I knew he was Stockton."

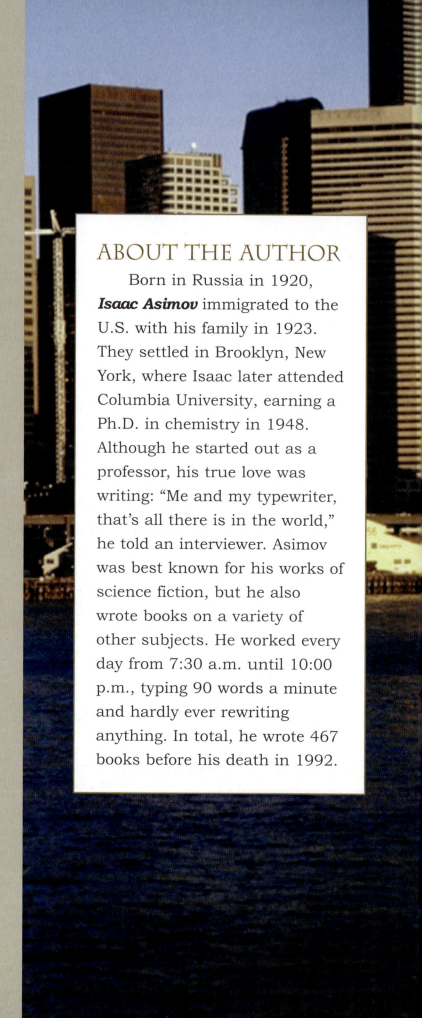

ABOUT THE AUTHOR

Born in Russia in 1920, **Isaac Asimov** immigrated to the U.S. with his family in 1923. They settled in Brooklyn, New York, where Isaac later attended Columbia University, earning a Ph.D. in chemistry in 1948. Although he started out as a professor, his true love was writing: "Me and my typewriter, that's all there is in the world," he told an interviewer. Asimov was best known for his works of science fiction, but he also wrote books on a variety of other subjects. He worked every day from 7:30 a.m. until 10:00 p.m., typing 90 words a minute and hardly ever rewriting anything. In total, he wrote 467 books before his death in 1992.

Studying the Selection

FIRST IMPRESSIONS
If you had been there, do you think you could have figured it out?

QUICK REVIEW

1. How old is the boy who narrates the story?

2. What does his father do for a living?

3. What is the boy's first name?

4. What kind of business is on the third floor of the building?

FOCUS

5. There is an expression, "it's all in the details." Larry solves the mystery by noticing details and drawing conclusions. Make a list of all the details Larry sees or hears that lead him to the discovery of the criminal.

6. Without logical thinking, even Larry's ability to notice details would not have helped him solve the mystery. Take each detail that you listed in question #1 and write next to it what conclusion you think Larry drew from each one.

CREATING & WRITING

7. You are writing your first detective story. What is the mystery or the "crime"? In a few sentences, describe the mystery or crime, how it will be "covered up," and how it will be solved.

8. Now that you have settled on the crime, invent an interesting detective. Give him or her (or them) a name, and tell us how he, she, or they look. Next, describe the setting in which the mystery takes place. This should include the place, approximate year, time of day, and some added details, such as the weather and the lighting.

9. You are publishing a detective magazine. Use the title the class made up in their discussion of the story—or make up a new title. Then, draw a cover that you think will make people want to read the stories inside. You may wish to write the story you outlined in the questions above, and place it under the cover.

LESSON IN LITERATURE . . .

CAUSE AND EFFECT

- A **cause** is any action, speech, or thought that causes something to happen.

- An **effect** is the result of that action, speech, or thought.

- A fiction or nonfiction story will usually present the cause first and the effect second.

- A mystery or detective story will often give the effect first; revealing the cause, is what the rest of the story is all about.

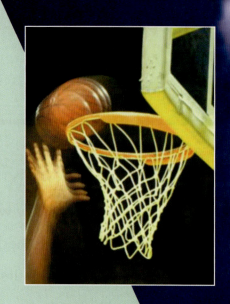

THINK ABOUT IT!

1. Michael did not make the basketball team. What was the cause?

2. Rodney Everett had been injured in the war. What was the immediate effect?

3. Rodney Everett *did* play again. What do you think was the cause?

4. Michael wants a certain "effect" very much. What is that effect? How will he cause it to happen?

What a Difference

Failing to make the school basketball team was the most embarrassing experience of Michael's life. Especially because he was the tallest kid in the school.

"A bit too slow," Coach Gregory said.

"Just doesn't make the shots," Coach Johnson said.

"Forget basketball," Michael said.

Michael's father didn't say much about Michael's not making the team, but one night a few weeks later, he brought a guest home for dinner, a guy he'd served with in the war. Michael had never met the man before, but he sure knew who he was.

Rodney Everett had been a football player when the war broke out. Putting his football career on hold to serve in the army, he returned to the U.S. after less than a year with injuries so severe his doctors told him he might never walk again. He went on not only to walk, but to play again, leading his team to two championships.

Michael couldn't believe he was talking to Rodney Everett right here in his own kitchen! And when Mr. Everett said, "Your dad tells me you're pretty disappointed about basketball this year," Michael found himself saying, "Yeah, but I'm going to work real hard in the off season to get ready for next year."

Even before the weather warmed up in the spring, Michael started spending every afternoon after school at his basketball hoop. He practiced dribbling. He practiced lay-ups. He practiced his jump shot. And he always ended with free throws, refusing to go inside until he could hit five in a row without a miss.

Michael worked hard on his skills all spring and summer. In addition, he started running as well, alternating between long, slow runs to work on endurance and shorter, faster runs to improve his speed.

Michael's hard work paid off. By the time tryouts came in November, there was no question Michael would make the team.

"With his height—and his quickness—this guy's going to be a team leader," Coach Gregory said.

"You see that jump shot?" said Coach Johnson. "What a difference a year makes."

Blueprint for Reading

INTO . . . *The Speckled Hen's Egg*

In folktales, characters believe things that seem very silly to us today. If you found a mark on the outside of an egg, would you believe it had an important, secret meaning? Do you believe that people have special, "noble" blood in their veins, if their parents or grandparents or great-grandparents were members of royalty? Do you believe in omens— "signs" that tell us what is going to occur in the future? Well, Madame Roberge does, in *The Speckled Hen's Egg*. But then again, Madame Roberge lived "once in another time," once upon a time.

EYES ON . . . *Cause and Effect*

Have you ever heard the expression "cause and effect"? It means the reason something happened—the cause, and what actually *did* happen—the effect.

Here's a simple example of cause and effect: Jim was hungry, so he ate an apple.

The cause: Jim was hungry. The effect: he ate an apple.

Every story includes at least one cause and its effect. Some stories start with the cause and then describe the effect. Other stories start with the effect and then reveal the cause. When you have read *The Speckled Hen's Egg*, ask yourself: which came first in this story, the cause or the effect?

The Speckled Hen's Egg

Natalie Savage Carlson

Once in another time, a very strange thing happened to Madame Roberge.[1]

Madame gave great care to her chickens because they laid well, and she sold their eggs at the store for a good price.

She was miserly with her egg money and hoarded it in the closet in a fluted[2] silver bowl which was an heirloom. It was shaped something like a fan, and one said that it had been brought from Quebec in the long ago by her great-grandfather, Lazare Proutte.[3]

Madame was very proud of the bowl and she was also proud of all the coins that her eggs made for her. So it was fitting that the coins should be saved in the silver bowl.

---

1. *Madame Roberge* (Muh DAHM roe BAIRZH)
2. A *fluted* bowl is one whose sides have decorative grooves.
3. *Lazare Proutte* (lah ZARR PROOT)

WORD BANK	
miserly (MY zer lee) *adv.:* stingy
hoarded (HOHRD ed) *v.:* hid and carefully guarded a supply of something—often, money or food
heirloom (AIR loom) *n.:* a family possession handed down from one generation to another

One day when Madame went out to her henhouse to gather the eggs, the scrawny old speckled hen was on the nest. Madame shooed her with her lips and a fling of her skirts. The hen jumped off the nest and ran away, flapping her wings and cackling puck-puck-puck-a-a-puck-puck-a-a.

Madame was displeased to see that there was only one egg in the nest.

"That worthless creature!" said Madame Roberge. "This is the first egg she has laid in a week. She is no longer worth her feed. I will put her in my stewpot Sunday."

Madame was about to drop the egg into her apron when she noticed a strange thing about it. There was a picture on the egg, just as surely as if it had been painted there. She studied it carefully. Yes, the picture on the egg was certainly of something. But what?

The next time she went to the store in the village with her eggs, she took the unusual one with her.

"This one is not for sale," Madame told Henri Dupuis,[4] the storekeeper. "It is a very strange egg laid by my old speckled hen. See, there is a picture on it. What would you say it is?"

Henri Dupuis looked at the egg closely. Others who were in the store gathered around.

"Perhaps you aren't feeding your hens the right food," said Henri. "Now I have a new kind of chicken feed that—"

But André Drouillard,[5] who had taken the egg in his own hands, interrupted.

"It is surely some omen," he said. "See those long lines that curve like feathers—like an Indian war bonnet?"

---

4. *Henri Dupuis* (on REE dew PWEE)
5. *Andre Drouillard* (on REE drew YARR)

WORD BANK   **omen** (OH mun) *n.:* a sign that something will happen; an omen can be "good" or "evil"

"Perhaps there will be an Indian uprising," cried Angéline Meloche[6] in terror, "and a massacre! Oh, my poor husband on the road somewhere and my unprotected children picking berries in the woods!"

But the pop-eyed Eusibe Latrop[7] must have his say.

"You are all wrong," he said. "This is a crown on the egg. See! A royal crown. Perhaps it means that Madame Roberge has noble blood in her veins and does not know it."

Madame immediately believed this explanation because it sounded closer to the truth.

"My great-grandfather, Lazare Proutte, was a rich man," she remembered, "but everyone thought it strange that he had nothing to say of his life before he came here. Perhaps he was a *comte*[8] or a *duc*[8] in disguise. No doubt the King was displeased with him over some matter and he had to hide in the New World. Yes, I am sure of it. One said he always seemed a little uneasy when strangers were around."

Madame proudly went home and put the wonderful egg in a prominent place on her parlor table. Instead of stewing the speckled hen, she made a special pet of her and build her a runway all for herself. She planted flowers in it and saw that the water dish and feed bowl were always full.

Then a great change came over Madame. She no longer sold eggs at the store because she said that was quite beneath a noblewoman. She took in an orphan girl to do her work so that she would have more time for her embroidery, which was a genteel pastime. She even began to call herself Madame de Roberge, which had a more aristocratic sound, even though the crown on the egg had nothing to do with her husband's family.

She took to walking about with the wart on her nose so high she no longer could see many of her old friends. She walked about with a la-la-de-da air and carried her handkerchief, so!

---

6. *Angeline Meloche* (on zhay LEEN may LOSH)
7. *Eusibe Latrop* (uh ZEEB lah TROP)
8. A *comte* (KOMT) is a count. A *duc* (DUK) is a duke.

> WORD BANK
> **prominent** (PRAH mih nent) *adj.:* standing out so as to be easily seen
> **genteel** (jen TEEL) *adj.:* well-bred; polite (today, used to mean overly polite)
> **aristocratic** (uh RISS tuh KRATT ik) *adj.:* belonging to a class of people who are educated, wealthy, and "well-born"

Sometimes her needle would snag in the fancy handkerchief she was embroidering and her eyes would have a faraway look.

"Perhaps I am really a *comtesse* or a *marquise*[9] or even a *princesse*," she would dream to herself. "If only Great-grandpére[10] Proutte had not made such a secret of his life before he came here!"

She began to wonder why the egg with the crown had been laid on that certain day—no sooner, no later. It was an omen all right. But what did it mean?

Omens often had to do with death. Perhaps the death of some important person back in old France. Death in noble families meant money and castles and titles changing hands.

Perhaps—could it be—was it possible? Yes, that was it! Some high and rich relative in France had died. The crown on the egg meant that it was time for her to claim her inheritance.

She puzzled over this for a few days. Then she made up her mind. She would take her egg money and make the long trip to the big records hall in

---

9. A *comtesse* (kum TESS) is a countess. A *marquise* (mar KEES) is the wife of
a marquis, who ranks below a duke and above a count.
10. *Great-grandpere* (grahn PAIR) is great-grandfather.

Quebec where they kept the documents and records of the past. She would learn the secret of her noble blood.

She hitched Coquin,[11] the wheezy horse, to the two-wheeled cart and set forth on the trip to Quebec. She would go to the old clerk and have him look up the family record of the Prouttes. Her egg money would be spent for food and lodging along the way.

Madame de Roberge set off in high spirit. She sat straight on the edge of the hard seat, with the reins in her hands and her wart in the air, so!

It was as if the two-wheeled cart pulled by the wheezy Coquin had become a fine coach drawn by four spirited white horses. And Madame the Marquise rode forth in silks and brocades and jewels.

---

11. *Coquin* (co KAH)

WORD BANK	**brocades** (broe KAYDZ) *n.:* expensive fabrics with raised designs, often woven with gold or silver threads

From time to time, she passed people on the road. To them she gave a stiff little bow of the head and half a smile, as if saluting her humble peasants.

At night Madame sought shelter in farmhouses, where the owners were overcome with awe and hospitality when they learned that their guest was a distinguished noblewoman riding to Quebec to claim an inheritance across the sea. They would not even accept payment for food and lodging, so honored were they. And the Marquise still had enough of the peasant left in her to be glad that she could hold fast to her egg money.

When Madame drove Coquin down the cobbled streets[12] of Quebec to the big records hall, she had no feeling of the country bumpkin come to the city. Rather she sat proudly erect, with her la-la-de-da air and her wart high in the air, so!

She twirled her embroidered handkerchief daintily as she told the clerk that she had come to seek records of the noble Proutte family so that she could rightfully claim an inheritance in France.

He led her into a cellar beneath the building where all the old papers and records were kept. He pulled out drawers, fussed through yellow papers and

_____

12. *Cobbled streets* are paved with round stones called cobblestones.

adjusted his spectacles on his Roman nose. So old were most of the documents that fine, dry dust blew from the drawers and Madame must from time to time use her fancy handkerchief with a vigor that was not so la-la-de-da.

"Proutte, Proutte, Proutte," chanted the clerk as if he were saying his litany. "Ah, here we have him. Guillaume Proutte, who came to the New World with Champlain."

"Yes, yes," cried Madame impatiently, "that must be the one. Was he a *duc* or a *marquis?*"

The clerk pinched his eyebrows together and popped the tip of his tongue out of his lips. He studied the fine handwriting. He shook his head sadly.

"Alas!" he said. "This Guillaume Proutte was released from a Paris prison on condition that he sail to the New World and turn over a new leaf."

Madame hastily leaned over his shoulder and strained her own eyes on the handwriting.

WORD BANK **litany** (LITT uh nee) *n.:* a long prayer in which many of the lines are repeated

"Tut! Tut!" said the clerk. "It seems that Guillaume did not turn his leaf over, for he was up before the council three times for stealing beaver skins from the Indians. And you must know, my daughter, that beaver skins were the coin of the country in those days."

"How disgusting!" exclaimed Madame. "That must be some other family of Prouttes. Look further, my man. What about Lazare Proutte?"

The clerk dug through some more documents.

"Here is another Proutte," he said. "Yes, it is your Lazare."

"That's the one!" exclaimed Madame. "He was my great-grandfather."

The clerk slowly and laboriously read the document. He mumbled from time to time. Certain phrases crawled into Madame's ears like stinging ants.

"Apprenticed to Marc Nadie, the silversmith. Disappeared from Quebec at the same time as the silver plate of the Sieur de Mare, which had been left with the smith for polishing."

WORD BANK	**laboriously** (luh BORR ee us LEE) *adv.*: with much difficulty and effort

"But—but there must be some mistake," Madame stammered.

Then she told the clerk about the wonderful egg with the crown on it which her speckled hen had laid.

"I have it here in my bag," she said, "wrapped in a piece of musquash[13] fur." She carefully took it out of the fur and held it up.

"See," she said, "a distinct crown. It must mean something."

The clerk pinched his brows together again and pushed his glasses higher on his Roman nose.

"But Madame is looking at it upside down," he said. "Turn it around—like this! Now what does it look like to you?"

"It—it looks like the fluted silver bowl my great-grandfather, Lazare—er—ah—the bowl I keep my egg money in."

"There, you have it, my lady," said the clerk with a twinkle in his eye. "The sign on the egg is a warning that one of Proutte blood should never let money get too strong a hold on her."

---

13. A *musquash* is a muskrat, which is a large rodent resembling a beaver. Its fur is brown and thick.

So when Madame drove back to her village, the two-wheeled cart was no longer a coach and Coquin no longer divided himself into four prancing white steeds. And Madame the Marquise had been left behind in the dusty records cellar. The return trip dug quite deeply into the egg money, too, for while it is a rare privilege to entertain a *marquise,* it is nothing but a nuisance to have ordinary persons turning in from the road to crowd one's table and beds.

Madame Roberge's wart came down, her la-la-de-da manner was gone and her handkerchief had been left where it fell in the cellar of the big hall in Quebec. She found a position for the orphan girl and went back to her own scrubbing and cooking.

She began to sell eggs at the store again, and spoke in a friendly manner to everyone. It was noticed that she became a bit more generous with her charity, and she no longer took pleasure in hoarding money. Perhaps this was because she no longer had a fine bowl to save it in, since the silver one was turned into a water pan for the chickens. And the old speckled hen disappeared from the fancy runway only to find herself in the stewpot one Sunday.

So you see, my friends, it is not a good thing to hold one's nose high and go about with a la-la-de-da air, for a turn of the egg can easily change a crown into a stolen bowl.

The End

ABOUT THE AUTHOR

Natalie Savage Carlson wrote more than forty novels and picture books for children. Born in Virginia in 1906, Natalie was raised on a farm in Maryland. As a child, she was enchanted by the legends and folktales told by her French-Canadian mother. In the late 1920s, Natalie married Daniel Carlson, a member of the U.S. navy. His career took the couple to many places, including Paris, France. Mrs. Carlson's love of folktales and her vivid memories of France can be seen in *The Speckled Hen's Egg*. She died in 1997.

Studying the Selection

FIRST IMPRESSIONS
Does it make sense to you that Madame Roberge became more friendly and generous at the end of the story, when she had to go back to the hard work of scrubbing and cooking?

QUICK REVIEW

1. What is the main character's name? Make sure you can pronounce it properly.

2. Give the name of her great-grandfather. Make sure you can pronounce it properly.

3. Where does she keep her egg money?

4. What is the picture on the egg?

FOCUS

5. Why does Madame Roberge feel superior to other people, when she believes she has "royal blood" in her veins?

6. Why does Madame Roberge travel to Quebec?

CREATING & WRITING

7. You are Madame Roberge. Earlier today, you learned that your great-grandfather was a thief. You are in a barn, where a farmer's family has invited you to spend the night. Tomorrow, you will drive home, but right now, you wish to put down your thoughts in your journal. What do you write about? How do you feel? What are your plans for when you arrive home? Don't forget to refer to yourself as **I**.

8. Have you ever owned a thing: clothing, jewelry, or a special book, for example, that made you feel better about yourself? Write about it in two or three paragraphs.

9. Draw a picture of the famous egg with the crown (or silver bowl). Don't forget to give your picture a caption, as it is to be hung in a museum.

PREDICTING

- Predicting is a form of guessing what will happen in the future.

- Good predictions are based on the facts that we have been given combined with our own experience.

- In a story, the author often provides many facts or clues to help us *predict* what will happen, but not enough to make us *sure* of what will happen.

- In stories with surprise endings, the readers' predictions often turn out to be wrong!

THINK ABOUT IT!

1. In Part I of "Camping Trip," the author describes one weekend in the life of a family. Write down three facts about the family. Then, make two predictions based on the facts in the story and what your own experience has taught you.

2. Look back at the story and review the events it describes. Write down three events. Even small, seemingly unimportant actions, may be included.

3. Think again about the action in the story. Is there any action that might be a clue to a future event? What is it, and what is your prediction?

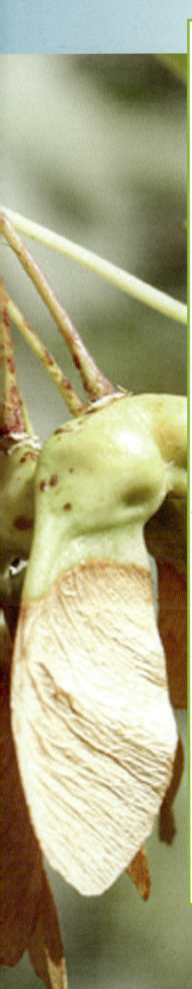

Camping Trip, Part 1

As Mom and Dad packed the car for the camping trip, little Sally lay on the ground, her body a landing pad for the maple helicopters fluttering to the ground like a gentle green snow. Baby John sat contentedly in his car seat, looking out the window and babbling happily. The packing completed, Dad nosed the car out of the driveway and headed down the two-lane highway that connected the family's five acres to the rest of the world.

After miles and miles of fields and farmhouses, Dad turned into a gas station to check his directions. On the other corner sat a country store, but there was no need to cross the street for refreshments. Mom had thought of everything. Opening the trunk to pour some lemonade, she noticed a cluster of green maple helicopters, and with one swipe, scooped them out and tossed them into the grass nearby. Delighted, Sally rescued a handful of the seeds and put them into her pocket.

"Perfect," Dad said, back from his chat with the gas station attendant. "It's just down this road here. Let's go."

More fields, more farms, and suddenly a small wooden sign announcing "Monhegan State Park." Dad turned right onto a dirt road that wound through a meadow that seemed to Sally to go on forever.

"Guess I expected a few more campers," Mom said. "You think it'll be alright?"

Dad nodded. "We've got the place to ourselves."

While Mom and Dad pitched the tent, it was Sally's job to keep an eye on the baby. She took the maple helicopters from her pocket. Sally stood straight and tall, the only "tree" on this flat stretch of grass. Sally reached way up high and, one at a time, let the helicopter go. As the blade of each seed fluttered to the ground, the baby, on his back on a blanket, squealed in delight.

Blueprint for Reading

INTO . . . *The Black Stallion*

Alexander Ramsay is going home on a tramp steamer that is traveling from India to England. When the *Drake* docks at a small Arabian port, a terrified black stallion is dragged aboard ship and locked into a small makeshift stall on deck. The horse is beautiful, powerful, and frightening. Alexander is the only passenger aboard the *Drake* that befriends the horse. Even though Alec is afraid of the horse's strength and wildness, he is drawn to him and wants to help him. When the ship sinks, he tries to save the horse. As it turns out, the horse saves *him!*

EYES ON . . . *Predicting*

What is *predicting*? *Predicting* is guessing what is going to happen before it happens. Usually, predicting is based on what we see, what we know, or what we ourselves have experienced. When you read a story, you may be able to predict what will happen at the end, from clues that the author has put in the story. Predicting can be fun, but it can also spoil the fun of reading. A good author will give you enough information to keep you guessing, but not enough to ruin the ending for you.

From THE BLACK STALLION

Walter Farley

The tramp steamer[1] *Drake* plowed away from the coast of India and pushed its blunt prow[2] into the Arabian Sea, homeward bound. Slowly it made its way west toward the Gulf of Aden. Its hold[3] was loaded with coffee, rice, tea, oilseeds, and jute. Black smoke poured from its one stack, darkening the hot cloudless sky.

---

1. A *tramp steamer* is a vessel that can be rented to take a load of goods from one port to another.
2. The *prow* (PROW) of a ship is the front part of it, also called "the bow."
3. The *hold* of a ship is the "basement" of the ship. It is a space below the lower deck used for cargo.

Alexander Ramsay, known to his friends back home in New York City as Alec, leaned over the rail and watched the water slide away from the sides of the boat. His red hair blazed redder than ever in the hot sun; his tanned elbows rested heavily on the rail as he turned his freckled face back toward the fast-disappearing shore.

It had been fun—those two months in India. He would miss Uncle Ralph, miss the days they had spent together in the jungle, even the screams of the panthers and the many eerie sounds of the jungle night. Never again would he think of his uncle's work as easy work. No, sir, you had to be big and strong, able to ride horseback for long hours through the tangled jungle paths. Alec glanced down proudly at the

WORD BANK

blazed (BLAYZD) *v.:* gleamed or glowed brightly

eerie (EER ee) *adj.:* strange, mysterious, and somewhat frightening

hard muscles in his arms. Uncle Ralph had taught him how to ride—the one thing in the world he had always wanted to do.

But it was all over now. Rides back home would be few.

His fist opened. Lovingly he surveyed the pearl pocketknife he held there. The inscription on it was in gold: *To Alec on his birthday, Bombay, India.* He remembered, too, his uncle's words: "A knife, Alec, comes in handy sometimes."

Suddenly a large hand descended on his shoulder. "Well, m'boy, you're on your way home," a gruff voice said, with a decidedly English accent.

Alec looked up into the captain's wrinkled, wind-tanned face. "Hello, Captain Watson," he answered. "It's rather a long way home, though, sir. To England with you and then to New York on the *Majestic.*"

"About four weeks' sailing, all in all, lad, but you look like a pretty good sailor."

"I am, sir. I wasn't sick once all the way over and we had a rough crossing, too," Alec said proudly.

"When'd you come over, lad?"

"In June, sir, with some friends of my father's. They left me with my uncle in Bombay. You know my Uncle Ralph, don't you? He came aboard with me and spoke to you."

"Yes, I know your Uncle Ralph. A fine man, too....And now you're going home alone?"

"Yes, sir! School opens next month and I have to be there."

The captain smiled and took Alec by the arm. "Come along," he said. "I'll show you how we steer this ship and what makes it go."

WORD BANK

surveyed (sur VAYD) *v.:* looked at; inspected
descended (dee SEND ed) *v.:* came down

The captain and crew were kind to Alec, but the days passed monotonously for the homeward-bound boy as the *Drake* steamed its way through the Gulf of Aden and into the Red Sea. The tropic sun beat down mercilessly on the heads of the few passengers aboard.

The *Drake* kept near the coast of Arabia—endless miles of barren desert shore. But Alec's thoughts were not on the scorching sand. Arabia—where the greatest horses in the world were bred! Did other fellows dream of horses the way he did? To him, a horse was the greatest animal in the world.

Then one day the *Drake* headed for a small Arabian port. As they approached the small landing, Alec saw a crowd of Arabs milling about[4] in great excitement. Obviously it was not often that a boat stopped there.

---

4. When a group of people move around aimlessly, they are *milling about*.

WORD BANK

monotonously (muh NOT uh nuss lee) *adv.:* dully and boringly

mercilessly (MURR suh luss lee) *adv.:* without pity

But, as the gangplank went down with a bang, Alec could see that it wasn't the ship itself that was attracting all the attention. The Arabs were crowding toward the center of the landing. Alec heard a whistle—shrill, loud, clear, unlike anything he had ever heard before. He saw a mighty black horse rear on its hind legs, its forelegs striking out into the air. A white scarf was tied across its eyes. The crowd broke and ran.

White lather ran from the horse's body; his mouth was open, his teeth bared. He was a giant of a horse, glistening black—too big to be pure Arabian. His mane was like a crest, mounting, then falling low. His neck was long and slender, and arched to the small, savagely beautiful head. The head was that of the wildest of all wild creatures—a stallion born wild—and it was beautiful, savage, splendid. A stallion with a wonderful physical perfection that matched his savage, ruthless spirit.

> WORD BANK
> **savage** (SA vudg) *adj.:* wild; fierce
> **ruthless** (ROOTH luss) *adj.:* without pity; cruel

Once again the Black screamed and rose on his hind legs. Alec could hardly believe his eyes and ears—a stallion, a wild stallion—unbroken, such as he had read and dreamed about!

Two ropes led from the halter on the horse's head, and four men were attempting to pull the stallion toward the gangplank. They were

going to put him on the ship! Alec saw a dark-skinned man, wearing European dress and a high, white turban, giving directions. In his hand he held a whip. He gave his orders tersely in Arabic. Suddenly he walked to the rear of the horse and let the hard whip fall on the Black's hindquarters. The stallion bolted so fast that he struck one of the Arabs holding the rope; down the man went and lay still. The Black snorted and plunged; if ever Alec saw hate expressed by a horse, he saw it then. They had him halfway up the plank. Alec wondered where they would put him if they ever did succeed in getting him on the boat.

Then he was on! Alec saw Captain Watson waving his arms frantically, motioning and shouting for the men to pull the stallion toward the stern. The boy followed at a safe distance. Now he saw the makeshift stall into which they were attempting to get the Black—it had once been a good-sized cabin. The *Drake* had little accommodation for transporting animals; its hold was already heavily laden with cargo.[5]

Finally they had the horse in front of the stall. One of the men clambered to the top of the cabin, reached down and pulled the scarf away from the stallion's eyes. At the same time, the dark-skinned

---

5. A ship's *cargo* is the goods the ship is carrying.

> WORD BANK
>
> **tersely** (TURSS lee) *adv.:* briefly
> **bolted** (BOLT ed) *v.:* suddenly tried to break free
> **plunged** (PLUNJD) *v.:* threw himself about
> **makeshift** (MAYK shift) *adj.:* temporary
> **accommodation** (uh KOM uh DAY shun) *n.:* place for housing and feeding
> **laden** (LAY dun) *adj.:* very full of something

man again hit the horse on the hindquarters and he bolted inside. Alec thought the stall would never be strong enough to hold him. The stallion tore into the wood and sent it flying; thunder rolled from under his hoofs; his powerful legs crashed into the sides of the cabin; his wild, shrill, high-pitched whistle filled the air. Alec felt a deep pity steal over him, for here was a wild stallion used to the open range imprisoned in a stall in which he was hardly able to turn.

Captain Watson was conversing angrily with the dark-skinned man; the captain had probably never expected to ship a cargo such as this! Then the man pulled a thick wallet from inside his coat; he counted the bills off and handed them to the captain. Captain Watson looked at the bills and then at the stall; he took the money, shrugged his shoulders and walked away. The dark-skinned man gathered the Arabs who had helped bring the stallion aboard, gave them bills from his wallet, and they departed down the gangplank.

Soon the *Drake* was again under way. Alec gazed back at the port, watching the group gathered around the inert form of the Arab who had gone down under the Black's mighty hoofs; then he turned to the stall. The dark-skinned man had gone to his cabin, and only the excited passengers were standing around outside the stall. The black horse was still fighting madly inside.

The days that followed were hectic ones for Alec, passengers, and crew. He had never dreamed a horse could

| WORD BANK | **inert** (in URT) *adj.:* still; unmoving |
| | **hectic** (HEK tik) *adj.:* rushed and confused |

have such spirit, be so untamable. The ship resounded far into the night from the blows struck by those powerful legs. The outside of the stall was now covered with reinforcements. The dark-skinned man became more mysterious than ever—always alone, and never talking to anyone but the captain.

The *Drake* steamed through the Suez into the Mediterranean.

That night Alec stole out upon deck, leaving the rest of the passengers playing cards. He listened carefully. The Black was quiet tonight. Quickly he walked in the direction of the stall. At first he couldn't see or hear anything. Then as his eyes became accustomed to the darkness, he made out the pink-colored nostrils of the Black, who was sticking his head out of the window.

Alec walked slowly toward him; he put one hand in his pocket to see if the lumps of sugar he had taken from the dinner table were still there. The wind was blowing against him, carrying his scent away. He was quite close now. The Black was looking out on the open sea; his ears pricked forward, his thin-skinned nostrils quivering, his black mane flowing like windswept flame. Alec could not turn his eyes away; he could not believe such a perfect animal existed.

The stallion turned and looked directly at him—his black eyes blazed. Once again that piercing whistle filled the night air, and he disappeared into the stall. Alec took the sugar out of his pocket and left it on the window sill. He went to

WORD BANK **resounded** (ree ZOWND ed) *v.*: echoed

his cabin. Later, when he returned, it was gone. Every night thereafter Alec would steal up to the stall, leave the sugar and depart; sometimes he would see the Black and other times he would only hear the ring of hoofs against the floor.

The *Drake* stopped at Alexandria, Bengasi, Tripoli, Tunis, and Algiers, passed the Rock of Gibraltar and turned north up the coast of Portugal. Now they were off Cape Finisterre on the coast of Spain, and in a few days, Captain Watson told Alec, they would be in England.

Alec wondered why the Black was being shipped to England—perhaps for stud, perhaps to race. The slanting shoulders, the deep broad chest, the powerful legs, the knees not too high nor too low—these, his uncle had taught him, were marks of speed and endurance.

That night Alec made his customary trip to the stall, his pockets filled with lumps of sugar. The night was hot and still; heavy clouds blacked out the stars; in the distance long streaks of lightning raced through the sky. The Black had his head out the window. Again he was looking out to sea, his nostrils quivering more than ever. He turned, whistled as he saw the boy, then again faced the water.

Alec felt elated—it was the first time that the stallion hadn't drawn back into the stall at sight of him. He moved closer. He put the sugar in the palm of his hand and hesitantly held it out to the stallion. The Black turned and once again whistled—softer this time. Alec stood his ground. Neither he nor anyone else had been this close to the stallion since he came on board. But he did not care to take the chance of extending his arm any nearer the bared teeth, the curled nostrils. Instead he placed the sugar on the sill. The Black looked at it, then back at the boy. Slowly he moved

WORD BANK
customary (KUSS tuh MAIR ee) *adj.*: usual
elated (ee LAY ted) *adj.*: immensely happy

over and began to eat the sugar. Alec watched him for a moment, satisfied; then as the rain began to fall, he went back to his cabin.

He was awakened with amazing suddenness in the middle of the night. The *Drake* lurched crazily and he was thrown onto the floor. Outside there were loud rolls of thunder, and streaks of lightning made his cabin as light as day.

His first storm at sea! He pushed the light switch—it was dead. Then a flash of lightning again illuminated the cabin. The top of his bureau had been swept clear and the floor was covered with broken glass. Hurriedly he pulled on his pants and shirt and started for the door; then he stopped. Back he went to the bed, fell on his knees and reached under. He withdrew a life jacket and strapped it around him. He hoped that he wouldn't need it.

WORD BANK
lurched *v.*: swayed or tipped suddenly
illuminated (ill LOO mih NAY ted) *v.*: lit up

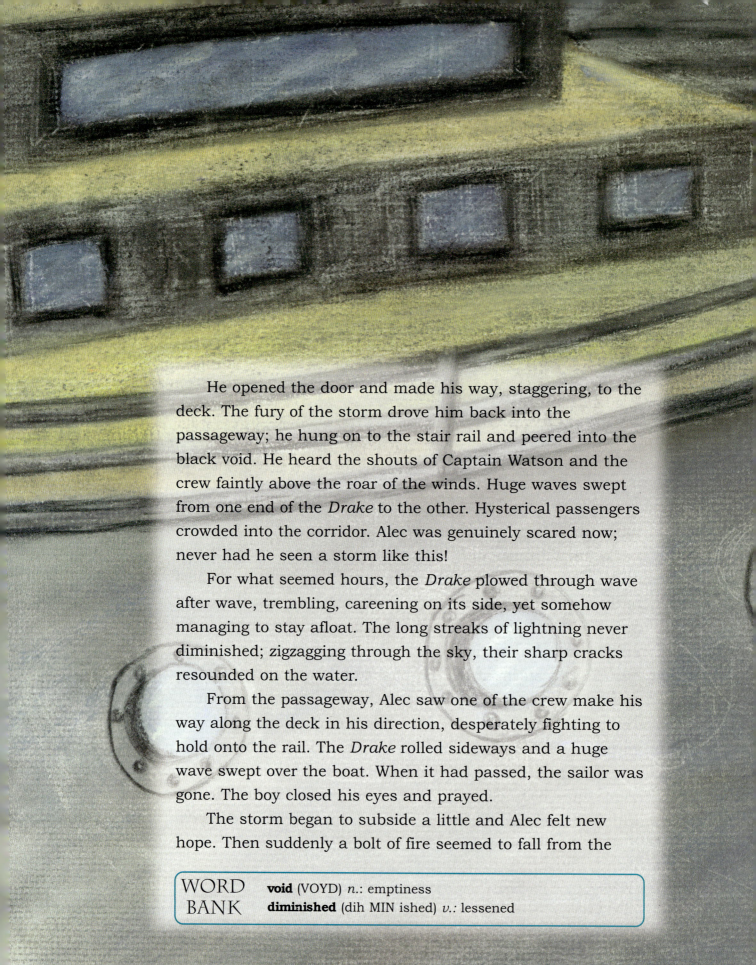

He opened the door and made his way, staggering, to the deck. The fury of the storm drove him back into the passageway; he hung on to the stair rail and peered into the black void. He heard the shouts of Captain Watson and the crew faintly above the roar of the winds. Huge waves swept from one end of the *Drake* to the other. Hysterical passengers crowded into the corridor. Alec was genuinely scared now; never had he seen a storm like this!

For what seemed hours, the *Drake* plowed through wave after wave, trembling, careening on its side, yet somehow managing to stay afloat. The long streaks of lightning never diminished; zigzagging through the sky, their sharp cracks resounded on the water.

From the passageway, Alec saw one of the crew make his way along the deck in his direction, desperately fighting to hold onto the rail. The *Drake* rolled sideways and a huge wave swept over the boat. When it had passed, the sailor was gone. The boy closed his eyes and prayed.

The storm began to subside a little and Alec felt new hope. Then suddenly a bolt of fire seemed to fall from the

WORD BANK	**void** (VOYD) *n.*: emptiness
	diminished (dih MIN ished) *v.*: lessened

heavens above them. A sharp crack and the boat shook. Alec was thrown flat on his face, stunned. Slowly he regained consciousness. He was lying on his stomach; his face felt hot and sticky. He raised his hand, and withdrew it covered with blood. Then he became conscious of feet stepping on him. The passengers, yelling and screaming, were climbing, crawling over him! The *Drake* was still—its engines dead.

Struggling, Alec pushed himself to his feet. Slowly he made his way along the deck. His startled eyes took in the scene about him. The *Drake*, struck by lightning, seemed almost cut in half! They were sinking! Strange, with what seemed the end so near, he should feel so calm. They were manning the lifeboats, and Captain Watson was there shouting directions. One boat was being lowered into the water. A large wave caught it broadside and turned it over— its occupants disappeared in the sea. The second lifeboat was being filled and Alec waited his turn. But when it came, the boat had reached its quota.[6]

_____

6. The *quota* (KWOE tuh) is the number of people the lifeboat can hold.

WORD BANK **broadside** (BROAD side) *n.:* the whole side of a ship above the water line

"Wait for the next one, Alec," Captain Watson said sternly. He put his arm on the boy's shoulder, softening the harshness of his words.

As they watched the second lifeboat being lowered, the dark-skinned man appeared and rushed up to the captain, waving his arms and babbling hysterically.

"It's under the bed, under the bed!" Captain Watson shouted at him.

Then Alec saw the man had no life jacket. Terror in his eyes, he turned away from the captain toward Alec. Frantically he rushed at the boy and tried to tear the life jacket from his back. Alec struggled, but he was no match for the half-crazed man. Then Captain Watson had his hands on the man and threw him against the rail. Alec saw the man's eyes turn to the lifeboat that was being lowered. Before the captain could stop him, he was climbing over the rail. He was going to jump into the boat! Suddenly the *Drake* lurched. The man lost his balance and, screaming, fell into the water. He never rose to the surface.

The dark-skinned man had drowned. Immediately Alec thought of the Black. What was happening to him? Was he still in his stall? Alec fought his way out of line and toward the stern[7] of the boat. If the stallion was alive, he was going to set him free and give him his chance to fight for life.

The stall was still standing. Alec heard a shrill whistle rise above the storm. He rushed to the door, lifted the heavy bar and swung it open. For a second the mighty hoofs stopped pounding and there was silence. Alec backed slowly away.

Then he saw the Black, his head held high, his nostrils blown out with excitement. Suddenly he snorted and plunged straight for the rail and Alec. Alec was paralyzed, he couldn't move. One hand was on the rail, which was broken at this point, leaving nothing between him and the open water. The Black swerved as he came near him, and the boy

---

7. *The stern* of the ship is the back end of the ship.

realized that the stallion was making for the hole. The horse's shoulder grazed him as he swerved, and Alec went flying into space. He felt the water close over his head.

When he came up, his first thought was of the ship; then he heard an explosion, and he saw the *Drake* settling deep into the water. Frantically he looked around for a lifeboat, but there was none in sight. Then he saw the Black swimming not more than ten yards away. Something swished by him—a rope, and it was attached to the Black's halter! The same rope that they had used to bring the stallion aboard the boat, and which they had never been able to get close enough to the horse to untie. Without stopping to think, Alec grabbed hold of it. Then he was pulled through the water, into the oncoming seas.

The waves were still large, but with the aid of his life jacket, Alec was able to stay on top. He was too tired now to give much thought to what he had done. He only knew that he had had his choice of remaining in the water alone or being pulled by the Black. If he was to die, he would rather die with the mighty stallion than alone. He took one last look behind and saw the *Drake* sink into the depths.

For hours Alec battled the waves. He had tied the rope securely around his waist. He could hardly hold his head up. Suddenly he felt the rope slacken. The Black had stopped swimming! Alec anxiously waited; peering into the darkness he could just make out the head of the stallion. The Black's whistle pierced the air! After a few minutes, the rope became taut again. The horse had changed his direction. Another hour passed, then the storm diminished to high, rolling swells. The first streaks of dawn appeared on the horizon.

The Black had stopped four times during the night, and each time he had altered his course. Alec wondered whether the stallion's wild instinct was leading him to land. The sun rose and shone down brightly on the boy's head; the salt water he had swallowed during the night made him sick to his stomach. But when Alec felt that he could hold out no longer, he looked at the struggling, fighting animal in front of him, and new courage came to him.

Suddenly he realized that they were going with the waves, instead of against them. He shook his head, trying to clear his mind. Yes, they were riding in; they must be approaching land! Eagerly he strained his salt-filled eyes and looked into the distance. And then he saw it—about a quarter of a mile away was a small island, not much more than a sandy reef in the sea. But he might find food and water there, and have a chance to survive. Faster and faster they approached the white sand. They were in the breakers. The Black's scream shattered the stillness. He was able to walk; he staggered a little and shook his black head. Then his action shifted marvelously, and he went faster through the shallow water.

Alec's head whirled as he was pulled toward the beach with ever-increasing speed. Suddenly he realized the danger of his position. He must untie this rope from around his waist, or else he would be dragged to death over the sand! Desperately his fingers flew to the knot; it was tight, he had

> WORD BANK
>
> **altered** (ALT urd) *v.*: changed

made sure of that. Frantically he worked on it as the shore drew closer and closer.

The Black was now on the beach. Thunder began to roll from beneath his hoofs as he broke out of the water. Hours in the water had swelled the knot—Alec couldn't untie it! Then he remembered his pocketknife. Could it still be there? Alec's hand darted to his rear pants pocket. His fingers reached inside and came out with the knife.

He was now on the beach being dragged by the stallion; the sand flew in his face. Quickly he opened the knife and began to cut the rope. His body burned from the sand, his clothes were being torn off of him! His speed was increasing every second! Madly he sawed away at the rope. With one final thrust he was through! His outflung hands caressed the sand. As he closed his eyes, his parched lips murmured, "Yes—Uncle Ralph—it did—come in handy."

ABOUT THE AUTHOR

"There is no way to explain the magic that some people have with horses," said **Walter Farley**, who loved horses and wrote about them throughout his life. At age eleven, he was writing stories about horses, and in high school, he wrote the first draft of his best-selling novel, *The Black Stallion.* Born in Syracuse, New York in 1915, Farley's youth was filled with horses. In addition to befriending the horses owned by his neighbors, he spent many hours visiting horses at nearby race tracks. Farley went on to write 16 Black Stallion books. Active until his death, Farley died in 1989.

Studying the Selection

QUICK REVIEW

1. Where does Alexander Ramsay normally live?

2. With whom has he spent the last two months? What will he miss?

3. What has his uncle given him as a gift? What is inscribed on it?

4. What is the name of the ship Alec will be taking from England to New York?

FOCUS

5. Why does Alexander visit the horse and bring him sugar?

6. Describe an incident or an object that is mentioned early in the story that is important for the way the story ends. Did you suspect that this was going to be a part of the story's ending? Did you do any predicting while you were reading the story?

CREATING & WRITING

7. What is the theme of this story? Remember, a theme is not an event or character in the story. It is the *idea* of the story, which the reader understands better and better as the story unfolds.

8. Your assignment is to do some research about horses and to write a two-page report. There are many topics you could choose. Some examples are: Horse Anatomy, Horse Behavior, How Horses Have Helped Human Beings Throughout History, How Horses Came to the Americas, Different Kinds of Horse Training. There are more than one hundred breeds of horses. You may choose a particular breed to write about. You may also write about the horse of a famous person.

9. Using your favorite medium (pencil, pen, crayons, pastels, paint, or clay), create a horse to go with your report.

LESSON IN LITERATURE . . .

UNIT REVIEW

- The three elements of plot taught in this unit—conflict, sequence, and cause and effect, work together to make a story interesting.

- The fourth element, predicting, is done by the reader as they are drawn into the story.

- In an exciting story, the two sides of the conflict are almost equally strong, making it difficult for the reader to predict the outcome.

- The stronger the link between cause and effect, the more powerful the story will be.

THINK ABOUT IT!

1. Refer to Part 1 of "Camping Trip." Who is John? Who is Joe? Where are the two cars headed?

2. Which of the predictions that you made in Part 1 turned out to be true?

3. What was the most important clue in Part 1? Why is Sally amazed when she sees all the maple trees?

4. Can you explain why sequence is so important to understanding cause and effect? Can you explain why cause and effect is so important to predicting? Can you explain why a story without conflict is rather boring?

Camping Trip, Part 2

Pointing at a crumpled sheet of directions scrawled thirty years earlier, John poked his head in the window of his sister's car. "I'm telling you, Sal, the interstate gets us there twice as fast."

In the car ahead, John, his wife, and his three kids sat in the rush-hour traffic they'd hoped to avoid, fifteen feet ahead of Sally, Joe, and their two kids.

Sally sighed. "If you're sure you're going to be able to find the town."

John just smiled and shot back into his car.

An hour later John put on his turn signal, and Sally followed him off the highway. At the bottom of the exit ramp was a crowded intersection, with car dealerships on three corners. When they pulled into a gas station with a SuperMart, Joe said, "I'll go get us some snacks."

The kids poured out of both cars, and headed for the patch of grass next to the station. While the girls threw a Frisbee, the boys climbed the large maple tree next to the parking lot.

John was back, a state map in his hand. "The attendant says we turn right here. It's down on the right just past the mall."

"Mall?" Sally said, looking around at the intersection. "This doesn't look anything like—"

"I know. It's a four-lane highway now," John explained.

Everyone piled back into the cars and they headed down the highway past new housing developments and, on the right, a mall.

They almost missed the green painted metal sign at the park entrance.

They drove down the paved, single-lane road that wound through the campground until John pulled into a numbered campsite.

He approached Sally's car with a puzzled look on his face. "I think this is the right place," he said. "But I don't remember all these trees. You remember these trees, Sal?"

Sally looked around in amazement at all the maple trees. She had a far-off look on her face, as if she were remembering a time long past.

"Yeah, actually. I do remember them, now that you ask."

Blueprint for Reading

INTO . . . By the Shores of Silver Lake

Does the natural world play a part in your life? Do you look at the moon and stars in the night sky, or fill with excitement as you watch the snowflakes fall? How does it feel when the wind blows through the trees? What do we mean when we exclaim, "Oh what a beautiful day!"?

By the Shores of Silver Lake was written about a time when wolves roamed freely in the wilderness. In the story, two little girls are frightened when they see a wolf watching them. The older girl, Laura, cannot quite say why, but she does not want her father to kill the wolf she saw. Delicately, she expresses her feelings for an animal that never did her harm.

EYES ON . . . *Pulling It All Together*

When we *pull it all together,* we look for each of the literary components in a single story, and see how they work together in that story.

In *Gold-Mounted Guns,* we talked about **conflict**. Remember that conflict can take place inside a person or outside a person. What is Laura's inner struggle or conflict? The *external* conflict for the characters in *By the Shores of Silver Lake* is the presence of a wolf that might hurt someone.

In *The Disappearing Man,* we talked about **sequence**. Sequence is the order in which events occur. What is the sequence of events in *By the Shores of Silver Lake?*

In *The Speckled Hen's Egg,* we focused on **cause and effect**. The **cause** is what happened that results in the **effect**. In *By the Shores of Silver Lake,* what occurs that results in Mr. Ingalls' finding a homestead?

In *The Black Stallion,* we looked at **predicting**. While reading a story, we try to figure out what will happen at the end. Can you predict the end of *By the Shores of Silver Lake?*

By the Shores of Silver Lake

Laura Ingalls Wilder

Wolves on Silver Lake

There came a night when moonlight shone silver clear. The earth was endless white and the wind was still.

Beyond every window the white world stretched far away in frosty glitter, and the sky was a curve of light. Laura could not settle down to anything. She didn't want to play games. She hardly heard even the music of Pa's fiddle. She did not want to dance, but she felt that she must move swiftly. She must be going somewhere.

Suddenly she exclaimed, "Carrie! Let's go slide on the ice!"

"In the night, Laura?" Ma was astonished.

"It's light outdoors," Laura replied. "Almost as light as day."

"It will be all right, Caroline," Pa said. "There's nothing to hurt them, if they don't stay too long and freeze."

So Ma told them, "You may go for a quick run. Don't stay until you get too cold."

Laura and Carrie hurried into their coats and hoods and mittens. Their shoes were new and the soles thick. Ma had knit their stockings of woolen yarn, and their red flannel underclothes came down over their knees and buttoned in a snug band around each stocking. Their flannel petticoats were thick and warm, and their dresses and their coats were wool, and so were their hoods and mufflers.

WORD BANK   **mufflers** *n.:* scarves

Out of the warm house they burst into the breathtaking air that tingled with cold. They ran a race on the snowy path down the low hill to the stables. Then they followed the path that the horses and the cow had made when Pa led them through the snow to water at the hole he had cut in the lake ice.

"We mustn't go near the water hole," Laura said, and she led Carrie along the lake shore until they were well away from it. Then they stopped and looked at the night.

It was so beautiful that they hardly breathed. The great round moon hung in the sky and its radiance poured over a silvery world. Far, far away in every direction stretched motionless flatness, softly shining as if it were made of soft light. In the midst lay the dark, smooth lake, and a glittering moonpath stretched across it. Tall grass stood up in black lines from the snow drifted in the sloughs.[1]

The stable lay low and dark near the shore, and on the low hill stood the dark, small, surveyors' house, with the yellow light in the window twinkling from its darkness.

"How still it is," Carrie whispered. "Listen how still it is."

Laura's heart swelled. She felt herself a part of the wide land, of the far deep sky and

---

1. *Sloughs* (SLOOS) are areas of soft, muddy ground, similar to swamps.

| WORD BANK | **radiance** (RAY dee unts) *n.:* shining brightness |
| | **motionless** (MO shun luss) *adj.:* not moving, still |

the brilliant moonlight. She wanted to fly. But Carrie was little and almost afraid, so she took hold of Carrie's hand and said, "Let's slide. Come on, run!"

With hands clasped, they ran a little way. Then with right foot first they slid on the smooth ice much farther than they had run.

"On the moonpath, Carrie! Let's follow the moonpath," Laura cried.

And so they ran and slid, and ran and slid again, on the glittering moonpath into the light from the silver moon. Farther and farther from shore they went, straight toward the high bank on the other side.

They swooped and almost seemed to fly. If Carrie lost her balance, Laura held her up. If Laura was unsteady, Carrie's hand steadied her.

Close to the farther shore, almost in the shadow of the high bank, they stopped. Something made Laura look up to the top of the bank.

And there, dark against the moonlight, stood a great wolf!

He was looking toward her. The wind stirred his fur and the moonlight seemed to run in and out of it.

"Let's go back," Laura said quickly, as she turned, taking Carrie with her. "I can go faster than you."

WORD BANK

bank *n.:* the slope or high ground next to a river

She ran and slid and ran again as fast as she could, but Carrie kept up.

"I saw it too," Carrie panted. "Was it a wolf?"

"Don't talk!" Laura answered. "Hurry!"

Laura could hear their feet running and sliding on the ice. She listened for a sound behind them, but there was none. Then they ran and slid without a word until they came to the path by the water hole. As they ran up the path, Laura looked back but she could see nothing on the lake nor on the bank beyond.

Laura and Carrie didn't stop running. They ran up the hill to the house, opened the back door and ran into the lean-to.[2] They ran across that, burst through the door into the front room and slammed it shut behind them. Then leaned against it, panting.

Pa sprang to his feet. "What is it?" he asked. "What has frightened you?"

"Was it a wolf, Laura?" Carrie gasped.

"It was a wolf, Pa," Laura gulped, catching her breath. "A great, big wolf! And I was afraid Carrie couldn't run fast enough but she did."

"I should say she did!" Pa exclaimed. "Where is this wolf?"

"I don't know. It is gone," Laura told him.

Ma helped them take off their wraps. "Sit down and rest! You are all out of breath," she said.

_____

2. A *lean-to* is a shack attached to the side of a building. Its roof slopes down, away from the building, to the opposite wall of the shack.

"Where was the wolf?" Pa wanted to know.

"Up on the bank," Carrie said, and Laura added, "The high bank across the lake."

"Did you girls go clear there?" Pa asked in surprise. "And ran all the way back after you saw him! I had no idea you would go so far. It is a good half-mile."

"We followed the moonpath," Laura told him. Pa looked at her strangely. "You would!" he said. "I thought those wolves had gone. It was careless of me. I'll hunt them tomorrow."

Mary sat still, but her face was white. "Oh, girls," she almost whispered. "Suppose he had caught you!"

Then they all sat silent while Laura and Carrie rested.

Laura was glad to be safe in the warm room with the desolate prairie shut out. If anything had happened to Carrie, it would have been her fault for taking her so far across the lake.

But nothing had happened. She could almost see again the great wolf with the wind ruffling the moonlight on his fur.

"Pa!" she said in a low voice.

"Yes, Laura?" Pa answered.

"I hope you don't find the wolf, Pa," Laura said.

"Why ever not?" Ma wondered.

"Because he didn't chase us," Laura told

WORD BANK   **desolate** (DEH suh lut) *adj.*: empty, deserted, and lonely

her. "He didn't chase us, Pa, and he could have caught us."

A long, wild, wolf howl rose and faded away on the stillness.

Another answered it. Then silence again.

Laura's heart seemed to turn over with a sickening flop and she found herself on her feet. She was glad of Ma's steadying hand on her arm.

"Poor girl! You are as nervous as a witch and no wonder," Ma said softly.

Ma took a flatiron[3] from the back of the stove, wrapped it tightly in a cloth and gave it to Carrie.

"It is bedtime," she said. "Here is the hot iron for your feet."

"And here is yours, Laura," as she wrapped another. "Be sure you put it in the middle of the bed so Mary's feet can reach it too."

As Laura shut the stair door behind them, Pa was talking earnestly to Ma. But Laura could not hear what he said for the ringing in her ears.

---

3. A *flatiron* is similar to our modern-day iron but is heated by being placed on a hot stove, not by electricity. Because the girls' room is freezing cold, their mother gives them flatirons wrapped in cloths to keep their beds warm.

WORD BANK
steadying (STED ee ing) *adj.:* calming
earnestly (UR nust lee) *adv.:* seriously, sincerely

Pa Finds The Homestead[4]

After breakfast next morning Pa took his gun and set out. All that morning Laura was listening for a shot and not wanting to hear it. All morning she remembered the great wolf sitting quiet in the moonlight that shimmered through his thick fur.

Pa was late for dinner. It was long past noon when he stamped the snow from his feet in the lean-to. He came in and put his gun on the wall, and hung his cap and coat on their nail. His mittens he hung, by their thumbs, to dry on the line behind the stove. Then he washed his face and hands in the tin basin on the bench, and before the small glass that hung above it he combed his hair and his beard.

"Sorry I kept dinner waiting, Caroline," he said. "I was gone longer than I thought. Went farther than I intended."

"It doesn't matter, Charles; I've kept dinner warm," Ma replied. "Come to the table, girls! Don't keep Pa waiting."

"How far did you go, Pa?" Mary asked.

"Better than ten miles, all told," said Pa. "Those wolf tracks led me a chase."

"Did you get the wolf, Pa?" Carrie wanted to know. Laura did not say anything.

---

4. A *homestead* is a piece of land on which a house can be built. In 1862, President Abraham Lincoln signed the Homestead Act. According to this new law, anyone who lived and worked on an area of government-owned land could become its owner. A settler was given 160 acres of land to farm in return for living on the land for five years.

WORD BANK

shimmered *v.:* glowed and softly shone with a flickering light

glass *n.:* mirror

Pa smiled at Carrie and said, "Now, now, don't ask questions. I'll tell you all about it. I went across the lake, followed the marks you girls made last night. And what do you suppose I found in that high bank where you saw the wolf?"

"You found the wolf," Carrie said confidently. Laura still said nothing. Her food was choking her; she could hardly swallow the smallest mouthful.

"I found the wolves' *den,*" said Pa. "And the biggest wolves' tracks I ever saw. Girls, there were two big buffalo wolves[5] at that den last night."

Mary and Carrie gasped. Ma said, "Charles!"

"It's too late to be scared now," Pa told them. "But that's what you girls did. You went right up to the wolves' den and there were the wolves.

"Their tracks were fresh, and all the signs show plain as day what they were doing. It's an old den, and from their size they're no young wolves. I'd say they'd been living there for some years. But they haven't been living there this winter.

"They came down from the northwest sometime yesterday evening and went pretty straight to that den. They stayed around it, in and out of it, maybe till this morning. I followed their tracks from there, down along Big Slough and out on the prairie, southwest.

"From the time they left the old den, those

_____
5. *Buffalo wolves* are very large wolves.

wolves never stopped. They trotted along, side by side, as if they had started on a long journey and knew where they were going. I followed them far enough to be sure that I couldn't get a shot at them. They've left for good."

Laura took a deep breath as though she had forgotten to breathe till now. Pa looked at her. "You are glad they got away, Laura?" he asked.

"Yes, Pa, I am," Laura answered. "They didn't chase us."

"No, Laura, they didn't chase you. And for the life of me, I can't figure out why they didn't."

"And what were they doing at that old den?" Ma wondered.

"They were just looking at it," said Pa. "My belief is they came back to visit the old place where they lived before the graders[6] came in and the antelope left. Maybe they used to live here before the hunters killed the last buffalo. Buffalo wolves were all over this country once, but there's not many left now, even around here. The railroads and settlements kept driving them farther west. One thing's certain if I know anything about wild animal tracks; those two wolves came straight from the west and went straight back west, and all they did here was to stop one night at the old den. And I wouldn't wonder if they're pretty nearly the last

_____

6. _Graders_ are machines that smooth out the ground and make it level enough to have a road paved over it.

buffalo wolves that'll ever be seen in this part of the country."

"Oh, Pa, the poor wolves," Laura mourned.

"Mercy on us," Ma said briskly. "There's enough to be sorry for, without being sorry for the feelings of wild beasts! Be thankful the brutes didn't do any worse than scare you girls last night."

"That isn't all, Caroline!" Pa announced. "I've got some news. I've found our homestead."

"Oh, where, Pa! What's it like? How far is it?" Mary and Laura and Carrie asked, excited. Ma said, "That's good, Charles."

Pa pushed back his plate, drank his tea, wiped his mustache, and said, "It is just right in every way. It lies south of where the lake joins Big Slough, and the slough curves around to the west of it. There's a rise in the prairie to the south of the slough, that will make a nice place to build. A little hill just west of it crowds the slough back on that side. On the quarter section[7] there's upland hay and plow land lying to the south; and good grazing on all of it, everything a farmer could ask for. And it's near the townsite, so the girls can go to school."

"I'm glad, Charles," said Ma.

"It's a funny thing," Pa said. "Here I've been looking around this country for months and

---

7. A *quarter section* is a quarter of a square mile of land, equaling 160 acres.

never finding a quarter section that just exactly suited me. And that one was lying there all the time. Likely enough I wouldn't have come across it at all, if this wolf chase hadn't taken me across the lake and down along the slough on that side."

"I wish you had filed on it last fall," Ma worried.

"Nobody'll be in here this winter," Pa said confidently. "I'll get out to Brookings and file on that claim[8] next spring before anybody else is looking for a homestead."

---

8. If a settler wanted to own a piece of land under the Homestead Act, he had *to file a claim* with the government. A *claim* is a statement declaring ownership of something. *Filing* a claim means giving the written statement of ownership to the government official in charge of claims.

ABOUT THE AUTHOR

Laura Ingalls Wilder was born in Wisconsin in 1867. Her father, a farmer, moved west to the Dakota Territory. Life was hard at first, and the family nearly starved one winter. Ingalls was unable to attend school and was largely self-taught. After she married Almanzo Wilder, the couple settled in the Ozarks. Not until she was 65 years old did Wilder, at the urging of her daughter, begin to write the eight Little House books. The series told the story of her life growing up on the American frontier. Wilder died in Missouri at the age of 90.

Studying the Selection

FIRST IMPRESSIONS
Would you like to live as the Ingalls family lives?

QUICK REVIEW

1. What is the setting of the story? Setting includes the place and the time. Give the approximate year, the season, and the time of day.

2. Who are the characters?

3. What does *this* family do when they want to hear music?

4. Which clothes do Laura and Carrie wear outside in the cold?

FOCUS

5. Explain in several sentences why Laura does not want her father to kill the wolf.

6. Choose one of the literary components we studied in Unit Two and answer one of the following questions:

   • What are the conflicts in the story? (conflict)

   • List the sequence of events. Try to limit yourself to ten events. (sequence)

   • Which events led the father to their future homestead? (cause and effect)

   • Did you predict the end of the story? Which clues pointed to it? (predicting)

CREATING & WRITING

7. In one or two paragraphs, write what lesson you think the story teaches.

8. Wolves are fascinating animals. They have a very strong family unit. The mother and father who lead a wolf pack remain together for all of their lives. Find out about wolves. Write a two-paragraph report.

9. Your family is moving West in a covered wagon. Your parents have loaded furniture and household goods onto the wagon. You may choose five items to take along. Write a list and explain why these things are special to you.

A
NICHE
IN THE
KITCHEN

Ouida Sebestyen

Some days my mother asks me,
How can she possibly cook
With me underfoot, and her
Cookbook full of pressed flowers,
5   And clay on the rolling-pin
From projects I'm doing at all hours
There in her kitchen?

She says, how can she move around
Anymore, surrounded by hobbies
10   And models and crafts and
Tools and messes, no matter
Which end she works in?

I tell her I don't know.
It's just more fun when I'm
15   Larking around in the kitchen,
Working where she's working and
Making things while she's baking things.

She says, yes, but where can she stand
Without standing in the spot where,
20   For instance, I'm sanding a new bird-feeder?
I tell her I don't know, but
I need her a lot. For company.
I keep saying I'd rather be
There where she's dicing carrots
25   And icing éclairs, in the kitchen,
Than making things upstairs.
Or anywhere.

She just glares.

So I say, can't I have even one
30   Little niche in the kitchen?
Even if I'm a bother? Please?
Even when I'm not helping? I say,
I don't mind getting down on my knees
To pick up any split peas that scatter,
35   (Won't they make a beanbag?) while she
Lets the hamburgers spatter
And tries to answer the phone.

I say it's neater,
Smelling what's cooking and
40   Looking for raisins in the cookie batter,
Than playing alone.

She says, what's wrong with your room,
Or the yard, or playing with Joan?

I explain to her, well, it's just nicer
45   Knowing she's right on my heels
Behind me, slicing bologna
Or spicing the applesauce.
But she's the boss,
And if that's how she feels
50   I'd better just gather my stuff up
And go.

She says, well…no.

I say, no?

She says, no, that time will come soon enough.
55   Too soon. So just bring your stuff
Back into the kitchen.

She smiles and gives me a taste of
Tomato paste and makes more room
On the counter beside her, so I can lace
60   The pieces of wallet from my leather kit
Or do some tooling.
Working together like that for a bit
Is great. I string beads
While she strings beans,
65   Or I glue seeds to plaques,
Or illustrate books between
Racks of cake-layers cooling.

My mother says, when she was young
A kitchen was where everyone hung around
70   Telling what happened that day
And feeling at home.
She says it had a table for schoolwork
And mending and crewel, and

A stool for cutting hair,
75 And not so much chrome.
She liked it there.

I say I like it here, too, in this kitchen,
And I'm glad it's okay if I stay.
We get on with whatever we're making—
80 Shaking the steak in flour and
Squashing papier-mâché in a tray—
Feeling like artists
And getting in each other's way.
She doesn't scream
85 When she opens the oven and
Steam pours out of the mouth
Of the scary mask I'm baking.
She only sighs when the poster I'm drying
Falls into the meat she's frying.

90 Every once in a while
She tells me it probably would be grand
To have a kitchen no bigger than a minute—
So small that only one person could fit in it.
But then she folds a slice of warm bread
95 And puts my favorite jam between,
And I know she doesn't mean it.

I know when she laughs and
Gives my hair a muss,
And swipes the counter to clear a spot,
100 She's saying our kitchen will always be
Large enough for both of us—
For her, and the things she likes a lot,
And the things I like a lot,
And me.

ABOUT THE AUTHOR

Ouida Sebestyen, an only child, was born in Vernon, Texas in 1924. Both her parents were teachers and, though she didn't like school much, she loved to read. In high school, she decided to become a writer. Her young adult years were spent writing, traveling through the American West and, during WWII, repairing airplanes for the U.S. air force. Sebestyen wrote many plays, stories, and books, but no one would publish them. When a story she wrote about a child was finally published, she decided to become a children's author. Since that time, Sebestyen has written poems, stories, and six novels for young adults. Sebestyen lives in Boulder, Colorado.

1. What is a *niche?*

2. What are you doing, when you *tool* leather?

3. What is this poem about? Just give a short, simple answer in two or three sentences.

4. How many sentences are in the first stanza?

5. Give five rhyming pairs or sets of words in the poem.

6. Describe four activities the child is involved in. Describe four activities the mom is involved in.

7. Where do you like to play or do homework? Why?

DO CHARACTERS HAVE DREAMS?

1. Pick one of the main characters from *Gold-Mounted Guns, The Disappearing Man, The Speckled Hen's Egg, The Black Stallion,* or *By the Shores of Silver Lake.* You are going to write down your character's dreams. For this, you will create a booklet with eight pages inside a cover. Fold a piece of 8½" x 11" colored paper in half across the middle, to create the front and back covers. Then fold two pieces of 8 ½" x 11" white paper in half and turn them sideways inside the cover. The cover of your booklet should say **My Character Book.** Don't forget to number your pages, using both the front and back of each piece of paper.

2. Pages 1 and 2 will be called **Vital Statistics.** On these pages, you write the name of the character, the character's age, whether the character is a boy or girl or a man or woman, and what your character looks like. Tell also where the character lives.

3. Pages 3 and 4 will be called **Family, Friends, Acquaintances, and Neighbors.** There, you will list the people who are important to the character in the story.

4. Pages 5 and 6 will be called **The Things I Like.** Make a list of the things you think the character likes based on your sense of the character as a person.

5. Pages 7 and 8 will be called **A Dream I Had.** This is a dream that you imagine your character had while he or she was sleeping. The dream should make sense in terms of the events of the character's life.

I CAN'T FIND MY STORY!
The Lost Character

1. You are one of the characters in one of the Unit 2 stories. You may be a major character or a minor character. You can even be an animal from *Gold-Mounted Guns, The Speckled Hen's Egg, The Black Stallion,* or *By the Shores of Silver Lake.* You should make or find some piece of clothing or a prop that helps you look like the character. You can also—with help from a grownup or a sibling—put on makeup to help you get into character, when the time comes for your presentation.

2. As it turns out, you can't remember who you are or which story (or poem) in Unit 2 you belong in. After you make your presentation to your class, it will be their job to tell you which story (or poem) you should go back to. But they can only do it if you give them the right information.

    *   Begin by saying, *Help! I can't find my story! Can you help me?* Then you give the following information.
    *   If you have a name, you will give your name, if you can remember it!
    *   Then describe the setting, where and when you were living when you were in the story.
    *   Tell who your friends or family are, if you have friends or family. Or, if you are an animal, who "owns" you.
    *   Next, say what you like, what you don't like, and, maybe, what you eat.

- Finally, tell your class what the last thing you remember is, before you popped out of the story into the here and now. What you remember can be more detailed than what is in the story, but it must be based on the situation in the story.
- Conclude by asking your class, "Where do I belong? Which story should I go back to?" Your presentation can be serious or funny.

3. Make notes on index cards for that moment when you are to be "The Lost Character." Practice your presentation. Don't forget to speak up so everyone in the classroom can hear you!

THE ANIMAL'S THE THING!

Learning as a Team / Teaching by Acting

1. Your teacher will help you and your class form small groups or teams.

2. Each group is going to choose from a list of animals that are in trouble. Your teacher will help, so that each team picks a different animal for a mascot. A *mascot* is an emblem or symbol of a team. Here are the animals you can choose from:

- Dolphins
- Polar Bears
- Whales
- American Black Bears
- Florida Panther
- Manatees
- Owls
- The California Condor
- Sea Otters
- The Sonoran Pronghorn

3. Each team, with the help of the teacher, should write a short letter to The Wildlife Conservation Society, asking for information about their animal. Their address is:

The Wildlife Conservation Society
2300 Southern Boulevard
Bronx, New York 10460

4. From the information they receive, each group should write a scene about the life of their animal. The team will rehearse together to act out the scene, with each team member assigned a part.

5. Each team must write an introduction and a conclusion for the scene. The introduction will be read aloud to the audience before the scene, by a team narrator. The conclusion will be read aloud after the scene, by a team narrator.

6. Do a good job with your presentation!

CHARACTER DEVELOPMENT

1. Think about the characters in each of the selections, including those in the poetry section.

2. In literature, some characters change and develop throughout the story or poem. Other characters remain the same from beginning to end.

    a. What are two examples of characters who do not change?
    b. What are two examples of characters who do change in some way?

3. Describe the characters who do not change. Choose the main trait that each one displays. Bring examples from the beginning and end of the story and poem to show how the character has not changed.

4. Describe the characters that do change. Choose the main trait that has changed in each one during the story or poem. Bring examples from the beginning and end of the story or poem to show how the character has changed.

unit 3

AIMING HIGH

CHARACTER

- The easiest way for us to know about a character is for the author to describe the character's looks, personality, and character traits.

- A more interesting way to learn about a character is to pay close attention to what the character says and does.

- At times, an author will let us in on a character's thoughts or feelings.

- In many stories, we learn about one character from another character.

THINK ABOUT IT!

1. Read the first paragraph of "We Love Our Marine." What are four facts that you have learned about PFC Escobar?

2. Read the rest of the story. What are two emotions PFC Escobar experiences in the story? How do you know this?

3. Does the author describe the physical appearance of Alejandro or Alicia? Does this add to or take away from the story?

4. What is one thing you learned about Mom from what she *says?* What is one thing you learned about Mom from what she *does?*

We Love Our Marine

Private First Class Alejandro Escobar stood on the sidewalk in the early morning sunlight. "We Love Our Marine!" the banner shouted to the world from the second story of his tiny house. Escobar walked up the short path to the front door. He started to knock, then looked at his watch. He should wait. Mom and Dad and his baby sister would still be sleeping. Despite all the pictures Mom had sent, in his mind Alicia had remained the mischievous two year old he'd left 17 months ago. Standing at his front door, he realized that Alicia was now a three and a half year old with little memory of her big brother.

Escobar looked in the picture window. Not even an extra folding chair in the small living room remained as evidence of last night's party. Mom, tired as she was, would never let herself go to sleep with the house a mess. Nonetheless, he knew it had been a big party. He could hear that when he had called. The music, the laughter, the noise.

"Don't say it's me," he instructed her. "Take the phone somewhere you can talk."

She did as he asked. There was fear in her voice when she finally spoke. "Alejandro? Where are you?"

"I just can't face the crowd tonight," he explained. "It's just a lot to get used to all of a sudden."

"Where are you," she asked again. This time he wasn't sure if it was fear or irritation in her voice.

"My bus got in a few hours ago. I've just been walking for a while."

"Everyone's been waiting," was all she said.

Escobar started to knock again, then stepped away from the door and sat down on a porch swing. He was so happy to be home, but he was nervous, too.

The front door swung open. Mom. She smiled at her son, then, without a word, she hugged him. A moment later, Dad held him in a hug so tight it almost took his breath away. No one spoke as Mom, Dad, and even Alejandro wiped tears away. Then, all three began to laugh. This was the welcome home party he needed. Escobar breathed a deep sigh of relief. Everything was going to be okay.

Blueprint for Reading

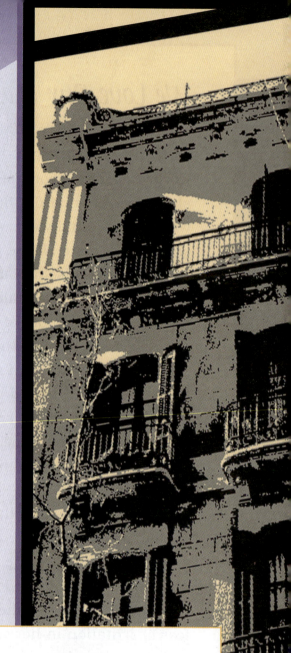

INTO . . . *Gramp*

Do you have grandparents or great-grandparents? Are you close with them? What do your grandparents or great-grandparents do each day? Have you ever thought about what it is like to be a very old person?

Many older people continue to work at their jobs and live in their own homes. But others are unable to do many of the things they used to do and are unable to live alone. If they live in a place for older people, they must obey the rules of the place where they live. They may not even be able to have a dog or a cat for company. Sometimes, older people feel that they cannot be themselves any longer and have lost control of their lives.

EYES ON . . . *Character*

In our everyday lives, we usually get to know people little by little. Often, we may have an intuition—a sense or a feeling—about a person. We can *sense* the person's character. However, we ordinarily form our opinions based on what someone says and does.

We get to know a character in a book the same way. We learn quite a lot about the character, because we see them in a variety of situations. What's more, in a story, we are often told what the character is thinking. Because of this, we may feel as though we know a fictional character better than we know some of our own friends.

If the story is a good one, we will feel that, even though the character is imaginary, they have very important lessons to teach us.

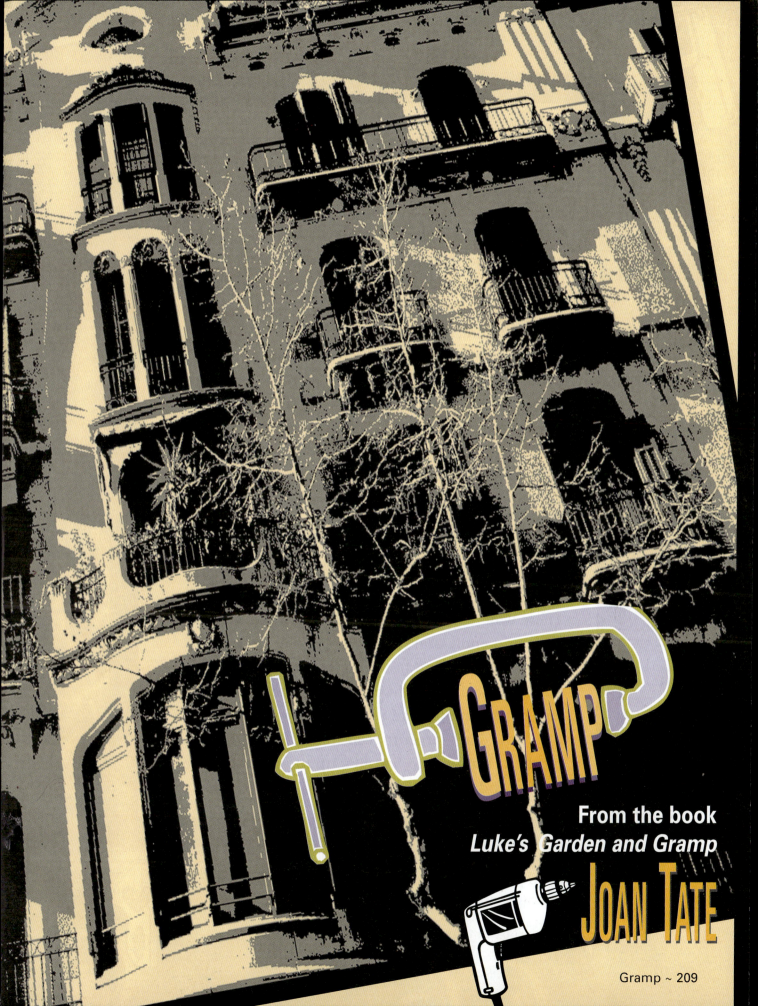

GRAMP

From the book
Luke's Garden and Gramp

JOAN TATE

That summer when Simon was ten was a time full of new things. Gradually, the apartment became home. Gramp and Mum put everything right and soon Simon was quite used to the differences, even liking his room in the sky, and going up and down in an elevator, or even sometimes running the whole way down the stairs, hundreds of steps, to arrive breathless and panting at the bottom, dizzy with it all.

The school took some getting used to, but it had a good playing field. Simon sometimes went there after school, too, because there was no space to play around the apartments, or at least nowhere to play without getting chased away every five minutes. But the school was several streets away, and he only went there for scrimmage. Best of all, he had found a place for his guinea pigs.

Gramp had fixed it up. The shed down in the yard was very small, one of a row all alike, a very large closet with a door-sized door, that was all. There was just room for Dad's motorbike, some odds and ends, and a shelf at the end for cans of paint and that kind of thing. Gramp cleared the shelf, stacked the paint cans all at one side, cut the legs off the hutch, and put the guinea pigs there.

"Now don't forget to feed them," he said. "It's a bit dark, but not too bad. It's up to you to see they get fed and cleaned."

WORD BANK

hutch *n.:* a pen or enclosed coop for animals

Simon had a small plastic bucket up in the apartment and Mum put all the leftover green leaves and stale bread in it. Every day after school, Simon took the key from the hook inside the kitchen cabinet and went down to feed the guinea pigs. They were getting big now and needed quite a lot of food. Sometimes he wandered all over the building sites down the road, looking for dandelions and groundsel[1] and other wild greenstuff for them. Sometimes the greengrocer[2] gave him leftover cabbage leaves, or a carrot or two. So the guinea pigs did well. And Simon was pleased.

But it was not the same with Gramp. At first it was all right, as there was a lot to do to help Mum put the apartment to rights. But then the apartment was finished and it was easy to clean and look after too, much easier than the house. Mum got a part-time job, mornings only, and Gramp was alone a lot. He sat in his room or in the living room, not even watching television, but just sitting there, staring out the window, or staring at nothing, not even smoking his pipe.

Sometimes he sat on his bed, staring at his feet, and Simon went in to talk to him, to tell him about his guinea pigs.

"They're big now, Gramp," he said. "Why don't

----

1. *Groundsel* is a weed that has small yellow flowers.
2. A *greengrocer* is someone who sells fresh fruits and vegetables.

you come down and look?"

Gramp looked up at him.

"That's good, boy," he said. "That's good."

"Come down and look," said Simon again.

Gramp shook his head.

"Too far down there," he said.

"But there's the elevator. It'd only take five minutes."

But Gramp shook his head.

"What's the matter with you, Gramp?"

"Nothing's the matter," he said. "Nothing, that's it."

"You mean you've nothing to do?"

"That's it," said Gramp, looking at his hands. "Nothing."

"Why don't you put a bench[3] up here?" said Simon.

Gramp looked around.

"In here?" he said. "In this room? There's not room."

"You could have a small one," said Simon. "Just so that you could fasten the vise[4] on, anyhow."

"The mess, boy," Gramp said. "The mess. She

---

3. When Simon says *bench*, he means a workbench, a strong, sturdy table fitted with tools, at which a person can do carpentry or repairs.
4. A *vise* is an instrument or tool used to hold an object firmly while work is being done on it.

wouldn't stand for it. You can't do that sort of thing indoors, in an apartment like this."

"We could keep it clean," persisted Simon.

"You don't know what you're talking about," said Gramp curtly, and then he just turned his head away, refusing to talk anymore, not looking at Simon.

"Gramp!"

But it was no good. Gramp had been talking in a way he had never talked before. Then he gradually got more and more silent and would not speak to any of them sometimes, for days on end. Even Dad could not get a word out of him if he was feeling in that mood. Gramp began to sit in a chair at his window, all day long, sitting there with a small hammer in his hands, turning it over and over, rubbing it with his hands, polishing the wood over and over again and resting the head against his thumb, the hammer which he never used anymore. Simon could not bear seeing him sitting there, mumbling to himself, but he did not know what to do.

Mum just said that he was getting old and she told Simon not to bother him.

"He's always been old," protested Simon. "And he never minded me bothering him before."

"Older, then," said Mum. "You get like that when you're old."

WORD BANK

persisted (pur SIS ted) *v.*: continued to make a point in spite of opposition

curtly (KURT lee) *adv.*: briefly and a bit rudely

screws • nuts • bolts • nails • hooks • washers • hinges • staples • sandpaper • drill bits

drill • wire cutter • miter box • staple gun • safety glasses • chisel • utility knife • file • grinder

"Like what?"

"Like Grandpa."

"But he wasn't like that before."

"Before what?"

"Before we came here."

"What d'you mean, before we came here?" said Mum. "He's better off here than where we were before. The room's lighter and cleaner and not so damp. It's warmer too."

Simon fell silent. She didn't understand. Then he looked at his mother, standing by the table in the kitchen, mixing something in a big bowl. He watched her turning the mixture over and beating at it with a spoon, then slicing through it with a knife. She moved quickly and took things out of the kitchen drawer, shut the drawer, darted across the kitchen, fetched a baking tin, switched the oven on, came back.

"What are you standing there staring at?" she said. "Go on down and out into the fresh air."

"Gramp would be all right if he had a bench. Like you," said Simon, holding his breath, knowing his mother would be cross.

"Oh, you and Grandpa and that bench!" she said. "Where can you find a workbench in a place like this?"

"We could try."

Simon did not know why he went on about it,

WORD
BANK

cross *adj.:* angry

because he knew his mother was right. But he kept thinking of their old shed, of him and Gramp talking and working, sometimes saying nothing, and now it had all gone. He had no one to talk to and Gramp didn't like it, either. His mother leaned across the table and knocked a small bowl off the edge by mistake. It fell to the tiled floor and broke.

"Oh!" she said. "Look what's happened now! That bowl belonged to your grandmother! Get along now."

Mum took a deep breath, then went to find the broom. She swept the floor in short, sharp movements. After every sliver of china had been picked up, she straightened up and said, "If it's that important to you, why don't you go out and find him a bench yourself? Go on, go and find him one for yourself!"

"All right," said Simon slowly. "All right," he repeated with more conviction. "I *will* find him one," he said, his voice strong and determined. "You've all got things to do and maybe you just don't have time to worry about him, too."

"Now you know that's not true," said Mum. "You know it. Just you say you're sorry now."

But Simon felt it *was* true. Without a word, he dashed out of the kitchen. He felt hot and impatient and he couldn't wait for the elevator. He began stamping down the stairs, crashing his feet on each step, until they were both sore.

"I'll find him one somewhere," he said to himself. "I will. I'll find him one. I'll get one somewhere, so he can use his tools again and we can talk again." He stumped down the road, not quite sure where he was going to start looking, his hot face slowly cooling. Where did you look? Where did you find things like that? Where did people do their odd jobs when they lived in apartments? Perhaps they didn't have odd jobs to do. Perhaps Gramp *was* too old. Perhaps they would put him in a home[5] next. Simon felt cold at the thought. His friend Ken's granddad had gone to a home and had hated it, Ken said. Simon didn't know what a home was, but he knew he didn't want Gramp to go to one, knew he would hate it too. Who would teach him to use the tools then? Not Dad, because he wasn't interested, and no one in the whole world used tools as well as Gramp did.

The other blocks of apartments on the opposite side of the road were going up fast. The one opposite Simon's was complete on the outside and the crane had gone from the top of it. There were painters and decorators inside it now. The next two blocks were about halfway up, and the next two just beginning to grow out of the ground. Simon

---

5. *Home* here means an old age home, a place where elderly people who cannot take care of themselves are cared for.

saw them every day from his window, and on his way to school, and each day they were a little higher. Soon they would all be full of people.

He stopped and looked through the gap in the fencing. The site was dry and dusty and the doors of all the builders' sheds were open in the sunlight. There were workers standing about everywhere, as it was payday and they were just getting off work.

The sheds?

They were fine sheds, wooden and sturdy, much larger than the shed they had had at home. In fact, some of them were almost as large as a small house. Surely one of them would have enough room inside for a bench for Gramp? Surely he wouldn't be in the way there? And he might even be useful, mending and making things for the men and the engineers.

Simon moved inside the fence. He knew you weren't supposed to go in, but no one seemed to notice him. He waited until the workers had gone away and then he moved over toward one of the huts.

It was big and roomy and had a kind of desk inside it. There were charts and papers all over the walls, and papers everywhere. There were chairs against the desk, just like an office. There wasn't much room for anything else. He turned around and began to walk toward the next one.

WORD BANK **gap** *n.:* a break or opening in a row of objects or in a wall

"Hi, you!" a voice cried out. "What are you up to over there?"

Simon turned around. A man was standing in the doorway of a smaller hut near the gateway.

"Get on out of there!" the man shouted. "You've no business here. Beat it!"

Simon walked slowly over toward him, trying to think what he would say. If he ran away now, he'd never find anywhere for Gramp. What should he say? Have you got a workbench to spare? The man would laugh.

"I was just looking," he said, as he came nearer the man.

"Well, just you go off and do your looking somewhere else. You're trespassing, you know. I could put the police onto you."

"I suppose it wouldn't be possible for my grandpa to have a bench anywhere here?" he said, boldly looking straight at the man.

"A *what*, did you say?"

"A bench, a workbench, where he could have his tools. Where he could come every day and do a bit of work at the bench."

"What? Here? On a building site?"

The man looked puzzled now. Now that he was closer to him, Simon could see that the man was rather like Dad, a little older perhaps but not much.

WORD BANK

trespassing (TRESS pass ing) *v.:* entering someone's property without the owner's permission

site (SYT) *n.:* area or exact place where something is to be located or built

"My grandpa," he went on. "We've come to live in the apartments there." He pointed back the way he had come. "And Gramp hasn't got a shed for his tools and a bench. And he's...he's..."

For some reason he couldn't go on. He couldn't understand why tears had come into his eyes, and he hurriedly wiped them away with his sleeve. Perhaps it was because the man in front of him wasn't looking angry anymore, and that he looked rather like Dad. All he could think of was Gramp sitting there in a chair, rubbing his hands up and down the handle of a small hammer. The one he used for tacks and little brass pin-nails.

"I'm looking for a place for him—somewhere near. Where he can put his bench. A new bench. He's got all his tools and nowhere to use them."

"Well," said the man, scratching his head, "I've heard some pretty funny things here, but you're the first to come and ask for a place for a bench."

"It wouldn't take up much space," said Simon. "And he wouldn't be a lot of trouble. He's awfully tidy. He just wants somewhere to come every day for a while. He would be useful, too. He's very good with the tools. He's teaching me. Or he was."

The man just shook his head.

"I know just what you mean, son," he said. "But I can't help you. This is a building site and it's as much as my job's worth to let your granddad come on the site even, much less use a bench. You can see for yourself that these huts are all used. The men use them. The engineers have that one, this one is an office, and the others are all full of supplies. We can't have old gents coming along here to do their carpentry, now, can we?"

"I suppose not."

"I know what you mean," he said. "The old man doesn't like the apartments, I suppose. They never do, the old ones. I know. But I can't do anything about it. I've got my own worries. And anyhow all these sheds will be gone soon. Now, you scat along now and get back to your mum."

He gave Simon a push toward the gap in the fencing.

Simon went home. There was nothing else he could do. When he got there, he closed his eyes and waited for the row[6] that was going to fall on his head. But his mother said nothing but "Tell Grandpa his tea's ready, will you?"

Gramp was sitting in his room, the hammer in his hand.

"Tea's ready, Gramp," he said.

The old man didn't even turn his head.

That night Simon dreamed he had found a bench for Gramp, down at the end of the road, in

---

6. A *row* is a noisy quarrel. Here, however, the word is used to mean a scolding. Simon waited for the scolding he thought he was going to get—but it never came.

one of the factories there. The dream was so clear that when he woke he could hardly believe that it wasn't true.

Simon tried the factory the next morning. He felt he knew just where Gramp would go, and just what they would say, it had all been so real the night before. He walked straight down the road to the far end and then turned in at the factory gate. For the first time, he hesitated, suddenly not so hopeful.

The factory looked large and not what Gramp would like at all. But he would have to try. He couldn't go back without even trying.

The gatehouse[7] had two men in it, one of them in a peaked cap. Simon went up to the open window.

"Well, my young feller, me lad, what can I do for you this fine morning? Looking for a job, are you?"

It was the man in the peaked cap speaking, and Simon saw him wink across the room.

Simon drew a deep breath. It was not easy to explain. He thought he would try the other way around this time.

"I've come to live in the new apartments," he said.

"Oh, yes, and how do you like that, eh?"

"Oh, it's all right, but it's not that."

---

7. A *gatehouse* is a small building placed at the entrance to a large area. People who wish to enter the area must be admitted by the guard in the gatehouse.

WORD BANK

peaked (PEEKD) *adj.:* having a pointed top

"What's not that?"

"It's not that I've come about. It's my grandfather."

"Oh, indeed. And what can I do for your grandfather, may I ask?"

"At our old place, where we used to live on the other side of town, we had a bit of garden and a shed. It was Gramp's shed, really. He used it all the time and had his bench and tools in it. He made all sorts of things and mended things for Mum."

"Here, come and listen to this, Jim. Here's someone with some rigmarole about his granddad."

The other man came over to the open window too, and they both leaned out and looked down at Simon.

"Well, go on then. Does your granddad want a job, or something?"

"Oh, no," said Simon, "Nothing like that. He just wants somewhere where he could put his bench and tools."

"Is that all?" said the second man. "So you came along here, did you? Smart young chap you are, aren't you?"

Simon's hopes began to rise. Perhaps they would find a small space somewhere. Perhaps they understood. Perhaps they even had an old bench that Gramp could use just like that. He went on.

"He wouldn't be a nuisance. He would just come every day for a while to use the bench. He

| WORD BANK | **rigmarole** (RIG muh rohl) *n.*: confused or meaningless talk |
| | **chap** *n.*: fellow, guy |

wouldn't be in the way. It's just that he hasn't anything to do when he hasn't got a bench, you see! You can't have workbenches in those apartments."

"You can't indeed," said the man in the peaked cap. "You're dead right there."

"There isn't room, you see."

"Yes, indeed I see," said the peaked cap man again. "And so you came along here to see if we had a bench to spare for your poor old granddad eh? Is that it?"

"Yes, please."

Both men suddenly burst out into loud raucous laughter, loud laughs which rained down over Simon's ears like hailstones.

"Oh, my, I've not heard such a good one for a right long time," gasped one of the men. "Old people's home, that's what we'd be in no time at all. Lor' help us, just imagine, every old person for miles traipsing in through the gate for their little bit of workshop!"

Both the men stopped laughing and the man in the peaked cap frowned.

"Now, look here, my lad," he said. "Just you get cracking and get off these premises. If you think this is a place to dump your granddad, then you're dead wrong, see? This is a factory, and a couple of thousand men work here for their living, see? Just think what'd happen if every granddad

WORD BANK

raucous (RAW kus) *adj.:* loud and harsh
traipsing (TRAYPS ing) *v.:* tramping through
premises (PREH mi suz) *n.:* a building and its grounds

for miles around came around here asking for a bench. Now, off you go, and grow up a bit. Go on, scram!"

Simon had already turned around to go. He felt hot and uncomfortable and he hated the two men. They'd made a fool of him. Perhaps he was childish and silly. Perhaps he was a fool after all. Perhaps it was hopeless and Mum was right. Perhaps Mum knew all the time and when she said, "What can *I* do about it?" she knew that she couldn't do anything. Perhaps she knew that Gramp was miserable, but she hadn't asked to move to the apartment, had she? It hadn't been her idea. She'd been sent there.

He walked slowly back toward the apartments. He did not want to go in. He didn't want Gramp and Mum and Dad to see that he hadn't been able to do anything either. He didn't want them to laugh at him, too. He went to the yard shed to look at his guinea pigs. But then he remembered that he hadn't got the key. He thought about going into town to the park, but then he couldn't be bothered. It was too far to walk and he hadn't any money on him for the fare. He wandered about and then finally pushed his way through the big glass doors into the hall of the building. Neither of the elevators was down, so he stood there waiting. There was no one there at all.

Just as he heard the elevator coming down, a man came in through the main doors and headed for the stairs that led down to the basement, where there was a notice saying

KEEP OUT

Simon knew who the man was. It was Mr. Gideon, who lived on the ground floor around the other side, and Mr. Gideon was the caretaker. He sometimes kept some greenstuff for Simon's guinea pigs.

"'Lo, Simon," he said.

"'Lo," said Simon.

"Well, that's a long face to pull on this fine morning. Anything wrong with those guinea pigs of yours?"

"No," said Simon.

"If you wait there a minute, I've got some greens for them," said Mr. Gideon. "Hang on a moment and I'll be back."

He started off down the basement steps. Then he stopped and came back again.

"Like to have a look around?" he said.

"What? Me?" said Simon, in surprise, because he knew Mr. Gideon didn't allow anyone down there, especially boys.

"Yes. Come on, then," said Mr. Gideon. "I'll show you."

---

8. A person who looks sad is said to have *a long face.*

Simon followed him down the stone steps. At the bottom there was a heavy metal door which Mr. Gideon opened with a key, and suddenly they were in a different world altogether. This was where the heating of the whole building came from and Mr. Gideon was in charge of it all.

There were pipes everywhere, and great tanks and boilers and things that looked like clocks with handles below them. It was all quite clean and Simon was surprised, for the only other boiler house he had ever seen had been the one at his old school, a dirty place, full of dust. Mr. Gideon kept this place clean and spent a lot of time down here in the winter, adjusting the heating and the flow of oil. He almost lived down here, as it was his job, and he had been caretaker for the block ever since it had been built.

Mr. Gideon took Simon around and showed him how the heating system worked. Of course it was not all turned on now, as it was summer, but the smaller boiler for water heating was working. Pipes snaked all around, some of them as thick as drainpipes, others smaller, disappearing up through the ceiling to the apartments above. Mr. Gideon had three boiler houses to look after, but this one was the biggest.

"Looks like a factory, doesn't it?" he said as Simon bent his head all the way back to look up at

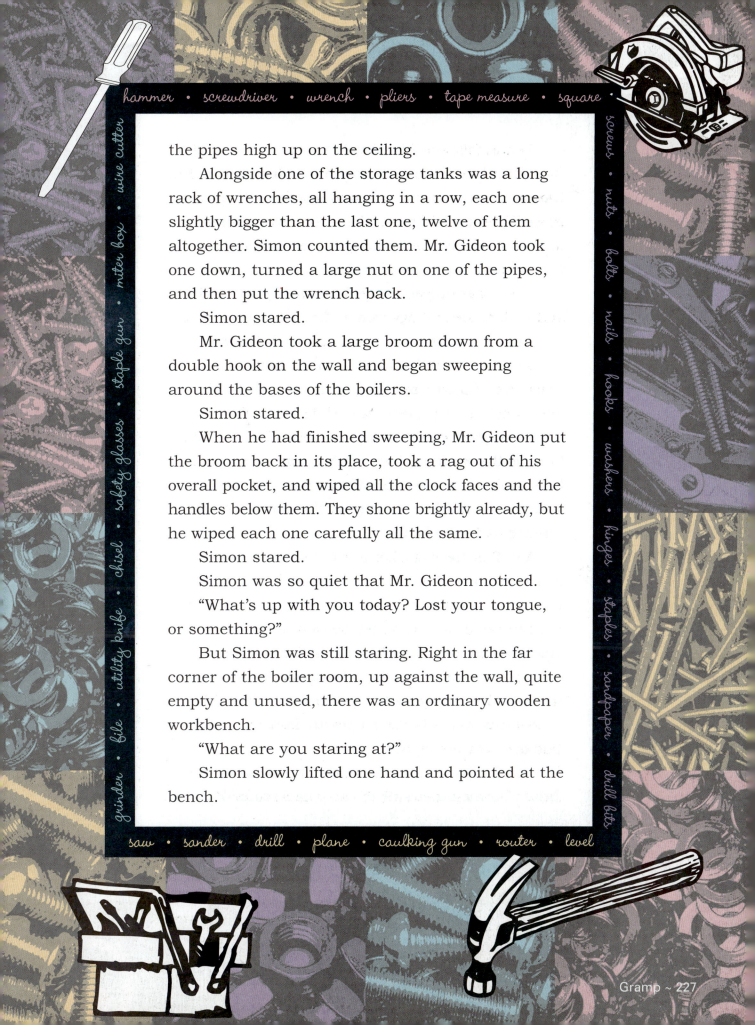

the pipes high up on the ceiling.

Alongside one of the storage tanks was a long rack of wrenches, all hanging in a row, each one slightly bigger than the last one, twelve of them altogether. Simon counted them. Mr. Gideon took one down, turned a large nut on one of the pipes, and then put the wrench back.

Simon stared.

Mr. Gideon took a large broom down from a double hook on the wall and began sweeping around the bases of the boilers.

Simon stared.

When he had finished sweeping, Mr. Gideon put the broom back in its place, took a rag out of his overall pocket, and wiped all the clock faces and the handles below them. They shone brightly already, but he wiped each one carefully all the same.

Simon stared.

Simon was so quiet that Mr. Gideon noticed.

"What's up with you today? Lost your tongue, or something?"

But Simon was still staring. Right in the far corner of the boiler room, up against the wall, quite empty and unused, there was an ordinary wooden workbench.

"What are you staring at?"

Simon slowly lifted one hand and pointed at the bench.

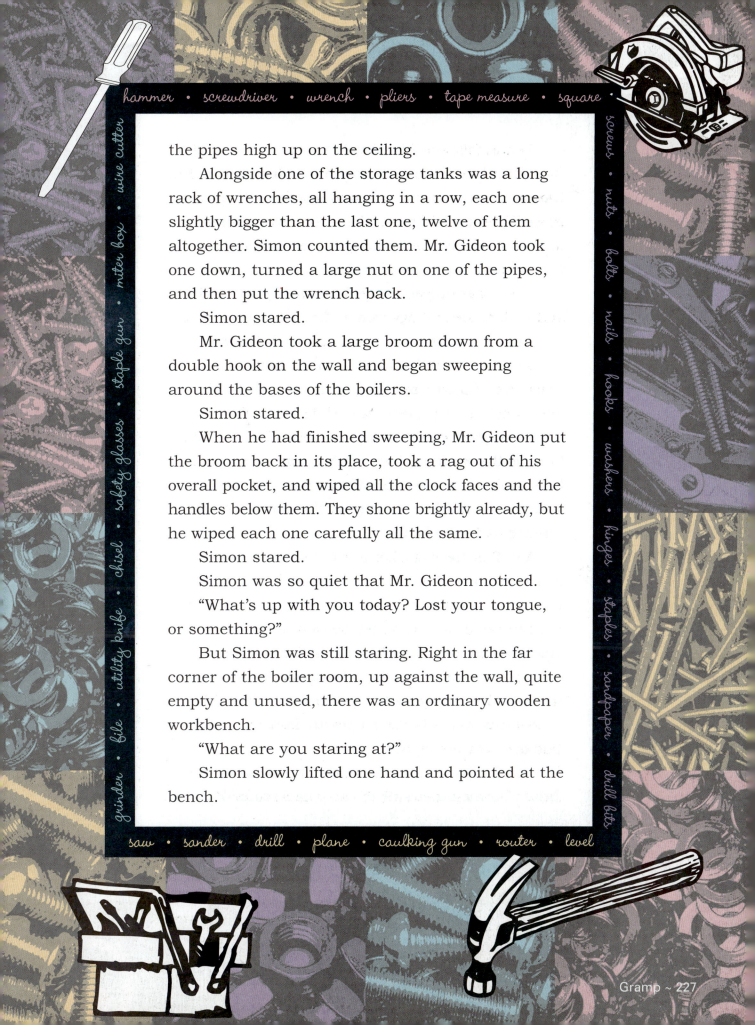

"That bench. Is it yours?"

"Oh, that," said Mr. Gideon. "That's been here all the time. Only use it now and again. It's for repairs, smaller ones. But since everything is new here, I've had nothing much to repair so far."

"Do you know my granddad?" said Simon.

"Didn't even know you'd got one. Here, do you mean? Here in the apartments?"

"Yes, I told you. He helped me make my hutch."

"Oh yes, I remember now. But I didn't know he was here. Does he live with your mum and dad, then?"

"Yes," said Simon.

"Well, of course, I wouldn't know which he was, would I? I can't tell one granddad from another, can I? And they're mostly younger here."

"He doesn't like it and he doesn't go out much now, either. He's lost his workbench and has nothing to do."

"That's bad."

"I've been out today and yesterday," said Simon, "looking for a place for him to have a bench, you see? He used to have one in the garden shed, you see? And now he's got his tools up in the storeroom and nowhere to put them. He couldn't...he couldn't...?"

Mr. Gideon turned around and looked at the bench on the other side of the boiler room.

"So that's what it's all about, is it? Thought you were in a bit of a state[8] about something," he said. "Well, no one uses it. Except me, and I haven't got any tools down here as yet. It's an idea. I don't see why not. Bring him down one day and we'll see what we can do. He'd have to fit in with my times, mind you, because I lock up when I go out of here. Got to keep you young mischiefs out of the place, haven't I?"

"You mean he could? Can I go and get him down now?"

"If you like. No time like the present. I've got about another half hour down here. After that, I'll have gone."

Simon ran as he had never run before. He ran up the basement steps and around to the elevators. As usual, both were up somewhere. He couldn't wait. He began running up the stairs, but soon found he was puffing and panting like a grampus and his legs felt weak and feeble. He slowed down and struggled on up the stairs, his chest heaving and his face scarlet. But he got there in the end and in his excitement could hardly get his key into the lock.

No one was home except Gramp.

Simon rushed into Gramp's room, trying to calm down a little.

_____

9. A person who is slightly excited is *in a bit of a state.*

WORD BANK

grampus (GRAMP us) *n.:* a large dolphin
feeble (FEE bul) *adj.:* weak
scarlet (SKAHR lut) *adj.:* deep red

"You been running up them stairs, or something," said Gramp, looking up as Simon appeared so suddenly.

Simon nodded.

"What's all the hurry today then?"

"I...I...I..."

"Come on, then, out with it. What's the excitement?"

"I've found a bench for you."

"What did you say?"

"I've found a bench and a place for your tools. I think."

"What d'you mean, a bench? And what d'you mean, you think?"

"Well, you may not like it."

"A bench?"

"Yes."

"A workbench."

"Yes."

"Where?"

"Come with me. I'll show you."

"Are you pulling my leg[9]?"

"Gramp!"

"Oh, all right, then. What, now?"

"Yes."

"Where?"

---

9. Gramp is asking Simon if Simon is fooling him, which he calls *pulling his leg.*

saw • sander • drill • plane • caulking gun • router • level

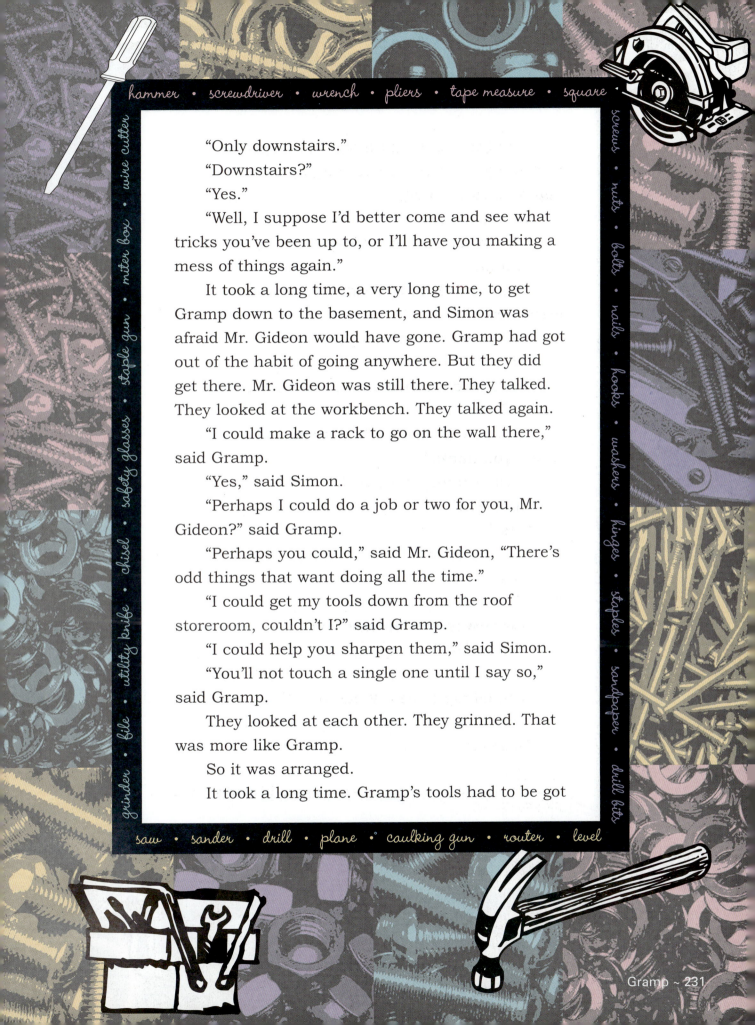

"Only downstairs."

"Downstairs?"

"Yes."

"Well, I suppose I'd better come and see what tricks you've been up to, or I'll have you making a mess of things again."

It took a long time, a very long time, to get Gramp down to the basement, and Simon was afraid Mr. Gideon would have gone. Gramp had got out of the habit of going anywhere. But they did get there. Mr. Gideon was still there. They talked. They looked at the workbench. They talked again.

"I could make a rack to go on the wall there," said Gramp.

"Yes," said Simon.

"Perhaps I could do a job or two for you, Mr. Gideon?" said Gramp.

"Perhaps you could," said Mr. Gideon, "There's odd things that want doing all the time."

"I could get my tools down from the roof storeroom, couldn't I?" said Gramp.

"I could help you sharpen them," said Simon.

"You'll not touch a single one until I say so," said Gramp.

They looked at each other. They grinned. That was more like Gramp.

So it was arranged.

It took a long time. Gramp's tools had to be got

out and that meant waiting for Dad to get back. Then Gramp had to make a rack for them, and that took a lot of mornings down there in the basement. Gramp had got slow. Then he had to clean and sharpen all his tools and put them in the new rack. Then it was ready.

Each day, Gramp seemed a little younger, a little quicker. Each day he moved a little more quickly. Each day he went down to the basement in the same building and each day he got his tools down and made something, mended something, or put something in order.

Each day, he told them what he had done.

"I found Gramp a shed in the end, didn't I, Mum?" said Simon, one night, long afterward, at tea.

"You certainly did," she said.

"You certainly did," said Dad. "Some shed, too."

"You certainly did," said Gramp. "Biggest blooming shed in the whole wide world, I'd say."

His old blue eyes were bright.

ABOUT THE AUTHOR

Joan Tate was born in Kent, England, in 1922. While living for three years in Sweden, she learned to speak, read, and write Swedish so perfectly that she later became an English translator of Swedish books. She also wrote books in English for teenagers. Joan and her family lived in Shrewsbury, England. Joan died in 2000.

Studying the Selection

FIRST IMPRESSIONS
Do you think it is unusual for a person Simon's age to try so hard to find a solution to his grandfather's problem?

QUICK REVIEW

1. When the story opens, what major event has recently taken place in the lives of the characters?

2. What was "best of all" for Simon, in the new situation?

3. How had Gramp helped Simon with the guinea pigs?

4. How does Simon feed his guinea pigs?

FOCUS

5. Is it easy for Simon to try to find a workbench for Gramp?

6. Simon encounters several different types of people as he tries to help his grandfather. Which person did you like the least? Why? Which did you like the most? What was there about his behavior that made you like him?

CREATING & WRITING

7. When Simon finds Gramp a workbench, Gramp is not the only one whose life improves. In several short paragraphs, write about who is helped and how.

   • *Your first paragraph* can be something like, "When Simon helps Gramp, he also helps . . . . *Your second* can be about how this helps Simon, himself. *The third* could be about how it helps his Mum. *The fourth* could be about how it helps Mr. Gideon, or Simon's Dad. (You choose the people or situations.) *In the final paragraph* write how we are all helped when another person is no longer suffering.

8. What do you know about Gramp? Imagine that he keeps a diary. What does he write in his diary after he learns about the workbench in the basement?

9. Make a collage about growing old.

CONFLICT

- A conflict is a clash of ideas, emotions, or forces.

- An *external* conflict is a conflict between a person and something outside of the person.

- An *internal* conflict is a conflict that takes place entirely inside a person's mind and emotions.

- In a story, the conflict makes the story interesting and exciting. A story without a conflict is hardly a story at all!

THINK ABOUT IT!

1. What is Jake's reaction the first time Bobby teases the new boy?
   What is his reaction the second time? What are his conflicting feelings towards Bobby?

2. What changes in Jake's reaction the third time Bobby is mean to Charles?
   Why didn't Jake act the first two times? How do you think he felt about himself each time he remained silent?

3. When Jake picks up his tray to move next to Charles, he probably is experiencing several conflicting emotions. Can you think of three things he is probably feeling?

4. What effect does Jake's action have on Bobby? Did you expect this reaction? Why or why not?

An Old Camp Trick

As Bobby and Jake left their cabin for the swimming pool, they practically bumped into the new kid.

"Watch yourself, Four Eyes," Bobby said.

Jake could hardly believe his ears. He and Bobby had been best friends at camp every summer since they were eight, and in all those years, Jake had never known Bobby to say a mean word. Jake didn't say anything, but he felt bad for the new kid.

Later, on their way into the dining hall for lunch, Jake saw Bobby stick out his foot at the last minute and trip the new kid. Jake was getting madder, but still he said nothing. What Bobby was doing was wrong, but Jake didn't want to lose his best friend.

At dinner that night, the new kid sat by himself at the end of the table where Jake and Bobby were sitting with their friends. When the boy got up to get something, Bobby grinned mischievously and shot quickly over to the new boy's tray, pouring salt and hot sauce into his milk.

Jake's face burned.

When the boy returned to his seat, the others watched as he took a bite of his food. Jake's friends giggled. The new boy looked up. His eyes met Jake's. Jake said nothing. Jake looked away, as angry with himself for saying nothing as he was with Bobby for playing this mean trick.

Finally, the new boy picked up his milk.

Jake couldn't hold back any longer. "Don't!"

The boy looked up uneasily.

"We put some stuff in your milk," he said. He looked at Bobby. Bobby stared back in disbelief. "It's an old camp trick. Don't drink it."

The boy looked confused, but he set the glass down.

Jake grabbed his tray and moved down next to the new boy.

"I'm Jake," he said.

"I'm Charles," the boy said, pushing up his glasses. "I'm from Evanston."

"Hey, Bobby's from Evanston." Jake looked over at his friend and gestured toward himself and the new boy.

Bobby looked at the other guys, then at Jake. He picked up his tray and moved toward Jake and Charles. "C'mon, guys," he said.

Blueprint for Reading

INTO . . . *After School*

Often, we think that it is the *events* of our lives that are important. When we write a letter, and nothing exciting has taken place, we write, "I don't have much to say. Nothing has happened lately." However, as we shall see in *After School,* most of "what happens" in our lives is our thoughts, our feelings, our friendships, and how we deal with other people.

Close your eyes. Focus on your breathing, in and out, in and out. How long can you do that with your mind turned off? How soon do the thoughts begin? Does it seem as though your mind has a life of its own? Thinking is almost as natural as breathing. It is the central activity of our lives.

EYES ON . . . *Conflict*

A **conflict** is a struggle. It can be a struggle between different ideas, needs, or emotions. It can also be a struggle between people and nature. It is what every story is about. Conflict is what makes a story suspenseful.

A conflict with anything that is outside, or *external* to, a person, is called an **external conflict.** A sailor caught in a storm at sea has an external conflict. He must battle the waves and the wind. Will he sink or survive? The conflict creates a suspenseful tale.

A struggle that takes place entirely *inside* a person's *mind* is called an **internal conflict.** When what we want to do is not what we ought to do, we experience an internal struggle. There are many combinations of thoughts and feelings that can create internal conflict. Can you think of some?

After School
V. Zheleznikov

When school was dismissed, I went to the classroom for first graders. I would not have gone there but our neighbor had asked me to look after her little son when school was over. After all, it was the first of September and the first day of school.

I ran into the classroom and found it empty. Everyone had already left. I was about to turn around and go on my way when I noticed someone sitting in the last row. Very little of her could be seen above her desk.

It was a little girl—and not at all the little boy for whom I had come. As is the custom for girl first graders on the first day of school, she wore a white apron and white bows in her hair—big ones.

It was strange for her to be sitting there alone. All the other children had gone home and were probably already eating soup or jello while they were telling their parents and other members of the family circle about the wonders of school. But this one sat there waiting for heaven knew what.

"Little girl," I said, "why don't you go home?"

No answer.

"Have you lost something?"

She continued her silence and sat there like a stone statue.

I didn't know what to do. I tried to think of a way to make this "stone statue" move. I went to the blackboard and began to draw.

I drew a first-grade girl who had come home from school and was having her dinner. Then I drew a mommie, a daddy, and two grandmas. The girl was eating with relish, both cheeks bulging with

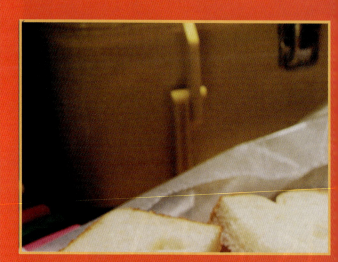

WORD BANK	**relish** (RELL ish) *n*.: great enjoyment

some delicious food, while the others were looking at her, straight into her mouth. It turned out to be an amusing picture.

"You and I," I said, "are hungry. Isn't it time for us, too, to go home?"

"No," she replied. "I'll not go home!"

"I suppose you're going to sleep here all night?"

"I don't know."

Her voice was sad and low, more like a mosquito buzz than a human voice.

I looked again at my picture and my stomach began to rumble. I was getting very hungry.

"Well, too bad, she is a strange one," I said to myself. I left the room and was on my way to the exit when my conscience began to nag, and I turned back.

"Listen," I said to her, "If you don't tell me why you are sitting there, I'll call the school doctor. And he—one, two, three,—he'll call 'Emergency,' there will be an ambulance, the siren, and off to the hospital you'll go." I decided to scare her a little. I am scared of the school doctor myself. He forever says: "Breathe, don't breathe…," and he sticks the thermometer under your arm. It is as cold as an icicle.

"All right," she blurted out, "so

I'll go to the hospital!"

"Can't you tell me," I almost shouted, "what's happened?"

"My brother is waiting for me. He's in the yard…"

I looked out—and, sure enough, a little boy was sitting there on a bench. The yard was deserted.

"So what?"

"So this—I promised to teach him today all the letters of the alphabet."

"Boy, you sure can make promises," I said. "In one day—the whole alphabet?! Perhaps you're planning to finish the whole school in one year. You're quite a liar."

"I didn't lie. I just…didn't know."

I could see that she was about to cry. She lowered her eyes and shook her head in a certain way which meant the tears were on their way.

"It takes weeks to learn to write all the letters. It's not so simple."

"Mother and Father went far away, and my brother Seryozha[1] misses them terribly. And so I told him, 'I'll start going to school, I'll learn all the letters, and we'll write Mommie and Daddy a letter. He has already told all the boys on our street about it. But all we wrote all day in class today is sticks!" She

___
1. *Seryozha* (sehr YOH zha)

barely managed to hold back the tears.

"Sticks!" I said, "that's fine, that's simply great! Letters are made out of sticks." And I went over to the board and wrote the letter "A"—I printed it. "This is the letter 'A.' It is made out of three sticks."

Well, I never intended to become a teacher, but I had to distract her somehow so that she would not start crying.

"And now," I said, "let's go to your brother. I'll explain everything to him."

We left the room, went to the school yard, and walked over to her brother. We walked like little kids, holding hands. She had thrust her tiny hand into mine. It was a soft little hand, with fingers like tiny pillows, and warm.

I thought to myself: if any of the boys saw me they'd laugh at me for walking hand in hand with a first-grade girl. But how could I push her hand away?—after all, she was a human being.

And this important Seryozha sat there, swinging his legs. He pretended not to see us.

| WORD BANK | **distract** (diss TRAKT) *v.*: draw someone's attention away |

"Listen, fellow," I said to him. "I want to explain something to you. ... You know, it takes almost a whole year to learn the whole alphabet. It's not so easy...."

"That means she didn't learn it!" he said and looked at his sister with scorn. "Then she didn't have to promise."

"We wrote only sticks all day," the little girl said desperately, "but letters are made out of sticks."

He didn't even listen to her. He rose from the bench, put his hands in his pockets, lowered his head, and shoved off like a duck. He had paid no attention to me. I got tired of the whole affair. I always seemed to get mixed up in other people's business.

"I did learn the letter 'A'!" his sister cried after him. But he didn't even turn around.

I caught up with him.

"Listen," I said. "You can't blame her. Learning is complicated. When you start school you'll find out. Do you think that the astronauts Gagarin and Titov mastered the whole alphabet in one day? They, too, sweated it out. And you complain..."

"All day I've been memorizing the letter I was going to write my Mommie," he said.

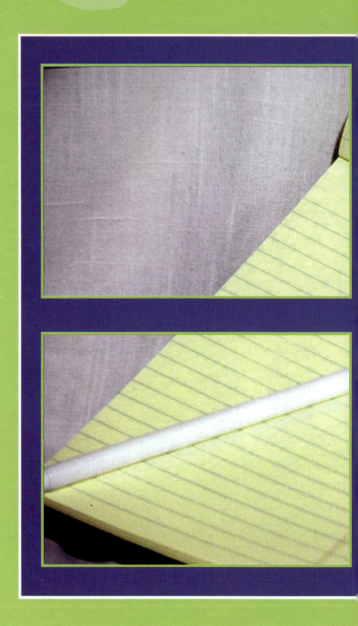

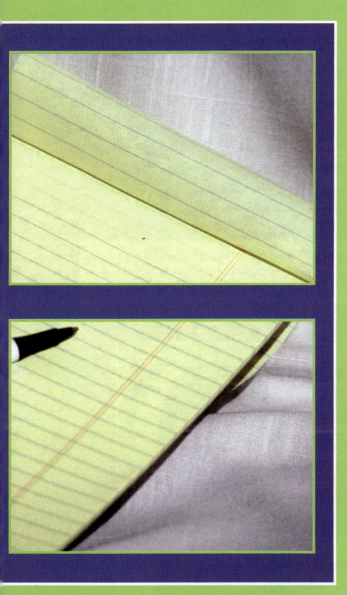

His face looked so gloomy that I thought it was wrong of his mother to have left him behind. If parents go off to distant places, let them take their children along. Children don't get scared of long trips or fierce frosts.

"Don't worry," I said to him. "I'll come over after supper, and I'll write everything down just as you dictate it."

"Good!" the little girl said. "We live in that house behind the iron fence. Won't that be good, Seryozha?"

"All right," Seryozha nodded, "I'll wait for you."

I saw them enter their courtyard. Their little figures soon began to disappear behind the iron fence and some bushes.

Then I heard a loud voice, the teasing voice of a boy: "Well, Seryozha, did your sister learn the whole alphabet today?"

Seryozha stopped, and his sister ran into the house.

"Do you know how long it takes to learn the whole alphabet? It takes a whole year!" Seryozha shouted.

WORD BANK

dictate (DIK tayt) *v.*: say or read aloud words so that they can be written down, typed, or recorded

"Oh, is that so? Then your letter will have to wait a whole year—and your parents, too," the other boy said in a nasty way.

"No, I have a friend. He finished the first grade long ago, and he will come this evening and write my letter!"

"You're lying," the other boy said. "You're a big liar! Can you tell me his name?"

Silence.

In another second I expected to hear the triumphant cry of the tease, but I didn't let this happen. I climbed up to the stone ledge below the iron fence and stuck my head through the bars.

"Do you want to know his name? It's Yurik," I said.

The tease's mouth fell open with surprise. Seryozha said nothing. He was not the kind to kick someone who was down.

I jumped off the ledge and started for home.

I didn't know why, but I was in a pretty good mood. I even felt like singing.

WORD BANK	**triumphant** (try UMF unt) *adj.:* expressing joy over a success or victory

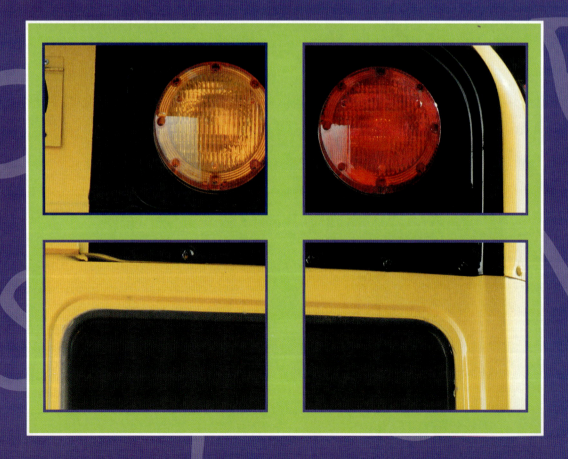

Studying the Selection

FIRST IMPRESSIONS

Are you surprised that the narrator, a young person himself, cares so much about what happens to other people?

QUICK REVIEW

1. Why does the narrator go to the classroom for first graders when school is dismissed?

2. What does he find when he goes to the classroom?

3. Who is waiting for the little girl in the school yard?

4. When do we learn the narrator's name?

FOCUS

5. Why does the narrator threaten the little girl by saying that he will call the school doctor?

6. Although the story tells of many small problems and conflicts, the children face a real problem, which casts a shadow over everything they do. What is that problem?

CREATING & WRITING

7. Why do you think the narrator helps the girl? What does he mean when he says that he was on his way to the exit "when my conscience began to nag, and I turned back"?

8. You are Yurik. Write out the letter that the little girl and her brother, Seryozha, dictate to you for their parents. Begin: *Dear Mommie and Daddy...*

9. Where is Russia? Using a globe or an atlas, draw your own map of Russia. Label the map to show the names of the countries that are on Russia's borders.

LESSON IN LITERATURE . . .

DIALOGUE

- Dialogue is the conversation between the characters of a story, book, or play.

- The word, "dialogue," indicates that two or more people are speaking to one another. (The prefix *di* means "two.") A speech by a single character is called a "monologue." (The prefix *mono* means "one.")

- Dialogue tells the reader about the characters, and may be used to move the plot along.

- All dialogue is placed inside quotation marks.

THINK ABOUT IT!

1. How are the two speakers in the dialogue related?

2. What do we learn about the younger speaker from what is said?

3. How can the reader tell when a new speaker is speaking?

4. Without using any dialogue, describe, in two or three sentences, what is happening in the story.

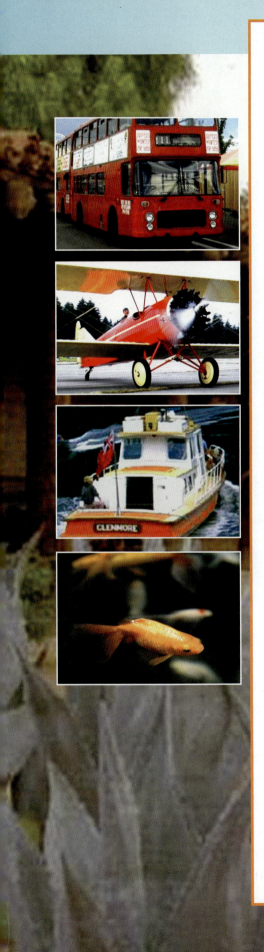

CARPOOL

"Daddy, why do you think Ben is taking so long to get here?"

"I bet he's getting into his car seat to come pick you up right now."

"What if they forget to pick me up today?"

"If they forget to pick you up, I'll take you to school today."

"If you drove me, maybe our car would break down—by the zoo!"

"If the car broke down, we'd have to catch a city bus to get you to school."

"Maybe the bus would take us to Grandma's house instead!"

"If the bus took us to Grandma's house, we'd have to take an airplane to get you to school."

"Maybe the airplane would take us to Australia instead!"

"If the airplane took us to Australia, we'd have to charter a boat to get you to school."

"But Daddy, what if the boat took us to a lost city deep beneath the sea?"

"Oh, that's easy. We'd simply take the tunnel that leads from the lost city deep beneath the sea . . . directly into your classroom."

"Oh."

[Car pool arrives.]

"Hey, Ben's here. Time to go to school."

"Okay.

"Have a great day."

"You too, Daddy."

"Hey Sweetie—nice try."

"Thanks, Daddy."

Blueprint for Reading

INTO . . . *One Throw*

Sometimes, in stories, one character tries to tempt another to do something wrong. Why does a writer create a story like this? The author wants to tell the story of a person being tested. The reader goes through the character's struggle against temptation, and is anxious about the outcome.

Is real life ever like that? It certainly is! Have you ever been tested by a little internal voice that says, "well, maybe it's really okay," or by a friend who wants you to go along with something that isn't right?

The suspense in *One Throw* comes from wondering how one of the characters is going to handle a strong temptation to be dishonest. We won't know the whole truth until we read the last line in the story.

EYES ON . . . *Dialogue*

Dialogue is the conversation in a story. Why do stories have dialogue? Characters in stories are supposed to be like people in real life. In real life, people talk to one another. There is no narrator to tell each of us what everyone else is thinking—or to tell everyone else what we are thinking. We speak in order to be understood!

Dialogue tells us as much about a character as do his or her actions—*if* the character is telling the truth. Good dialogue is believable and can be hard to write. If you write down an ordinary conversation, you will discover that it is not very interesting to read. An author has to make the dialogue sound real, while at the same time, making it clearer, briefer, and more to the point than everyday dialogue.

One Throw is nearly all dialogue. Notice, as you read, that every time a character speaks, the words are set off with quotation marks. Notice, too, that when a new character starts to speak, a new paragraph begins.

ONE Throw

I checked into a hotel called the Olympia, which is right
on the main street and the only hotel in the town.
After lunch I was hanging around the lobby,
and I got to talking to the guy at the
desk. I asked him if this wasn't
the town where that kid
named Maneri
played ball.

W. C. Heinz

"That's right," the guy said. "He's a pretty good ballplayer."

"He should be," I said. "I read that he was the new Phil Rizzuto."[1]

"That's what they said," the guy said.

"What's the matter with him?" I said. "I mean if he's such a good ballplayer what's he doing in this league?"

"I don't know," the guy said. "I guess the Yankees know what they're doing."

"What kind of a kid is he?"

"He's a nice kid," the guy said. "He plays good ball, but I feel sorry for him. He thought he'd be playing for the Yankees soon, and here he is in this town. You can see it's got him down."

"He lives here in this hotel?"

"That's right," the guy said. "Most of the older ballplayers stay in rooming houses,[2] but Pete and a couple other kids live here."

He was leaning on the desk, talking to me and looking across the hotel lobby. He nodded his head. "This is a funny thing," he

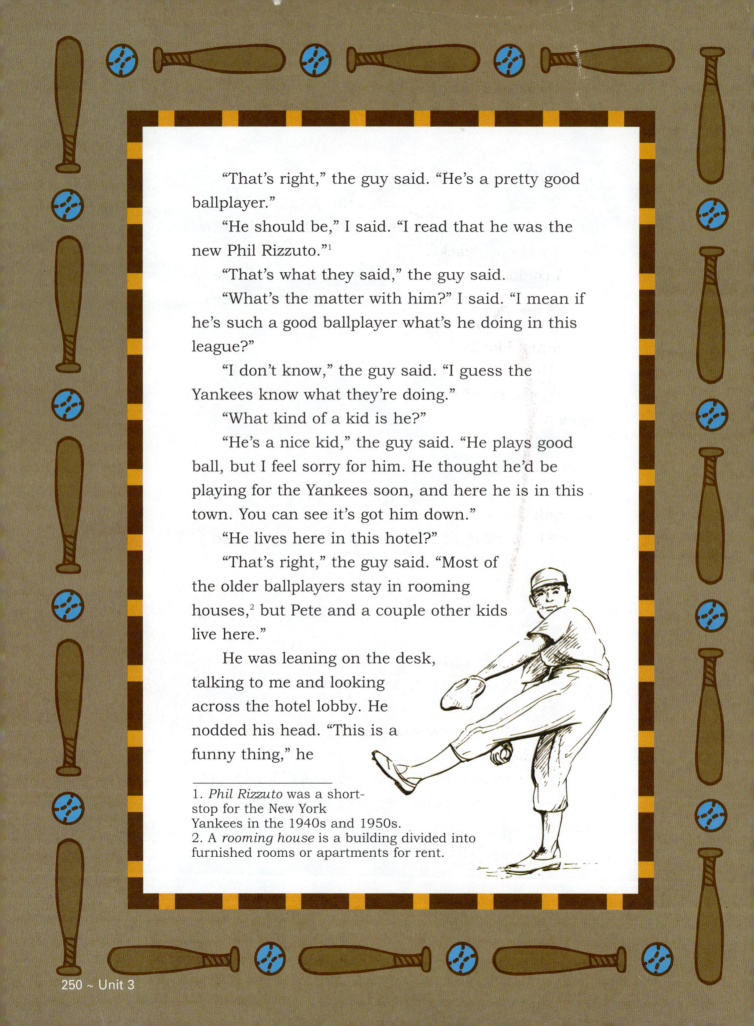

---

1. *Phil Rizzuto* was a short-stop for the New York Yankees in the 1940s and 1950s.
2. A *rooming house* is a building divided into furnished rooms or apartments for rent.

said. "Here he comes now."

The kid had come through the door from the street. He had on a light gray sport shirt and a pair of gray flannel slacks.

I could see why, when he showed up with the Yankees in spring training, he made them all think of Rizzuto. He isn't any bigger than Rizzuto, and he looks just like him.

"Hello, Nick," he said to the guy at the desk.

"Hello, Pete," the guy at the desk said. "How goes it today?"

"All right," the kid said, but you could see he was exaggerating.

"I'm sorry, Pete," the guy at the desk said, "but no mail today."

"That's all right, Nick," the kid said. "I'm used to it."

"Excuse me," I said, "but you're Pete Maneri?"

"That's right," the kid said, turning and looking at me.

"Excuse me," the guy at the desk said, introducing us. "Pete, this is Mr. Franklin."

"Harry Franklin," I said.

"I'm glad to know you," the kid said, shaking my hand.

"I recognize you from your pictures," I said.

"Pete's a good ballplayer," the guy at the desk said.

"Not very," the kid said.

"Don't take his word for it, Mr. Franklin," the guy said.

"I'm a great ball fan," I said to the kid. "Do you people play tonight?"

"We play two games," the kid said.

"The first game's at six o'clock," the guy at the desk said. "They play pretty good ball."

"I'll be there," I said. "I used to play a little ball myself."

"You did?" the kid said.

"With Columbus," I said. "That's twenty years ago."

"Is that right?" the kid said.

That's the way I got to talking with the kid. They had one of those pine-paneled taprooms[3] in the basement of the hotel, and we went down there. I had a couple and the kid had a soda, and I told him a few stories and he turned out to be a real good listener.

"But what do you do now, Mr. Franklin?" he said after a while.

"I sell hardware," I said. "I can think of some things I'd like better, but I was going to ask you how you like playing in this league."

"Well," the kid said, "I suppose it's all right. I guess I've got no kick coming."[4]

---

3. A *taproom* is a room in a hotel where drinks and snacks are served.
4. *I've got no kick coming* is an expression meaning: "I've got no reason to be angry or resentful."

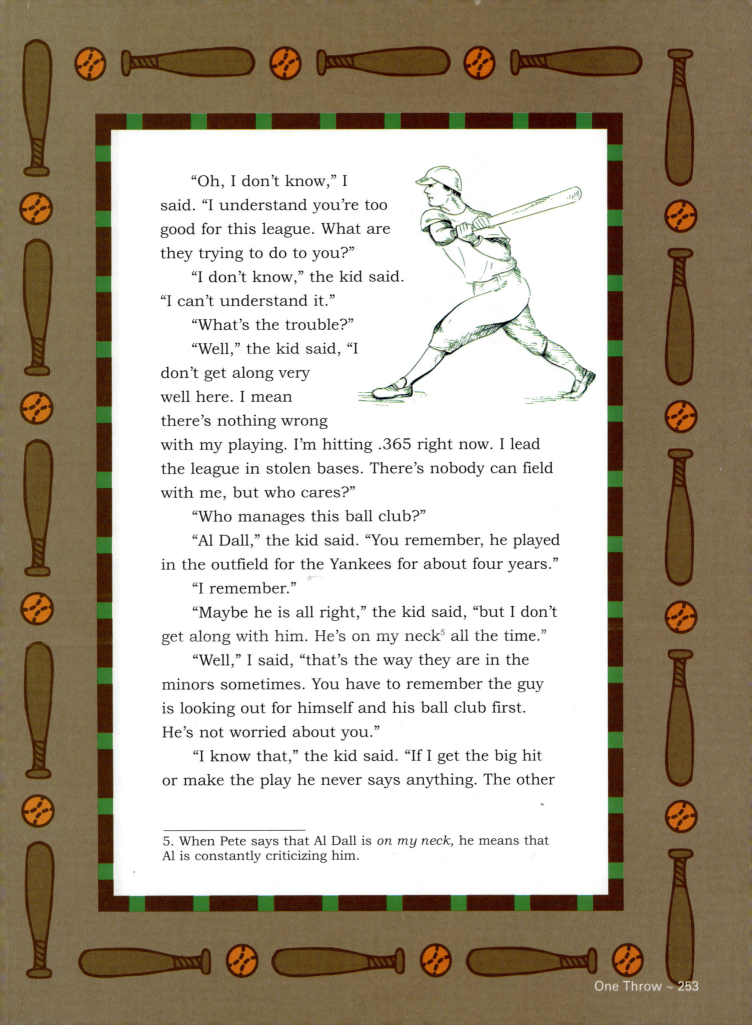

"Oh, I don't know," I said. "I understand you're too good for this league. What are they trying to do to you?"

"I don't know," the kid said. "I can't understand it."

"What's the trouble?"

"Well," the kid said, "I don't get along very well here. I mean there's nothing wrong with my playing. I'm hitting .365 right now. I lead the league in stolen bases. There's nobody can field with me, but who cares?"

"Who manages this ball club?"

"Al Dall," the kid said. "You remember, he played in the outfield for the Yankees for about four years."

"I remember."

"Maybe he is all right," the kid said, "but I don't get along with him. He's on my neck[5] all the time."

"Well," I said, "that's the way they are in the minors sometimes. You have to remember the guy is looking out for himself and his ball club first. He's not worried about you."

"I know that," the kid said. "If I get the big hit or make the play he never says anything. The other

_____

5. When Pete says that Al Dall is *on my neck,* he means that Al is constantly criticizing him.

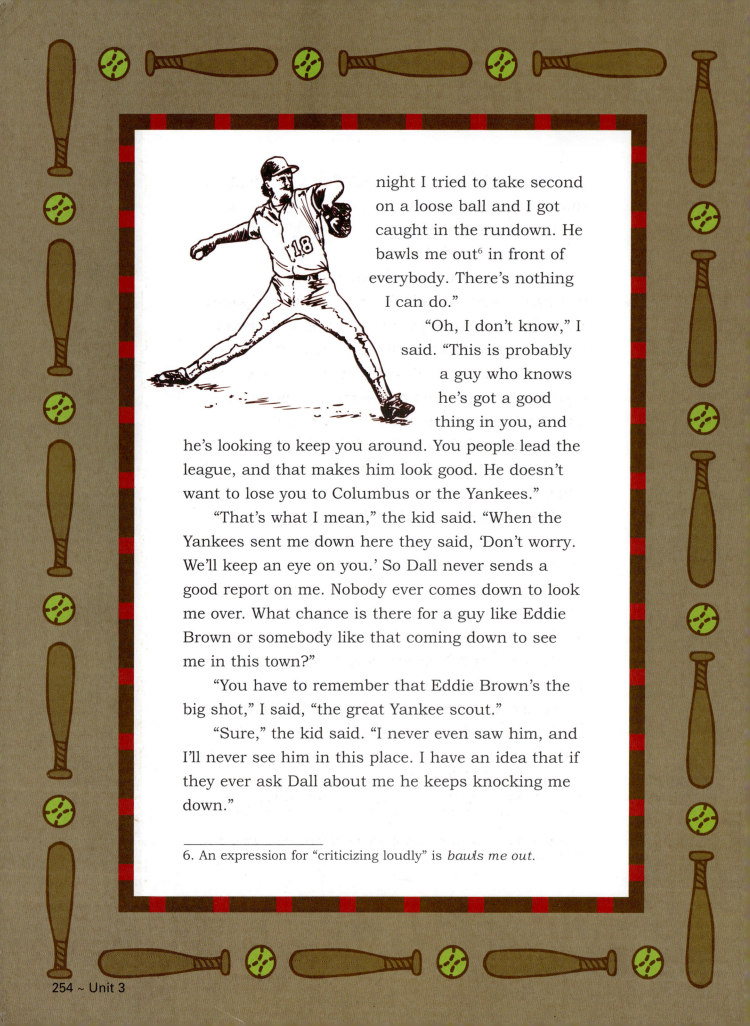

night I tried to take second on a loose ball and I got caught in the rundown. He bawls me out[6] in front of everybody. There's nothing I can do."

"Oh, I don't know," I said. "This is probably a guy who knows he's got a good thing in you, and he's looking to keep you around. You people lead the league, and that makes him look good. He doesn't want to lose you to Columbus or the Yankees."

"That's what I mean," the kid said. "When the Yankees sent me down here they said, 'Don't worry. We'll keep an eye on you.' So Dall never sends a good report on me. Nobody ever comes down to look me over. What chance is there for a guy like Eddie Brown or somebody like that coming down to see me in this town?"

"You have to remember that Eddie Brown's the big shot," I said, "the great Yankee scout."

"Sure," the kid said. "I never even saw him, and I'll never see him in this place. I have an idea that if they ever ask Dall about me he keeps knocking me down."

_____

6. An expression for "criticizing loudly" is *bawls me out*.

"Why don't you go after Dall?" I said. "I had trouble like that once myself, but I figured out a way to get attention."

"You did?" the kid said.

"I threw a couple of balls over the first baseman's head," I said. "I threw a couple of games away, and that really got the manager sore. I was lousing up his ball club and his record. So what does he do? He blows the whistle[7] on me, and what happens? That gets the brass[8] curious, and they send someone down to see what's wrong."

"Is that so?" the kid said. "What happened?"

"Two weeks later," I said, "I was up with Columbus."

"Is that right?" the kid said.

"Sure," I said, egging him on.[9] "What have you got to lose?"

"Nothing," the kid said. "I haven't got anything to lose."

"I'd try it," I said.

"I might try it," the kid said. "I might try it tonight if the spot comes up."

I could see from the way he said it that he was madder than he'd said. Maybe you think this is

---

7. When someone *blows the whistle* on another, he is reporting that that person is doing something wrong.
8. *The brass* is a slang expression meaning "the authorities, the people in power."
9. Harry Franklin is encouraging Pete to behave badly. This is called *egging him on.*

mean to steam a kid up[10] like this, but I do some strange things.

"Take over," I said. "Don't let this guy ruin your career."

"I'll try it," the kid said. "Are you coming out to the park tonight?"

"I wouldn't miss it," I said. "This will be better than making out route sheets and sales orders."

It's not much of a ball park in this town—old wooden bleachers and an old wooden fence and about four hundred people in the stands. The first game wasn't much either, with the home club winning something like 8 to 1.

The kid didn't have any hard chances, but I could see he was a ballplayer, with a double and a couple of walks and a lot of speed.

The second game was different, though. The other club got a couple of runs and then the home club picked up three runs in one. They were in the top of the ninth with a 3-2 lead and two outs when the pitching began to fall apart and they loaded the bases.

I was trying to wish the ball down to the kid, just to see what he'd do with it, when the batter drives one on one big bounce to the kid's right.

The kid was off for it when the ball started. He made a backhand stab and grabbed it. He was deep now, and he turned in the air and fired. If it goes

---

10. Harry is trying to make Pete angry, to *steam a kid up*.

over the first baseman's head, it's two runs in and a panic—but it's the prettiest throw you'd want to see. It's right on a line, and the runner goes out by a step, and it's the ball game.

I walked back to the hotel, thinking about the kid. I sat around the lobby until I saw him come in, and then I walked toward the elevator like I was going to my room, but so I'd meet him. And I could see he didn't want to talk.

"How about a soda?" I said.

"No," he said. "Thanks, but I'm going to bed."

"Look," I said. "Forget it. You did the right thing. Have a soda."

We were sitting in the taproom again. The kid wasn't saying anything.

"Why didn't you throw that ball away?" I said.

"I don't know," the kid said. "I had it in my mind before he hit, but I couldn't."

"Why?"

"I don't know why."

"I know why," I said.

The kid didn't say anything. He just sat looking down.

"Do you know why you couldn't throw that ball away?" I said.

"No," the kid said.

"You couldn't throw that ball away," I said, "because you're going to be a major-league ballplayer someday."

The kid just looked at me. He had that same sore expression.

"Do you know why you're going to be a major-league ballplayer?" I said.

The kid was just looking down again, shaking his head. I never got more of a kick[11] out of anything in my life.

"You're going to be a major-league ballplayer," I said, "because you couldn't throw that ball away, and because I'm not a hardware salesman and my name's not Harry Franklin."

"What do you mean?" the kid said.

"I mean," I explained to him, "that I tried to needle[12] you into throwing that ball away because I'm Eddie Brown."

---

11. Harry never *got more of a kick,* more real pleasure, out of anything than he did from seeing Pete's reaction.
12. If you stuck someone with a needle several times, that person would be really annoyed. That is why to annoy and provoke someone is called *to needle.*

About the Author

Wilfred Charles Heinz was born in Mt. Vernon, New York in 1915. After graduating from college he wrote articles for the *New York Sun*'s sports department. When the newspaper closed in 1950, Heinz began to write books and articles about sports and their players. "What I attempt to do in my writing," wrote Heinz, "is to set the scenes and put the characters in it and let them talk."

QUICK REVIEW

1. Where in the story do you first see the "kid's" last name? What is his last name? Where do you first see his first name? What is his first name?

2. When the narrator first sees the kid, what is he wearing?

3. When the kid played with the Yankees in spring training, who did he remind them all of?

4. What is the first name of the man working at the front desk of the hotel?

FOCUS

5. Why doesn't the kid throw the game?

6. To understand the way dialogue is written in a story, copy the paragraphs on page 254 in which the kid tells Harry Franklin why he is so upset with Al Dall, the manager of the ball club.

CREATING & WRITING

7. Imagine that the kid *did* throw the game. What would he and "Harry Franklin" talk about after the game? How would their conversation go? Write down their dialogue, as you imagine it would have been. Does Eddie still offer him a job with the Yankees?

8. You are Eddie Brown. Explain why you pretended to be someone other than who you *really* are, and why you tried to get the kid to throw the game. Tell us what you have learned about the kid that makes you want him for your team.

9. Draw a World Series scoreboard. Decide what two teams are playing, how many runs have already been scored, what inning it is, and who's at bat. If you want, you can even draw a company's ad above the scoreboard.

A CHARACTER'S INNER THOUGHTS

- We learn about a character's inner thoughts from the story's dialogue.

- We learn about a character's inner thoughts from the character's actions.

- We learn about a character's inner thoughts from the story's narration.

- As in real life, it may take us time to fully understand a character's inner thoughts.

THINK ABOUT IT!

1. How do we know that Matt had not meant to hurt Frankie?
   - From his words
   - From his actions
   - From what the story's narration tells us
   - All of the above

2. How does Matt *feel* when he hears that Frankie has been taken to the hospital?

3. What does Matt *do* to express how sorry he is?

4. What are two feelings that Frankie had towards Matt before Matt gave him the card?

Friends

Matt hadn't meant to hurt his friend. It all happened so fast. One minute he and Frankie were playing; the next, Frankie's father was rushing Frankie to the hospital.

Frankie was pretty sure he knew what happened. They had been playing soldiers, tossing sticks and stones at pretend enemies in the woods behind Frankie's house. In the fading light of the evening, it was getting harder and harder to see. Frankie's eye must have been hurt by something Matt threw. A sickish feeling, like a tight fist, began to form in his stomach.

The next morning, Mom opened the curtains of Matt's room early. "Frankie's home," she said. "He'll have a patch on his eye for a while, but he's going to be fine."

Matt felt like an enormous weight had been lifted from him. Still, he knew he had to tell Frankie the truth. He quickly went to his house.

When he arrived at Frankie's, his friend was on the couch.

"That's a big bandage," Matt said. "Does it hurt?"

"A little," said Frankie.

He gave Frankie a get-well card. Inside was a single baseball card, the card Frankie had been trying to trade him for all summer.

"Wow!" Frankie exclaimed. "Now I've got the whole set! Thanks, Matt."

Matt was glad the baseball card made Frankie happy, but the sick feeling in Matt's stomach wasn't going away.

Matt took a deep breath. "Last night, when your eye got hurt...I'm pretty sure it was a stick I threw that hurt your eye."

Frankie said nothing.

"I'm sorry," Matt continued. "I didn't mean to hurt you."

"You know, I kind of thought that's what happened," Frankie said.

"You did?" Matt asked. "Why didn't you say anything?"

"Same reason you didn't. I'd feel terrible if I threw the stick."

"I do feel terrible. Will you still be my friend?" he asked.

"That's a silly question," said Frankie. "Of course I will." Then he added, "Can I still keep the baseball card?"

"It's yours," Matt said.

Frankie smiled, and the sick feeling in Matt's stomach began to go away.

INTO . . . The Birds' Peace

When terrible things happen to people, they sometimes feel as though they can no longer be themselves. They know they must change to handle what has happened.

Kristy's father has left to fight in a war. How can this be? He doesn't even know how to shoot a gun! Her father is gone! This cannot be happening to her!

Kristy runs outside to a place where she and her father spent time together. As she weeps, she grows calmer and begins to notice the world around her. She hears the song sparrow. She listens and watches him. He seems to be in trouble. She tells him that she feels the way he feels. She watches again and learns something new.

. . . When a Character Speaks to Someone Who Can't Answer

When a character speaks out loud, the words are put in quotation marks. A character's spoken lines are usually part of a *dialogue,* a conversation between two or more characters. In *The Birds' Peace,* there is only one speaker—Kristy, but her lines are treated as though they are part of a dialogue.

At times, a character's *thoughts* are placed in quotation marks. It may be difficult for the reader to decide whether the character is thinking these words or actually speaking them. In real life, there is a great difference between the way we think and the way we speak. Our thoughts are lightning quick, and not expressed in complete sentences. Our speech, however, must be in words that another person can understand. That is why the thoughts expressed in a story are written more like spoken language than the language of thought.

The BIRDS' PEACE

Jean Craighead George

On the day Kristy's father went off to war, she burst out the back door and ran down the path to the woods. Her eyes hurt. Her chest burned. She crossed the bridge over the purling stream and dashed into the lean-to she and her father had built near the edge of the flower-filled woodland meadow.

She dropped to her knees, then to her belly.

Covering her face with both hands, she sobbed from the deepest well of her being.

Tears did not help. The pain went on and on.

A bird sang.

Kristy lifted her head. She recognized Fluter, the busy little song sparrow who lived in the bushes at the edge of the meadow. He seemed to be in trouble. His melodious song was loud and belligerent.

"I'm in trouble, too," she said. "My father had to go into the army. He's going to war. And I am scared." Fluter ignored her and sang on. From across the meadow, a strange song sparrow sang clearly and loudly. Kristy barely heard him.

"Daddy doesn't even know how to shoot a gun."

Fluter flew to a sumac bush, thrust out his spotted tan breast, and sang again.

"Suppose bombs fall on him." Kristy began to cry again. "Or an enemy tank shoots at him."

Fluter went on singing. After a few moments he flew across the meadow and boldly sang from a raspberry patch.

Dulce, his mate, flew off their nest in the thicket, where she had been

WORD BANK

purling (PURR ling) *adj.:* flowing with a curling or rippling motion, as a shallow stream over stones
melodious (muh LOE dee us) *adj.:* tuneful; sweet-sounding
belligerent (buh LIJ urr int) *adj.:* argumentative; displaying an eagerness to fight
thicket (THIK et) *n.:* a dense growth of bushes or small trees
incubating (IN kyew BAY ting) *v.:* sitting on (eggs) for the purpose of hatching

incubating their eggs. She ate a bristlegrass seed and serenely preened her feathers. She was quite at ease.

Fluter was not. He turned this way and that. He flicked his tail and raised his crest, then flew to the bracken fern and sang. He flitted briskly to the sugar maple limb and sang from a conspicuous twig. He winged to the dogwood tree and sang from a high limb. As he flew and sang, Kristy became aware of what he was doing. He was making a circle, an invisible fence of song around his meadow and his nest in the thicket.

Suddenly Fluter clicked out what Kristy's father had told her were notes of warning. Dulce became alarmed. She flattened her feathers to her body and flew silently back to their nest.

Kristy checked to see what was the matter. The strange song sparrow was in Fluter's raspberry bush. He was pointing his bill at Fluter, who crouched as if he were going to fly at the stranger. But he did not. Instead, he sang.

The stranger heard Fluter's "stay-off-my-property" song and swiftly departed. He flew over Fluter's invisible fence of song and alighted on his own sapling. Then he sang at Fluter.

WORD BANK

serenely (suh REEN lee) *adv.:* calmly; peacefully

preened *v.:* trimmed or smoothed feathers with the beak or tongue

flitted (FLITT ed) *v.:* flew swiftly from one place to another, settling only for a moment

conspicuous (kun SPIK yoo us) *adj.:* noticeable; standing out

sapling (SAPP ling) *n.:* a young tree

Fluter flew to the sugar maple limb on the border of his territory and sang right back at him. The stranger answered with a flood of melody from his trees and bushes. When each understood where the other's territory lay, they rested and preened their feathers.

Kristy was fascinated. She sat up and crossed her legs.

"Even Daddy doesn't know about this," she said.

Putting her chin in her hands, she watched the birds until the day's long shadows told her she must go home. And all that time, Fluter did not fly or sing beyond the raspberry bush, nor did the stranger come back to Fluter's territory. But sing they did, brightly and melodically, while their mates sat serenely on their brown-splotched eggs.

Dear Daddy, Kristy wrote that night. I know how the birds keep the peace.

> **WORD BANK**   **melodically** (muh LODD ih klee) *adv.:* tunefully; with a beautiful melody

ABOUT THE AUTHOR

Jean Craighead George was born in 1919 into a family of naturalists. As a child, she spent weekends camped in the woods near her Washington, DC home with her parents, brothers, aunts, and uncles, studying nature. When she grew up, she took a job as a newspaper reporter, married, and had three children. George collected wild animals to teach her children about nature. The 173 animals she kept in her backyard became characters in the more than 100 books she wrote! Her children grown, George now lives in Chappaqua, New York.

Studying the Selection

FIRST IMPRESSIONS
Did you find the ending of the story satisfying?

QUICK REVIEW

1. What happened to Kristy's father?

2. Two sentences describe physical feelings she has, as she runs out the back door that day. Which sentences are they?

3. What is it that gets Kristy's attention as she kneels in the grass sobbing?

4. What are Kristy's two fears for her father?

FOCUS

5. Why do you think Kristy stops sobbing when she hears the song sparrow sing?

6. When Kristy talks to Fluter, she is able to express her feelings. What does she tell Fluter? Describe the feelings and thoughts she shares with him. Don't write this as dialogue.

CREATING & WRITING

7. In the story, Kristy grows up a little. How does she grow up?

8. Write the dialogue that you imagine takes place between Fluter and the intruder sparrow. For this you will use dialogue format, with quotation marks. Use the usual "he said /she said" format, but remember they can squawk, cheep, chirp, or sing their words. Remember to use a new paragraph every time the speaker changes. If you wish, Dulce, Fluter's mate, can also be part of this discussion.

9. Make a mobile on a hanger with the three sparrows hanging at different levels.

POINT OF VIEW AND NARRATION

- The point of view of a story depends on who is telling the story.

- If the story is told by a character in the story, it is told in the first person and the character is the "I" of the story.

- If the story is told by a narrator, it is told in the third person with the pronouns he, she, they, and it.

- Sometimes an author will have different characters take part in the storytelling to show the different ways the same story could be told.

THINK ABOUT IT!

1. Who is telling the story? What is he called in the story?

2. When do the first and last sentence take place? Do you think the speaker is a child or an adult?

3. When does the middle of the story take place? Whose point of view does the storyteller try to express?

4. Why does Harold expect his father to be angry at him for playing the organ?

The Old Parlor Organ

An antique dealer came today to haul away the old parlor organ. The organ belonged to my grandfather's mother, who died the winter my grandfather turned nine. Harold, my grandfather, was a silent man. His silence was due in part to his having lost his hearing as an adult, but I imagine the silence began much earlier. Harold was an only child; he must have felt very lonely growing up on the farm after his mother died. Sometimes, staring at the old parlor organ in our basement, I try to imagine what it was like for him.

I picture Harold, perhaps seven, sitting next to his mother on the organ bench. A fire in the fireplace makes the little parlor glow with warmth against the cold Ohio winter. With her feet, his mother pumps the pedals that breathe air through the organ. Harold taps his toe to the tune, his face aglow with firelight and love. His world is complete.

Later, I imagine a hot afternoon the summer after Harold's mother died. Having worked in the fields with his father since sunrise, he's come inside to make lunch. For some reason, he feels drawn today to the parlor, to the silent organ. No one has been in this room since his mother died. Brushing dust off the bench, he sits. He lifts up the organ cover, and starts pumping. The pedals are stiff. He pumps as best as he can. He decides to play a note. The sound that comes from the organ is not the smooth sound his mother's even pressure on the pedals made. Rather, the organ releases a low moan, like the cry of a ghost. Harold feels the hair on his neck stand up.

Suddenly, he is aware of a presence.

Father! Harold hadn't heard him come in. Harold expects anger. Instead, his father offers a pained smile.

"Lunch?" his father asks.

Harold nods, relieved.

In my mind's eye, Harold pulls the lid shut tightly on that ghostly sound.

In time, Harold and his father would use the parlor again, but for the past 75 years, no one has played the organ.

It is time for a new player to make the organ sing again.

Blueprint for Reading

INTO . . . Hattie's Birthday Box

Have you ever made a promise you couldn't keep? How did you feel? Did your conscience bother you? Did you imagine the other person feeling disappointed? Did you tell yourself no one would really care? How careful are you to keep your word?

A young man gave his sister a box to take on her journey out West. He told her not to open it until things were their very worst. He said that there was something precious in the box that would help her through the worst times. As the years passed, he never asked if she'd opened the box, and never told her it was really empty. Now his sister is coming to visit. What will she say? What does she think of him? He is afraid.

EYES ON . . . Changing Point of View

You have read many stories in which one of the characters is also the narrator. You have seen events through the eyes of Samuel in *Samuel's Choice*, Craig in *The Silent Lobby*, Larry in *The Disappearing Man*, Laura in *By the Shores of Silver Lake*, Yurik in *After School*, and Harry Franklin in *One Throw*. Because each one of these characters is so different from the other, the narration of each is different, too.

The beginning and end of *Hattie's Birthday Box* is told to us by a character in the story who speaks in the first person. The middle of the story, however, goes back into the past. The first-person voice is not used, because that part of the story is being told by the author, not by a character.

HAPPY ONE HUNDREDTH BIRTHDAY
SPENCER MCCLINTIC

JULY 5 1847 - 1947

Hattie's Birthday Box

The sign stretching across the ceiling of the nursing
home's rec room says HAPPY ONE HUNDREDTH BIRTHDAY,
SPENCER McCLINTIC, and on the wall in bright numbers
and letters it says JULY 5, 1847 to 1947. Spencer McClintic
is my great-great-grandfather, and our whole family is
coming to celebrate.

Pam Conrad

Momma and I got here early because Momma wanted me to help her blow up balloons and tack up the decorations before everyone arrived. She says now that the war[1] is over and most everyone is back home and rations are a thing of the past, we're going to *really* celebrate.

But Grandaddy's nervous. He sits in his chair by the window, rubbing his hands together and asking my mother over and over, "Now who-all is coming, Anna?"

And she keeps reciting the list of everyone who's coming, and he ticks them off on his fingers, but before she's even through, he asks impatiently, "But is Hattie coming? My baby sister? Are you sure she's coming?"

"Hattie's coming, Grandaddy. Don't you worry. Hattie will be here."

Momma doesn't hear, but I hear him. He mumbles, "Oh, no, oh, no, not Hattie. She's gonna skin me alive."[2]

I pull up a stool near Grandaddy. "Don't you like Aunt Hattie, Grandaddy?"

"Oh, I love her to pieces," he answers. "But she's gonna have my hide.[3] Last time I saw Hattie, she was a bride of sixteen, heading out in a wagon with her new husband to homestead[4] in Nebraska. And I did a terrible thing, a terrible thing."

All the decorations are up, and now that Momma's sure everything is all set, she tells me to stay with Grandaddy and keep him calm while she runs home to get the cake and soda.

But there is no way to keep Grandaddy calm. "What'd you do that was so bad, Grandaddy? What was it?"

---

1. *The war* refers to World War II, which ended in 1945.
2. *She's gonna skin me alive* is a humorous slang expression meaning "she is so angry at me that she would like to hurt me in some way." The listener is supposed to understand that this is an exaggeration and that she would not really want to hurt him.
3. *Have my hide* is similar in meaning to "she's gonna skin me alive." Again, Grandaddy is saying that his sister is very angry at him.
4. In 1862, a law was passed whereby anyone who lived and worked on a piece of government-owned land for five years would be given that land. The land given to the person was called a *homestead*. The name of the law was the Homestead Act. Here, Grandaddy is using the word as a verb. Hattie and her husband went *to homestead,* meaning to settle a piece of land, in Nebraska.

I watch Grandaddy wringing his hands and tapping his slippered feet nervously. He keeps glancing out the window to the road outside, like he's waiting for some old lynch mob to come riding over the hill. This is the story I finally got out of him.

It had been a warm May morning in 1873, and Grandaddy's sister Hattie McClintic Burden was a new bride ready to set out for a life on the distant, promising plains of Nebraska. The sun hadn't quite risen yet, and she and her new husband, Otto, were loading the final things into the wagon. While it was a happy occasion in that Hattie and her husband were heading out for a new life, it was also a sad day, because no one knew when they'd ever see them again. Grandaddy, who was a young man at the time, didn't know it would be seventy-four years before he would finally see her. But no one ever knew that back then. No one knew how long it would be before they saw each other or if they would ever see each other at all. There were no telephones, no airplanes, just the U.S. mail, slow but reliable, carrying recipes for pumpkin bread and clippings of hair from new babies, and sad messages of deaths.

The night before Hattie and Otto left, everyone had tried to smile and be happy for them. There was a combination going-away party and birthday party for Hattie, who was just sixteen. Everyone brought special gifts—blankets and lanterns and bolts of cotton,[5] a pair of small sewing scissors, a bottle of ink, and even a canary in a shiny cage.

My grandaddy, who was then a young man of twenty-six, had stewed and brooded. He had been ten years old when Hattie was born, and she had always been his favorite. More than once he had carried her out into the barn on crystal-clear nights to

---

5. A *bolt of cotton* is a roll of many yards of cotton.

WORD BANK	**stewed** (STOOD) *v.*: fretted, worried, fussed
	brooded (BROO did) *v.*: worried about; thought about moodily

show her a calf being born. He had taught her to swim in the cool spring. And he had chased away anyone who came around to bother her. His heart was breaking that his little sister was going away, and he had wanted to give her the most special gift. The best gift of all. So she would always remember him and know how much he had loved her.

He would have given her a gold necklace, or a bracelet with diamonds, or earrings with opal jewels, but it had been a rough year, with a few of the cattle dying in a storm and a few others lost to a brief sickness. He had no money, nothing to trade, no real gift to give her. Not knowing what the gift would be, he had lovingly hammered together a small wooden box and carved her initials in it, thinking that whatever it would be, it would be about this size.

It was at the party that night that he realized there was nothing to give her and he concocted his tale. Finding her alone at the punch bowl, Spencer had clasped Hattie's small shoulders in his rough hands, looked straight in her face, and lied boldly.

"I got you something special, Hattie, something so special I think you'd better not open it right away. I want you to just hold on to the box, and don't open it unless times get hard, not unless things get to be their very worst, you hear me? And it will see you through."

Hattie had looked at him with such love and trust. He memorized her face, the same small face she had turned to him when a birth-wet calf had finally struggled to its feet, or when he had carried her out on snowy nights to turn her tongue to the swirling night sky.[6] Her face was soft with love, and he knew she

---

6. As children, Spencer and Hattie had played outside at night as the snow fell. Spencer had told Hattie to catch snowflakes on her *tongue* as they *swirled* down from the *night sky.*

> WORD BANK
>
> **concocted** (kun KAHK ted) *v.:* made up; put together many ingredients resulting in something new and different
> **clasped** *v.:* gripped; firmly grasped

must have thought his gift was something precious that she could sell if crops failed or some other disaster happened. But he lied, he lied.

So that morning before the sun rose, he helped Otto hook up the team to the wagon, and once Hattie was high on her perch beside her husband—looking for all the world like a little child playing farmhouse—my young grandaddy had slipped the sealed and empty wooden box into her lap and backed away. He waved goodbye and never saw her again.

Until today. Aunt Hattie's flying in from Nebraska with cousin Harold and his wife, Mary. Since she was sixteen, Hattie has never set foot off Nebraska soil.

"I meant to finally buy her something to put in the box, I really did," Grandaddy keeps saying. "I thought that as soon as things got a little better, as soon as I had a little money, I'd buy those earrings or that necklace and send it right off to her, explaining everything. But then I don't know. Soon I got married myself, and then there were my own children, and Hattie just

| WORD BANK | **team** (TEEM) *n.:* two or more horses, oxen, or other animals harnessed together to draw a vehicle |
| | **perch** *n.:* a high position or resting place |

never mentioned it in any of her letters." Grandaddy groans and lowers his head into his upturned hands. "Oh, mercy, Hattie's coming."

People are starting to arrive now, and the room is filling with children, laughter, and presents. Many of the people are my relatives who live right nearby, and a few came up from Jersey and Washington, people I'd normally see on holidays and such but never all together like this in one place.

And Grandaddy won't even look at them. He just gets up and walks slowly to another seat far from the window. Out the window I see an airport taxi pull up.

I post myself behind Grandaddy and watch. His hands are trembling more than usual, and I can tell he's not paying attention as little babies are brought to him to kiss and my father keeps taking flash pictures of him with everybody.

Suddenly a hush falls over everyone. Even the littlest children grow wide-eyed and still. The name "Hattie" is whispered across the room, like prairie wind over the flute of a stovepipe.[7]

"It's Hattie."

"Hattie's here."

"Hattie!"

I put my hand on Grandaddy's shoulder. "Don't worry, Grandaddy. She'll have to get through me first."

Grandaddy takes a deep breath, and his shoulders slump. He doesn't turn toward the door. He just waits in the silence that falls over the room. We can hear footsteps, Harold's and Mary's, and Hattie's. They stand in the doorway with Hattie in the middle, as though they support her, but when she sees Grandaddy sitting with his back to her, she gently withdraws her arms from them and comes toward us.

She doesn't look like she could swat a fly, and she's not packing a shotgun. The tiny thin net on her hat trembles as she takes tiny steps toward us. "Spencer?" she says softly.

---

7. A *stovepipe* is a pipe that conducts heat away from the stove to the chimney. A *flute* refers to a groove in a pipe. When the prairie wind blows over the groove in the stovepipe, it makes a soft, whispering sound.

"Grandaddy," I say more sharply, poking him in the arm. "Grandaddy, it's Hattie."

He turns then, ready to meet his Maker,[8] I guess, but I'm right there, right next to them, able to see both their faces, and there is nothing but pure love, pure and powerful and undeniable love.

"Why, Spencer, they told me you were an old man." She holds out her hands to him, and he takes them.

Tears stream down his cheeks and drip from his chin. "But no one told me you were still such a fine young lady," he says. Still lying, my grandaddy.

"Oh, Spencer, Spencer," she says, "there's been too much time and space." And I watch her as she steps towards her brother, as they gaze at each other, sharing their special connection. No one in the room is breathing. Then all of a sudden, one of the cousins starts to clap, and everyone, one at a time, joins in, until everyone is laughing and wiping tears, patting Grandaddy on the shoulder, and hugging Hattie.

I'm not about to leave Grandaddy's side. If she's ever going to give him the business[9] about the empty box, I want to hear it. Someone brings her a chair and sits her down right next to him, and no one stops me so I sit down between them right at their feet. And then I notice it. On her lap is a small wooden box, and the lid is off. Delicately carved into its varnished top are the initials HMcB. She holds the box in her hands, and I can see the varnish worn dull in spots where her fingers touch and must have touched for years.

Grandaddy sees it, too, and groans. "Oh, Hattie, do you hate me? Can you ever forgive me?"

"Forgive you for what?"

---

8. When a person is about to die, we say he is *going to meet his Maker,* meaning he is going to meet G-d, Who *made* him.
9. *Give him the business* is an old-fashioned expression for "scold him."

WORD BANK   **undeniable** (un dee NY uh bul) *adj.*: clearly real and true

"For the empty box."

"Forgive you? Why, Spencer, it was the best present I've ever gotten."

"An empty box?" Grandaddy is stunned.

"It wasn't an empty box. It was a box full of good things."

"How d'you figure that?" Grandaddy asks.

"Well, I put it in a safe place, you know. First I hid it under the seat in the wagon, and when we finally got our soddy[10] built, I had Otto make a special chink in the wall where I hid it and where it stayed for years. And I always knew it was there if things got really bad.

"Our first winter, we ran out of food, and I thought to open the box then and see if it would help us, but there were kind neighbors who were generous with us, and I learned to let people be neighborly.

"And then one summer we lost our whole crop in a prairie fire, and I thought of the box, but Otto was sure we could make it on our own, and I learned to let him have his pride. Then when our son drowned, just out of despair I almost opened it, but you had said to open it only if things got their worst, and I knew I still had my daughter, and there was another baby already stirring in me.

"No matter how bad things got, Spencer, they never got their worst. Even when Otto finally died a few years ago. Your box taught me that."

"But you did open it." He points to the box, open and empty in her lap.

"I opened it when I knew I'd be seeing you. I always thought maybe there'd be a brooch or a gold stickpin or something." Hattie smiles. I can almost imagine her with her open face turned up to a snowy sky. She laughs. "I was going to wear it for you!"

---

10. A *soddy* is a house made of tightly packed earth.

WORD BANK	**chink** (CHEENK) *n.:* crack; narrow opening

"I always meant to fill it, Hattie—"

"Hush now," she says. "They're bringing your cake."

And sure enough, Momma's wheeling over a metal table that has a big iced sheet cake on it. Hattie slips the cover back on her empty box and places it on the floor beside her feet, beside me. I stand to get out of the way of the rolling table and take the box.

Grandaddy and Aunt Hattie hold hands while everyone sings "Happy Birthday." Their hands are like old wisteria vines[11] woven into each other. I hold the empty box. I bring it to my face. I look inside. Nothing. It is empty. And then I smell it. At first I think it smells like wood, and then I smell all the rest—a young farmer's stubbornness, a pioneer mother's sorrow, and a wondrous wild and lasting hope.

---

11. *Wisteria vines* have beautiful bluish purple flowers and are often grown to cover walls.

About The Author

Pam Conrad was born in Brooklyn in 1947. She grew up in an apartment near her grandparents' home and, throughout her life, felt very close to them. Although Conrad wrote poetry and stories even as a girl, she didn't start her career as a writer until she was the mother of two children. Her first book was entitled *I Don't Live Here;* it was followed by more than twenty others. Conrad's appreciation for older people can be seen in *Hattie's Birthday Box.* Sadly, her own life was cut short by illness. She died in 1996.

Studying the Selection

FIRST IMPRESSIONS

Do you think Grandaddy is basically an honest or a dishonest person?

QUICK REVIEW

1. When the story opens, who is having a birthday party?

2. Who is telling the story?

3. What year is it, when the story opens?

4. When the story goes back in time, to what year does it return?

FOCUS

5. For many years Hattie believed that there was something in the box. What does the box represent to Hattie? Does it matter that the box is really empty?

6. Why do you think the author uses the past tense for pages 273-275? Why does she stop using the first-person voice on those pages?

CREATING & WRITING

7. Find a box to hold slips of paper. Whenever you feel that things are not going your way, do the following. On one side of the paper, write down what you wished had happened. On the other side, write down how things could have been worse!

8. You can learn something about how it felt to live 150 years ago. For one day, you will not use the telephone (unless you have an emergency or your parents request that you do). Every time you want to make a phone call, write a letter to the person you want to call. Have paper, envelopes, stamps, a pen, and addresses ready. Keep a record of your letters for your teacher.

9. Now is your chance to make a beautiful box. You will need a box with a lid, that you can use for your project. If you prefer, you may make a box yourself, using cardboard, oak tag, or another suitable material (and lots of tape!). Have fun. Do something wonderful!

LESSON IN LITERATURE . . .

PULLING IT ALL TOGETHER

- The plot is acted out by the story's **characters.**

- The characters must have **internal conflict, external conflict,** or both, if the story is to be exciting.

- One way we learn about the characters and their conflicts is through the story's **dialogue.**

- The story's **point of view** depends on who is telling the story. The story may be told by a narrator outside the story or by a character in the story.

THINK ABOUT IT!

1. What are two actions of Androcles that tell us about his character?

2. What internal conflict did Androcles have before he decided to escape?

3. What are two examples of how a character's inner thoughts are revealed to us through the dialogue?

4. In response to Androcles' words, the lion does something. If you put the lion's actions into words, what would the lion be saying?

Androcles and the Lion: A Fable Retold

Long ago, during the time of the Roman Empire, a young slave named Androcles had a very harsh master. No matter how hard Androcles worked, his master would whip him and push him harder. One day Androcles decided to escape.

"Though I may be executed if I am caught," Androcles reasoned, "it would be better to die than to live like this." That night, taking only the clothes on his back, he walked all night by the light of the moon, and by sunrise he was exhausted and very hungry. Stepping into a thicket of trees to find a place to hide, Androcles found himself face to face with a lion.

Androcles couldn't believe his bad luck, to have finally escaped slavery only to fall prey to a wild lion. But the lion did not pounce. Rather, the animal held up a front paw as if to shake hands. Androcles realized that the paw was soaked in blood.

"You poor creature," the young man said soothingly. "You're hurt."

As Androcles stepped carefully toward the lion, he saw the source of the problem: a very large thorn stuck in the lion's paw.

Androcles spoke in a low voice. "It's alright. All will be well." He gently took the lion's paw in one hand, and with the other quickly pulled out the thorn. The lion licked its paw, then, in thanks, licked Androcles' hand. From that moment on they were friends.

One day, however, when Androcles was out gathering food for his supper, he was captured by Roman soldiers and—as punishment—taken to the city to be thrown into the arena with hungry lions.

When the day arrived for his execution, Androcles was sent into the arena to face his death. A hush fell over the gathered masses as the Emperor gave the order to release the hungry lion. The fierce creature raced toward the helpless man. Androcles closed his eyes and prepared to be torn limb from limb by a beast certainly gripped with hunger and angry at having been caged. He waited. The attack never came.

Androcles opened his eyes to find the lion laying at his feet. Could it be? It was! Androcles knelt down and patted his friend.

"Poor thing," he said. "They must have captured you the same day they caught me."

Stunned by this escaped slave who could tame a lion, the Emperor ordered both Androcles and the lion to be freed. As Androcles and his friend left the arena together, the crowds roared their approval.

You never know when a kindness shown to another might be repaid.

Blueprint for Reading

INTO . . . The Whimbrel

Whimbrels are large birds with long down-curved bills. They live near the water and spend their summers in arctic climates. You are about to read a story about a whimbrel who was injured while making his way back north.

The setting of *The Whimbrel* is a small seaside town in Australia. In a small town everyone usually knows everyone else. The people feel at home with each other. It is a comfortable feeling.

In this story, Axel Jorgensen is the man people turn to when a wild creature needs help. He is the kind of person who always steps forward and does what needs to be done.

EYES   ON   . . . Pulling It All Together

After you have read *The Whimbrel*, ask yourself the following questions:

How do we get to know the characters?
- Is it through the words the author uses to tell the story?
- Through the dialogue?
- Through the characters' thoughts or actions, or reactions to other characters?

What is the conflict for each of the main characters?
- Do they have a conflict with people or events or within themselves?

How important is the dialogue in *The Whimbrel?*
- Do we read about their inner thoughts and feelings?
- Is there a narrator that speaks in the first person?
- Is the story written in the present tense or the past tense?

Are there any obvious symbols in the story?

The Whimbrel

Colin Thiele

About a hundred people lived in the little town of Snapper Bay in southern Australia. Some of them were young, and some of them were old, and some of them were in-between.

Axel Jorgensen was seventy-two, with a mop of white hair and a cotton-wool beard, and legs that bowed outward like bananas. He looked something like Father Time.

Tessa Noble was twelve, with a mop of brown hair and tapioca-freckled cheeks, and legs that bowed inward at the knees like bent sticks. She lived in a white house in the main street of Snapper Bay. There was only one street in the whole town, so it had to be the main one anyway. She lived with her father and mother and her grown-up brother, Jody, and Jody's wife, Bridget.

Axel Jorgensen lived by himself in a wooden hut far around the curve of the bay, away from the town. It was the place where the sandy beach ended and the first rocks reared up near the start of the Hammerhead Handle. He was a fisherman, and a forager, a boatman and a beachcomber, a talker and a teacher. He taught Tessa many

WORD BANK	**forager** (FOR uh jer) *n.:* one who wanders about looking for food, provisions, or some unexpected find
	beachcomber (BEECH kohm er) *n.:* one who looks carefully (combs) along the beach for objects of interest

things. When they walked along the coast together he taught her about seashells and albatrosses, and when they walked inland by the lakes and marshes he taught her about summer sedges, snails, and spoonbills in the wildlife sanctuary.[1] She thought he was one of the Wise People of the World.

She had called him Uncle Axel for as long as she could remember, even though they were not related. He often came to have a meal in Tessa's house, and Tessa's father went fishing with him whenever he could. She spent as much time pottering about near his shack as she did in her own little street in Snapper Bay.

---

1. A *wildlife sanctuary* is an area of land that is preserved in its natural state. There, the plants, birds, fish, and animals native to the area live and grow undisturbed. People may come to observe the wildlife, but may not interfere with it in any way.

WORD BANK	**marshes** (MAR shiz) *n.:* areas of waterlogged soil, having no trees and covered with rushes, cattails, and other grasses **pottering** (usually puttering, PUTT er ing) *v.:* doing "odds and ends" of small jobs

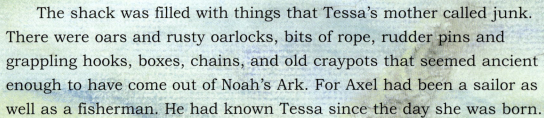

The shack was filled with things that Tessa's mother called junk. There were oars and rusty oarlocks, bits of rope, rudder pins and grappling hooks, boxes, chains, and old craypots that seemed ancient enough to have come out of Noah's Ark. For Axel had been a sailor as well as a fisherman. He had known Tessa since the day she was born.

---

2. A *rudder* is a blade that turns in the water at the stern (rear) of a boat. The rudder is used for steering the boat.

3. A *grappling hook* is an iron-clawed instrument attached to a rope. It is thrown from a boat onto an object such as a wall or an enemy ship. When the object is "hooked," it cannot move away from the boat.

Axel loved all living things—even Rump, the young wombat, who caused him a lot of trouble. Rump had been run over by a car near the Murray River, and the driver had picked him up and left him with Axel, just like a patient in a hospital. When Rump had recovered he had stayed on, burrowing in the bank behind the hut or wandering down to the town to thin out someone's vegetable garden.

"It's that potbellied wombat again," people used to say when they found out. "Take him back to Axel."

And so Rump would soon be back digging in his bank again or snuffling in a corner of the hut or scrabbling under the floor. Once Axel had disappeared completely into a new wombat hole while he had been stirring the porridge at the stove. But he was never angry with Rump. He wouldn't even call him a pet. He was a mate, he said, a friend and a companion.

One morning when Tessa walked around the long curve of the beach to Axel's hut she found him busy and excited. He was working at the vise on his bench near the door of his shack.

"What are you doing?" she asked. "What's up?"

"You'll never guess, Tessa girl," he said. She knew that something had happened, because he never called her Tessa girl unless he was excited.

"What is it, then?"

"Look inside." He nodded his head at the shack. "But move slowly."

She was suspicious and walked very carefully. "Is it a snake?"

WORD BANK	**burrowing** (BURR oh ing) *v.*: digging down
	vise (VYZ) *n.*: a tool with two jaws that can be adjusted to hold an object firmly

"Not a snake. Come and see."

At first she couldn't see anything at all in the shadow. She opened her eyes wide and then puckered them quickly to get a clearer view.

"I can't see anything."

"Not very smart, are you?" He chuckled. "Wouldn't take you out to see things in the marshes."

"Is it a . . . Oh!" Suddenly she saw it. There was a little silence while she took a breath and looked at it. Axel went on working busily at the vise on his bench.

WORD BANK **puckered** *v.:* drew together tightly, forming wrinkles

It was a bird with a long
curved beak, lying on its side in a
large wire cage, panting. It was
streaked brown and buff over the
wings and body, but its breast
was white and its crown had long
white stripes above the eyes. It
was beautiful—lovely mottled
feathers and bright frightened
eyes, and a long slender
downward-curved bill.

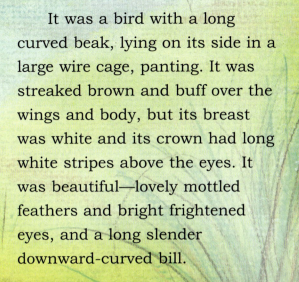

"What is it?" Tessa
asked at last.

Axel straightened up and stopped his filing
at the vise. "A whimbrel," he said.

"A whimbrel." Tessa tasted the name on her
tongue. "I like that. It's a name with meanings
in the sounds."

"Yes," Axel answered. "Speed and distance,
and lonely faraway cries in the night."

Tessa paused and looked at it again. "Is it
hurt?"

"Yes."

She sensed something in his voice. "Is it
very bad?"

"Pretty bad."

"Wings?" she asked.

WORD BANK **mottled** (MOTT uld) *adj.:* marked with spots
or blotches of different colors or shades

Axel took the thing he was making out of the vise, examined it, put it back, and turned toward her.

"He's lost a foot, Tessa. He can't stand up properly."

She was horrified. "A foot? How on earth could he have lost a foot?"

"Who knows?"

"A fish? Do you think maybe a barracuda bit it off?"

Axel shook his head. "It would have happened on the land— or in the air. He likes the inlets and the mud flats."

"A sharp piece of iron, then? Or a piece of wire—a power line he didn't see when he was flying fast?"

Axel's big mop of white hair trembled as he shook his head again. "No. A bullet, more likely."

Tessa was appalled. "Not a bullet!" she said quickly. "Nobody would shoot at a whimbrel!"

"No?" Axel rubbed angrily with a file. "Have you seen the way Tiny Hilbert or Joe Zucci handle a rifle around here? Like maniacs!"

"But not at a whimbrel. Surely they wouldn't shoot at a whimbrel."

"They'd shoot at anything. At a stilt or a curlew or an ibis or a pelican, at a spoonbill or a snipe or a swallow or a swan, at a post or a tin or a light bulb or a tank. They ought to be locked up."

"That's awful." She was silent for a while. "What's going to happen to him?"

Old Axel looked up sharply. "What do you think? He can't live as he is, can he? He has to fly all the way to Siberia or Canada in a few weeks time."

"But that's on the other side of the world!"

"Yes. Big enough trip to tackle with two legs."

She sat on an old box near the door and glanced back and forth from Axel to the whimbrel. "Can he land on one foot and take off again?"

"Most birds can stand on one foot—if it's not too windy. But his other foot is hurt too—the claw."

"Can't he stand at all, then?"

"He can tumble about and hop and flap and flop. But how could he live like that? How could he get enough food? It would be better to put him away than to let him starve to death."

Her eyes opened wide. "Put him away?"

"Yes. Kill him kindly."

"No," she said quickly. "Oh no, you wouldn't do that." She paused for a second and looked at the old man shrewdly. "You couldn't do that, could you?"

He seemed to be so busy at his vise that at first she thought he hadn't heard her. But after a while he went on without looking up. "Sometimes things have to be done even when you don't want to do them. Even when it's very hard."

"I know you wouldn't do it," she said confidently, "even if you could." She stood up and went over to him. "What are you making?"

He unfastened something very small from the vise and held it up. It was a foot. A tiny wooden foot—for a whimbrel.

Tessa held the whimbrel while Axel tried to fit the artificial foot. It was not an easy thing to do, even though the little piece of wood was carefully made, with three carved toes, and a hollow stem to fit over the stump of the leg.

Fortunately the whimbrel didn't struggle. Axel showed Tessa how to hold it firmly and gently with the wings wrapped against its body. Although it was frightened it seemed to know that they were trying to help. Its dark eyes blinked and flashed, and when its head moved jerkily its long bill darted about like a probe. Tessa was spellbound.

"It must be four inches long," she said.

Axel didn't even look up. "Four!" he said. "More like sixteen; nice streamlined bird, the whimbrel."

"Not the bird. The bill."

"What about the bill?"

"It must be four inches long."

"The bill is, yes. Not the bird."

"No, the bill, the bill."

"Well, why didn't you say so in the first place?"

Tessa snorted. "Really, Uncle Axel!" She was about to say much more, but decided to hold her peace. She looked down at the whimbrel again, at the great curving beak, as black as ebony, at the white breast, the mottled back, and the light stripe running above the eyebrows and over the curve of his head.

WORD BANK	**shrewdly** (SHROOD lee) *adv.:* sharply and cleverly

"Oh, you're a beautiful fellow," she said. But the bird suddenly struggled and she had to tighten her grip.

"Hold still, Willie," said old Axel gently. "We've nearly finished."

"Is that his name—Willie?"

"Suits him, I reckon. Will-he walk? Or won't he?"

"Will-he walk! That's a dreadful joke, Uncle Axel."

"Well, we'll soon know."

"Finished?"

"Finished."

Axel put his pliers and other tools aside and straightened up. "Put him down in his pen."

The whimbrel fluttered for a minute, but he settled down quickly and began to pace up and down in the cage. At first he lifted his leg with a high awkward step like a man learning to walk on skis, but before long he grew used to it and stomped about happily. Tessa had her nose pressed against the wire. "It works, Uncle Axel," she said excitedly. "It actually works."

"Of course it works," he answered haughtily.

"D'you think he'll be able to fly now, and land without somersaulting?"

"Give him a day or two to get used to it," Axel said. "It's not every day that a bird has to learn to fly with a wooden leg."

It was wise to wait. Two days later the wooden leg was useless. After Willie had walked in his tray of water a few times the light wood grew soggy and began to break up.

"Fat lot of use that was, Willie," said Axel. "Wouldn't have lasted you to Mount Gambier, let alone to the other side of the world. We'll have to do better than that."

So he worked at his bench for another whole day and made a metal foot—of aluminum. It was beautifully shaped, but it was too hard to fit to Willie's leg.

"Won't work," Axel admitted at last. "Might hurt him, probably do more harm than good."

Tessa was downhearted. "Whatever are we going to do, then? He looks so helpless when you take his foot away from him."

"We'll win yet. I've still got bags of ideas."

This time he made a plastic foot, cutting the shape carefully to match the real one, and melting out a hollow stem with a red-hot skewer. It fitted beautifully. But Axel was still not satisfied. He experimented for another two days, making more and more little feet and varying the length and diameter until it was perfect. It fitted snugly over the whole of the stump of Willie's leg and extended a half inch or so beyond it so that the two legs—the real one and the artificial one—were of exactly the same length. Then Axel fastened a tiny clamp around the stump to be doubly sure.

"Now, Willie," he said, "you ought to be able to dance to music."

Willie walked as if he was marching in a brass band. He looked so pleased that Tessa thought his big bill would break out into a long down-curving smile.

"He's all right this time," she said. "Now he really can look after himself."

Axel kept him for another week, checking the foot carefully every day. By now Willie was quite tame, standing quietly when they came near him and even eating out of their hands. Tessa could see that Axel was becoming so fond of him that soon he wouldn't be able to part with him.

"Are you going to keep Willie?" she asked slyly one day. "Or are you going to set him free?"

Axel looked at her quizzically.

Tessa was very uncomfortable. She knew she had been rude and she was certain that he knew it too.

"Come on then," he said suddenly, lifting Willie out of his cage.

"It's time you tested your new foot out in the wide world."

WORD BANK **quizzically** (KWIZ ik lee) *adv.:* questioningly

They carried the whimbrel inland over the dunes behind the shack until they came to the open flats beyond Snapper Bay. Then they stopped and both of them looked at Willie for the last time. His dark eyes were flashing and blinking. Tessa felt very sad, as if she was about to say farewell to a special friend forever.

"Good-bye, Willie," she whispered. "Look after yourself."

"Off you go," said Axel. "You'll be all right now."

He put Willie down on the firm clay near the edge of the mud flats. Willie stood for a second or two as if he was amazed at the sight of everything around him. Then he ran forward for a few steps and rose easily into the air. They both stood watching, holding their hands up to shade their eyes.

"Just look at him fly," Tessa said, "so fast and free."

"Beautiful," said Axel, watching intently. "Beautiful fellow."

They both remained with their hands to their eyes until the whimbrel curved downward at last

WORD BANK	**dunes** (DOONZ) *n.*: sand hills

toward the skyline by the marshes and they lost sight of him. Though the world was full of birds it was suddenly empty.

"Back home, Tessa," said Axel gently. He saw her eyes misting over and her lip trembling. "No need to be sad for Willie," he said quietly. "He's happy back with the other whimbrels—with all his friends. It wouldn't be right to keep him in a cage, especially when they all fly to the other side of the world. Think how lonely he would be then. You wouldn't like that."

She shook her head. "No, I wouldn't like that."

"And think what a hero he'll be. He'll be able to talk about his wooden leg for the rest of his life."

"His plastic leg."

"Just like old Mrs. Elliot with her operations."

Tessa smiled. "He will be sort of special, won't he?"

"Super special," said Axel. "There won't be another whimbrel like him in the whole world."

Animal Glossary

An *albatross* is a large, white bird with a broad wingspread and the ability to remain aloft for long periods of time.

A *sedge* is a grasslike plant that grows in wet places.

A *barracuda* is a long, slender fish with sharp teeth. It is known for its habit of biting any moving object within reach.

A *snipe* is a plump, long-billed shorebird.

A *cray* is a spiny lobster found in Australian waters. A *craypot* is used for trapping crays.

A *spoonbill* is a large wading bird with a long, flat bill that has a spoonlike tip.

A *curlew* is a large shorebird with a long bill that curves down.

A *stilt* is a black and white wading bird with long, pink legs and a long black bill.

An *ibis* is a large wading bird with a long, thin bill that curves down.

A *wombat* is an Australian marsupial (animals who carry their young in a pouch). The wombat has a thick, bearlike body and short legs.

About the Author

Colin M. Thiele was born in 1920 in a small, South Australian town called Eudunda. As a child, he loved to roam the countryside. His early love of nature is seen in most of his writings. Thiele fought for Australia in WWII. After the war, he worked as a teacher, principal, and college director. All the while, he was writing poetry, novels, storybooks, biographies, and plays. His hometown of Eudunda is so proud of him that, in their civic gardens, they have erected a sculpture of him, seated with a notebook and pencil, a pelican at his side.

Studying the Selection

FIRST IMPRESSIONS
Do you think Willie will do
well with his plastic foot?

QUICK REVIEW

1. What is the setting of the story?

2. Who are the three main characters?

3. What does the author think Tessa's mother would call the things in Axel's shack?

4. Who is Rump?

FOCUS

5. Why does Axel make an artificial foot for the whimbrel?

6. Imagine that Tessa is telling the story. She will speak in the first person. Rewrite at least five sentences from the story. Here is an example from page 287:

> I had called him Uncle Axel for as long as I could remember, even though we were not related. He often came to have a meal in **my** house, and **my** father went fishing with him whenever he could. I spent as much time pottering about near his shack as I did in **my** own little street in Snapper Bay.

CREATING & WRITING

7. Write several paragraphs in which you explain why helping animals is so important.

8. Choose one of the following elements of a story: character, conflict, dialogue, or first-person narration. Write a paragraph explaining the element you have chosen. Then, use one or two paragraphs to bring examples from the story of how the element is used in *The Whimbrel.*

9. Your assignment is to do an **Outside Bird Count.** You will need a pad and a pencil, and a quiet place outside. Spend half an hour counting the birds you see. Note the different types. If you don't know their names, describe them in brief notes. Count the different bird calls you hear. If you can, make some rough, quick sketches of the birds you see.

I AM WINDING THROUGH A MAZE

Jack Prelutsky

I AM WINDING THROUGH A MAZE, I'VE BEEN TRAPPED IN HERE FOR DAYS, AND I WONDER IF I EVER WILL GET OUT. I AM FEELING SOME DISMAY, FOR I'VE TRULY LOST MY WAY, AND MY FUTURE SEEMS TO BE A BIT IN DOUBT. AS I JOURNEY FORTH AND BACK, I'M COMPLETELY LOSING TRACK OF WHERE I'VE BEEN, AND WHERE TO GO. IS THE EXIT FAR OR NEAR? I AM CERTAIN I HAVE MISSED WHERE I OUGHT TO DIRECTION, IT I AM

A Tooter Tutor
Carolyn Wells

A tutor who tooted the flute
Tried to tutor two tooters to toot.
Said the two to the tutor,
"Is it harder to toot or
5   To tutor two tooters to toot?"

EVERY STEP I TAKE IS OBVIOUSLY WRONG. IT'S APPARENT THAT I AM IN A PICKLE, IN A JAM, IN A QUANDARY, IN A SCRAPE, A SQUEEZE, A SPOT. NOW I'M IN A CUL-DE-SAC, AND I HAVE TO DOUBLE BACK, BUT AT LAST I THINK I SEE WHERE THE EXIT JUST MIGHT BE, SO I'LL SOON BE OUT. . . WHOOPS! NO, I'M NOT. AND I WOEFULLY ACKNOWLEDGE I DON'T KNOW. AS I TAKE EACH TURN AND TWIST, HAVE BEEN GOING ALL ALONG IS TOTALLY UNCLEAR,

A Bear in Reverse

Anonymous

A cheerful old bear at the zoo
Could always find something to do.
When it bored him to go
On a walk to and fro,
5   He reversed it, and walked fro and to.

74th Street

Myra Cohn Livingston

Hey, this little kid gets roller skates.
She puts them on.
She stands up and almost
flops over backwards.
5   She sticks out a foot like
she's going somewhere and
falls down and
smacks her hand. She
grabs hold of a step to get up and
10   sticks out the other foot and
slides about six inches and
falls and
skins her knee.

And then, you know what?

15   She brushes off the dirt and the
blood and puts some
spit on it and then
sticks out the other foot

again.

THIS IS THE DAY

June Crebbin

This is the sort of day
I should like to wrap
In shiny silver paper
And only open when it's raining,

5   This is the sort of day
I should like to hide
In a secret drawer to which
Only I have the key,

This is the sort of day
10   I should like to hang
At the back of the wardrobe
To keep me warm when winter comes,

This is the day
I should like to last for ever,

15   This is my birthday.

ABOUT THE AUTHORS

Jack Prelutsky was born in Brooklyn, New York in 1910. Upon reaching adulthood, he could not decide upon a career. He tried carpentry, furniture moving, cab driving, bookselling, and even folk singing. Finally, he tried drawing. To accompany his drawings, he wrote some verses. When he took them to a publisher, she said "You are the worst artist I've ever seen"—but she loved his poems. Prelutsky became a children's poet, writing more than sixty books of poems for children. He lives in Olympia, Washington.

Carolyn Wells was born in New Jersey in 1869. At the age of six, she lost her hearing. As a young woman, she worked as a librarian, but for most of her life she was an author who wrote and wrote and wrote! She completed 180 volumes, most of which were either humorous verse or mystery novels. In 1918 she married Hadwin Houghton and moved to New York. Although her husband died the following year, she remained in New York until her death in 1942.

Myra Cohn Livingston was born in Omaha, Nebraska in 1926. Many of the poems she wrote later were based on her happy childhood in Omaha. As a girl, her main interests were writing and music. Livingston's first published poems were written while she attended Sarah Lawrence College in New York. While working at a bookstore, she decided to submit a manuscript of a children's book she had written to a publishing house. The book was published. It was the first of almost fifty books of poetry and nonfiction that Livingston wrote. She, her husband, and their three children lived in Los Angeles until her death in 1996.

Studying the Selection   POETRY

I Am Winding Through a Maze

1. What is a maze?

2. Write out the first four stanzas of the poem *I Am Winding Through a Maze.* Here are some clues:
   • The poem has 8 stanzas.
   • Each stanza has 3 lines.
   • The first two lines of each stanza rhyme.

To help you, here are the last two stanzas:

> It's apparent that I am,
> in a pickle, in a jam,
> in a quandary, in a scrape, a squeeze, a spot.

> But at last I think I see
> where the exit just might be,
> so I think I'll soon be out . . . whoops! No, I'm not.

3. Write a concrete poem. Remember, it doesn't have to rhyme or have a regular beat. There are lots of ways you can do this. A poem about a house could be in the shape of a house. A poem about a cat could be in the shape of a cat. Try to keep your "drawing" very simple. You will be drawing with lines of words. Here are other possibilities: the sun, the moon, a star, a tree, a box, a circle, a triangle, and so forth.

A Tooter Tutor • A Bear in Reverse

1. What does the tutor try to do in the limerick?

2. What question do the students ask the tutor—in your own words?

3. Write your own limerick. Just remember a limerick is five lines. Lines 1, 2, and 5 rhyme and have 8 beats. Lines 3 and 4 rhyme, and have 5 or 6 beats. Have fun with this.

74th Street

1. Why do you think the poet uses mostly one-syllable words?

2. Write down eight of the verbs in the poem.

3. What is the girl in the poem trying to do?

4. How do you think the poet feels about her?

This Is the Day

1. What is this poem about? Just give a short, simple answer in one or two sentences.

2. What are two phrases in the poem that are repeated?

3. Give an example from the poem of words that begin with the same letter.

4. What is the strongest picture you have in your mind from the poem? (There is no single correct answer to this question.)

WHAT MONTH IS IT? WHAT DAY?
HEY, WHAT KIND OF BIRD IS THAT?

Create a Calendar of Birds • Song Sparrow, Canary, Whimbrel

1. You have read three selections in this unit in which birds are mentioned. In *The Birds' Peace* and *The Whimbrel*, a song sparrow and a whimbrel are main characters. *In Hattie's Birthday Box*, a canary is briefly mentioned. Make a table like the one below. Using books from the library, or provided by your teacher, fill in all of the columns in the table. Make sure your third and fourth columns are big enough for your notes.

Selection	Bird	Color & Markings	Habits and Ways
The Birds' Peace			

2. Have you ever seen a calendar that hangs on the wall and has one particular subject? For each month, there is a picture related to the subject of the calendar. Below the picture, there is information about it. Underneath, is the calendar for that month. It looks like this: ⟶

Complete each of the steps below on a separate sheet of paper, so that if you make a mistake on one part, you can correct it before it is attached to the other parts.

Name of Bird

Information about the bird.

Name of Month

Sun	Mon	Tues	Wed	Thurs	Fri	Sat

a. Pick one bird for your calendar, and draw a picture of that bird.
Do this on its own sheet of paper.

b. Write a paragraph of information about your bird. Take the information from the research you did for your table in #1.
Do this on a separate piece of paper.

c. Choose one month of the year, and copy the page for that month from a calendar. Your teacher may wish to assign different months to different students so that, when the project is completed, the class will have a calendar of the entire school year to hang on the wall. **Again, do this on a separate piece of paper.**

d. Now, put all of the pieces together on one very large piece of paper or oak tag. When the month you have chosen comes, hang your bird calendar on the wall!

WHO ARE THESE TWO PEOPLE?

You and a Classmate Have Come From One of the Stories—Which One?

1. In each of the stories in this unit, two characters have a friendship or important connection. Your teacher will match people to be partners. Together, the two of you will pick one of the selections. Now, you and your partner are going to be one of the character pairs in the story you have selected. Bring some props and costumes. You may even wish to put on some makeup for your presentation.

2. Write down about five sentences each, describing "yourself."

3. Prepare a very short skit in which the two of you talk *to each other*. It must "feel" like part of the story from which your character is taken.

4. For the presentation, first tell the class about "yourself," from the sentences you have prepared. If you can do this without looking at your notes, all the better. Second, act out your skit together.

5. Conclude your presentation by asking your class together, "Who are we?" Don't be afraid to be funny.

6. Remember. It takes practice and rehearsing to do a good job on this.

DRAMATIC PERFORMANCE

The Curtain's Going Up: What Will It Be, Prose or Poetry?

1. Quickly review the six stories and the poems. What is your favorite passage of all?

2. Copy the passage down. (Your passage must be at least fifty words long.) Now, write a paragraph's worth of notes about why you like it. These do not need to be complete sentences, but should express your feelings.

3. Practice reading your passage aloud. Read it clearly and with proper expression.

4. Recite the passage of prose or poetry before your class. Then, with the help of your notes, tell them why this passage is your favorite.

AIMING HIGH

1. What does it mean to aim high?

2. Think about the main characters in each of the prose selections. All of them aim high, one way or the other. Who did you like the most?

3. Now it is time to write several paragraphs. In your first paragraph, explain what it means to aim high. For the final sentence of your first paragraph, write something like, "These words remind me of in _selection name_, and I am going to write about (him or her)." Use your second paragraph to give examples of ways in which your character aimed high. Use your third paragraph to conclude. Here is an example of a conclusion: "These are the reasons (character's name) was the person I liked most in these stories."

unit 4

THE
WORLD
AROUND
US

LESSON IN LITERATURE . . .

MOOD

- The mood of a story or a play is the atmosphere in which the story takes place.

- Many things contribute to the mood of the story. The setting, the dialogue, and the plot all contribute to the mood.

- In a play, lighting, music, scenery, and costumes can add even more power to the mood.

- Often, what we remember most about a story is its mood. We may say, "I don't remember the plot, but I remember that the book was scary/funny/sad/lighthearted," and so forth.

THINK ABOUT IT!

1. Describe the mood that is created by the phrase "dark and stormy night."

2. In the two paragraphs of Olive's story, there are several phrases that create a mood. Some create it through sound, some through sight, and some through feel or touch. Find one phrase for each of the above.

3. What mood is created by the words, "Footsteps. On the stairs."?

4. What is the mood at the end of the story?

Dark and Stormy Night

It was a dark and stormy night.

Olive knew it was a corny opening for a story, but it was a dark and stormy night. Although it wasn't the first time Olive's parents had let her stay home alone, she was feeling a little spooked. Maybe this wasn't the best time to work on her English assignment to write a scary story.

The fierce wind blew raindrops onto the princess' face as she stared longingly out her window in the castle tower. The moon seemed like a windblown candle that might flicker out at any moment.

It was so dark out that with her bedroom light on, Olive could see little more than her own reflection in the window. She turned off her desk lamp to get a better look outside.

Bad idea! A shiver ran up Olive's spine as she stood alone in the dark room. Fighting the urge to bolt from the room and call a friend, Olive felt around in the darkness until she found the switch for her desk lamp.

Outside the castle windows, the wind howled like a pack of wolves on the hunt. Huddled in the corner, the princess suddenly heard a thump. Then another. Then the creaking of a door opening and slamming shut.

Was someone in the house? Olive looked at her clock. 9:05. Her parents wouldn't be home this early. Who could it be?

Footsteps. On the stairs.

Terrified, she turned off the lamp and ran to her closet, pulling the door shut silently behind her. From inside the closet the footsteps were more muffled, but someone was definitely coming up the stairs.

Holding her breath, Olive heard the bedroom door opening. A pair of feet quietly padded into the room. She pulled herself into the tightest ball she could make in the corner of the closet. Suddenly, a finger of light forced its way under the closet door. Someone was looking for her.

"Ollllliiiive? Olive, honey, where are you?"

Mom.

Olive sheepishly pushed the closet door open with her foot. Her mother jumped, startled.

"Surprise," Olive said meekly.

INTO . . . The Day of the Turtle

In *The Day of the Turtle,* a young girl who lives on an island wants to rescue a stranded leatherback turtle. Unlike the horse in *The Black Stallion,* the turtle is not capable of showing loyalty, affection, or any emotion at all. It cannot wag its tail, or shake its mane, or purr to a friend. The turtle cannot even look grateful! Yet, the girl in the story and Granny May work very hard to save the turtle's life. They are thrilled when their efforts pay off.

What is it that makes a person care so much?

EYES ON . . . Setting and Mood

You may hear people talk about being in a good mood or a bad mood. But what do we mean when we talk about the mood of a story?

Have you ever been in a place where there is lots of screaming and shouting? What about entering a place where voices are hushed and people are studying silently? Is there a difference between a room that is very hot and airless and one that is cool and airy? In each of these places, there is a mood or atmosphere.

What is the mood, or atmosphere, in *The Day of the Turtle?*

The Day of the Turtle

Michael Morpurgo

September 8

Today I found a turtle. I think it's called a leatherback turtle. I found one once before, but it was dead. This one has been washed up alive.

Father had sent me down to collect driftwood on Rushy Bay. He said there'd be plenty about after a storm like that. He was right.

I'd been there for half an hour or so heaping up the wood, before I noticed the turtle in the tide line of piled seaweed. I thought at first he was just a washed-up tree stump covered in seaweed.

He was upside down on the sand. I pulled the seaweed off him. His eyes were open, unblinking. He was more dead than alive, I thought. His flippers were quite still and held out to the clouds above as if he was worshiping them. He was massive, as long as this bed, and wider. He had a face like a two-hundred-year-old man, wizened and wrinkled and wise, and a gently smiling mouth.

| WORD BANK | **driftwood** (DRIFT wood) *n.:* wood floating or cast ashore by a body of water |
| | **wizened** (WEE zund) *adj.:* withered; shriveled |

I looked around, and there were more gulls gathering. They were silent, watching, waiting; and I knew well enough what they were waiting for. I pulled away more of the seaweed and saw that the gulls had been at him already. There was blood under his neck where the skin had been pecked. I had got there just in time. I bombarded the gulls with pebbles and they flew off, protesting noisily, leaving me alone with my turtle.

I knew it would be impossible to roll him over, but I tried anyway. I could rock him back and forth on his shell, but I could not turn him over, no matter how hard I tried. After a while I gave up and sat down beside him on the sand. His eyes kept closing slowly as if he was dropping off to sleep, or maybe he was dying—I couldn't be sure. I stroked him under his chin, where I thought he would like it, keeping my hand well away from his mouth.

A great curling storm wave broke and came tumbling toward us. When it went hissing back over the sand, it left behind a broken spar. It was as if the sea was telling me what to do. I dragged the spar up the beach. Then I saw the turtle's head go back, and his eyes closed. I've often seen sea birds like that. Once their heads go back there's nothing you can do. But I couldn't just let him die. I couldn't. I shouted at him, I shook him. I told him that he wasn't going to die, that I'd turn him over somehow, that it wouldn't be long.

I dug a deep hole in the sand beside him. I would lever him up and topple him in. I drove the spar into the sand underneath his shell. I drove it in again and again, until it was as deep as I could get it. I hauled back on it and felt him shift. I threw all my weight on it and at last he tumbled over into the hole, and the right way up, too. But when I scrambled over to him, his head lay limp in the sand, his eyes closed to the world. There wasn't a flicker of life about him. He was dead. I was quite sure of it. It's silly, I know—I had only known him for a few minutes—but I felt like I had lost a friend.

I made a pillow of soft sea lettuce for his head and knelt beside him. I cried till there were no more tears to cry. And then I saw the gulls were back. They knew too. I screamed at them, but they just glared at me and moved in closer.

"No!" I cried. "No!"

I would never let them have him, never. I piled a mountain of seaweed on top of him, and my driftwood on top of that. The next tide would take him away. I left him and went home.

I went back to Rushy Bay this evening at high tide, just before nightfall, to see if my turtle was gone. He was still there. The tide had not come high enough. The gulls were gone though, all of them. I really don't know why, but I wanted to see his face once more. I pulled the wood and seaweed away until I could see the top of his head. As I looked it moved and lifted. He was blinking up at me. He was alive again! I could have kissed him, really I could. But I didn't quite dare.

He's still there now, all covered up against the gulls, I hope. In the morning—I had to stop writing because Father just came in. He hardly ever comes into my room, so I knew at once that something was wrong.

"You all right?" he said, standing in the doorway. "What've you been up to?"

"Nothing," I said. "Why?"

"Old man Jenkins. He said he saw you down on Rushy Bay."

"I was collecting wood," I told him, as calmly as I could. "Like you said I should." Lying is so difficult for me. I'm just not good at it.

"He thought you were crying— crying your eyes out, he says."

"I was not," I said, but I didn't dare look at him. I pretended to go on writing in my diary.

"You are telling me the truth, Laura?" He knew I wasn't; he knew it.

"Of course," I said. I just wished he would go.

"What do you find to write in that diary of yours?" he asked.

"Things," I said. "Just things." And he went out and shut the door behind him. He knows there's something, but he doesn't know what. I'm going to have to be very careful. If Father finds out about the turtle, I'm in trouble. He's only got to go down to Rushy Bay and look. That turtle would just be food to him, and to anyone else who finds him. We're all hungry. Everyone is getting hungrier every day. I should tell Father. I know I should. But I can't do it. I just can't let them eat him.

In the early morning, I'll have to get him back into the sea. I don't know how I'm going to do it, but somehow I will. I must. Now it's not only the gulls I have to save him from.

September 9

I shall remember today as long as I live. This morning I slipped away as soon as I could. No one saw me go and no one followed me, I made quite sure of that. I'd lain awake most of the night wondering how I was going to get my turtle back into the water. But as I made my way down to Rushy Bay while the morning fog was lifting off the sea, I had no idea at all how I would do it. Even as I uncovered him, I still didn't know. I only knew it had to be done. So I talked to him. I was trying to explain it all to him, how he mustn't worry, how I'd find a way, but that I didn't yet know what. He's got eyes that make you think he understands. Maybe he doesn't, but you never know. Somehow, once I'd started talking, I felt it was rude not to go on.

I fetched some sea water in my hat and poured it over him. He seemed to like it—he lifted his head into it as I poured. So I did it again and again. I told him all about the storm, about Granny May's roof, about the battered boats, and he looked at me. He was listening.

He was so weak, though. He kept trying to move, trying to dig his flippers into the sand, but he didn't have the strength to do it. His mouth kept opening and shutting as if he was gasping for breath.

Then I had an idea. I scooped out a long, deep channel all the way down to the sea. I would wait for the tide to come in as far as it could, and when the time came I would ease him down into the channel and he could wade out to sea. As I dug I told him my plan. When I'd finished I lay down beside him, exhausted, and waited for the tide.

The gulls never left us alone for a minute. They stood eyeing us from the rocks and from the shallows. When I threw stones at them, they didn't fly off anymore. They just hopped a little farther away, and they always came back. I didn't go home for lunch—I just hoped Father wouldn't come looking for me. I couldn't leave my turtle, not with the gulls all around us just waiting for their chance. Besides, the tide was coming in now, closer all the time. Then there were barely five yards of sand left between the sea and my turtle, and the water was washing up the channel just as I'd planned it. It was now or never.

I told him what he had to do. "You've got to walk the rest," I said. "If you want to get back in the sea, you've got to walk, you hear me?"

He tried. He honestly tried. Time and again he dug the edge of his flippers into the sand, but he just couldn't move himself.

The flippers dug in again and again, but he stayed where he was. I tried pushing him from behind. That didn't work. I

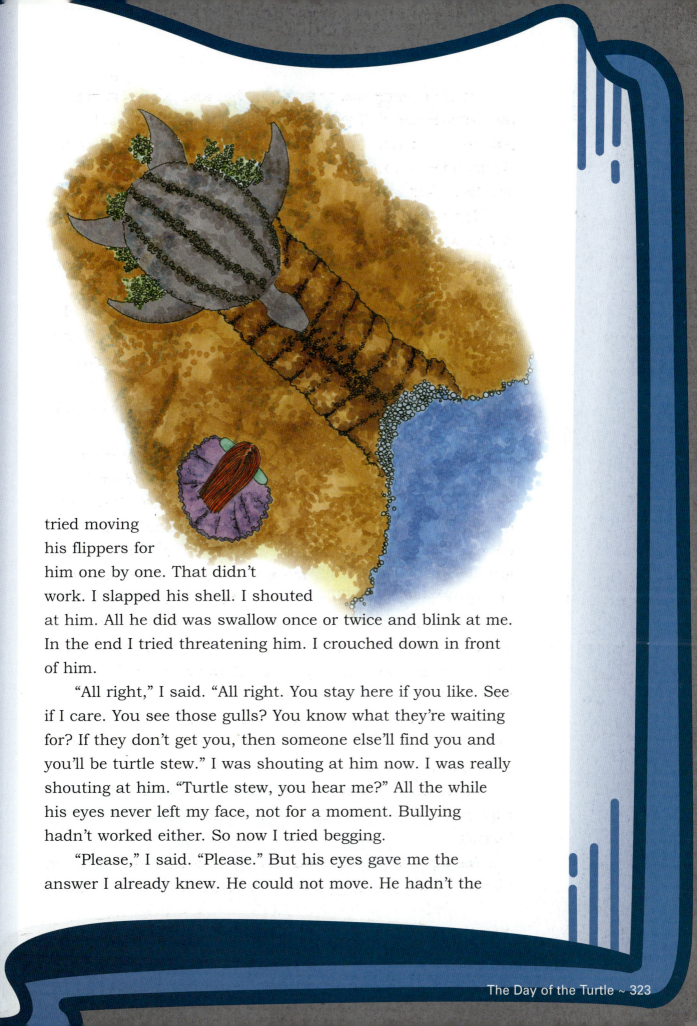

tried moving
his flippers for
him one by one. That didn't
work. I slapped his shell. I shouted
at him. All he did was swallow once or twice and blink at me.
In the end I tried threatening him. I crouched down in front
of him.

"All right," I said. "All right. You stay here if you like. See
if I care. You see those gulls? You know what they're waiting
for? If they don't get you, then someone else'll find you and
you'll be turtle stew." I was shouting at him now. I was really
shouting at him. "Turtle stew, you hear me?" All the while
his eyes never left my face, not for a moment. Bullying
hadn't worked either. So now I tried begging.

"Please," I said. "Please." But his eyes gave me the
answer I already knew. He could not move. He hadn't the

strength. There was nothing else left to try. From the look in his eyes I think he knew it too.

I wandered some way away from him and sat down on a rock to think. I was still thinking fruitlessly, when I saw the gig coming around Droppy Nose Point and heading out to sea. Father was there—I recognized his cap. Old man Jenkins was in Billy's place, and the Chief was setting the jibsail. They were far too far away to see my turtle. I came back to him and sat down.

"See that gig?" I told him. "One day I'm going to row in that gig, just like Billy did. One day."

And I told him all about the gig and the big ships that come into Scilly needing a pilot to bring them in safely, and how the gigs race each other out to get there first. I told him about the wrecks too, and how the gigs will put to sea in any weather if there are sailors to rescue or cargo to salvage. The strange thing is, I didn't feel at all silly talking to my turtle. I mean, I know it *is* silly, but it just seemed the natural thing to do. I honestly think I told the turtle more about me than I've ever told anyone before.

I looked down at him. He was nudging at the sand with his chin; his mouth was open. He was hungry! I don't know why I hadn't thought of it before. I had no idea at all what turtles eat. So I tried what was nearest first—seaweed of all sorts, sea lettuce, bladder wrack,[1] whatever I could find. I

---

1. *Bladder wrack* is the name of a common seaweed.

WORD BANK

fruitlessly (FROOT luss lee) *adv.:* unsuccessfully; with no useful outcome

gig (GIG) *n.:* a light boat rowed with four, six, or eight long oars

cargo (KAR go) *n.:* freight carried by a ship or airplane

salvage (SAL vuj) *v.:* to save from being destroyed or thrown out

dangled it in front of his mouth, brushing his nose with it so he could smell it. He looked as if he was going to eat it. He opened his mouth slowly and snapped at it. But then he turned his head away and let it fall to the ground.

"What, then?" I asked.

A sudden shadow fell across me. Granny May was standing above me in her hat.

"How long have you been there?" I asked.

"Long enough," she said, and she walked around me to get a better look at the turtle.

"Let's try shrimps," she said. "Maybe he'll eat shrimps. We'd better hurry. We don't want anyone else finding him, do we?"

And she sent me off home to fetch the shrimping net. I ran all the way there and all the way back, wondering if Granny May knew about her roof yet.

Granny May is the best shrimper on the island. She knows every likely cluster of seaweed on Rushy Bay—and everywhere else, in fact. One sweep through the shallows and she was back, her net jumping with shrimps. She smiled down at my turtle.

"Useful, isn't it?" she said, tapping him with her stick.

"What?" I replied.

"Carrying your house around with you. Can't hardly have your roof blowed off, can you?" So she did know. "It'll mend," she said. "Roofs you can mend easily enough. Hope is a little harder."

She told me to dig out a bowl in the sand right under the turtle's chin, and then she shook out her net. He looked mildly interested for a moment and then looked away. It was no good. Granny May was looking out to sea, shielding her eyes against the glare of the sun.

"I wonder," she murmured. "I wonder. I won't be long." And she was gone down to the sea. She was wading out up to her ankles, then up to her knees, with her shrimping net scooping through the water around her. I stayed behind with the turtle and threw more stones at the gulls. When she came back, her net was bulging with jellyfish, blue jellyfish. She emptied them into the turtle's sandy bowl. At once he was at them like a vulture, snapping, crunching, swallowing, until there wasn't a tentacle left.

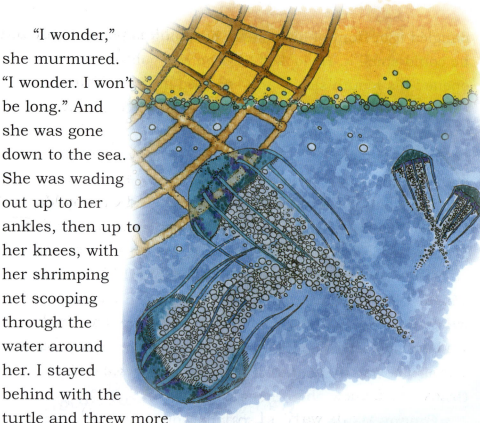

"He's smiling," she said. "I think he likes them. I think perhaps he'd like some more."

"I'll do it," I said.

I picked up the net and rushed down into the sea. They were not difficult to find. I've never liked jellyfish since I was stung on my neck when I was little and came out in a burning welt that lasted for months. So I kept a wary eye around me. I scooped up twelve big ones in as many minutes. He ate those and then lifted his head asking for more. We took turns after that, Granny May and me, until at last he seemed to have had enough and left a half-chewed jellyfish lying there, with the shrimps still hopping all around it. I crouched down and looked my turtle in the eye.

"Feel better now?" I asked, and I wondered if turtles burp when they've eaten too fast. He didn't burp, but he did move. The flippers dug deeper. He shifted—just a little at first. And then he was scooping himself slowly forward, inching his way through the sand. I went crazy. I was cavorting up and down like a wild thing, and Granny May was just the same. The two of us whistled and whooped to keep him moving, but we knew soon enough that we didn't need to. Every step he took was stronger and his neck reached forward purposefully. Nothing would stop him now. When he got near the sea where the sand was tide-rippled and wet, he moved, faster and faster, past the rock pools and across the muddy sand where the lugworms leave their curly cases. His flippers were under the water now. He was half walking, half swimming. Then he dipped his snout into the sea and let the water run over his head and down his neck. He was going, and suddenly I didn't want him to. I was alongside him, bending over him.

| WORD BANK | **cavorting** (kuh VORT ing) *v.*: jumping and prancing merrily about |
| | **purposefully** (PUR puss full lee) *adv.*: seriously, with a goal in mind; determinedly |

"You don't have to go," I said.

"He wants to," said Granny May. "He has to."

He was in deeper water now, and with a few powerful strokes he was gone, cruising out through the turquoise water of the shallows to the deep blue beyond. The last I saw of him he was a dark shadow under the sea making out toward Samson.

I suddenly felt alone. Granny May knew it I think, because she put her arm around me and kissed the top of my head.

Back at home we never said a word about our turtle. It wasn't an arranged secret—nothing like that. We just didn't tell anyone because we didn't want to. It was private somehow.

About the Author

Michael Morpurgo was born in Albans, England in 1943. When he was twenty years old, he took a job teaching and discovered that his students loved to hear him tell stories. He began to write down his stories and soon became a popular author of children's books. Between 1974 and 2000 he wrote nearly seventy books for children and teens. He and his wife started Farms for City Children, a program in which children can stay and work for several weeks at one of three farms the Morpurgos own. The couple have three children and live in Devon, England.

Studying the Selection

QUICK REVIEW

1. On what day of the year does this story take place? How do you know?

2. What kind of turtle does Laura find?

3. To what does Laura compare the turtle's face?

4. As it turns out, what does the turtle need to eat to get strong?

FOCUS

5. In the story, who feels the same way Laura does?

6. Why is the story so suspenseful?

CREATING & WRITING

7. Has there ever been a time in your life when help came from some unexpected place? Tell the story in several paragraphs. If that has never happened to you, write about a time when you wished someone would help you, but no one did.

8. Make a table like the one below. In Column 1, list three actions Laura takes to help the turtle. Give the page and paragraph numbers where the action begins. In Column 4 describe the result.

How Laura Tries to Help the Turtle	Page #	Par #	The Result

9. You are going to draw a comic strip. Take a large sheet of paper and draw three rectangles for pictures. From the chart you just filled out, draw a picture of each action in each of the three boxes. Put a caption that describes the picture beneath each box.

IMAGERY

- An image is a picture, sound, or feeling put into words.

- An image can describe the way something looks, feels, smells, sounds, or even moves.

- Authors use images to help you picture something or someone.

- A strong image may remain with the reader long after the story itself has been forgotten.

THINK ABOUT IT!

1. In the first paragraph, the author uses many descriptive words to help create images. Look at the following images: *howling wind; delicate skin; barely visible moon; flickering candle; wet blanket of clouds.* Which image(s) tells you how something looked? Which tells you how something sounded? Which tells you how something felt?

2. In the following phrases, descriptive words are used to create an image. Change the descriptive words to create a new image. *The <u>ancient</u> building; the <u>scorched</u> landscape; a <u>fire-breathing</u> dragon; a <u>single wooden</u> chair.*

3. To what are the following compared in the story: the howling wind; the moon; fear? Do you know what this type of comparison is called?

Olive's Story

Outside, the wind howled like a pack of wolves on the hunt. Very faintly, through the howling, the princess heard a commotion below. Frightened but determined to be brave, she approached the open window. The fierce wind pelted her delicate skin with raindrops as she squinted into the darkness below. The moon, barely visible through the soaking wet blanket of dark clouds, was like a candle that might flicker out at any moment. Suddenly, a dazzling display of lightning turned night into day, and the princess could see the barrenness of the countryside all around the castle to which she had been taken. Every single tree seemed scorched as if by fire. Nothing green grew around the castle for what seemed like miles.

The great crack of thunder that followed made the princess jump back from the window, but as the thunder slowly rumbled away, the princess heard another, more terrifying, sound. A thump, somewhere deep within the bowels of the ancient building. Then another. A door creaked open, then slammed shut. Now heavy footsteps pounded the castle stairs. Fear shot through her like a sword thrust.

She had not seen her captor, but the scorched landscape surrounding the castle could mean only one thing: a fire-breathing dragon. If a creature capable of laying that kind of waste to his own land was now headed up the stairs to her cell, she was certainly doomed. Scanning the dark cell for a weapon, her eyes fell on a single wooden chair. Raising the chair high over her head, she smashed it down onto the cold stone floor, breaking it into a dozen pieces. One of the pieces, a chair leg, had splintered off, leaving a sharp point.

At that moment, the door to her cell burst open. Instead of a fierce dragon, before her was a tall knight, clad from head to toe in armor, shiny even in the darkness of the cell. The knight lowered his sword and flipped up his visor.

"Brother!" she said, running to him. "Thank goodness. I'm rescued!"

Blueprint for Reading

INTO . . . *Prairie Fire*

The Laura Ingalls Wilder books are beloved by children and adults alike. Why? They are a firsthand record of pioneer life. Although the stories are written by the grown-up Laura Ingalls, she tells them as though she were still the girl in the story.

The books are very satisfying because they are *true*—she was there and this is what happened. We read about a family in which everyone works hard. There can be great sadness, but their lives are, on the whole, satisfying, secure, and full of love. Mr. and Mrs. Ingalls show their goodness in everything they do.

EYES ON . . . *Vivid Images*

What is an image? Our dictionary says, *a mental picture of something not actually present.* A *vivid image* is a strong, clear picture that we see in our mind's eye.

Prairie Fire is full of images. In the first paragraph we read, *Baby Carrie was playing on the floor in the sunshine, and suddenly the sunshine was gone.* When you read this sentence, you see a picture: of the baby, the floor, the sunshine, and the darkness that remains when the sunshine is gone. A story's images may last only a moment, or may stay with you forever.

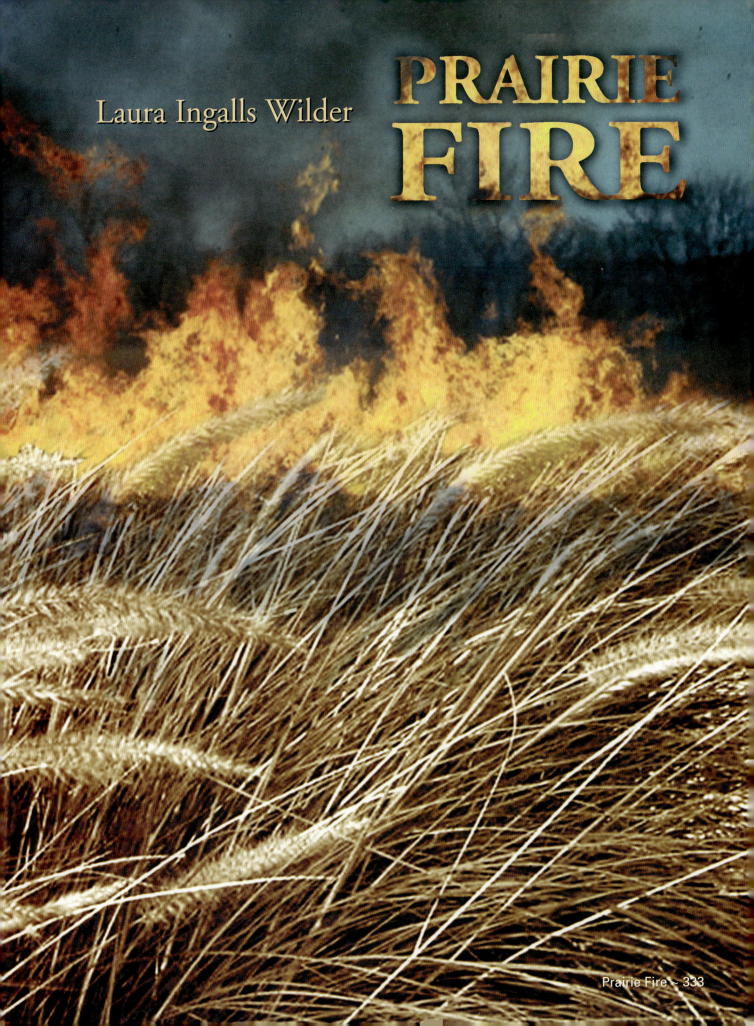

PRAIRIE FIRE

Laura Ingalls Wilder

One day Mary and Laura were helping Ma get dinner.
Baby Carrie was playing on the floor in the sunshine,
and suddenly the sunshine was gone.

"I do believe it is going to storm," Ma said, looking
out of the window. Laura looked, too, and great black
clouds were billowing up in the south, across the sun.

Pet and Patty, the horses, were coming running from
the field, Pa holding to the heavy plow[1] and bounding in
long leaps behind it.

"Prairie fire!" he shouted. "Get the tub full of water!
Put sacks in it! Hurry!"

Ma ran to the well, Laura ran to tug the tub to it. Pa
tied Pet to the house. He brought the cow and calf from

---

1. A breaking *plow,* also called a prairie breaker, is a plow with a long
low moldboard (curved piece of iron) that is designed to cut a wide,
shallow groove. The plow's blade lifts the soil and turns it over.

WORD BANK	
billowing (BIL oh ing) *v.:* swelling and puffing out
bounding (BOWND ing) *v.:* leaping in great steps and jumps

the picket-line[2] and shut them in the stable. Ma was pulling up buckets of water as fast as she could. Laura ran to get the sacks that Pa had flung out of the stable.

Pa was plowing, shouting at Pet and Patty to make them hurry. The sky was black now, the air was as dark as if the sun had set. Pa plowed a long furrow west of the house and south of the house, and back again east of the house. Rabbits came bounding past him as if he wasn't there.

Pet and Patty came galloping, the plow and Pa bounding behind them. Pa tied them to the north corner of the house. The tub was full of water. Laura helped Ma push the sacks under the water to soak them.

─────────
2. A *picket* is a pointed post or peg driven deep into the ground. An animal can be tied to the post by a long rope or *picket line*. This permits the animal to move around while preventing it from running away.

WORD BANK　　**furrow** (FUR oh) *n.:* a narrow groove made in the ground by a plow

"I couldn't plow but one furrow; there isn't time," Pa said. "Hurry, Caroline. That fire's coming faster than a horse can run."

A big rabbit bounded over the tub while Pa and Ma were lifting it. Ma told Laura to stay at the house. Pa and Ma ran staggering to the furrow with the tub.

Laura stayed close to the house. She could see the red fire coming under the billows of smoke. More rabbits went leaping by. They paid no attention to Jack, the dog, and he didn't think about them. He stared at the red undersides of the rolling smoke and shivered and whined while he crowded close to Laura.

The wind was rising and wildly screaming. Thousands of birds flew before the fire, thousands of rabbits were running.

Pa was going along the furrow, setting fire to the grass on the other side of it. Ma followed with a wet sack, beating at the flames that tried to cross the furrow.

WORD BANK **staggering** (STAG er ing) *v.:* walking unsteadily

The whole prairie was hopping with rabbits. Snakes rippled across the yard. Prairie hens ran silently, their necks outstretched and their wings spread. Birds screamed in the screaming wind.

Pa's little fire was all round the house now, and he helped Ma fight it with the wet sacks. The fire blew wildly, snatching at the dry grass inside the furrow. Pa and Ma thrashed at it with the sacks, when it got across the furrow they stamped it out with their feet. They ran back and forth in the smoke, fighting that fire.

The prairie fire was roaring now, roaring louder and louder in the screaming wind. Great flames came roaring, flaring and twisting high. Twists of flame broke loose and came down on the wind to blaze up in the grasses far ahead of the roaring wall of fire. A red light came from the rolling black clouds of smoke overhead.

Mary and Laura stood against the house and held hands and trembled. Baby Carrie was in the house.

WORD
BANK   **thrashed** *v.:* beat soundly; hit repeatedly

Laura wanted to do something, but inside her head was a roaring and whirling like the fire. Her middle shook, and tears poured out of her stinging eyes. Her eyes and her nose and her throat stung with smoke.

Jack howled. Pet and Patty were jerking at the ropes and squealing horribly. The orange, yellow, terrible flames were coming faster than horses can run, and their quivering light danced over everything.

Pa's little fire had made a burned black strip. The little fire went backing slowly away against the wind. It went slowly crawling to meet the racing furious big fire. And suddenly the big fire swallowed the little one.

The wind rose to a high, crackling, rushing shriek, flames climbed into the crackling air. Fire was all around the house.

Then it was over. The fire went roaring past and away.

Pa and Ma were beating out little fires here and there in the yard. When they were all out, Ma came to

WORD
BANK

quivering (KWIV er ing) *v.:* trembling; shaking

the house to wash her hands and face. She was all
streaked with smoke and sweat, and she was trembling.

She said there was nothing to worry about. "The
back-fire saved us," she said, "and all's well that ends
well."

The air smelled scorched. And to the very edge of the
sky, the prairie was burned naked and black. Threads of
smoke rose from it. Ashes blew on the wind. Everything
felt different and miserable. But Pa and Ma were cheerful
because the fire was gone and it had not done any harm.

Pa said that the fire had not missed them far, but a
miss is as good as a mile. He asked Ma, "If it had come
while I was in Independence, what would you have done?"

"We would have gone to the creek with the birds and
the rabbits, of course," Ma said.

All the wild things on the prairie had known what to
do. They ran and flew and hopped and crawled as fast as
they could go, to the water that would keep them safe

WORD
BANK   **scorched** (SKORCHD) *adj.:* slightly burned

from fire. Only the little soft striped gophers had gone down deep into their holes, and they were the first to come up and look around at the bare, smoking prairie.

Then out of the creek bottoms the birds came flying over it, and a rabbit cautiously hopped and looked. It was a long, long time before the snakes crawled out of the bottoms and the prairie hens came walking.

The fire had gone out among the bluffs. It had never reached the creek bottoms or the Indian camps.

That night Mr. Edwards and Mr. Scott came to see Pa. They were worried because they thought that perhaps the Indians had started that fire on purpose to burn out the white settlers.

Pa didn't believe it. He said the Indians had always burned the prairie to make green grass grow more quickly and traveling easier. Their ponies couldn't gallop through the thick, tall, dead grass. Now the ground was clear. And he was glad of it, because plowing would be easier.

WORD BANK   **bluffs** *n.:* cliffs

Pa said he figured that Indians would be as peaceable as anybody else if they were let alone. On the other hand, they had been moved west so many times that naturally they hated white folks. With soldiers at Fort Gibson and Fort Dodge, Pa didn't believe these Indians would make any trouble.

"As to why they are congregating in these camps, Scott, I can tell you that," he said. "They're getting ready for their big spring buffalo hunt."

He said there were half a dozen tribes down in those camps. Usually the tribes were fighting each other, but every spring they made peace and all came together for the big hunt.

"They're sworn to peace among themselves," he said, "and they're thinking about hunting the buffalo. So it's not likely they'll start on the warpath against us. They'll have their talks and their feasts, and then one day they'll hit the trail after the buffalo herds. The buffalo will be

<table>
<tr><td>WORD
BANK</td><td>congregating (KAHNG ruh gay ting) v.: meeting; assembling</td></tr>
</table>

working their way north pretty soon, following the green grass. By George! I'd like to go on a hunt like that, myself. It must be a sight to see."

"Well, maybe you're right about it, Ingalls," Mr. Scott said, slowly. "Anyway, I'll be glad to tell Mrs. Scott what you say."

Studying the Selection

FIRST IMPRESSIONS
If someone said something unfair or untrue about a group of people that everyone dislikes, would you speak up?

QUICK REVIEW

1. Which characters are introduced in the first paragraph?

2. Who are Pet and Patty, and what is Pa doing when he enters the scene?

3. What is Pa doing in the sixth paragraph? Make a list of his actions.

4. What are the rabbits doing, and why?

FOCUS

5. What do you think the story shows us about this family? Think of four phrases that describe something about the family.

6. List the ten images you thought were most vivid. Indicate the page number.

CREATING & WRITING

7. Write a paragraph about three of the Ingalls family's character traits. Then, bring examples from the story of those traits at work.

8. A writer brings a scene to life by using strong images. You could write a sentence such as this:

   My mother is cooking dinner.

   Or you could write a sentence like this:

   My mother is moving about the kitchen quickly trying to make dinner while she holds my baby brother tightly in her left arm.

   Now it's *your* turn. Write three sentences to describe three different scenes from your life. Write simple, boring sentences first. Then try to make your sentences vivid!

9. Find the passage you like the most. It should be about two paragraphs long. Practice reading it out loud. Read slowly, carefully, and loudly. After you have practiced several times, you are ready to read to the class.

PARAPHRASING

- Paraphrasing is putting something you have read or heard into your own words.

- Quotation marks are not used in paraphrasing.

- Even though you have changed the way something was written or said, you must still let the reader or listener know that the idea is not your own.

- When faced with a difficult piece of writing, paraphrasing it in clear, simple language will help you understand it.

THINK ABOUT IT!

1. In the phrase "I am one cup of sugar *shy* of what I need," what is the meaning of the word "shy"?

2. When Thomas "paraphrases" Mrs. Baker's words, what mistake does he make?

3. What is the difference between what Auntie Fay does and paraphrasing?

4. This humorous story could have been longer if the captain of the fire department had "paraphrased" Auntie Fay's words. What might he have thought she said, which would lead to another funny scene? Make up a line or two.

Cook and Ladder

Mrs. Baker, who was baking a cake, called her son, Thomas, into the kitchen. "Thomas, the oven's hot, but I am one cup of sugar shy of what I need. Please run over to Auntie Fay's and ask if you may borrow one cup of sugar."

Thomas ran down the lane to Auntie Fay's.

"Auntie Fay," he gasped. "Mother's feeling very shy, but the oven's already hot, so she sent me to ask for a cup of sugar so she can cook the batter."

Auntie Fay, who didn't hear very well, held her hand to her ear. "What'd you say, boy, speak up?"

"Mama needs a cup of sugar," shouted Thomas, "SO SHE CAN COOK THE BATTER!"

The old woman's face became very serious. "I'll take care of it right away." She took off down the lane as fast as she could to the volunteer fire department. She rang the alarm bell. "Mrs. Baker's oven is on fire," she shouted. "Quick— bring the Hook and Ladder!"

By this time, Thomas had quite forgotten about the cup of sugar. A squirrel had caught his eye, and Thomas had chased it into a tree. From his perch, Thomas saw the village's Hook and Ladder carrying the entire volunteer fire department toward his house! In the front seat with the captain was Auntie Fay. He was not sure what had happened, but he was pretty sure it was somehow his fault.

When Mrs. Baker heard all the commotion, she came outside, wiping her hands on her apron.

"Quick, out of the way, Mrs. Baker!" shouted the fire captain. "Where's the fire?"

"The only fire I know of is in my oven, where I've just about finished baking a cake," said Mrs. Baker.

The captain looked at Auntie Fay, who shrugged and looked at Thomas, who had come down from the tree and was looking very confused.

Mrs. Baker smiled. "No harm done," she said. "I was able to borrow some sugar from Mrs. Twickenham. The cake will be out any minute. Anyone care for a piece?"

INTO . . . *How to Bring Up a Lion*

Most children have some idea of how to bring up a baby. Many have baby sisters or brothers of their own, and most have observed babies being brought up at the homes of their friends and relatives. But how many people know how to bring up a lion? For that matter, how many people would *want* to bring up a lion? Would you?

EYES ON . . . *Paraphrasing*

Paraphrasing is taking what someone else has said or written, and repeating it or rewriting it in other words.

Paraphrasing can be very helpful when you are trying to understand what someone has written. You may have already tried your hand at paraphrasing to help you understand poetry. If there is a line or several lines you do not understand, you can look up the words in the dictionary, and rewrite the passage in your own words. When it is *really* hard to understand what an author has written, paraphrasing can be like translating from a foreign language!

How to Bring up a Lion

Rudyard Kipling

Now this is a really-truly tale.
It all truthfully happened,
and I saw it and heard it.

Once there was a
mother lion that lived in a cage
halfway up a mountain in Africa,
behind the house where I was living, and
she had two little baby lions. She bit one of
them so hard that it died. But the keeper in
charge of the cages pulled out the other little lion
just in time and carried him down the hill. He put him
in an egg box, along with a brindled[1] bulldog puppy,
called Budge, to keep him warm.

When I went to look at the little thing, the keeper said,
"This baby lion is going to die. Would you like to bring up this

---

1. A *brindled* (BRIN dld) animal is gray or brownish yellow with darker
streaks or spots.

baby lion?" And I said,
"Yes," and the keeper said,
"Then I will send him to your house
at once, because he is certainly going to
die here, and you can bring him up by hand."

Then I went home and found Daniel and Una,
who were little children, playing. I said, "We are
going to bring up a baby lion by hand!" and both
children said, "Hurrah! He can sleep in our nursery and
not go away for ever and ever."

Then Daniel and Una's mother said to me, "What do you
know about bringing up lions?" And I said, "Nothing
whatever." And she said, "I thought so," and went into the
house to give orders.

Soon the keeper came, carrying the egg box with the baby
lion and Budge, the brindled bulldog pup, asleep inside. Behind
the keeper walked a man with iron bars and a roll of wire
netting and some picks and shovels. The men built a den for
the baby lion in the backyard, and they put the box inside
and said, "Now you can bring the lion up by hand. He is
quite, quite certain to die."

The children's mother came out of the house with a
bottle, the kind that you feed very small babies from,
and she filled it with milk and warm water. She said,
"I am going to bring up this baby lion, and he is
not going to die."

She pulled out the baby lion (his eyes
were all blue and watery and he
couldn't see), and she turned

him on his back and
tilted the bottle into his little
mouth. He moved all his four little
paws like windmills, but he never let go of
the bottle, not once, until it was quite empty
and he was quite full.

The children's mother said, "Weigh him on the
meat scales," and we did. He weighed four pounds,
three ounces. She said, "He will be weighed once every
week, and he will be fed every three hours on warm milk
and water—two parts milk and one part water. The bottle
will be cleaned after each meal with boiling water."

I said, "What do you know about bringing up lions by
hand?" and she said, "Nothing whatever, except that this lion is
not going to die. *You* must find out how to bring up lions."

So I said, "The first thing to do is to stop Daniel and Una
from hugging and dancing around him because if they hug him
too hard or step on him he will surely die."

For ten days the baby lion ate and slept. He didn't say
anything; he hardly opened his eyes. We made him a bed of
wood shavings (they are better than straw), and we built
him a real little house with a thick roof to keep the sun
off. And whenever he looked at all hungry, it was time
for him to be fed out of the bottle.

Budge tried to make him play, but the little
lion wouldn't. When Budge chewed his ears too
hard, he would stretch himself all over the
puppy and Budge would crawl from
under him, half choked.

We said, "It is an
easy thing to bring up a lion,"
and then visitors began to call and
give advice.

One man said, "Young lions all die of
paralysis of the hindquarters."[2] And another man
said, "They perish of rickets,[3] a condition that comes
on just as they are cutting their first teeth."

We looked at the baby lion, and his hind legs were
very weak indeed. He rolled over when he tried to walk, and
his front paws doubled up under him. His eyes were dull and
blind.

I went off to find someone who knew about animals'
insides. "You must give him broth," I was told. "Milk isn't
enough for him. Give him mutton broth at eight in the morning
and four in the afternoon. You must also buy a dandy brush,[4]
same as they brush horses with, and brush him every day to
make up for his own mother not being able to lick him with
her tongue."

So we bought a dandy brush (a good hard one) and
mutton for broth, and we gave him the broth from the

---

2. A baby lion that is unable to move the back half of his body has
paralysis (puh RAL uh sis) of the *hindquarters*.
3. *Rickets* is a disease that may be found in both man and
animal. It is caused by lack of vitamin D and too little
exposure to sunlight. The disease causes the bones to
soften and bend.
4. A *dandy brush* is a stiff brush used for cleaning
horses.

WORD BANK	**perish** (PAIR ish) *v.*: die

bottle. In two days he was a different lion. His hind legs grew stronger, and his eyes grew lighter, and his furry, woolly skin grew cleaner.

We all said, "Now we must give him a real name of his own." We inquired into his family history and found that his parents were both Matabele[5] lions from the far north and that the Matabele word for lion was "umlibaan." But we called him Sullivan for short, and that very day he knocked a bit of skin off his nose trying to climb the wire fence.

He began to play with Daniel and Una—especially with Una, who walked all around the garden, hugging him till he squeaked.

One day, Una went out as usual and put her hand in Sullivan's house to drag him out, just

_____

5. The *Matabele* (mat uh BEE lee) people live in Zimbabwe, a country in southern Africa.

as usual, and Sullivan flattened his little black-tipped ears back to his thick woolly head and opened his mouth and said "Ough! Ough! Ough!" like a monkey.

Una pulled her hand back and said, "I think Sullivan has teeth. Come and look." And we saw that he had six or eight very pretty little teeth about a quarter of an inch long, so we said, "Why should we give up our time to feeding this monarch of the jungle every few hours with a bottle? Let him feed himself."

He weighed eight pounds, eight ounces, and he could run and jump and growl and scratch, but he did not like to feed himself.

For two days and two nights, he wouldn't feed himself at all. He sang for his supper, like little Tommy Tucker,[6] and he sang for his breakfast and his dinner, making noises deep in his chest, high noises and low noises and coughing noises. Una ran about saying, "Please let my lion have his bottle!"

Daniel, who didn't speak very plainly, would go off to the lion's den, where poor Sullivan sat looking at a plate of cold broth. He would say, "Tullibun, Tullibun, eat up all your dinner or you'll be hungry."

---

6. The author is referring to the line "Little Tommy Tucker/ sang for his supper," from the well-known children's poem, *Little Tommy Tucker*.

WORD BANK	**monarch** (MAHN ark) *n.:* king; ruler

At last Sullivan made up his mind that bottles would never come again and he put down his little nose and ate for dear life. I was told that the children's mother had been out in the early morning and dipped her finger in mutton broth and coaxed Sullivan to lick it off. She discovered that his tongue was as raspy as a file. Then we were sure he ought to feed himself.

So we weaned Sullivan, and he weighed ten pounds, two ounces, and the truly happy times of his life began. Every morning, Una and Daniel would let him out of the den. He was perfectly polite so long as no one put a hand into his house. He would come out at a steady, rocking-horse canter that looked slow but was quicker even than Una's run.

He would be brushed, first on his yellow tummy and then on his yellow back, and then under his yellow chin where he dribbled mutton broth, and then on his dark yellow mane. The mane hair of a baby lion is a little thicker than the rest of his hair, and Sullivan's was tinged with black.

After his brushing, he would go out into the garden to watch Daniel and Una swing. Or he would hoist himself

WORD BANK

raspy (RASP ee) *adj.:* not smooth; rough and grating

weaned (WEEND) *v.:* ended the period of time when a baby was fed only milk; introduced the baby to solid food

canter (KAN ter) *n.:* an easy gallop

hoist (HOYST) *v.:* raise; lift

up on the porch to
watch their mother sew or he
would go into my room and lie under
the couch. If I wished to get rid of him I
had to call Una, for at her voice he would
solemnly trundle out with his head lifted and help
her chase butterflies among the hydrangeas. He
never took any notice of me.

One of the many queer things about him was the way
he matched his backgrounds. He would lie down on the
bare tiled porch in the full glare of the sun, and you could
step on him before you saw him. He would sit in the shadow
of a wall or slide into a garden border, and, till he moved, you
could not tell that he was there. That made him difficult to
photograph.

Sudden noises, like banging doors, always annoyed him. He
would go straight backward almost as fast as he ran forward,
till he got his back up against a wall or a shrub. There he
would lift one little broad paw and look wicked until he heard
Una or Daniel call him.

If he smelled anything in the wind, he would stop quite
still and lift his head high into the air, very slowly, until he
had quite made up his mind. Then he would slowly steal
upwind with his tail twitching a trifle at the very end.

The first time he played with a ball he struck
it just as his grandfather must have struck at

WORD	**broad** (BRAWD) *adj.:* wide
BANK	**trifle** (TRY fl) *adj.:* a bit

the big Matabele oxen in the far north—one paw above and one
paw below, with a wrench and a twist—and the ball bounced
over his shoulder.

He could use his paws as easily as a man could use his
arms, and much more quickly. He always turned his back
on you when he was examining anything. That was a
signal that you were not to interfere with him.

We used to believe that little lions were only big
cats, as the books say. But Sullivan taught us that
lions are always lions. He would play in his own
way at his own games, but he never chased
his tail or patted a cork or a string, or
did any foolish, kitten tricks. He
never forgot that he was a

lion, not a dog or a
cat, but a lion.
When he lay down, he would
cross his paws and look like the big
carved lions in Trafalgar Square.[7] When he
rose and sniffed, he looked like a bronze lion, and
when he lifted one paw and opened his mouth and
wrinkled up his nose to be angry (as he did when we
washed him all over with carbolic[8] and water because of
fleas), he looked like the lions the old Assyrians[9] drew on
stone.

He never did anything funny. He was never silly or
amusing (not even when he had been dipped in carbolic and
water), and he never behaved as though he were trying to show
off. Kittens do.

He kept to himself more and more as he grew older. One
day I shall never forget, he began to see out of his eyes—really
see. Up till then his eyes had been dull and stupid, just like a
young baby's eyes. But that day—I saw them first under the
couch—they were grown-up lion's eyes, soft and blazing at
the same time, without a wink in them, eyes that seemed to
look right through you and out over all Africa.

---

7. *Trafalgar Square* is a public square in London, England. In
it stands a monument called Nelson's Column, surrounded
by four statues of lions.

8. *Carbolic* (car BAH lik) is a soap used as a
disinfectant.

9. The *Assyrians* were an ancient people who
lived in southwestern Asia.

Though he had
been born in captivity, as were
his parents, and though the only
home he had ever known was on the
slopes of the big Table Mountain where Africa
ended, we never saw him once look up the hill
when he lay down to do his solemn, serious
thinking. He always faced squarely to the north, to the
great open plains and the ragged, jagged mountains
beyond them—looking up and into the big, sunny, dry
Africa that had once belonged to his people.

That was curious. He would think and he would sigh,
exactly like a man. He was full of curious, half-human noises,
grunts and groans and mutters and rumbles.

He grew to weigh more than fifteen pounds when we had to
leave him. We were very proud of this, and triumphed over the
keeper and the other people who had said we could never bring
him up by hand.

"You've certainly won the game," they said. "You can have
this lion if you like and take him home and give him to the
Zoological Gardens in London."

But we said, "No, Sullivan is one of the family, and if
he were taken to a cold, wet, foggy zoo, he'd die. Let
him stay here."

WORD BANK	**captivity** (kap TIV ih TEE) *n.:* being held as a prisoner **triumphed** (TRY umft) *v.:* rejoiced over a victory

The End

ABOUT THE AUTHOR

Rudyard Kipling was born in 1865 in Bombay, India. When he was six years old, his English parents sent him back to England for his schooling. Even as a schoolboy he wrote poems and essays. By the time he was 22, he had published seven volumes of short stories. Kipling wrote about English people who lived in India, about Indian natives, and about British soldiers in many countries. He also wrote many popular children's books and poems, including *The Jungle Books, Captains Courageous,* and *Kim.* He was the first English writer to receive the Nobel Prize for Literature. Rudyard Kipling died in 1936.

Studying the Selection

QUICK REVIEW

1. What is the first sentence of the story?

2. Where did the mother lion live?

3. How did the keeper carry the baby lion down the hill?

4. What did the keeper say?

FOCUS

5. In what ways does this story sound like a folktale or a fable? In what way does it sound like nonfiction?

   Paraphrase the fifth paragraph from the end of the story.

   (a) First look up the words you don't know, and write down their definitions and synonyms.

   (b) Break the long sentences into shorter sentences.

   (c) Write each of these shorter sentences in your own words.

CREATING & WRITING

6. Daniel and Una learned a lot about life's challenges from bringing up Sullivan. Can you name at least two lessons they learned? How does their final decision about Sullivan show their love for him?

7. What do you know about lions? Find five facts about lions in a book or encyclopedia. Write two paragraphs about lions, using the facts you have learned.

8. Draw a picture to illustrate your two-paragraph report on lions.

ESTABLISHING SETTING

- Setting, as we learned in Unit One, includes place, time, and mood.

- In a drama, the scenery and dialogue create the place.

- The scenery, costumes, and dialogue tell us when the drama takes place.

- The lighting, background music, plot, and dialogue create the mood.

THINK ABOUT IT!

1. In the story *Prairie Fire,* what tells you where the action takes place?

2. In the story "Rock Face," how does the reader identify the "place" of the action?

3. At what time of day, time of year, and period of history does "Rock Face" take place?

4. If you had to choose a "mood" for this story, which of the following would it be: scary; lazy; hurried; mysterious; exciting; easygoing. Explain your answer.

Rock Face

"I CAN'T DO IT!" Bill shouted down over his shoulder. His right foot dangled into the fifty feet of air separating him from his fellow campers. The toes of his left foot were jammed into a small crevice. Three fingers of his right hand clutched a small crag not more than an inch thick. Bill's left hand gripped his best hold—a handle of granite that stuck out a full five inches. For an experienced climber, a hold this easy and this high up would have felt like cheating. But Bill was no experienced climber. He was a first timer, and he was panicked.

"You're perfectly secure in the harness." The camp counselor's voice billowed up from below. "Just push off and let yourself drop. It's the only way down."

"I CAN'T. I'M SCARED."

The afternoon sun blazing into the canyon seemed to squeeze the water right out of Bill's body.

"Hang on, dude," said a voice. "I'm coming up."

Bill risked a peek over his shoulder. Pete?

Pete was a quiet, skinny boy from his school back home. He was often the last boy chosen when teams were picked, but here he was scaling the rock face like it was a staircase. Within minutes Pete was by his side.

"Alright, listen," Pete began. His voice was calm, authoritative. "We can climb all the way to the top, or we can drop."

Pete looked skyward. "I do some climbing back home, and I'm telling you, we're not going to get up those last thirty feet."

Bill just nodded. He couldn't hold on much longer.

"Let's drop together," Pete said.

"Okay."

"These ropes are secure," Pete said, tugging at his own harness. "Trust me. I've taken my share of falls. Without this harness, I wouldn't be here."

Bill nodded.

Pete reached his left hand out toward Bill. "Take my hand."

With his right hand, Bill clutched at Pete's as if it were a life preserver.

Pete smiled. "One. Two."

Bill took a deep breath.

"THREEEEEEEEE!" they shouted together as they pushed back from the rock face and fell to safety below.

INTO . . . *The Streets are Free*

In the play you are about to read, you will see that a group of children can work to make a change in the city where they live. How do they do this? What does the story say about politicians? About the press?

The Streets are Free seems to be based on events that actually occurred in Caracas, Venezuela. Children usually have to wait for adults to improve things. But in *The Streets are Free,* it is the children who start a project and work at it until it is a success.

EYES ON . . . *Drama*

A play is written to be performed before an audience. A play allows us to *see* and *hear* what is occurring. A play is divided into sections called acts. The acts are numbered: Act One, Act Two, and so forth. Every act is divided into sections called scenes. The scenes are also numbered: Scene One, Scene Two, and so on. The script of a play begins with a list of characters in the order in which they appear on stage. After the list of characters, the playwright describes the setting and props in italics, and may also give stage directions.

THE STREETS ARE FREE

In the hills above the city of Caracas, Venezuela, thousands of people live crowded together in neighborhoods called barrios. The children of the barrio of San José de la Urbina had a problem. More than anything else they wanted a place to play. *The Streets Are Free* is the true story of how they worked to make their wish come true.

CHARACTERS

Kurusa

Carlitos[1]	Guard	Cheo's Mother
Cheo[2]	Mayor	Carlitos's Father
Camila[3]	Reporter	(Children, Officials, Police
Neighbor	Cheo's Father	Officers, Mayor's Aide,
Librarian	Camila's Mother	and Photographers)

---

1. *Carlitos* (kar LEE toss)
2. *Cheo* (TCHAY oh)
3. *Camila* (kah MEE lah)

> **WORD BANK** **aide** (AYD) *n.:* an assistant or helper

SCENE 1

(The play takes place in the barrio of San José, a neighborhood at the edge of the city of Caracas, Venezuela. The play opens on a street in the barrio with the sound of a loud truck horn. Carlitos, Cheo, and Camila look to the right at an imaginary truck that has just passed by.)

CARLITOS. *¡Caray!*⁴ That was close!

CHEO. That truck nearly ran us over!

CAMILA *(Yelling to driver)*. *¡Epa!*⁵ Why don't you watch where you're going?

CHEO. I guess we can't play in the street.

CARLITOS. I thought the streets were supposed to be free.

CAMILA. Not for us, they aren't.

CHEO. Well, where else can we play?

CAMILA. Don't ask me.

CARLITOS. How about flying kites up on the hill?

---

4. *Caray* (kah RY) is a Spanish word that means "Gee! Gosh!"
5. *Epa!* (AY pah) is Spanish for "hey!"

CAMILA. Impossible. If we go up there, on the hill, the kites will get tangled in the power lines.

CHEO. And I don't feel like getting electrocuted.

CARLITOS. How about playing catch right here? Hey, Cheo! Catch! *(He throws a ball to* Cheo, *but it lands in a* Neighbor's *laundry basket.)* Uh-oh. *(He goes to get ball, and gets in the* Neighbor's *way.)*

NEIGHBOR. You kids get out! Go on! Scram! You're always getting in my way!

CAMILA. We can't help it! There's nowhere else to go!

NEIGHBOR. That's not my problem. I have my laundry to do! And after that I've got to go shopping at the market or I'll never get supper on the table! And after that...

CHEO. Come on, Camila. Let's just leave her alone.

(The Children *sit down on the steps of the library.)*

CARLITOS *(Gloomily).* There must be somewhere we can play.

CHEO. Maybe we can go to City Hall and ask the Mayor.

CAMILA *(Sarcastically).* Oh, sure. Do you really think the Mayor's going to listen to a bunch of kids?

CARLITOS. We can ask our parents to come with us.

CHEO. My parents are working.

CAMILA. So are mine. They're always busy.

CARLITOS. I guess mine are, too.

CAMILA. So much for that idea.

(They sigh and sit in silence. Librarian *comes out.)*

LIBRARIAN. Why all the sad faces?

CHEO. There's no place to play.

LIBRARIAN. Hmmm. You're right. *(Librarian sits down next to them.)* Did you know that this entire hillside, was once covered with forests, streams, and trails? The trouble is, our city grew up so fast that the streets and buildings just took over. No one had time to plan a playground.

CAMILA. Well, why doesn't somebody plan one now?

CHEO. I know a great place—that empty lot near the bottom of the hill.

CAMILA. That one with all the garbage and broken glass? Who would want to play there?

CARLITOS. If someone fixed it up it wouldn't be bad.

LIBRARIAN. What would *you* do to fix it up, Carlitos?

CARLITOS. Who, me? I don't know. Maybe if we planted those tall *apamate*[6] trees and some shrubs...

LIBRARIAN. Wait! You should write this down! I'll get a pencil and a pad of paper.

(Librarian *runs into the library.)*

CAMILA. What's the use of writing it down? Who's going to read it?

CARLITOS. Maybe the Mayor will!

CAMILA. Here we go with the Mayor again.

(Librarian *returns with paper and pencil.)*

LIBRARIAN. Here, Camila. I appoint you official list-maker.

CAMILA *(Sighing and taking the pencil and paper)*. Fine. Go ahead.

CARLITOS. Our playground should have swings and slides!

---

6. An *apamate* (ah pah MAH tay) is a tree that grows in Venezuela.

CHEO. And room to play baseball and volleyball and soccer.

CARLITOS. And tag, and hide and seek, and places to fly kites, and run around!

CHEO. And benches for our parents to sit and visit.

CAMILA. Slow down!

CARLITOS. And don't forget the *apamate* trees and shrubs.

LIBRARIAN. Don't you have any suggestions, Camila?

CAMILA. Yes. I suggest we forget the whole thing. What good is planning a park if we can't get our parents to help us?

CARLITOS (*Boldly*). We don't need their help. We'll go to City Hall by ourselves. We can round up all our friends...

CHEO (*Caught up in the spirit*). And we can make a banner!

CARLITOS. Right! It can say, "Give us a playground or else!"

LIBRARIAN. Maybe something a little less threatening would be better.

CHEO. What about, "We have nowhere to play. We need a playground"?

LIBRARIAN. Perfect. You can use the paint and crayons I have in the library.

CHEO (*Enthusiastically*). Great! Come on, Camila. You're good at making posters.

CAMILA (*Reluctantly standing up*). Fine, I'll help, but I'm telling you, you're wasting your time.

WORD BANK   **banner** *n.:* a large sign painted on cloth

SCENE 2

(The setting is in front of City Hall. Carlitos, Cheo, Camila, and their friends are marching in a circle. They are carrying the banner they made.)

We need A PLAYGROUND

CHILDREN *(Chanting)*. We need a playground! We need a playground!

GUARD *(Gruffly)*. I told you before. No one gets in to see the Mayor.
Especially not a bunch of kids off the street. Go home!

CAMILA. We need somewhere to play.

GUARD. Then go somewhere to play. But not here!

CHEO. The streets are free! We're not leaving until we see the Mayor.

GUARD *(Losing his patience)*. That does it. I'm calling the police!

(The Guard *blows a whistle. The* Children *continue to shout. Five* Police
Officers *enter. The* Children *stop chanting.)*

CARLITOS. The police!

CAMILA. *¡Que bueno!*[7] Now we'll have our playground in jail.

GUARD. Arrest these kids!

(Police officers try to grab the Children, *who run around trying to avoid
them. In the middle of the confusion the* Librarian *and several worried*
Parents *rush in.)*

LIBRARIAN. There they are!

_____

7. *Que bueno* (KAY BWAY no) is Spanish for "great!"

CHEO'S FATHER. What is going on here?

CHEO (*Pointing at the* Guard). He won't let us talk to the Mayor about our playground!

GUARD. These kids are disturbing the peace! (*To* Police Officers) Take them away!

(Police Officer *takes hold of* Camila's arm.)

CAMILA'S MOTHER (*Stepping forward*). Oh, no you don't. If you put a hand on these children, you'll have to arrest me, too.

CARLITOS'S FATHER. And me!

LIBRARIAN. And me!

(Children *and* Parents *cheer.* Police Officers *stand there, uncertain. Children begin to chant,* "We want a playground!" *The* Mayor, Mayor's Aide, a Reporter, *and* Photographers *appear at the door of City Hall.*)

MAYOR. What's all this ruckus? What is going on out here?

CARLITOS. It's the mayor!

GUARD. Your Honor, these people are starting a riot.

CHEO'S FATHER. They're trying to arrest our children!

CHEO. We need a playground!

MAYOR. ¡Un momento!⁸ Wait a minute! One at a time!

LIBRARIAN. Let the children speak first.

REPORTER. Yes, I would be very interested to hear what they have to say. (Reporter *takes out notebook and pen.*)

CHEO. We came to ask you for a playground.

CAMILA. The barrio of San José is too crowded!

---

8. *Un momento* (OON moe MENT oh) means "just a moment!" in Spanish.

WORD BANK

ruckus (RUCK iss) *n.:* uproar; a noisy commotion

riot (RY itt) *n.:* a noisy, violent public disorder caused by a crowd of people

CARLITOS. The streets are dangerous. There are too many cars and trucks.

CAMILA. But the streets are the only place we have!

CARLITOS. We just want a place to play baseball and volleyball and soccer and fly kites.

CHEO *(Cheerfully)*. That's all.

MAYOR. A playground. Hmmmmm. *(To Aide)* Is there a space for them to have a playground?

CARLITOS. *¡Si!*[9] We know the perfect place!

CHEO. It's an empty lot at the bottom of the hill.

CARLITOS. It's beautiful!

CAMILA *(Amazed)*. You think that empty lot is *beautiful?*

CHEO. Well, with a little work, it could be beautiful.

CARLITOS. We even made a list. (Carlitos *begins reading from the list.*) It should have apamate trees and shrubs and flowers and benches and a field for playing.

REPORTER *(While writing in pad)*. You children have been doing your homework.

MAYOR. Hmmmm. "Mayor Builds Playground for City Children." *(The* Mayor *smiles.)* I like the sound of that. *¡Si!* I'll look into it first thing tomorrow. Remember, I am always here to serve you. Now, line up and I'll let you shake my hand. Then you can leave.

(The Mayor *shakes everyone's hand and leaves, along with* Aide.*)*

REPORTER. I'd like to take a look at this playground of yours.

CHEO. Come on! We'll take you there!

(Cheo, Reporter, and Photographers *leave.)*

CARLITOS. Isn't it great, Camila? We've practically done it!

CAMILA. I'll bet nothing happens. Just you wait and see.

(Carlitos and Camila *follow after* Cheo.*)*

---

9. *Si* (SEE) is Spanish for "yes."

SCENE 3

(The setting is the vacant lot at the bottom of the hill. It is one week later. The lot is scattered with garbage. Carlitos, Cheo, and Camila are standing at the edge of the lot.)

CAMILA. I told you nothing would happen. Check it out. This lot is the same ugly garbage dump that it was one week ago.

CHEO (Discouraged). And after all that work we did. The banner, the list, the marching...

CARLITOS. Maybe we should have made the banner bigger.

(The Librarian rushes in, waving a newspaper.)

LIBRARIAN. Hey, you three! Take a look at this!

CARLITOS. ?Qué pasa?[10]

CAMILA. What is it?

LIBRARIAN. Today's newspaper. Read the front page.

CHEO (Reads from newspaper). "Children of San José take on City Hall. They demand park, but Mayor doesn't budge."

CHEO. The children of San José! That's us!

CARLITOS. We're famous!

CHEO (Laughing). Look at this picture of the Mayor. He looks as if he just swallowed an arepa.[11]

CARLITOS. And there's me, right behind him. Look, Camila.

CAMILA (Glancing at the paper and speaking sarcastically). Ah, sí. That's a nice picture of the back of your head, Carlitos.

CARLITOS. At least the back of my head is in the newspaper.

CHEO. We're all in the newspaper! They'll have to take us seriously now.

CAMILA. Come on, Cheo, wake up. They're still not going to do anything.

LIBRARIAN. You may be wrong, Camila. Look who's coming.

(The Mayor enters, wearing a new suit. He carries a huge pair of scissors. His Aide, Officials, the Reporter, and Photographers are with him. The Aide carries a sign and a long red ribbon.)

---

10. Qué pasa? (KAY PAH sah) is Spanish for "what's going on?"
11. An arepa (ah RAY pah) is a cornmeal cake.

CARLITOS. *¡Beunos días!*[12] Mr. Mayor.

MAYOR *(To* Photographers)**.** Stand over there so you can get the whole picture. Hurry up now, we don't have all day.

CARLITOS *(Craning his neck)***.** What does the sign say? I can't see!

CAMILA. "This Site Reserved for the Children's Park of San José."

CHEO. You see, Camila? Everything's working out fine!

(The Officials *unwind the red ribbon and hold it in front of the* Mayor. *The* Mayor *takes out a piece of paper, clears his throat, and reads.)*

MAYOR. *Señoras señores.* The children of San José are unhappy. And when the children are unhappy, I am unhappy.

CAMILA *(Rolling her eyes)***.** Oh, give me a break.

MAYOR. My friends, the barrio of San José has become too crowded! The streets are dangerous. But the streets are the only place the children have to play!

CAMILA. Wait a minute. Haven't I heard this somewhere before?

MAYOR. They need a place to play baseball and volleyball and soccer and fly kites.

CAMILA. He's saying the exact same things *we* said!

MAYOR. *Señoras y señores,* the children need a playground. And I intend to give them one.

(Light applause, mostly from Aide *and* Officials.)*

MAYOR *(Holding hands up modestly)***.** Thank you. My friends, I have come up with a wonderful idea. I am reserving this vacant lot for the children of San José. A playground will make the future brighter for you—and you—and you. (Mayor *points to the three* Children.) Now, turn around and smile for the cameras, children.

CAMILA *(Smiling a fake smile)***.** This is so silly.

*(Mayor *cuts the ribbon with the giant scissors. The cameras flash.)*

---

12. *Buenos dias* (BWAY noss DEE ahs) is Spanish for "good day."

WORD BANK   site *n.:* the place on which something is to be built

MAYOR. How about another shot of me with the children? *(To Children, as he poses)* Well, my young friends, are you happy with your new playground?

CHEO AND CARLITOS. Very happy, Mr. Mayor.

MAYOR. What about you, little girl?

CAMILA. New playground? *(Scornfully)* It still looks like a garbage dump to me. It just has a pretty new sign, that's all. You can't fool me. There's an election coming up. I'll bet after this ceremony you don't do anything.

MAYOR *(Embarrassed).* ¡Qué va!¹³ You have it all wrong, little girl! I'm always here to serve you! Now, line up and I'll shake your hands, and then you'll have to leave. I'm very busy!

(The Mayor hastily shakes some hands and then walks off with Photographers, Aide, Reporter, and Officials.)

LIBRARIAN. Well, children, it looks as if your hard work has finally paid off.

CARLITOS. Yes! We're going to get a playground!

CAMILA. Don't count on it.

---

13. *Qué va* (KAY VAH) means "not at all" in Spanish.

SCENE 4

(It is four weeks later. The sign the Mayor left has faded in the sun. The letters are barely visible. The lot is even dirtier than before. Camila kicks a can across the stage.)

CAMILA. I told them, I warned them, but they didn't believe me. Maybe they'll believe me now. It's been over a month. Where are the swings? Where are the playing fields? Where are the flowers? There's more garbage and junk in this lot than there was before our march! It's hopeless!

(Carlitos *enters.*)

CARLITOS. No, it's not, Camila!

(Cheo, *the* Librarian, *the* Children *and* Parents *of San José enter behind* Carlitos *carrying hammers, wood, trees, flowers, shrubs, paint buckets, and shovels.*)

CAMILA. What's going on?

CHEO'S MOTHER. We had a meeting last night.

CARLITOS'S FATHER. We decided to build the playground ourselves!

CHEO. Who needs City Hall?

CARLITOS. All it takes is a little teamwork!

CAMILA. Teamwork? Come on! No one ever cooperates in San José, not even to clean the sidewalks.

CAMILA'S MOTHER. Well, that's going to change. I brought some wood I had lying around.

CARLITOS'S FATHER. I have some flowers and a few saplings.

LIBRARIAN. I brought my shovel and some tools.

CHEO. And I made a brand new sign to put up over the old one.

WORD BANK   **saplings** (SAPP lings) *n.:* young trees

(*Cheo and* Carlitos *and some of the* Parents *hammer the new sign up. It says, "San José Playground. Everybody come and play."*)

LIBRARIAN. *Bueno*, what do you say now, Camila?

CAMILA. What do I say? I'll tell you what I say. (*Pause.*) I say—that I always knew we could do it!

(*Everyone cheers. People begin digging, planting, painting, and cleaning up as the curtains close.*)

THE END

ABOUT THE AUTHOR

Kurusa is the pseudonym (pen name; a name that is not the author's real name) of a Venezuelan writer and editor. She was born in Caracas in 1942 and spent the first few years of her life in Caracas, the United States, and Costa Rica. Currently, she lives in Caracas with her daughter, Daniella, and her two dogs. Kurusa is the president of a non-profit organization that publishes legends of the Pemon and Guajiro Indians of Venezuela. She also writes realistic stories about the difficulties children face growing up in Caracas.

Studying the Selection

FIRST IMPRESSIONS
Does the play sound realistic to you?

QUICK REVIEW

1. When the play opens, where are the characters?

2. What are the names of the children?

3. Who else appears in the play?

4. Why can't the children play on the street?

FOCUS

5. In the end, it is the parents (along with the Librarian) who help the children. Describe an incident in which someone in your family came through for you. You may also describe an incident in which someone else helped you out.

6. Since your class will be performing this play, make sure you know the pronunciation of the Spanish words, and their English definitions. If you include the word *barrio*, that's thirteen words.

CREATING & WRITING

7. In *The Streets are Free,* the Guard and the Police do not behave very nicely. Are you surprised by how they treat the children? In one or two paragraphs, describe how they could have been more helpful.

8. In many big cities, people live in apartment buildings and they have no backyards. Why are playgrounds and parks important?

9. You are the Photographer for the daily newspaper, *The Caracas Chronicle.* In your black and white "photo," show how the playground looks when the parents are finished. Don't forget to include the new sign in the photo and a caption at the bottom. (If you prefer, you can take a "before" picture!)

PULLING IT ALL TOGETHER

- Any story, fiction or nonfiction, if well written, will create a "place" in your memory.

- The mood, the images, and the setting may be remembered more clearly than the plot.

- For example, although you may not remember the details of *One Day in the Desert* (the story you are about to read), you will probably remember the heat, the desert, and the lion.

- This tells us that a good story is far more than just a plot.

THINK ABOUT IT!

1. Describe the setting of "Clean-up."

2. List five vivid images that are present in the story.

3. Paraphrase the story, telling only the plot.

4. Paraphrase the story, including setting and images. Which is more interesting—the answer to #3 or #4?

Clean-up

Bill and Pete had been best friends ever since Pete had climbed up the rock face at camp and helped Bill muster the courage to come down. Back home, they played ball, they rode bikes, and Pete had even taken Bill rock climbing. One day, Bill decided to take Pete to someplace very special. Every summer when his grandfather was alive, Bill and his grandfather had fished together on Tyson's Creek, but Bill had not been there in two years.

It was a perfect day, not a cloud in the sky. As they pedaled down the old dirt road toward the covered bridge, the fresh scent of pine filled their noses. Dumping their bikes near the bridge, they scrambled down the hillside to the creek, fishing poles in tow.

They were greeted by the stench of stagnant water and rotting fish. In the August sun, the creek was nearly dry. Bill's disappointment was deepened by the litter he could see strewn all along the creek bed. He and his grandfather always picked up any odd litter they saw when they were down here, but now with the water level so low, Bill could see that people used the creek as a dumping ground for all sorts of stuff: plastic soda bottles, bits of broken glass of all colors, string, even rusted tin cans.

Bill was crushed. "It really used to be a great place. Sorry."

Pete shrugged. "Let's clean it up."

So, they rode back to Pete's house, left their fishing rods, and returned to the creek with a wagon, a bunch of large plastic garbage bags, and work gloves. Before the afternoon was over, they had filled three large garbage bags.

The creek wouldn't be restored to its full natural beauty again until next spring, when the cleansing snow of winter melted and filled the creek bed to overflowing, but as the boys headed back into town towing the wagon behind them, Bill was filled with the satisfaction of a job well done.

INTO . . . One Day in the Desert

Walk outside your home on a spring day. All is quiet. Nothing is happening. True? False! Just below the surface, living things in the air, the trees, the grass, and the earth are running here and there to find food, seek shelter, fight enemies, and care for their young.

One Day in the Desert gives you a close-up view of a variety of animals, birds, and insects that live in the desert. Each starts the day by going about its daily routine. But today is the hottest day of the year, and suddenly, these creatures are in a life and death struggle for survival against the heat, the drought, and then—the storm.

EYES ON . . . Pulling It All Together

This story is not an ordinary one. Most stories have strong plots and character development, with a short description setting. In One Day in the Desert, the plot is simple and there is no character development. Setting, however, is very important. The desert—its dryness, its heat, its sudden turns of weather, its beauty, and its cruelty—is at the center of the story.

In this story, there is no good or evil, no reward or punishment. It is the story of the natural world, in which some creatures live and others die, as the world goes on: changing, yet still largely the same.

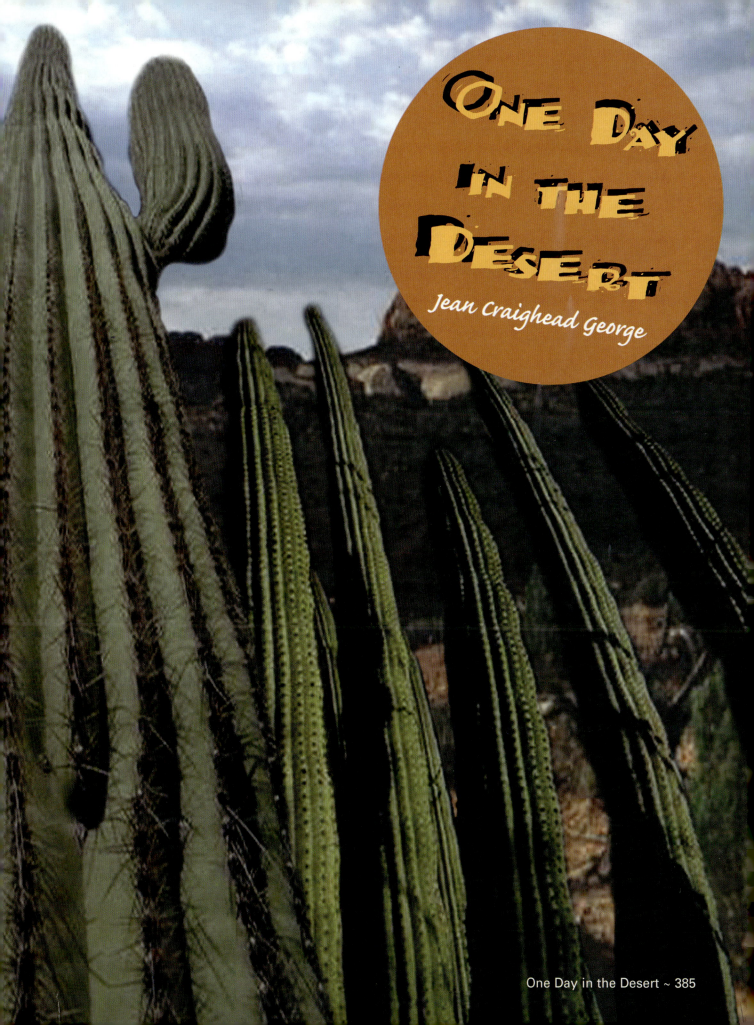

One Day in the Desert

Jean Craighead George

*Papago Indian Hut **

*Gila Woodpecker **

*Cactus Wren **

At daybreak on July 10th a mountain lion limped toward a Papago[1] Indian hut, a small structure of grass and sticks on the bank of a dry river in the Sonoran Desert of Arizona. Behind it rose Mount Scorpion, a dark-red mountain. In all directions from the mountain stretched the gray-green desert. It was dry, hot and still.

The cactus wrens began to sing. The Gila woodpeckers squawked to each other across the hot air, arguing over their property lines. The kit foxes who had been hunting all night retreated into underground dens. The bats flew into caves on the mountain and hung upside down for the day.

The lion was hungry and desperately thirsty. A poacher's bullet had torn into the flesh of his paw, and for two weeks he had lain in his den halfway up the mountain nursing his feverish wound. As the sun arose this day, he got to his feet. He must eat and drink.

The desert stretched below him. He paused and looked down upon the dry river called an arroyo. It was empty of water, but could be a raging torrent in the rainy season after a storm. He twisted his ears forward. A Papago Indian

---

1. *Papago* (PAP uh GO)

WORD BANK

retreated (rih TREE ted) *v.*: withdrew; drew back to a place of greater safety

poacher (POE cher) *n.*: one who hunts illegally on property belonging to someone else

torrent (TAW rent) *n.*: a huge, rushing stream of water

girl, Bird Wing, and her mother were walking along the bank of the dry river. They entered the hut.

The lion smelled their scent on the air and limped toward them. He was afraid of people, but this morning he was desperate.

Six feet (1.8 meters) in length, he stood almost 3 feet (a meter) tall. His fur was reddish brown above and white beneath. A black mustache marked his face. The backs of his ears and the tip of his tail were also black.

He growled as he came down the mountain, which was a huge clinker thrown up from the basement of the earth by an ancient volcano. Near its summit were pools where beaver and fish lived in the desert and which the mountain lion normally visited to hunt and drink. But today he went down, for it took less energy than going up.

The rising sun burned down from space, heating the rocks and the soils until they were hot even through the well-padded feet of the lion. He stood in the shade of a rock at 8 A.M. when the temperature reached 80 Fahrenheit (26.6 Celsius).

This day would be memorable. Bird Wing, her mother, the lion and many of the animals

Mountain Lion *

Long-nosed Bat *

Teddy-Bear Cholla *

Nevada Sagebrush

Agaves *

below Mount Scorpion would be affected by July 10th. Some would survive and some would not, for the desert is ruthless.

The Sonoran Desert is one of four deserts marked by distinctive plants that make up the great North American Desert, which extends from central Mexico to almost the Canadian border. The North American Desert covers more than 500,000 square miles (1,300,000 square kilometers).

All of the four deserts have one thing in common—little rain. Less than 10 inches (24 centimeters) a year fall on the greater parts of these deserts. The temperatures, however, vary from below freezing to the low 120s F. (about 50 C.).

Each one is slightly different. The Great Basin desert of Oregon, California, Idaho, Nevada, Utah and Wyoming—the most northern and the coldest—is largely covered with sagebrush, a plant that has adapted to the dry cold.

The Mojave[2] Desert of California is the smallest and driest, with less than 4 inches (10 centimeters) of rain a year. The teddy-bear cactus called cholla (choy-ya), a cactus so spiny

---

2. *Mojave* (mo HAH vee)

WORD BANK

ruthless (ROOTH less) *adj.:* without mercy; without any reluctance to do something wrong

distinctive (diss TINK tiv) *adj.:* unusual; having a special quality or style

it seems to have fur, dominates this desert.

The third, the Chihuahuan (chee-wa-wan) Desert, lies largely in Mexico. Only 10 percent of it is in the United States, in New Mexico, Arizona and Texas. On this desert the yuccas and agaves, or century plants, have adapted and grow abundantly, lending a special look to the land.

The fourth and most magnificent is the Sonoran Desert of Mexico and Arizona. Unlike the other deserts, it has two rainy seasons— showers in March and deluges in July and August. The rains nourish magnificent plants that support a great variety of creatures. The outstanding plant in this desert is the giant saguaro cactus, a tall plant that resembles a telephone pole with upturned arms. All the cacti—the saguaro, barrel, teddy bear and prickly pear—are unique to North America. They exist nowhere else in the world.

The North American Desert is dry because it is robbed of rain by the Pacific coast mountains. The clouds coming in from the ocean strike the high cold peaks and dump most of their moisture on the western side of the mountains. Practically no rain reaches the eastern side, which is in what is called the "rain shadow" by scientists.

Yucca *

Saguaro Cactus *

Prickly Pear Cactus *

Barrel Cactus

WORD BANK

dominates (DAHM ih nayts) *v.:* rules over; controls

adapted (uh DAPP ted) *v.:* suited by nature or design to a particular use or situation

deluges (DELL yooj iz) *n.:* huge rainstorms

Kangaroo Rat *

Coyote *

Ring-tailed Cat *

White-tailed Deer *

Kit Fox *

All deserts are lands of extremes: too hot, too dry, too wet. Yet they abound with living things that have adjusted to these excesses. To fight dryness, plants store water in their tissues or drop their leaves to prevent evaporation from their broad surfaces. They also grow spines, which do not use much water and which cast shadows on the plant to protect it from the blazing sun. They thicken stems and leaves to hold water.

The animals adapt by seeking out cool microclimates, small shelters out of the terrible heat. The microclimates are burrows in the ground where it is cool, crevices and caves in rocks, or the shade. Because of the dryness, the thin desert air does not hold heat. Shady spots can be 20 F. (11 C.) cooler than out in the sun.

A few animals adapt to the harsh conditions by manufacturing water from the starch in the seeds they eat. The perky kangaroo rat is one of these. Others move in the cool of the night.

The coyote hunts in the dark, as do the deer, ring-tailed "cat" (cacomistle), desert fox, raccoon and lion. The honeypot ant, on the other hand, has such a tough outer skeleton that it can walk in extremely hot sunshine.

WORD BANK

abound (uh BOWND) *v.:* are filled or supplied with

excesses (EX sess iz) *n.:* extremes; unusually large amounts or degrees of something

burrows (BURR ohz) *n.:* holes or tunnels in the ground made by an animal

crevices (KREH viss iz) *n.:* long, deep cracks

On July 10th the wounded mountain lion was forced to hunt in the heat of the day. He could not wait for darkness. He made his way slowly down the trail toward the Papago Indian hut.

By 9 A.M. he was above the dwelling on a mountain ledge. The temperature climbed another degree. He sought the shade of a giant saguaro cactus and lay down to rest.

The scent of lion reached the nose of a coyote who was cooling off under the dark embankment of the dry river not far from the Papago Indian hut. He lifted his head, flicked his ears nervously and got to his feet. He ran swiftly into his burrow beneath the roots of the ancient saguaro cactus that grew beside the hut.

The huge cactus was over 100 years old, stood 75 feet (22.5 meters) tall and weighed more than 6 tons (5.5 metric tons). The last of its watermelon-red fruits were ripe and on the ground. Bird Wing and her mother were going to gather them and boil them in the water they had carried in buckets from the village. The fruit makes a sweet, nourishing syrup.

At 11 A.M. they stretched out on their mats in the hut. It was much too hot to work. The temperature had reached 112 F. (44.4 C.).

Raccoon *

Honeypot Ant *

Saguaro Cactus Fruit *

Roadrunner *

Peccary *

Paloverde Tree

The old cactus was drying up in the heat. It drew on the last of the water in the reservoir inside its trunk and shrank ever so slightly, for it could expand and contract like an accordion.

The mountain lion's tongue was swollen from lack of moisture. He got to his feet again.

A roadrunner, a ground-dwelling bird with a spiny crest and a long neck and legs, saw the lion pass his shady spot in the grass. He sped down the mountain, over the riverbank and into the dry riverbed. He stopped under the embankment where the coyote had been. There he lifted his feathers to keep cool. Bird feathers are perhaps the best protection from both heat and cold, for they form dead air space, and dead air is one of the best insulations.

The roadrunner passed a family of seven peccaries, piglike animals with coarse coats, tusks and almost no tails. They stay alive in the dry desert by eating the water-storing prickly pear cactus, spines and all. They were now lying in the cool of the paloverde trees that grow in thickets. Like the pencil-straight ocotillo and almost all the desert leafy plants, the paloverdes drop their leaves when the desert is extremely hot and dry. On July 10th they began falling faster and faster.

WORD
BANK

reservoir (REZ urv WAHR) *n.:* a place where water is stored

The scent of the lion reached the old boar. He lifted his head and watched the great beast. The lion turned away from the peccary family and limped toward the Indian hut. All the pigs, big and little, watched him.

A warm moist wind that had been moving northwest across the Gulf of Mexico for a day and a night met a cold wind blowing east from the Pacific coast mountains. The hot and cold air collided not far from the Mexico-Arizona border and exploded into a chain of white clouds. The meeting formed a stiff wind. It picked up the desert dust and carried it toward Mount Scorpion.

As the lion limped across the embankment under which the roadrunner was hiding, the air around him began to fill with dust.

Near the coyote den dwelled a tarantula, a spider almost as big as a man's fist and covered with furlike hairs. She looked like a long-legged bear, and she was sitting near the top of her burrow, a shaft she had dug straight down into the ground. The hot desert air forced her to let go with all eight of her legs. She dropped to the bottom of her shaft, where the air was cooler. The spider survives the heat by digging underground and by hunting at night. The moist crickets and other insects she eats quench her thirst.

Ocatillo *

Tarantula *

WORD BANK

shaft *n.:* a passageway leading deep into the ground

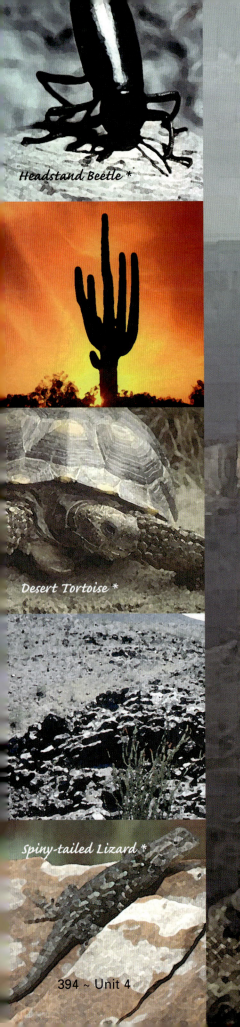

Headstand Beetle *

Desert Tortoise *

Spiny-tailed Lizard *

A headstand beetle felt the heat of the day and became uncomfortable. He stopped hunting in the grass and scurried into the entrance of the tarantula hole. He was not afraid of the spider, with her poison fangs that kill prey, but he was wary of her. Hearing the spider coming up her shaft to see who was there, the headstand beetle got ready to fend her off. He stood on his head, aimed his rear end and mixed chemicals in his abdomen. The tarantula rushed at him and lifted her fangs. The headstand beetle shot a blistering-hot stream of a quinonoid chemical at the spider. She writhed and dropped to the bottom of her den. The headstand beetle hid under a grass plant by the tarantula's door.

The temperature rose several more degrees. At 12:30 P.M. a desert tortoise, who was protected from the heat by two unusually thick shells of bone, went on eating the fruit of a prickly pear cactus. He was never thirsty. The moisture from the plants he ate was stored in his enormous bladder, a reservoir of pure water that desert tortoises have devised over time to adapt themselves to the dry heat. The water cools the reptiles on the hottest days and refreshes them on the driest.

WORD BANK   **writhed** (RYTHD) *v.*: twisted and turned in pain

The temperature reached 117 F. (47.2 C.). At last the tortoise felt warm. He turned around and pushed up on his toes. On his short legs he walked to his burrow under the paloverde bushes where the peccaries hunched, their eyes focused on the lion.

Inside his burrow the tortoise came upon a cottontail rabbit who had taken refuge there out of the hot sun. The tortoise could not go on. The heat poured in, and to lower the temperature he plugged up the entrance with his back feet. On the ceiling above his head clung a spiny-tailed lizard and a Texas banded gecko, reptiles who usually like the heat. At 12:30 P.M. on July 10th they sought the protection of the tortoise's burrow.

The temperature rose one more degree. A cactus wren who had sung at dawn slipped into her nest in a teddy-bear cactus at the edge of the paloverde thicket. She opened her beak to release heat.

The peccaries heard soft sounds like rain falling. Hundreds of small lizards who usually hunted the leaves of the paloverde, even on the hottest days, could no longer endure the high temperature. They were dropping to the ground and seeking shelter under sticks and stones.

Texas Banded Gecko

Desert Cottontail Rabbit

WORD BANK   **labyrinth** (LAB uh rinth) *n.:* a complicated and confusing set of paths, through which it is difficult to find one's way

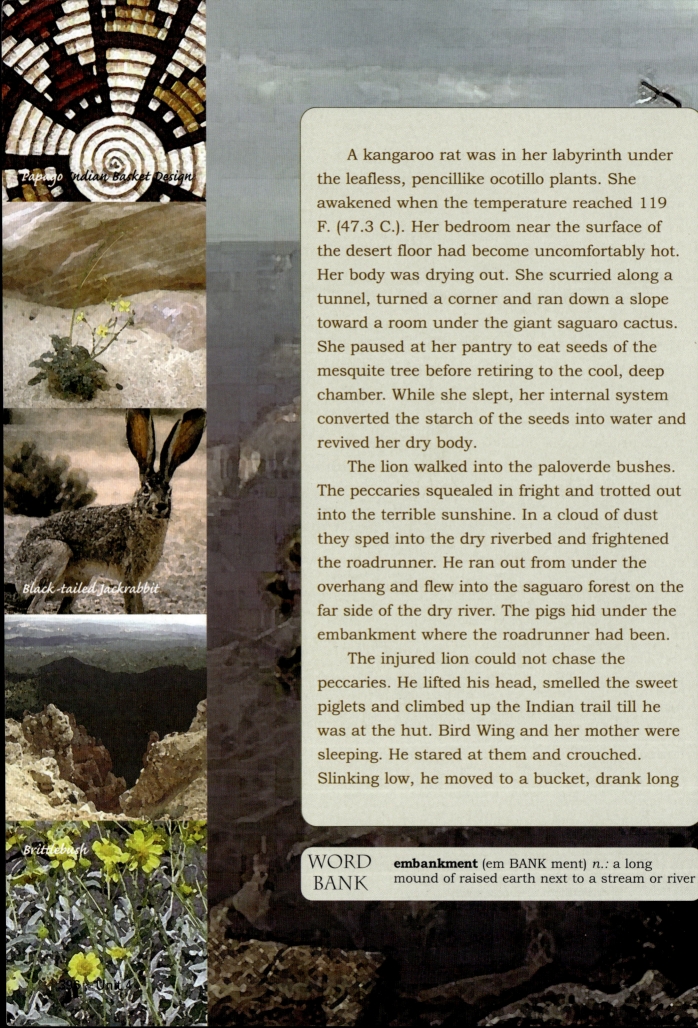

Papago Indian Basket Design

Black-tailed Jackrabbit

Brittlebush

A kangaroo rat was in her labyrinth under the leafless, pencillike ocotillo plants. She awakened when the temperature reached 119 F. (47.3 C.). Her bedroom near the surface of the desert floor had become uncomfortably hot. Her body was drying out. She scurried along a tunnel, turned a corner and ran down a slope toward a room under the giant saguaro cactus. She paused at her pantry to eat seeds of the mesquite tree before retiring to the cool, deep chamber. While she slept, her internal system converted the starch of the seeds into water and revived her dry body.

The lion walked into the paloverde bushes. The peccaries squealed in fright and trotted out into the terrible sunshine. In a cloud of dust they sped into the dry riverbed and frightened the roadrunner. He ran out from under the overhang and flew into the saguaro forest on the far side of the dry river. The pigs hid under the embankment where the roadrunner had been.

The injured lion could not chase the peccaries. He lifted his head, smelled the sweet piglets and climbed up the Indian trail till he was at the hut. Bird Wing and her mother were sleeping. He stared at them and crouched. Slinking low, he moved to a bucket, drank long

WORD BANK **embankment** (em BANK ment) *n.:* a long mound of raised earth next to a stream or river

and gratefully, then lay down in the doorway of the hut.

The temperature climbed one more degree. The birds stopped singing. Even the cicadas, who love hot weather and drum louder and faster in the heat, could no longer endure the fiery temperature. They stopped making sounds with their feet and wings and sat still. The Gila woodpecker flew into his hole in the giant saguaro. Below him, in one of his old nests, sat the sparrow-sized elf owl. He opened his beak and lifted his feathers.

Bird Wing was awakened by thirst. She tipped one of the water buckets and drank deeply. The desert was so quiet she became alarmed.

Clouds were racing toward Mount Scorpion. They were black and purple. Constant flashes of lightning illuminated them from within. She crept to the back of the hut and lay down beside her mother. She closed her eyes.

At 1:20 P.M. the temperature reached 121 F. (49.4 C.).

This hour on July 10th was the hottest hour on record at the bottom of Mount Scorpion.

Even the well-insulated honeypot ants could not tolerate the temperature. They ran

Desert Mistletoe

Elf Owl *

toward the entrance of their labyrinth near a pack rat nest by the hut. Some managed to get underground in the caverns where sister ants hung from the ceilings. Forager honeypot ants store the sweets from plants they have gathered in the bellies of hanging ants, some of which became as round as balloons and as big as marbles. The last two foraging ants ran across the hot soil to get home. They shriveled and died in seconds.

The peccaries under the embankment dug into the earth to find coolness.

The clouds covered the sun.

Instantly, the temperature dropped four degrees.

The tortoise shoveled more dirt into the mouth of his burrow.

The thunder boomed like Indian drums.

The kangaroo rat felt the earth tremble. She ran to her door, smelled rain on the air and scurried to a U-shaped tunnel. She went down it and up to a room at the top. There she tucked her nose into her groin to sleep.

The temperature dropped five more degrees. A rattlesnake came out of the pack rat's nest and slid back to his hunting spot at the rear of the hut. The cicadas sang again. The cactus

Rattlesnake *

Desert Lavender

wren looked out of the entrance of her ball nest in the teddy-bear cactus.

A thunderclap exploded sharply. Bird Wing awoke. She saw the lion stretched in the doorway. She took her mother's arm and shook her quietly until she awoke. Signaling her to be quiet, she pointed to the mountain lion. Bird Wing's mother parted the grass at the rear of the hut and, after pushing Bird Wing out, backed out herself.

The rattlesnake buzzed a warning.

The sky darkened. Lightning danced from saguaro cactus to saguaro cactus. Bird Wing's mother looked at the clouds and the dry arroyo.

"We must get out of here," she said. "Follow me up the mountain." They scrambled over the rocks on hands and feet without looking back.

Huge raindrops splattered onto the dust. Bird Wing and her mother reached an overhanging rock on the mountain. Lightning flashed around them like white horsewhips.

The thunder cracked and boomed. Then water gushed out of the sky. The rain fell in such torrents that Bird Wing and her mother could not see the dry river, the hut or the old saguaro. They sat quietly, waiting and listening.

Man-in-maze Basket Design

arroyo *

Ocotillo Flowers

A flash of lightning shot out of a cloud and hit the old saguaro cactus. It smoked, split and fell to the ground. The elf owl flew into the downpour. His wings and body became so wet, he soared down to the grass beneath the paloverde bushes. The woodpecker stayed where he was, bracing himself with his stiff tail.

The crash of the saguaro terrified the coyote. He darted out of his den under the tree and back to the dry riverbed. The peccaries dug deeper into the embankment. The roadrunner took to his feet and ran up the slope beyond the giant saguaro forest.

The rain became torrents, the torrents became waterfalls and the waterfalls cascaded out of the sky until all the moisture was wrung from the clouds. They drizzled and stopped giving rain. The storm clouds rumbled up the canyon above the dry riverbed.

The sun came out. Bird Wing and her mother did not move. They listened. The desert rocks dripped and the cacti crackled softly as they swelled with water. Cactus roots lie close to the surface, spreading out from the plants in all directions to absorb every possible drop of water. The roots send the water up into the trunks and barrels and pads to be stored.

Chuparosa

Spiny-tailed Iguana

Desert Lavender

A drumroll sounded up Scorpion Pass.

The peccaries heard it and darted out from under the embankment. They struggled up the bank and raced into the saguaro forest.

The lion got to his feet. He limped through the door.

The coyote rushed out of the dry riverbed. The wet elf owl hooked his beak around a twig of a paloverde and pulled himself upward toward higher limbs.

Water came bubbling and singing down the arroyo. It filled the riverbed from bank to bank, then rose like a great cement wall, a flash flood that filled the canyon. It swept over the embankment, over the hut, over the old saguaro cactus. It rose higher, thundered into the paloverdes and roared over the rocks at the foot of the mountain. It boomed into the valley, spread out and disappeared into the dry earth.

The coyote was washed out from under the embankment. He tumbled head over heels, swam to the surface and climbed onto an uprooted mass of prickly pears. On this he sailed into the valley and was dropped safely onto the outwash plain when the water went into the ground. Stunned, he shook himself and looked around. Before him the half-drowned

Willow Leaf Groundsel

Collared Lizard

Woolly Daisy

Zebra-tailed Lizard

Fishhook Pincushion Cactus

pack rat struggled. Recovering his wits, the coyote pounced upon him.

The lion was lifted up by the flood and thrown against a lump of ocotillo. He clung to it for a moment, then, too weak to struggle, slipped beneath the water.

The flash flood that had trickled, then roared, trickled and then was gone. The banks of the arroyo dripped. Bird Wing and her mother walked to the spot where their hut had been. There was no sign of house, pack rat nest, saguaro, or lion.

"But for the lion, we would be dead," said Bird Wing. "We must thank him." She faced the mountain and closed her eyes for a moment. Her mother picked up an ocotillo stick and turned it over in her hand.

"We will rebuild our house up the mountain above the flood line," she said. Bird Wing nodded vigorously and gathered sticks, too.

The kangaroo rat sat in her room above the U trap that had stopped the water from reaching her. She waited until the floodwaters seeped into the ground. Then she began to repair her labyrinth.

The peccaries came out of the saguaro forest and rooted for insects among the billions of seeds that had been dumped on the land by the flood. The land was greening, the sky was blue. The roadrunner came back to the saguaro forest, ran down a young snake and ate it. The cactus wren and owl did not call. The rattlesnake did not rattle. They had not survived the wrath of the desert on this day, July 10th.

Bird Wing walked to the arroyo edge. The earth trembled at her feet. She looked down. Plugs of sand popped out of the wet bank like corks. In each hole sat a grinning spadefoot toad, creatures who must grow up in the water. Then what were they doing in the desert? Waiting for just this moment.

They hopped into the brilliant sunshine and leaped into the puddles in the arroyo. Quickly they laid eggs and quickly they ate and dug backward into the sand with the spades on their feet. Far underground their skins secreted a sticky gelatin that would prevent them from drying up. In this manner they survived in the hot waterless desert.

The warm sunlight of late afternoon heated the water in the puddles, speeding up the development of the toad eggs. They must hatch into pollywogs and change into toads before the blazing heat dried up the puddles.

WORD BANK

wrath (RATH) *n.:* fierce anger

Spadefoot Toad

Pollywogs *

At 7:33 P.M. soft blue and purple light swept over the beautiful desert. In the puddles pollywogs swam.

Studying the Selection

FIRST IMPRESSIONS
How does the story make you feel?

QUICK REVIEW

1. Where does the story take place?

2. To what tribe of Indians did Bird Wing and her mother belong?

3. When the story opens, the mountain lion is injured. What has happened to him?

4. What is the name of the dark-red mountain that rises behind the Sonoran Desert?

FOCUS

5. Why does the mountain lion come down to the Papago Indian hut, when he is limping and feverish?

6. Who or what is the most important character in this story? Who or what do you think is the next most important character? Why?

CREATING & WRITING

7. Read through the story again and write down every reference to the saguaro cactus (with the page and paragraph number in parentheses). Now write two paragraphs about the saguaro cactus in the story. Begin with a description of the cactus. Then describe how it provides for the desert animals and people. Finally, describe how it is killed.

8. You are Bird Wing. You want to speak to tell the mountain lion that you are grateful to him for saving you from the flood. Write down what you want to say.

9. Draw a picture of the desert, the mountain lion, and the cactus.

Agaves

Most agaves bloom only once. They have large leaves arranged in a spiral along a small stem. They channel water down the thick, wax-covered leaves to the roots.

Headstand Beetle

Beetles have the funniest names! There is the telephone-pole beetle, the wrinkled bark beetle, the whirligig beetle, and the clown beetle, just to name a few!

Arroyo

An arroyo is a gulch with steep sides and a flat floor. It fills with water when it rains, but most of the time, it is dry.

Honeypot Ant

These ants survive in the desert by overfeeding some of the worker ants during the rains. In the dry season, the other ants feed off of the worker ants.

Cactus Wren

The cactus wren is Arizona's state bird. About eight inches long, it builds several nests in the giant saguaro cactus. It lives in one and uses the others for decoys!

Kangaroo Rat

These animals often fight each other by leaping in the air and slashing at each other with their powerful hind feet. When fleeing from danger, they jump like kangaroos.

Coyote

The coyote is a member of the dog family. In size and shape it is like a Collie dog. At night, coyotes howl to communicate with other coyotes.

Kit Fox

The kit fox is only about 15 inches long and is considered the second smallest dog in the world. It is among the fastest carnivores.

Desert Cottontail Rabbit

Tan or gray in color, this rabbit's tail looks like a ball of white cotton. When in danger, it raises its tail as a warning signal to other cottontails.

Long-nosed Bat

These brown or gray bats roost in caves, abandoned buildings, or mines. They feed on fruit, agave flowers, and the juice of the saguaro or organ pipe cacti.

Desert Tortoise

The desert tortoise is around a foot long. It can live in places with temperatures up to 140 degrees F. because of its ability to dig deep underground to escape the heat.

Mountain Lion

At one time found in all of North America, the mountain lion now exists only in the western states. The home range of the male is as much as 100 square miles.

Elf Owl

This is the smallest owl in the world. It comes out at night and leaves the U.S. during the winter. Its eyes are lemon yellow.

Ocotillo

An ocotillo is a desert shrub found in the American Southwest and Mexico. At the tip of each branch, it has a tight cluster of red flowers.

Gila Woodpecker

Each year, the Gila woodpecker makes a nesting hole in the stem of saguaro or cardon cacti. After it abandons the hole, other birds move in.

Papago Indian Hut

The Papago house was a rectangular hut made of adobe mud. The summerhouse was a shelter made of brush, built to give protection from the heat.

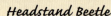

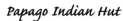

Peccary

The peccary is a wild, pig-like mammal. It weighs about 50 pounds, has gray or brown hair, boasts extremely sharp teeth, and smells like a skunk!

Prickly Pear Cactus

This cactus has yellow, red, or purple flowers. Its leaves are loaded with juice, but covered with thorns. Candy, jelly, and syrup are made from the juice.

Pollywog

A pollywog is a tadpole. These baby frogs have gills and tails like fish before they develop into mature frogs, which are amphibians.

Raccoon

Raccoons have a distinctive black robber's mask across the eyes and a black banded tail. They are known for their unusual habit of washing their food.

Rattlesnake

In the spring, the rattlesnake basks in the sun, but as the weather warms, it becomes more active at night. Its diet includes small mammals, birds, reptiles, and amphibians.

Ring-tailed Cat

The ring-tailed cat, or cacomistle, is a small, alert cousin of the raccoon with shorter limbs and soft thick fur. Its name means "nimble thief" in the Aztec language.

Roadrunner

The roadrunner is New Mexico's state bird. This comical bird prefers running to flying, is about 22 inches long, and eats insects, lizards, centipedes, mice, and snakes.

Saguaro Cactus

While a young saguaro takes nearly ten years to reach one inch tall, over time, it can grow up to fifty feet. A very old cactus can weigh over 8 tons!

Saguaro Cactus Fruit

In mid-April, buds appear on the saguaro. By early June, large white flowers appear, and then, bright red fruit. Each fruit contains about 2000 black seeds.

Spadefoot Toad

Using the spade on its hind foot, a spadefoot can quickly bury itself in loose, sandy soil. It burrows in the ground to avoid the heat, but the female comes up after a storm to lay eggs.

Spiny-tailed Lizard

This lizard tends to be nasty and not tamable. Juveniles are green, but within a year, they turn brown, gray, or black. They like temperatures near 100 degrees.

Tarantula

Tarantulas are large, hairy spiders, 1-3 inches long. Their abdomens are covered with poisonous stinging hairs. The tarantula can launch these hairs into the air at a target.

Teddy-Bear Cholla

This cactus is covered with long, sharp, shiny spines. The branches or "joints" break off easily and root to form a new plant. The flowers and fruit are green or yellow.

Texas Banded Gecko

This lizard is pinkish brown with bands of brown and yellow. It comes out at night to look for insects and spiders. The female is larger than the male.

White-tailed Deer

The white-tailed deer stands about 3 1/2 feet tall. Males, called bucks, weigh up to 400 pounds. Their antlers are shed each year and later regrow.

Yucca

Yuccas are in the Agave family. They have stiff leaves and creamy-white, waxy flowers.

Choose a Color

Jacqueline Sweeney

If I were brown I'd be cattail
or turtle deep burrowed
in mud.

If I were orange
5   I'd be a newt's belly.

If yellow a willow
in Fall.

If pink I'd be a flamingo
or salmon
10   leaping upstream.

If I were blue
I'd be glacier.

If purple a larkspur
in Spring.

15   If I were silver
I'm sure I'd be river
        moonshattered
in liquid surprise.

If I were green
20   I'd be rainforest,

tree canopied.

If green I would help
the world

breathe.

Beverly McLoughland

For Crows and Jays

I sing a song
Of thanks and praise
For cranky crows
And feisty jays
5   Who could have lived
A life of ease
Sailing on a southern breeze
But gave up warm and
Sunny skies
10 To stay behind and
Criticize
November's damp
And bitter cold—
With squawk, and
15 Bellyache, and
Scold.

One Day

One day is like another to a cow—
the long and languid grazing in the meadow,
the patient chewing of the cud,
the gazing out upon the world with quiet eyes—
5   the leisurely turning
of the whole green meadow
into a wide and flowing river of milk.

Beverly McLoughland

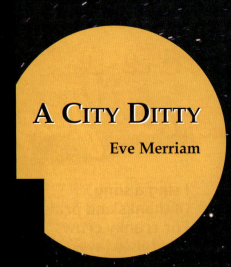

A City Ditty

Eve Merriam

Blackout in the buildings,
the big fuse blew;
no electric current,
what will we do?

5   Can't use the telephone,
can't make toast,
can't use the stereo,
boo, you're a ghost.

Frozen juice cans
10   getting runny,
frozen meat is
smelling funny.

Traffic signals out
and headlights on the cars,
15   but what do you know?
We can see the moon and stars.

Afternoon on a Hill

Edna St. Vincent Millay

I will be the gladdest thing
   Under the sun!
I will touch a hundred flowers
   And not pick one.

5 I will look at cliffs and clouds
   With quiet eyes,
Watch the wind bow down the grass,
   And the grass rise.

And when lights begin to show
10   Up from the town,
I will mark which must be mine,
   And then start down!

ABOUT THE AUTHORS

Author, poet, playwright, professor, speaker, radio writer, magazine editor, and conductor of a weekly radio program on modern poetry, **Eve Merriam** loved words, rhymes, and language throughout her life. Born in Philadelphia in 1916, Merriam moved to New York in 1937 and began to work as a radio writer. At the same time, she began to write poetry, first for adults, and then for children. Merriam's poetry presented her ideas on war, pollution, television, and many other issues. In all, Merriam wrote over 65 books for children and more than 25 books for adults. She died in New York in 1992.

Born in Maine in 1892, **Edna St. Vincent Millay** was raised by her mother, Cora Millay. Cora gave her children music lessons and urged them to excel at their studies. At first, Edna hoped to become a concert pianist, but then took up writing poetry. In 1912, a school director was so impressed when she heard Millay recite her poetry and play her own compositions for piano, that she promised to pay part of Millay's college tuition. Upon completion of her studies, Millay wrote book after book of poetry, becoming one of America's foremost poets. After an intense, emotional life, Edna St. Vincent Millay died in Steepleton, New York, in 1950.

Studying the Selection   POETRY

Choose a Color

1. What is this poem about? Answer in two or three sentences.

2. How many stanzas does the poem have? How many sentences? How are the sentences divided among the stanzas?

3. Where does the poet repeat words?

4. Where does the poet repeat the sound, *uhr*? (Spelling of the sound is not important.)

5. What is the strongest picture you have in your mind from the poem? (There is no single correct answer to this question.)

For Crows and Jays & One Day

1. What do *cranky* and *feisty* mean? Please use each word in a sentence.

2. Which words rhyme in *For Crows and Jays?* Which words rhyme in *One Day?*

3. How does a green meadow turn into a river of milk?

A City Ditty

1. What event has occurred in the poem that causes all of the other things to happen?

2. The poet seems, at first glance, to have made a mistake in the line "and headlights on the cars." After all, are car headlights affected by a blackout? Why might the scene described by the poet be true to life, in spite of what appears to be a mistake?

3. Write your own stanza about what happens in a blackout. The second and fourth lines should rhyme.

Afternoon on a Hill

1. The first two lines of the poem show us that the poet is excited and enthusiastic. A punctuation mark and one particular word are used to show the poet's excitement. Identify the punctuation mark and the word.

2. Why do you think the poet will not pick any flowers?

3. Can you give an example of opposites from the poem?

A GUIDE TO THE PLANTS OF THE SONORAN DESERT

1. There is a saying that *everyone has a book in them.* Hopefully you have more than one book in you, because you are about to make a book and you are only in fifth grade!

    a. Make a table like the one below.
    b. Write a list of **all** the plants mentioned in *One Day in the Desert.* Put them in alphabetical order. In the **Plant** column of your table, enter each of your plants.
    c. In the **Description** column, write down the information about each plant that you find in the story. Fill in the last column.

Plant	Description	Who Needs This Plant
saguaro cactus	can grow to be 75 feet tall lives more than 100 years has fruit	elf owls
ocotillo		
paloverde		

2. Draw a picture of each plant.

3. Using information from your table, write a paragraph about each of the plants you have drawn. Each paragraph should be on its own page, and pasted into your book opposite the plant it describes.

4. Now it is time to construct your book. What is going into your book?

   a. a front cover with the name of your book and the name of the author and illustrator
   b. a back cover with a very short biography of the author
   c. a Table of Contents that tells what is in your book and on which page it is located
   c. the table of plants that you have created
   d. your illustrations and information about three plants
   e. any other information you wish to add

   Count the number of pages you will need. With your teacher's help, construct a booklet with a front and back cover and the required number of blank pages. Paste the table, drawings, information, and all the other material you have prepared onto the blank pages. Decorate the cover and you have your very own book of plants!

WHO AM I? WHERE AM I?

You Have Come from One of the Stories in This Unit— and Ended up by Mistake in the Wrong Story!

1. Make a list of the stories.

2. Now, add to your list, the characters in each story: human, animal, insect, or spider. You may do this as a table, or make a very neat list.

3. Think hard. Who could you be and do a good job of it? You will need to get into the role of the person or creature and perhaps add some costumes or props.

4. Write some lines that you can say in front of the class. Although you will not be speaking to the class directly, they should be able to identify you by what you say. This is **Scene I.**

5. Now, write your **Scene II.** In Scene II, you have gotten lost in someone else's story. Think of ways you will be able to suggest where you are, with words, actions, and props.

6. Conclude your presentation by slapping your hand to your forehead— or making some other gesture of despair—and saying, "Where am I? How do I get home?" Don't be afraid to be very dramatic or very funny.

7. Remember, if the class cannot figure out who you are, where you came from, and where you have ended up, you will never be able to go home! But don't make it too easy for them!

DRAMATIC PERFORMANCE
Time for Reciting Poetry

1. This unit has five poems. Pick two poems and practice reciting them.

2. Now, take a tape recorder and record yourself reading the poem.

3. Listen to your tape of yourself. **Do not erase this recording,** no matter how awful you think it is. What do you think? Is it good? Is it embarrassing? How could you make it better?

4. Now you are going to record yourself again. **Do not erase your first recording!**

5. Listen to your second recording. Have you improved?

THE WORLD AROUND US

1. Go outside. Try to shut out all of the things that are man-made. What is left? What do you see? Now close your eyes for several minutes. What do you hear? What do you smell? If it is raining or snowing, or if the wind is blowing, or if the warm sun is beating down, what physical sensations do you have? Now, either remaining outdoors or going indoors, write down what you saw, heard, smelled, and felt.

2. Think about how each story and each poem in this unit is connected with the world around us. Select three of the stories or poems that you have not yet worked with in the Wrap-Up.

3. Now it is time to write several paragraphs. In your first paragraph you are going to say which works you have chosen. In paragraph two, three, and four, you will talk about how the world around us is described in each piece. Your final paragraph will be your summary.

unit 5

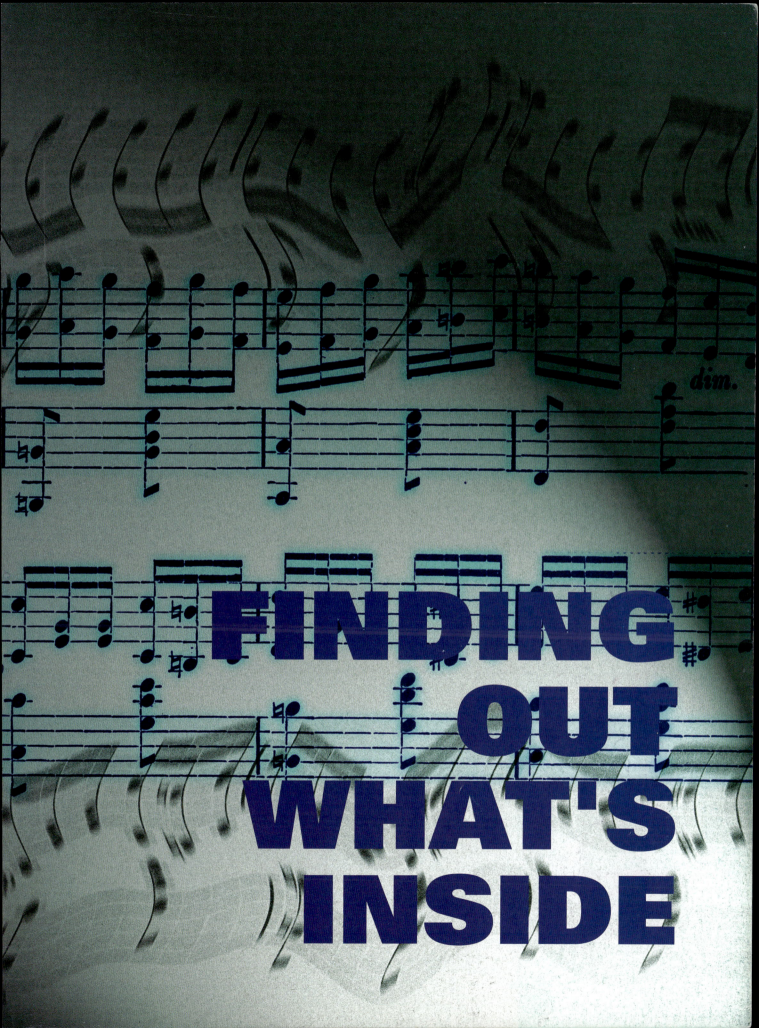

FINDING
OUT
WHAT'S
INSIDE

SYMBOL

- A symbol is an object or picture that represents an idea or feeling.

- Some symbols, such as a country's flag, have the same meaning for many people.

- Some symbols have meaning only to one or a few individuals.

- A symbol is a convenient way to express an important idea or feeling in a brief or simple way. It can take many words to say what one symbol says.

THINK ABOUT IT!

1. What picture does the name "Peter Rabbit" bring to mind?

2. Why did Peter have a special dread of this name?

3. What does a lion symbolize to you? Did it symbolize that to Tommy?

4. What does an eagle symbolize to you? Did it symbolize that to Peter?

I Am An Eagle

Only fifteen minutes into fifth grade, Peter was filled with dread. Peter suffered from a cleft palate, a mild deformity which had, from birth, left him with the characteristic scar right down the center of his upper lip. That, together with two tremendous buck teeth, had earned him the nickname "Peter Rabbit." All summer he had been filled with the hope that the move to the middle school would give him a chance to make a new start. But sitting across the room from Robert Adams—one of his cruelest tormentors from last year—Peter felt doomed.

And to make matters worse, Mrs. Mahoney was asking students what kind of animal they would be if they could become any animal at all. It was supposed to be a fun icebreaker, but to Peter it felt like a cruel joke. He was sure that by lunch time Robert would have spread the "Peter Rabbit" nickname to all his new classmates.

"I'm Tommy," one boy said. "I'd like to be a lion, because I am an excellent hunter. Last summer with my dad I—"

Peter barely heard a word. He was desperate to think of an animal, but he couldn't get "Peter Rabbit" out of his head.

I like model airplanes, he thought. What kind of animal likes model airplanes? And I like math, but animals don't use math, do they?

"Peter?"

It was Mrs. Mahoney. Peter's hands felt sweaty. His heart raced.

"What kind of animal would you like to be?"

He looked over at Robert. Robert was leaning back in his chair and staring out the window.

"An eagle." Peter surprised himself with the perfect answer. "I would like to be an eagle, because I love airplanes, and one day I would like to be a pilot."

"Thank you, Peter," said Mrs. Mahoney. "It's a pleasure to have you in my class."

Wow! Just like that. No one had laughed.

Peter looked at the boy called Tommy. Tommy smiled at him. Peter smiled shyly back.

Maybe fifth grade wouldn't be so bad after all.

Blueprint for Reading

INTO . . . The Memory Box

It may be hard to describe an experience.

Sometimes, this is because we don't have the right words. So here is a new word that describes the story, *The Memory Box: poignant.*

First of all, *poignant* is pronounced POY nyent. You don't say the **g**, and the accent is on the first syllable. The **ny** sound is just like the sound you make when you say *onion.*

Poignant refers to a story or an experience that affects your feelings. You feel pain, sadness, and, at the same time, sweetness.

EYES ON . . . Rite of Passage

All communities have ceremonies for major life events. In your community, what do people do when a baby is born? When a young person comes of age? When people marry? When a person dies?

What people do at these times are called *rites of passage.* A rite of passage is a series of actions that we perform with life-changing events. Everyone in a community knows these rituals.

Change is difficult, especially when it means suffering. Authors write about rites of passage, because they are central to our lives.

In this story, Gramps has Alzheimer's disease. As a rite of passage, the family creates a memory box.

The Memory Box

Mary Bahr

When I woke up this morning, I knew it was going to be a great vacation. Gramps was standing by my bed, holding the tackle box.

"Already too hot for catching walleye," he said.

"I bet Zach would like to throw out a line anyway, this being his first day," Gram argued from the doorway. She was holding a plateful of butter-dripping cinnamon rolls. As I said, it was going to be a great vacation. Three weeks of fishing Gramps's lake and eating Gram's cooking.

Now, from the boat, I could see Gram waving at us fishermen from the dock on the sky blue lake. Behind her on the hillside sat their berry red house in the middle of the dark green northern woods. The colors reminded me of a painting I saw once.

WORD BANK	**tackle** (TAH kuhl) *n.:* equipment for fishing, such as lines and hooks

Gramps and I rested our bamboo poles on the side of the boat. Our bobbers[1] rode the glittery waves.

"It's a Memory Box day," Gramps said as we waited for the perch to decide if they were hungry.

"What's a Memory Box?" I asked, dangling my hands in the cool water. I wondered if fish ever nibbled fingers.

"Remind me to tell you after the fish fry we're gonna have tonight. Now let's get quiet and catch 'em."

And we did. We got so quiet I could hear the fish circling our night crawlers.[2] But it still took three hours of sweaty, itchy stillness before we hauled in enough to fill Gram's skillet.

"Don't forget the Cook's Rule," Gram said as we unloaded our catch. We always cleaned ourselves and the fish in the lakeside shed. But every summer Gram reminded us, anyway! "Nothing but good smells at my dinner table," she'd say, pushing us back out if we tried to sneak in without washing first.

In the shed, for the first time ever, Gramps handed me the long filet knife, the knife that's about a hundred years old. The one I hope will be mine someday.

"I think you're old enough to handle the blade," he said, "and to hear the true tale of the Cook's Rule." He guided my fingers as I gutted my fish. "That first time I caught fish for Gram to cook, I brought them into the kitchen to clean. I don't think she was prepared for fish eyes staring back at her out of the sink. She screamed so loud I dropped the frypan and broke my toe. After that, the fish and I went to the shed."

---

1. A *bobber* is a small object that floats on the water. The fisherman attaches it to a fishing line to attract fish.
2. *Night crawlers* are earthworms, used here as bait.

WORD BANK	**hauled** (HAWLD) *v.*: pulled or tugged with force
	filet knife (fih LAY NYF) *n.*: a knife used to remove the bones of meat or fish
	gutted *v.*: removed the inner parts, such as the stomach and intestines

We laughed. Everybody knew Gramps usually made up most of his "true tales."

After dinner, we dragged our fish-full bellies to the porch to watch the sun slip into the lake. Crickets fiddled and owls hoo-ooted, but the rest of the world was quiet. All except Gram and Gramps and me in our rickety rockers on the wooden porch.

"Hmm-mmmm-m." Gramps was settling in, getting ready for another true tale. He's a great storyteller. Gram thinks so, I know, because she always puts down her cross-stitch[3] when he begins.

"It was your Great-Gram who told me about the Memory Box," Gramps said, staring at the sunset sky. "It's a special box that stores family tales and traditions. An old person and a young person fill the box together. Then they store it in a place of honor. No matter what happens to the old person, the memories are stored forever."

---

3. The first stitch learned in embroidery is usually the *cross-stitch,* which is a little, embroidered *x.* Here, the author calls the entire piece of embroidery that Gram is working on cross-stitch.

"What do you mean, 'no matter what happens'?" I asked Gramps. I didn't like his story much.

The sun practically disappeared before Gramps answered. "Do you know this old body just flunked a physical exam for the first time?"

Gram stopped rocking.

"This old person must make his Memory Box," Gramps said after a long silence. He stopped rocking, too, and looked me square in the eye. "Is this young person ready?"

"I guess. Sure." The words stuck in my mouth like caramel from a candied apple.

Gram disappeared into the house and made a pot-and-pan racket.

"Zach? The door, please?" she called through the screen. "I emptied an old recipe box so we can start *our* Memory Box," she said, handing me a treasure chest a pirate would love. "Now I'll leave my men alone."

My fingers traced the designs carved in the smooth, shiny wood.

"I gave that to your grandmother on our wedding day," was all Gramps said. Then we sat in the dark and watched the fireflies

dart past the porch. Maybe Gramps was already searching his mind for memories to put in the box. He never said.

But for the rest of my vacation, we remembered, Gramps and Gram and me. We especially remembered when we were fishing. "Thoughts come faster when bobbers are jumping," Gram said as she wrote our memories on paper scraps.

"How about the time I climbed the water tower?" I asked Gramps. "Mom said no, but you turned your back so I could make it to the top."

"You nearly fell off, as I recall." He scratched the whiskers that appeared on his face for the first summer ever. I wondered about those whiskers. Didn't Gramps tell me once how much Gram hated it when he didn't shave?

"How about the time I laid my freshly picked blueberries on the porch to sun-dry?" Gram remembered. "Zach came in from his swim and squished a path right through those juicy berries."

"Looked like an old blue rug to me," I said, remembering how Gram's face had turned red and my feet had turned blue at the same time.

It was Gramps's job to add photos and souvenirs to the Memory Box. He found a picture of my second birthday party when I had taken a bite off the top of the cake. There was a shot of Gram in her wedding dress with flowers in her hair and one of Dad in his football uniform when he still *had* hair. Another was of Gramps and Mom the day he had taught her to ride a bike. She had ridden it too. Right over his foot!

We added other important stuff, like my first soccer medal and Gram's chocolate-chip cookie recipe.

We added new memories too.

We wrote about the morning the three of us rolled green

WORD BANK   **dart** *v.*: move swiftly and suddenly

apples down the hill for a herd of deer that rested in the long grass.

And the time we watched a raccoon bandit watch *us* as she ate a trayful of cookies that Gram had set to cool on the picnic table.

And a picture of the trophy walleye[4] I caught the morning we put the boat on the lake before the sun even got up.

As the days passed, I noticed something different about Gramps. A major small change, if you know what I mean. One afternoon I saw him sitting in the swing that hung between two giant pines. I headed on over. But I stopped when I heard him talking to somebody else. Gramps was telling Francie how to reel in a northern pike that was fighting her hook. He was talking to

---

4. A *walleye* is a large fish sought after by fishermen. A *trophy walleye* is a walleye so big it deserves to win a prize or trophy.

WORD BANK | **bandit** *n.:* an outlaw, a robber

her as if she were right there. But nobody was. Especially not *Francie*—she's my mom.

And one afternoon we hiked to find nature stuff I could take back to school. Gramps wandered off the trail into a poison ivy patch as if he didn't even see it. I yelled until he stopped, but he wouldn't come back. I had to go get him and take him by the hand. That day it seemed like his body walked with me, but his thoughts strolled somewhere else.

None of it made sense until the morning Gram shook me awake.

"Get dressed, Zach. Help me find Gramps. He's been gone too long."

"Probably just fishing." I stared at Gram as if she were a crazy lady.

"But he forgot his shoes." She looked back at me as if *I* were the crazy one. "Check the shed. Whistle if you find him first."

I ran toward the lake, even faster when I saw the shed door swinging. But Gramps wasn't inside.

Outside again, I stopped to listen, the way hunters do. I thought I heard noises out back, so I circled the woods around the shed. When I found Gramps, I whistled loud. He was sitting on the ground like a scout[5] in front of a campfire. His feet were bare, and one was bleeding.

"Forgot my shoes." He tried to hide his face. It was shiny with tears.

Gram moved the fastest I'd ever seen. She sat on the ground beside Gramps while I ran back for his slippers. We helped him back to the house. Led him, if you want to know the truth. While we bandaged his foot and made him lie down on his bed, Gramps was quiet. We waited until the snoring began before Gram and I

---

5. Since Boy Scouts and Girl Scouts are trained to camp out, Gramps is compared to a *scout* when he is found sitting on the ground outside.

WORD BANK   **reel** *v.*: to pull out of the water by winding a fishing line around a small wheel or spool

tiptoed out of the room.

"Remember that first Memory Box night?" Gram asked. She sat in the kitchen. "Gramps was trying to tell you about Alzheimer's disease...when the body stays but the mind leaves."

She stared off, and I just waited until she looked at me again.

"The mind doesn't go all at once, or all the time, but it never comes back quite the same way. When Dr. Johnson suggested Gramps might have Alzheimer's, it explained so many things about this past year—Gramps forgetting to shave, his talking to me like we were kids again, his getting lost on trails he'd hiked for years."

I thought about the poison ivy and Francie's fishing lesson.

"It scares Gramps, knowing he'll forget. That's why the Memory Box is so important."

When Gramps woke up, he called me. I stood at his bedroom door. He sat on the bed.

"Did Gram tell you about this useless old man? And how he needs to find a home for special things like this?" He handed me the old fishing knife from the shed. "I forgot the sheath, so I went back...and got lost."

"Thanks," I whispered, holding the knife the way Gramps had taught me. My own, very first knife. I'd always wanted one. *This* one. But now it didn't seem so important.

"Your mom's going to hurt," Gramps said. "When it gets bad, bring out our Memory Box. Show her what I remember."

I hugged Gramps. We both felt better.

The rest of my vacation bolted like a fawn when you try to sneak too close. The day Dad and Mom came to take me back for school, we had such a great barbecue that we decided it should be part of the Memory Box. I could tell Dad already knew about Gramps because he shot a zillion photos of Gramps and Gram.

WORD BANK	**sheath** (SHEETH) *n.:* a close-fitting case for the blade of a knife or sword
	bolted *v.:* moved suddenly in a rush to escape

When it was time to leave, Gramps squeezed me hard.

Gram squeezed me soft. "Add things to the Memory Box you want Gramps to remember," she whispered as she handed it to me. "And bring it with you next summer. We'll need it, you and I."

I waved as our car drove away—away from the best and worst summer ever. This time Gramps and Gram had taken care of me. Next summer, Gram and I would take care of Gramps. And the summers after that...well, we'd figure out something.

As the car hit the top of the hill, I watched Gramps slowly disappear into the horizon.

And I hugged my Memory Box.

WORD BANK **horizon** (huh RI zun) *n.:* the place in the distance where the sky and earth appear to meet

About The Author

Born in Minnesota in
1946, **Mary Bahr** always
wanted to be a nurse. But in her
first year of training, a favorite patient
died suddenly. This upset her so much and
for so long that she realized she had to find
another career. In the years that followed, she took a
job as a librarian, married, and had four sons. Having
young children of her own made her recall her own
childhood. She began to write stories about and for children.
She has written four books and numerous stories and articles.
The Bahrs live in Colorado Springs, Colorado.

QUICK REVIEW

1. Where has Zach gone for his vacation?

2. Which two things does Zach imagine he is going to be doing for three weeks?

3. Describe his grandparents' house and its surroundings.

4. The first time Zach and Gramps go out in the boat, what kind of day does Gramps say it is?

FOCUS

5. What is the purpose of the memory box?

6. How is Zach forced to grow up in this story?

CREATING & WRITING

7. Why does the author write about something sad? In one or two paragraphs, explain why it is important to write about sad events as well as happy or thrilling ones.

8. Explain what a rite of passage is. In different cultures, children have different rites of passage. For example, a rite of passage of an Eskimo boy might be participating in a whale hunt for the first time. Find out about a culture different from your own, and write about the rite of passage of an imaginary boy or girl of that culture.

9. Create a collage using the kinds of things you would put in a scrapbook or a memory box: ticket stubs, school productions, photographs, parts of letters, printed words, vacation scenes.

LESSON IN LITERATURE . . .

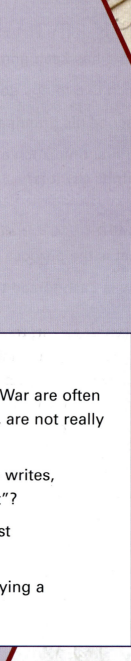

AUTHOR'S VIEWPOINT

- When reading nonfiction, ask yourself whether the story is completely true.

- Did the author write about the topic in a way that was too simple? It may be more complicated than it seems.

- Have all the facts been presented? The author may have left out "the other side of the story."

- Is the author's conclusion the only one that is possible? The facts may point to more than one conclusion.

THINK ABOUT IT!

1. What two statements about the Civil War are often made which, according to the author, are not really true at all?

2. What does the author mean when he writes, "The truth is more complex than that"?

3. How does the author disprove the first "oversimplified" statement?

4. How can an author avoid oversimplifying a true story?

The Truth, The Whole Truth, and Nothing But the Truth

In an effort to make the world understandable to ourselves, we often oversimplify complicated situations. For example, a typical student might say that slavery was a terrible *Southern* institution and that *in order to free the slaves,* President Lincoln led the North in a Civil War against the South. The truth is more complex than that. Let's look at the following statements.

Slavery existed only in the South.

Although we always connect slavery with plantation life in the South, slavery existed for a very long time in the North as well. For example, Philadelphia, the very city in which the Declaration of Independence was written, was itself a slaveholding city. By 1700, approximately one in every fourteen Philadelphia families owned slaves, and slavery was not officially outlawed in Pennsylvania until 1780. In 1789, slavery was written right into the U.S. Constitution as a fact of American life.

Lincoln freed the slaves.

It is true that in 1863, in the midst of the Civil War, Lincoln issued the famous Emancipation Proclamation, but most people do not realize that the Emancipation Proclamation did not free *all* slaves. It only freed slaves in the states that had seceded, or broken away from, the United States. In slaveholding states that had stayed with the Union (Delaware, Maryland, and Kentucky, for example), the Proclamation had no effect. In fact, Lincoln's goal in fighting the Civil War was to preserve the Union—to keep the country together—*not* to end slavery. Proclaiming the freedom of the slaves in rebelling states was a way to help win the war by weakening the South. Slavery was not officially outlawed nationwide until the 13th Amendment to the Constitution was passed in December 1865, eight months after Lincoln's death and the end of the Civil War.

If history is to help us understand our world better, good historians must look deeply into events, not just repeat simple explanations they have heard from others.

Blueprint for Reading

INTO . . . *The Greatest Snowball Fight in History*

This story is about a snowball fight that takes place on a battlefield. It is written in a style called *tongue-in-cheek.* Put your tongue in your cheek and look at your face in a mirror. Imagine you had this expression on your face as you were telling someone a story. Would that person take you seriously?

This story, though almost true, has a sly, humorous twist to it. In *The Greatest Snowball Fight in History,* words of war are used to describe a snowball fight. The reader wonders: is the author being serious? Did the soldiers feel like they were fighting a real war? You be the judge!

EYES ON . . . Historical Fiction

This story is historical fiction. Or is it? We *know* that the Civil War occurred. We know that generals named in the story were actual Confederate generals. The Battle of Fredericksburg was fought near the Rappahannock River in Virginia. *That* battle occurred on December 13, 1862. The Texas Brigade was there. There are diary entries and letters that describe snowball fights among the Confederate soldiers. But which generals were actually there? What was the actual date of the snowball fight?

This is what is so interesting about historical fiction: Part of it is true and part of it is not. But which is which?

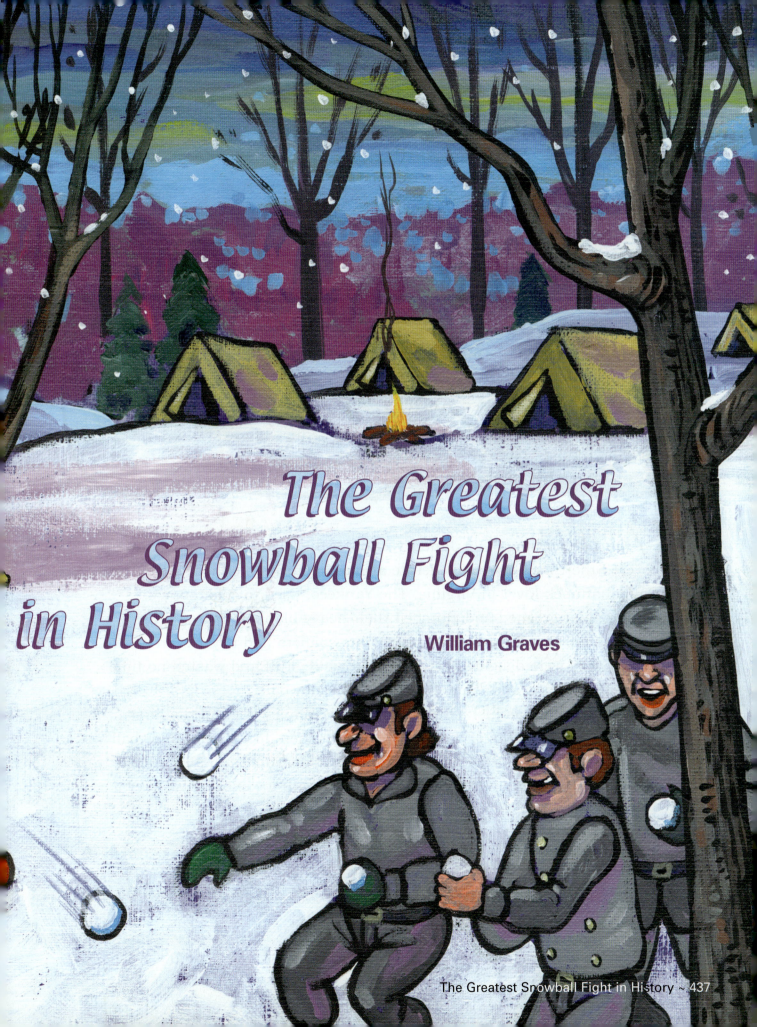

The Greatest Snowball Fight in History

William Graves

On the morning of 29 January 1863, a thick, wet blanket of snow covered the Union and Confederate armies camped on either side of the Rappahannock River in Virginia. The Yankees, used to cold, snowy winters, just groaned and clutched their heavy blankets more tightly about them. But many of the Confederate soldiers had never seen snow before; they were delighted with the cold white stuff and wasted no time leaving their huts and tents to throw a few snowballs.

It started out as just a small fight between a few men in the First and Fourth Regiments of the Texas Brigade. Then, like a giant snowball rolling down a mountain, the fight gained momentum until all the men in the two regiments were pelting each other with icy snowballs. After a

WORD
BANK

momentum (mo MENT um) *n.:* a feeling or energy that increases once the action is underway

regiments (REJ ih ments) *n.:* a unit of soldiers in an army; several regiments make up a brigade

while they joined forces to attack the still-sleeping Fifth Regiment and, with a murderous barrage of iceballs, charged their fellow Texans. The Bloody Fifth, never one to avoid a fight, counterattacked vigorously.

It wasn't long before someone yelled, "Let's get the Porkers!" and with a shout of laughter the fight expanded still further. Even the officers entered into it now; some of them directing the enlisted men in preparing a huge supply of snowball ammunition, others sending out scouts and forming the wings as the three regiments prepared to descend on the unsuspecting "Porkers" of the Third Arkansas Regiment (also part of the Texas Brigade).

General John Bell Hood, commander of the entire brigade, watched the Texans attack the boys from Arkansas, but he stayed neutral as his

WORD BANK	**barrage** (buh RAZH) *n.:* a heavy, prolonged attack
	vigorously (VIG uh russ LEE) *adv.:* energetically; forcefully
	brigade (brih GAYD) *n.:* a unit of an army having two or more regiments; several brigades make up a division

men fought it out with thousands of sailing snowballs. Then, smiling, Hood turned to his staff and whispered instructions.

A great cheer arose from the men as the brigade battle flag unfurled in the crisp winter air. Bugles, fifes, and drums sounded as Hood's staff hurried to carry out orders. The enlisted men followed their general's instructions and formed into battle array, stuffing their haversacks with snow and ice and packing plenty of snowballs to carry in their arms.

Then, led by General Hood himself, the laughing, stumbling Texas Brigade pushed through two feet of snow for a surprise attack on General G. T. Anderson's Georgia Brigade which was calmly eating breakfast.

WORD BANK   **array** (uh RAY) *n.*: an orderly grouping or arrangement, especially for troops

Studying the Selection

FIRST IMPRESSIONS

Can you explain why battle-hardened soldiers could take a snowball fight so seriously?

QUICK REVIEW

1. In which state did the snowball fight take place?

2. The armies of the North and the South were on opposite sides of which river?

3. Were soldiers from both the North and the South taking part in the snowball fight?

4. What was the Georgia Brigade called?

FOCUS

5. Why is this piece humorous?

6. Quote four phrases in which it sounds as if this fight were part of a real war.

CREATING & WRITING

7. Why is this piece sad?

8. Two Confederate generals, General Lafayette McLaw and Brigadier General William Barksdale were known to sometimes wander over to the Rappahannock riverbank at night and listen quietly to the Yankee bands playing. Write an imaginary conversation they might have had on one of those nights.

9. Make a shadow box of a snowy woods with snowy hills in the background. If you want, you can put the frozen Rappahannock River to the side or in the distance. Draw your soldiers on paper (the stiffer, the better) and cut them out. Leave a flap attached to their shoes (or boots) that you can fold and paste to the "ground," so that they will stand up. Do not use plastic figures. Make everything in this box yourself. Think about materials, such as cotton balls for snow, that will bring your scene to life.

THEME IN NONFICTION

- The theme of a nonfiction piece ties the story together.

- The theme is usually introduced in the first or second paragraph.

- The author will select facts that help the reader understand the theme. Facts that are not directly related to the theme will take away from the story.

- Often, the author will draw conclusions from the facts presented. The conclusions are opinion, not fact.

THINK ABOUT IT!

1. Read the first paragraph. What do you think will be the theme of this essay?

2. What does the Habitat for Humanity do?

3. Which of Jimmy Carter's qualities does the author mention?

4. What makes the last sentence a good concluding statement?

Jimmy Carter Builds a Habitat for his Fellow Man

It is easy to imagine that after occupying the office of President of the United States, perhaps the most powerful position in the world, it would be hard to find meaningful, satisfying work. However, since leaving office in 1980, Jimmy Carter, the 39th president, has made it look easy. He has established the Carter Center in Atlanta as a place where world leaders could meet—sometimes even in secret—to work out differences in a peaceful manner. But perhaps the work for which Carter has become most well-known since leaving office is his volunteering with Habitat for Humanity.

Habitat for Humanity is a non-profit, non-denominational (not limited to a particular religious group) organization which builds homes for needy people both in the United States and around the globe. Those who would like to be homeowners are not simply given a house, however. They work hard to help Habitat's volunteers to build it, putting in at least 250 hours of "sweat equity," a down payment made not in dollars but in hard work.

Always interested in the plight of the less fortunate, Jimmy Carter and his wife Rosalyn first got involved in Habitat for Humanity in 1984. "Rosalyn and I are proud to work for one week each year side by side with other volunteers and the families who will realize their dream of home ownership," Carter has explained. Indeed, since 1984 the Carters have dedicated one week each year to what has become the organization's biggest annual event, the Jimmy Carter Work Project.

In 1994, Carter's volunteerism hit a personal note, when a flood destroyed the home of Annie Mae Rhodes, then 77, who had been the Carter family's cook and housekeeper for 22 years. As soon as a Red Cross volunteer let Carter know Ms. Rhodes' home had been destroyed, Carter set to work on building her a new home. Despite her arthritis, Ms. Rhodes was able to participate in the construction.

Through his work at home and abroad, Jimmy Carter has set the standard for a meaningful life of service after retirement.

Blueprint for Reading

INTO . . . *Founders of the Children's Rain Forest*

Many people feel helpless to make the world a better place. Some say it's more important to help people than to help plants and animals or worry about the rain forest. But both are very important, and we can do both. We must have the water, the oxygen, and the weather patterns that the rain forest produces. *Founders of the Children's Rain Forest* is the true story of first- and second-grade students in Sweden who tackled a global problem: the worldwide destruction of the rain forests. These children are a model for us all.

Founders of the Children's Rain Forest

From *It's Our World, Too!*
Phillip Hoose

EYES ON . . . *Nonfiction and Theme*

It is clear from this piece that nonfiction can also have a theme. What is the message in this story?

Costa Rica

Arenal National Park

Monte Verde

Children's
Eternal
Rain Forest

It all began in the first week of school when Eha Kern, from the Fagervik School, in the Swedish countryside, showed her forty first- and second-grade students pictures of hot, steamy jungles near the Equator. It was there, she said, that half the types of plants and animals in the whole world could be found. She read to them about monkeys and leopards and sloths, about snakes that can paralyze your nerves with one bite, about strange plants that might hold a cure for cancer, about the great trees that give us oxygen to breathe and help keep the earth from becoming too hot.

And then she told them that the world's rain forests were being destroyed at the rate of one hundred acres a minute. In the past thirty years, she said, nearly half the world's rain forests have been cut down, often by poor people who burn the wood for fire. Sometimes forests are cleared to make pastures for cattle that are slaughtered and sold to hamburger chains in the U.S. and Europe. Sometimes the trees are sold and shipped away to make furniture and paper. More often they are just stacked up and burned. At this rate, there might not be any rain forests left in thirty years!

the world's rain forests are being destroyed at the rate of one hundred acres a minute

The children were horrified. The creatures of the rain forest could be gone before the students were even old enough to have a chance to see them. It didn't matter that they lived thousands of miles away in cold, snowy Sweden. It seemed to them that their future was being chopped and cleared away.

During the autumn, as the sunlight weakened and the days became short, the Fagervik children continued to think about the rain forest. Whenever they went on walks past the great fir trees on the school grounds, they imagined jaguars crouched in the limbs just above them, their long tails twitching impatiently.

They begged Mrs. Kern to help them think of something—anything— they could do to rescue the creatures of the tropics. And then one afternoon during a music lesson, a student named Roland Tiensuu asked suddenly, "Can't we just *buy* some rain forest?"

The lesson stopped. It was a simple, clear idea that all the others understood at once. The class began to cheer, and then they turned to their teacher. "Please, Mrs. Kern," they said. "Please, won't you find us a forest to buy?"

Mrs. Kern had no idea how to find a rain forest for sale. But then, the very weekend after Roland's idea, she was introduced to an American biologist named Sharon Kinsman. As they chatted, Ms. Kinsman explained that she had been working in a rain forest called Monte Verde,[1] or Green Mountain.

When Mrs. Kern told Ms. Kinsman of the nearly impossible mission her students had given her, she expected the biologist to laugh. Instead her expression turned serious. "Oh," she said quickly, "please buy mine."

Ms. Kinsman said that some people in Monte Verde were trying desperately to buy land so that more trees wouldn't be cut. Much land had already been protected, but much more was needed. Land was cheap there, she said—only about twenty-five dollars per acre.

Ms. Kinsman agreed to visit the Fagervik School. She would bring a map and slides of the Monte Verde forest and tell the children where they could send money to buy rain forest land. When Mrs. Kern told the children what had happened, they

1. *Monte Verde* (MAHN tuh VAIR dee)

some people in Monte Verde were trying desperately to buy land so that more trees wouldn't be cut

didn't even seem surprised. As they put it, "We knew you would find one."

In the days before Sharon Kinsman's visit, the Fagervik students began to think about how to raise money. They asked Mrs. Kern to write down all their ideas. As she picked up a piece of chalk, several students spoke at once.

"Pony rides!"

"Let's collect old things, and sell them!"

"What about a rain forest evening here at school?"

"Dog washing!"

Dog washing? They began to laugh. "That would never work," someone said. "Who would give money for that?" Mrs. Kern put her chalk down. "Look," she said. "Let's make this our rule: there are no bad ideas. The only bad thing is if you have an idea and don't say it. Then we can't use it." She returned to the blackboard. Were there more ideas?

"A rabbit jumping contest!"

"Rabbit jumping?" said Mrs. Kern. "Be serious. You can't *make* a rabbit jump."

"Oh, yes, we all have rabbits. We can train them. We can. We *can!*"

Mrs. Kern tried to imagine someone actually paying money to

watch children try to make rabbits jump. She couldn't. This idea was crazy.

"Mrs. Kern...there's no such thing as a bad idea...remember?" She did. "Rabbit jumping," she wrote, dutifully putting her doubts aside.

On November 6, 1987, Sharon Kinsman arrived at the Fagervik School. She was just as enthusiastic as the students. They put on skits for her about rain forests and showed her the many books they had written about tropical creatures. Then at last, it was her turn to show them slides of the Monte Verde forest.

First she unfolded a map of the forest and pointed to the area their money could preserve from cutting. She told them that 400 bird species live in the forest, more than in all of Sweden, as well as 490 kinds of butterflies and 500 types of trees. Monte Verde is also the only home in the world, she said, for the golden toad, a creature that seems to glow in the dark.

Then she showed her slides. As the room became dark, the students were swept into a hot, steamy jungle half the world away. The slides took them sloshing along a narrow, muddy trail, crisscrossed with roots and

400 bird species live in the forest, as well as 490 kinds of butterflies and 500 types of trees

vines. A dark canopy of giant trees, thick with bright flowering plants, closed in above them.

They saw giant spiders and deadly snakes. Ms. Kinsman's tape recorder made the forest ring with the shriek of howler monkeys calling to each other and with the chattering of parrots above the trees. They saw the golden toad, the scarlet macaw, and the red-backed poison-arrow frog.

And they saw the forest disappearing, too. They saw hard-muscled men, their backs glistening with sweat, pushing chain saws deep into the giant trees. They could almost smell the smoke of burning tree limbs and feel the thunder of thick, brown trunks crashing down. Behind great piles of ragged wood, the tropical sky was hazy with smoke. Time seemed very short.

When the lights came on, the students were back in Sweden, but they were not the same. Now they had seen their forest—and the danger it faced. There was no time to lose. Mrs. Kern had inspired them with a problem, and Roland had given them

WORD BANK **canopy** (KAN uh pee) *n.:* the cover formed by the leafy upper branches of the trees in a forest

an idea they could work with. Sharon Kinsman had shown them their target. Now it was up to them.

Two weeks later, more than a hundred people crowded into an old schoolhouse near the Fagervik School for a rain forest evening. Students stood by the door and collected ten crowns (about $1.50) from each person. Special programs cost another crown. Even though it was winter, rain splattered steadily onto the roof, just as it must have been raining in the Monte Verde forest. To the students, rain was a good sign.

First they performed a play containing a dramatic scene in which trees of the rain forest were cut and creatures killed. That way guests would understand the problem they were trying to help solve. As the applause died down, the children passed an old hat around, urging audience members to drop money in it.

Then they sold rain forest books and rain forest poems. "We were not afraid to ask for money," remembers Maria Karlsson, who was nine. "We knew what we wanted was important." One boy stood at a table keeping track of how much they were making. Whenever a classmate would hand over a fresh delivery of cash, he

they had raised enough money to save about twelve football fields worth of rain forest

would count it quickly and shout above the noise, "Now we've got two hundred crowns!!" "Now it's three hundred!!"

The evening's total came to 1,600 crowns, or about $240. The next day, they figured out that they had raised enough money to save about twelve football fields worth of rain forest. It was wonderful…but was it enough space for a sloth? A leopard? They all knew the answer. They needed more.

They filled up another blackboard with ideas and tried them out. Everything seemed to work. Mrs. Kern brought in a list of prominent people who might make donations. Two girls wrote a letter to the richest woman on the list. A few days later, a check arrived. Someone else wrote to the king of Sweden and asked if he would watch them perform plays about the rain forest. He said yes.

One day they went to a recording studio and made a tape of their rain forest songs. From the very beginning, Mrs. Kern and a music teacher had been helping them write songs. They started with old melodies

WORD BANK **prominent** (PRAHM ih nent) *adj.:* leading, important, or well-known

they liked, changing them a little as they went along. As soon as anybody came up with a good line, they sang it into a tape recorder so they wouldn't forget it by the end of the song. They rehearsed the songs many times on their school bus before recording them, then designed a cover and used some of their money to buy plastic boxes for the tapes. Within months, they had sold five hundred tapes at ten dollars each.

The more they used their imaginations, the more money they raised. They decided to have a fair. "We had a magician and charged admission," remembers Lia Degeby, who was eight. "We charged to see who could make the ugliest face. We had a pony riding contest. We had a market. We had a lady with a beard. We had the strongest lady in the world. We tried everything." The biggest money maker of all was the rabbit jumping contest, even though each rabbit sat still when its time came to jump! Even carrots couldn't budge them. One simply flopped over and went to sleep, crushing its necklace of flowers.

Soon they needed a place to put all the money they had earned. Mrs. Kern's husband, Bernd, helped them form an organization called Barnens

inspired by the students, the Swedish government gave a grant of $80,000 to Monte Verde

Regnskog, which means Children's Rain Forest. They opened a bank account with a post office box where people could continue to mail donations.

By midwinter, they had raised $1,400. The children addressed an envelope to the Monte Verde Cloud Forest Protection League, folded a check inside, and sent it on its way to Costa Rica. Weeks later, they received a crumpled package covered with brightly colored stamps. It contained a map of the area that had been bought with their money. A grateful writer thanked them for saving nearly ninety acres of Costa Rican rain forest.

In the early spring, the Fagervik students performed at the Swedish Children's Fair, which led to several national television appearances. Soon schools from all over Sweden were joining Barnens Regnskog and sending money to Monte Verde. At one high school near Stockholm, two thousand students did chores all day in the city and raised nearly $15,000. And inspired by the students, the Swedish government gave a grant of $80,000 to Monte Verde.

After another year's work, the children of Fagervik had raised $25,000 more. The families who

could afford it sent their children to Costa Rica to see Monte Verde. Just before the holidays, ten Fagervik children stepped off the plane, blinking in the bright Costa Rican sunlight. It was hot! They stripped off their coats and sweaters, piled into a bus, and headed for the mountains.

A few hours later, the bus turned onto a narrow, rocky road that threaded its way through steep mountains. The children looked out upon spectacular waterfalls that fell hundreds of feet. Occasionally they glimpsed monkeys swinging through the trees.

Ahead, the mountaintops disappeared inside a dark purple cloud. For a few moments they could see five rainbows at once. Soon it began to rain.

The next morning, they joined ten Costa Rican children and went on a hike through the Monte Verde rain forest. Sometimes the thick mud made them step right out of their boots. But it didn't matter. "There were plants everywhere," says Lia. "I saw monkeys and flowers."

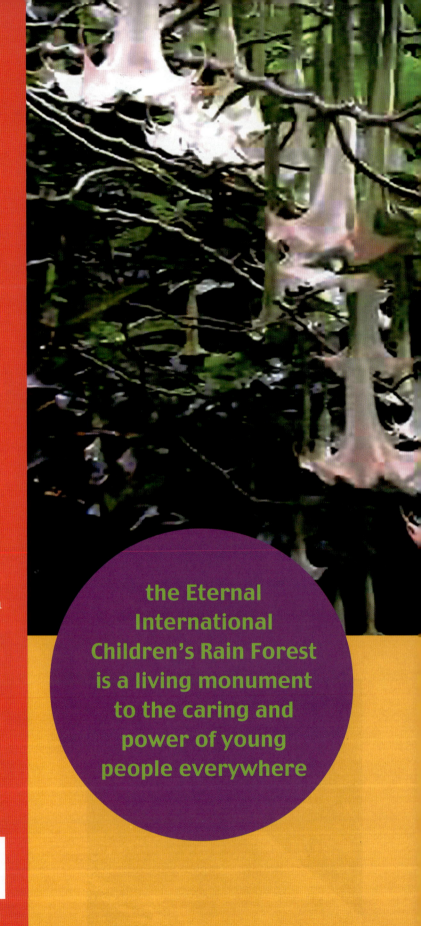

the Eternal International Children's Rain Forest is a living monument to the caring and power of young people everywhere

WORD BANK	**threaded** (THRED ed) *v.*: made its way past or around obstacles

On the holiday, the children of the Fagervik School proudly presented the staff of the Monte Verde Cloud Forest with their check for $25,000. They said it was a holiday present for all the children of the world.

The Monte Verde Conservation League used their gift, and funds that had been donated by other children previously, to establish what is now known as El Bosque Eterno de los Ninos,[2] or the Eternal International Children's Rain Forest. It is a living monument to the caring and power of young people everywhere. So far, kids from twenty-one nations have raised more than two million dollars to preserve nearly 33,000 acres of rain forest, plenty of room for jaguars and ocelots and tapirs. The first group of Fagervik students have now graduated to another school, but the first- and second-graders who have replaced them are still raising great

---

2. *El Bosque Eterno de los Ninos*
(el BOSK ee TAIR noh de los NEEN yos)

WORD BANK

monument (MAHN yoo ment) *n.:* any lasting evidence or outstanding example of something

sums of money. The school total is now well over $50,000.

The Fagervik students continue to amaze their teacher. "I never thought they could do so much," Mrs. Kern says. "Sometimes I say to them, 'Why do you work so hard?' They say, 'I think of my future.' They make me feel optimistic. When I am with them, I think maybe anything can be done."

WORD BANK

optimistic (OPP tuh MISS tik) *adj.:* hopeful; positive; having a feeling that all will turn out well

About the Author

Phillip Hoose (pronounced Hose) has two main interests: conservation and music. Born in South Bend, Indiana in 1947, he grew up in an area famous for its popular high school basketball teams. The first book Hoose wrote was *The Fabulous Basketball Life of Indiana.* He later published a collection of stories about children and teens who made a difference in such areas as feeding the homeless, opposing racism, and ending gang violence. In addition to writing children's books and books on conservation, Hoose is a songwriter and a performing musician.

Studying the Selection

QUICK REVIEW

1. About how old were the children who started this project?

2. In which country do the students live? Can you find it on a world map?

3. According to Mrs. Eha Kern, the teacher in the story, how much of the rain forest has been cut down in the last thirty years?

4. Look through the story, and find out what year the story begins.

FOCUS

5. Give three reasons why the children's achievement was really amazing. (There are many right answers.)

6. What do the students say when Mrs. Kern asks them why they work so hard on raising money for the rain forest?

CREATING & WRITING

7. Write two or three paragraphs about why saving the rain forest is important.

8. Do some research. In a book or other source of information, read about one living thing—plant or animal—that is now extinct. Write two paragraphs that describe that plant or animal and tell how the plant or animal came to be extinct.

9. Make a brief presentation to your class about the organization you wrote to before reading this selection. Use at least one drawing, photograph, or map for your talk.

BIOGRAPHY

- A biography is the story of one person written by another person.

- Material for a biography is gathered from books, letters, speeches, interviews, and anything else written or said by the *subject* of the biography.

- In addition, a biographer may use books, letters, and anything else that have been written by *others* about the subject of the biography.

THINK ABOUT IT!

1. The author writes that Gertrude Bonnin "lived her life between two worlds." What two worlds were those?

2. How did the author learn about Bonnin's experience at the government school in Indiana?

3. By reading Bonnin's collection of short stories, what did the biographer learn about Bonnin?

4. List five biographical facts about Gertrude Bonnin that are included in the story.

Gertrude Bonnin: A Voice for Her People

From the day that she was taken from her mother's teepee in South Dakota to be educated in the East, Native American writer Gertrude Bonnin lived her life between two worlds. Although the change from her traditional Sioux home to the wider American world was difficult, Bonnin turned this pain into good, devoting her life to helping Americans understand her native culture and trying to gain full rights for her people.

Gertrude Bonnin, who often published under the pen name "Zitkala-Sa" (a Lakota Sioux word for "red bird") was born in 1876 on the Yankton Sioux Reservation in South Dakota. Bonnin had a pleasant childhood among the Sioux, but when the opportunity arose in 1884 to attend a government-sponsored school in Indiana, she jumped at the chance.

Although she was excited at first, Bonnin soon discovered that attending school would be a difficult and sometimes painful experience. In a series of three essays, Bonnin wrote movingly of her experiences at the school, where she was forced to cut her long hair (a sign of shame among her people), to wear American-style clothing (which to her felt horribly immodest), and where she was not permitted to speak her native language.

Neither fully accepted in the white world, nor—as a result of her education—fully able to feel at home on the reservation, Bonnin felt all alone. Rather than wallow in self-pity, Bonnin chose to make the best of her situation, putting her knowledge of both cultures to good use. In addition to a collection of short stories entitled *American Indian Stories,* she published *Old Indian Legends,* a collection of old Sioux tales translated for an English-reading audience.

Later in life, Bonnin moved to Washington, D.C., as secretary of the Society of American Indians (SAI). In the nation's capital, Bonnin worked tirelessly to gain political rights for Native Americans, editing *American Indian Magazine* for SAI, testifying before Congress, and writing and editing the *Indian News Letter* for the National Congress of American Indians.

Her life and her stories offer the reader a window not only into her Sioux culture, but into the wider American culture as well.

Blueprint for Reading

INTO . . . *Jessica Govea*

Jessica Govea worked in the fields of California from the time she was a little girl. By the time she was a young teen, she fully understood what it meant to do hard physical labor for low pay and no guarantee that the job would last longer than the day she was hired. One might think that such a difficult start in life would have crushed her spirit. It did not! It gave her strength and the determination to help others. Can you imagine yourself working in a hot field, picking crops from morning to night?

EYES ON . . . *Biography Created from Interview*

A **biography** is the story of one person's life written by another person. The author uses the pronouns "he" or "she." An **autobiography** is the story of one person's life written by that same person. The author uses the pronoun "I."

Although *Jessica Govea* is a biography, much of it is written with the pronoun "I." This is because the author, Phillip Hoose, interviewed Jessica Govea and decided to use some of Jessica's own words to tell her story. That is why this biography sounds a bit like an autobiography!

JESSICA GOVEA: EDUCATION OF A UNION ORGANIZER
PHILLIP HOOSE

Bakersfield, California, late 1960s

In 1965, California grape pickers made ninety cents an hour. Most were of Mexican heritage and were treated as inferiors by whites. Their average age at death was forty-nine. Migrant workers—those who traveled from field to field—lived in unheated shacks, without indoor plumbing or cooking stoves, segregated by race. Thousands of children worked in fields that had been sprayed with poisons to kill insects, and many died in accidents that could have been prevented. In the late 1960s, farmworkers formed a union and stood up to the growers who owned the fields. One of the first to work full-time for the Farm Workers Association was a girl still in her teens. But in her case, age didn't matter. Jessica Govea was already an experienced organizer.

"It was always dark when mother would wake me up. I'd pull on homemade pants and a long-sleeved shirt to protect my arms from scratches and bugs, splash water on my face and get in the car. Every day we went hoping we'd get work but not knowing for sure. The earlier you went, the better your chance, so it would still be dark when we'd get to the field. While we waited mother would give us breakfast—tacos made from tortillas, filled with eggs and pinto beans or potatoes.

"I worked every summer from the time I was four until I was about fifteen. The first time I picked was in a cotton field near Bakersfield, California. Adults carried sacks that would hold a hundred pounds of cotton. Mom made me a twenty-five-pound sack. I threw cotton bolls[1] into it until it dragged behind me like a tail. Prunes were the worst: The foreman would shake the tree and knock

1. *Cotton bolls* (BOHLZ) are the round pods or vessels of the cotton plant. When the plant matures, the boll opens up to reveal fluffy white cotton.

them on the ground. Then we had to crawl around on our hands and knees and put them into buckets. The sweet fruit attracts wasps and we were scared to death of getting stung. Tray grapes were bad, too. You go down the row and cut bunches of grapes with sharp pruning clippers. Sometimes you got nicked by the clippers. Almost all tray grape pickers were children. There may have been child labor laws, but we kids worked because our families needed the income.

"My skin would itch and burn, but I didn't know why. I thought it was because it was hot. I smelled funny smells on the grapes and vines and on the ground. Often I could see them spraying pesticides on the plants that grew in the next field. They

never sprayed us while we worked but our plants were covered with chemicals. The thing I hated most, though, was that there was no privacy for my personal needs. I just had to find a place to be alone.

"I worked hard. I was like my mother, disciplined and fast. I had one treat to look forward to: Every day on the way home we would stop at a gas station and my mom would buy me an ice-cold bottle of Nehi orange pop."

When Jessica was seven, labor organizers Fred Ross and Cesar Chavez formed the Community Service Organization (CSO) in her hometown of Bakersfield. Bakersfield was a center for farm labor, and it attracted many poor Mexicans and Mexican-Americans. CSO set out to help them find places to live, medical care, food, and legal aid.[2] CSO also encouraged them to register to vote. Jessica's father was a well-respected leader in the Mexican-American community, so Chavez looked him up right away. Jessica says:

"I could tell Cesar Chavez was important by the way others respected him, but there was nothing about him that made you afraid of him. It didn't matter that I was young, he sat down and talked with me. And when he did I knew that he really cared about what I was saying, and about me. It came through in his eyes, and in his face.

"I went door-to-door with my father when he worked for CSO and listened to him talk with people. My father never talked down to people. He listened carefully and spoke respectfully. People told him stories of how they had been discriminated against in jobs,

---

2. Sometimes, a poor person needs the advice or services of a lawyer, but cannot afford to pay for them. The government or some organization will often provide these services free of charge or for a very small fee. The help the person receives is called *legal aid.*

WORD
BANK
discriminated (dis KRIM ih NAY ted) *v.:* were treated unfairly because of prejudice

hospitals, schools, public offices. He had no
room in his heart for injustice. I learned a lot
about organizing just from listening to these
conversations.

"I had similar problems in my own life. At
my school, we Mexican-Americans were
punished when we spoke Spanish, even though

that was the language we spoke at home. We were stood in a corner, or we got smacked. My father was asking people to join together through CSO to try to make some changes. To protest. To register to vote. To become strong by acting together. It all made sense to me.

"I became his assistant when I turned nine. I helped him produce leaflets, one sheet at a time on a machine with purple ink. 'Register to vote,' they would say, or 'come to a meeting.' Then I learned to type them myself. I started speaking before large crowds when I was very young. I recited patriotic poems at Mexican holiday celebrations. Some were ten or twenty minutes long, and I could deliver them from memory and with great expression.

"I grew more and more confident and independent. A bunch of farmworker kids and other working-class kids formed 'Junior CSO.'

We had our own officers and meetings. I was president. Our first campaign was for a new park. When I was in eighth grade my best friend, Virginia, got run over by a speeding truck while she was taking her little brothers and sisters to a park, three miles away, that could only be reached by crossing a dangerous road. She just had time to throw the children aside but she couldn't save herself. We drew up a petition to convince county officials to make a park closer to us and went around door-to-door and asked people to sign.

"The lessons I had learned with my father came back to help me. I was always very clear about why I was at someone's door. I knew how to listen patiently and to express my own view. I knew

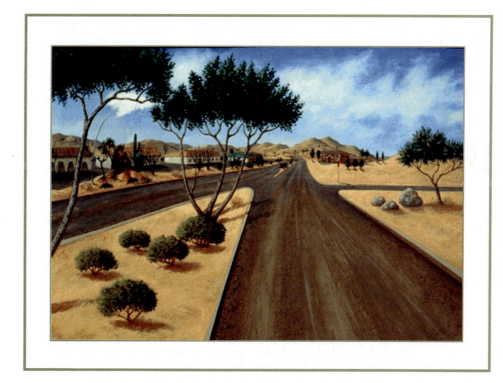

how to discuss an issue and come to an agreement. Basically, I knew how to express democracy. I knew that the most successful actions are those in which you figure out a way for everybody to make a contribution. One old man was especially mean to us. He kept saying, 'I'm not gonna sign anything...Get away from me.' I made him my personal project. And I signed him up, though it took a long time. Four years after Virginia's death, the county supervisors passed a resolution to make a park. They took all the credit—which was fine—but we Junior CSO'ers did it.

"In the middle 60's Cesar Chavez left CSO to organize a new labor union for farmworkers. Our family supported him. We knew for ourselves what it meant to work in the fields—the long hours, the lousy conditions, the poor pay. People sometimes met in my backyard when they were afraid to be seen meeting with Cesar at their homes. They feared they would be 'blacklisted,' which meant that no grower would hire him. They felt safe talking with him in our home. Many important plans were made in a little circle of chairs in our backyard.

"One night after I graduated from high school, Cesar invited my dad to a meeting. He couldn't go, so I represented our family. We gathered in a little house about thirty miles out of Bakersfield. They were going to organize a union for farmworkers. The conversation so excited me that I started volunteering right away in the small office they set up, but I wanted to do more. I told my father, 'Dad, I want to go work full-time with Cesar.' At first he said no—college was his dream for me—but my mind was made up. For a while there was a lot of tension around home. Finally he agreed, but he said just for a year. A year turned into sixteen. After I started, it didn't take long for my mom and dad to support me.

"I moved to Delano, California, and joined the staff of the National Farm Workers Association [later renamed the United Farm Workers]. We urged workers to strike—not to pick table grapes until they got better pay and working conditions. I was still in my teens but I had a lot of work and responsibility. I started

every morning at a field, carrying signs and marching in a picket line, urging the pickers who showed up to join us and not work in the fields that day. Then I worked in the service center, where we helped families of farmworkers. One of my first jobs was to act as a translator for a family whose toddler had been killed by the pesticides. She had inhaled them from her dad's clothes by hugging him when he got home from work.

"That life wasn't easy. Room and board often meant sleeping on someone's floor or in the basement, and food sometimes meant nothing. I got paid five dollars a week. But I believed in what I was doing, and I was good at what I did. The lessons I had learned as a girl had prepared me well."

WHAT HAPPENED TO JESSICA GOVEA?

She worked for the United Farm Workers for sixteen years and became one of the group's key leaders. "Our union wasn't about high tech or computers," she recalls. "It started as a small group of dedicated people with a very clear message. We turned it into a lot of people with a similar message." Twenty-six growers ended up signing contracts with the union. Jessica taught workers, community groups, and college students how to organize.

Jessica Govea Thorbourne wrote the following about labor organizing:

"You have to draw a picture so that people understand your story and your struggle, and you have to give them something they can do about the problem you are presenting....I learned that people will help if they are asked."

New York, N.Y. — Jessica Govea Thorbourne, a labor educator with Cornell University's School of Industrial and Labor Relations in New York City and a founding organizer of Cesar Chavez's United Farm Workers (UFW) Union, died January 23, 2005 of cancer at age 58. A resident of West Orange, N.J., at the time of her death, she had played a central role in making the UFW one of the nation's strongest labor organizations and a source of pride to several generations of Mexican-Americans.

CORNELL NEWS, FEBRUARY 1, 2005

Studying the Selection

FIRST IMPRESSIONS

If you thought that you would be fired if you protested against terrible working conditions, would you protest anyway?

QUICK REVIEW

1. At what age did Jessica Govea begin working?

2. In what country does this story take place?

3. Name three difficult things that occurred when Jessica was working.

4. What happened to Mexican-American children if they spoke Spanish in school?

FOCUS

5. How does Jessica Govea describe her father?

6. What qualities did Jessica possess that made her so successful at organizing people?

CREATING & WRITING

7. Interview someone you know. Ask about the person's childhood. Write out the interview. Then, take your interview, and use it to write a brief biography of that person.

8. Find out about Cesar Chavez and write a short biography of his life. Your essay should be six to eight paragraphs long.

9. With three other students, act out one of these mini-dramas for your class:

(a) The four of you are holding petitions for people to sign. Your petitions will be sent to a well-known wine company. The petition asks the company to pay adult migrant workers at least $5.00 an hour. The four of you are trying to persuade people on the street to sign the petitions.

(b) One of you is a teacher and three of you are children who have missed school because you were working in the fields with your parents. The teacher has asked the three children, a little impatiently, why they have been out of school. The three must answer, explaining what their life is like.

Make sure that each person on your team has at least two lines to speak in the mini-drama. Use information from the story.

PULLING IT ALL TOGETHER

- A well-written story, whether it is fiction or nonfiction, will have a strong theme. The theme will be supported by the plot, characters, symbols, setting, and dialogue.

- Symbols such as flags and uniforms help the author express complicated ideas in one or two words.

- Although many pieces are written as though they are historical fact, the reader should remember that they are written from the author's point of view.

THINK ABOUT IT!

1. What symbol tells the boy that the wounded soldier is the enemy?

2. In your opinion, why doesn't the writer tell us when or where this story takes place?

3. As you read the story, did you place the action in a particular war? Why did you think the story took place then?

4. What is the theme of "The Enemy"?

The Enemy

The boy stared the enemy in the face. He had never seen the enemy before, but the rifle and the flag on the uniform said this soldier, who lay bleeding and unconscious at the edge of the boy's cornfield, was the enemy. The boy's heart raced. He felt strong, and a little older, as he used the enemy's knife to saw the flag patch from the man's right shoulder. Before running home to show off his prize, the boy removed the enemy's belt and tied one of the man's hands to the wooden fence. He couldn't take a chance of this man wandering off when he awoke, or worse, wandering into their village.

The boy had to struggle to make the man's other hand reach the fence, and as he tugged at the arm, the man's hat, crusted in blood, dropped into the dust. Inside the hat was a photograph. Pictured were a young man—perhaps the enemy himself, a woman, and three girls, about the same age as the boy. He reached down and picked up the photograph. It was the enemy.

Confusion muddled his brain as he walked through the woods to his village. He loved his country. Of course he did. And he loved his brother, off fighting to defend it from these invaders. But in all the years he'd heard the grownups talk of the enemy, he'd never considered that the enemy might actually be a person. With a wife. Kids.

When he got home, no one was in the kitchen. He knew instantly what to do. Working quietly, he filled a sack with some bread, fruit, and cheese. This fallen soldier would certainly be hungry when he awoke. He filled a bucket with water and hurried back through the woods.

Taking off his own shirt, he cut it into strips and soaked a strip in water. The boy mumbled a silent apology to his brother at the front. Daubing the blood from the man's face and head, he wondered if in all the months of fighting, his brother had yet discovered that the enemy has families, too.

Blueprint for Reading

INTO . . . The Street Boy

Do you ever see homeless people? What is your reaction? Do you turn away, because they make you feel uncomfortable? Do you feel bad? Sad? Angry? Do you hope that someone will help them? Do you try to forget them as soon as you have passed them? Have you ever wondered why some people are homeless?

EYES ON . . . Fantasy

The Street Boy is a fantasy. What is a fantasy? It is a story that is in some ways realistic, but which could never be true, because something in it is too good or too terrible or too strange to be real. Fantasy is a little bit like a dream.

A fantasy must make sense on some level. In *The Street Boy*, the characters, setting, and theme are true to life. Because they are so believable, they make the plot, which is pure fantasy, seem like something that *could* have happened.

THE STREET BOY   Silverman

The city where Hedley lived, like most other cities, sprawled out in all directions, had a huge number of inhabitants, and had streets that were always busy. For Hedley, it was home. He lived there with his father, mother, and younger sister, Serena.

Their comfortable house overlooked a subway station and from his upstairs bedroom window, Hedley could see the rush of commuters setting out every day for work. Each evening he would

| WORD BANK | **inhabitants** (in HAB ih tunts) *n.:* people or animals who live in a place |
| | **commuters** (kum YOO ters) *n.:* people who travel to and from work |

see them all return. It was like the tide of an ocean going out and coming in every day, waves of people flowing first in one direction, then the other.

One day, Hedley noticed a boy no older than himself sitting on the sidewalk outside the station. There was a scruffy dog beside the boy and a cap laid upside down in front of him with a few coins sprinkled in it. The boy looked like he didn't wash very often, and his clothes were shabby.

The boy was there again the following day and every day after that. Sometimes he sat there with his dog next to him, or he talked to the newspaperman, an old man with no teeth, who sat at a little table most of the time, selling the daily papers.

Hedley never spoke to the street boy, but he saw him every day on his way to and from school. Hedley also watched him from his upstairs bedroom window.

Very few people threw coins into the boy's cap, but some did, and every now and then the boy would remove most of the coins and slip them in his pocket. At night, the street boy slept in the doorway of a store that was boarded up and empty. He lay on a

few sheets of cardboard and slept in a dark green sleeping bag that had seen better years.

Hedley's parents had also noticed the street boy.

"This area's going downhill," Hedley's father complained.

"They shouldn't be allowed to beg here!" his mother grumbled.

But the boy was always there, and near him, his faithful dog. The dog never wandered off on its own. It was a white terrier with black markings. Actually, the dog was not that white. More like yellowish brown. Once, Hedley saw them share a bag of chips.

When Hedley's parents asked him what he wanted for his birthday, which was only a few weeks away, Hedley answered, "A dog."

"A dog's out of the question," his mother said. "No one could look after it when we're at work and you're at school."

"Why don't you ask for a bike," his father suggested. "Then you could ride to school."

So Hedley said, "Okay, a bike."

"I want a bike, too." His little sister, Serena, pouted.

 WORD BANK **pouted** (POW ted) *v.*: showed discontent or ill humor in a gloomy and silent way

But before his birthday came along, the weather turned freezing cold. There was a shimmering of frost on the grass in the morning, and puddles turned into sheets of ice that cracked if you stepped on them. Flurries of snow fell from time to time. Hedley wore his fur-lined parka and put on gloves and a scarf to go to school.

The street boy huddled in his sleeping bag during the day, hugging his dog closely for extra warmth. Hedley thought it was unfair that the boy should be out there in the freezing cold.

"Can't we help him?" he asked his parents.

"I don't think so," his father said. "It's his choice to live out there on the streets."

"Can't we at least give him some warmer clothes?" Hedley persisted.

"No!" his mother said adamantly. "Then he'd never stop pestering us for more."

The severe cold continued for sixteen days. A biting north wind added to the misery of being outdoors.

From his upstairs window, Hedley looked down at the street boy and his dog. The boy was lying in a ball in his sleeping bag, with the dog curled up next to him.

Then, one morning, on his way to school, Hedley noticed that the boy wasn't there! The green sleeping bag was lying in a heap at the entrance of the boarded-up store, and the dog was lying on it, whining.

A feeling of panic rushed through Hedley's heart. He knew something was horribly wrong.

At school, Hedley couldn't keep his mind on his schoolwork. He kept wondering what had happened to the street boy. He wouldn't have left his dog there all alone!

WORD BANK	**adamantly** (ADD uh munt LEE) *adv.*: firmly and insistently; strongly and definitely **panic** (PAN ik) *n.*: a sudden, overwhelming fear

On the way home, he stopped at the subway station. His parents had told him to always come directly home, but Hedley couldn't help himself.

The boy still wasn't there. And the dog looked so miserable on its own.

"Where's the boy who's always with that dog?" he asked the newspaperman.

"He's sick," the old man explained. "Gone to the hospital, poor kid."

An awful feeling went through Hedley's body when he heard this.

"When's he coming back?"

"Dunno," the old man replied.

Hedley crossed the road and went indoors. He lay down on his bed, his head aching.

By the time his mother came home from work, he was weak and pale. She called for a doctor, who examined Hedley, then prescribed some medicine.

Hedley's condition worsened during the night, and he spent fitful hours tossing and turning, passing in and out of sleep, tortured by dreams of the street boy in the hospital.

The next day, Hedley was feverish. At times, he seemed to lose consciousness altogether. When he came around, he asked only for sips of water as the thought of food made him nauseous. During the following night, his family was worried about him. He ranted and raved, complaining that they shouldn't have left him out in the snow during such freezing weather. He didn't recognize his mother or father.

For three days, Hedley was delirious. But on the morning of the fourth day, he woke up feeling much better. The dizziness was gone, the nightmares had vanished, and the fever had dropped.

He sat up, but he could hardly believe his eyes!

Where was he?

He was outdoors!

He was shocked to find himself lying on a few sheets of cardboard, huddled inside a dark green sleeping bag.

He recognized the entrance of the boarded-up store. Curled up beside him was a scruffy dog, who wagged its tail joyfully when it saw that Hedley had woken up.

WORD BANK   **delirious** (dih LEER ee us) *adj.*: a state of illness in which a person is unconscious but has strange, dreamlike visions

Hedley couldn't figure out what had happened. But here he was, dressed in clothes that were old and shabby, huddled in a sleeping bag, while people walked past without even noticing him.

"Morning, kiddo."

It was the toothless newspaperman.

"You're looking a lot better today," he added cheerfully.

"How did I get here?" Hedley asked.

"The same guy who took you to the hospital brought you back," the old man explained.

Hedley wanted to say he'd never gone to the hospital. But at that moment he noticed his father emerging from the house across the road.

Hedley climbed out of his sleeping bag and rushed to greet him. The dog immediately followed. Hedley had to pick it up, so that they could cross the road safely. He had to wait for a break in the traffic, and by the time Hedley reached his father, he was just getting into the car. Hedley's father deliberately pulled the car door shut and started the engine.

| WORD BANK | **deliberately** (de LIB uh rut LEE) *adv.:* carefully and knowingly |

"Dad!" Hedley shouted.

Hedley's father barely looked at him as he drove off.

Hedley was stunned. His father had not recognized him!

He marched up to the front door of his house and rang the doorbell.

His mother came to the door and opened it.

"What do you want?" she asked.

"Mom, don't you know who I am?" Hedley said.

Hedley's mother tried to shut the door, but Hedley put his foot out and prevented it from closing.

"Mom, it's me. Hedley!"

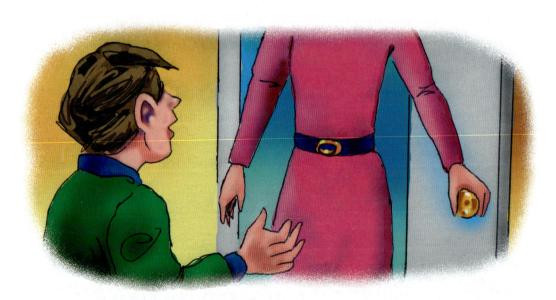

"Don't be ridiculous!" his mother said, looking at him with terror in her eyes. "Hedley's upstairs."

Hedley hardly knew what to say or do.

"Please let me in, Mom!"

"Go away!" his mother screamed. "Leave us alone or I'll call the police."

Hedley backed away. His mother closed the door. He crossed the road back to the subway station. The dog snuggled up against him. He lay there, cold and confused.

A while later, Hedley noticed the curtains being opened in the upstairs room across the road. A boy looked out of the window. Hedley recognized him. It was the street boy! In Hedley's room!

Hedley felt very strange. What was going on?

His stomach was growling with hunger.

"I'm starving," he said to the newspaperman.

"You've forgotten to put out your cap," the old man responded. "But here, you can have this in the meantime."

The old man took out half a sandwich from his pocket.

"Thanks," Hedley said.

WORD BANK   **responded** (ree SPOND ed) *v.*: answered

Hedley found a cap under his sleeping bag and laid it out in front of him. The morning rush hour had started, but no one dropped any money into Hedley's cap.

The front door of the house across the street opened, and the street boy emerged, dressed for school. He looked so clean! He walked past the station and disappeared around the corner.

The day passed slowly. Eventually, Hedley's cap contained some coins. He bought a bag of chips from the station snack stand and shared it with the dog.

Later in the day, the street boy returned from school. Hedley saw him coming and intercepted him.

"Why are you living in my house?" Hedley asked him.

The street boy looked at Hedley as if he were a dangerous maniac.

"Leave me alone!" the boy said.

"No!" Hedley said firmly. "You stay here with your dog and give me the front door key so I can go home."

WORD BANK	**emerged** (ee MURJD) *v.*: came out from
	intercepted (IN ter SEP ted) *v.*: stopped someone or something on the way to its destination

The street boy pulled away from Hedley, but Hedley grabbed hold of him and tried to get the key that he knew was in the boy's jacket pocket.

"Stop it!" the street boy shouted.

The two boys started pulling at each other, punching and hitting.

The newspaperman hobbled over and separated them.

"Enough of that, boys!"

The street boy straightened himself up and crossed the road.

"You shouldn't be allowed to live on the streets!" he yelled back, as he let himself in the front door.

That night, Hedley slept outdoors. He huddled in his sleeping bag and hugged the dog for warmth. He thought of going to the police himself to tell them he was the real Hedley. But, of course, they wouldn't believe a boy dressed in shabby clothes.

Hedley found it difficult to sleep on the concrete. It was too cold, for one thing. And uncomfortable. And noisy. The cars going past made a terrific racket. When Hedley finally did fall asleep, he was woken after just a few hours by some drunk men who were passing by. They poured beer all over his sleeping bag, just for a laugh. The men made fun of Hedley and swore at him for a while before staggering off. Hedley didn't sleep much the rest of the night; he was too damp.

The next morning, after the rush hour, Hedley was wondering how to get through the day, when, suddenly, he heard a voice.

"Hey!" the voice. "Let's go to the food kitchen."

Hedley looked to see where the voice was coming from. The only thing nearby was the scruffy dog.

"Well, you comin' or what?"

It was the dog!

Hedley stashed his sleeping bag in a corner of the shop entrance.

"You can talk?" Hedley said.

WORD
BANK   **staggering** (STAG er ing) *v.:* walking unsteadily; tottering

"Well, no point going on and on about it," the dog said. "Let's get going."

The dog knew the way. He had traveled there every day for months.

At the food kitchen, Hedley stood in a line of street people. All of them had spent their night somewhere on the streets. Some of them looked in really bad condition, coughing and hacking. Others looked like ordinary people, Hedley thought.

Inside the building, Hedley downed a carton of milk and ate some beans on toast. It brought some life back to his aching body. One or two street people spoke to him and asked him where he hung out. But on the whole, he kept to himself.

After the meal, the dog said, "Hey, what about something for me?"

So Hedley asked the person behind the counter if they had any scraps or leftovers.

"Here you are, Mutt," the woman said, offering the dog some cold french fries and half a burger from the trash can.

Hedley spent the rest of the day begging outside the station. In the afternoon, he spent what he had earned on a secondhand sweater he found in a thrift shop.

One day followed after another. In a story, days can pass as quickly as this, but for Hedley, each day was a long, hard day of real time.

Most people walked past him without a comment. Several older men in suits made nasty comments about boys begging for money from decent people. But often, young people stopped, spoke to him, and gave him money. At night, he grew accustomed to the noise of cars, but still he was woken by cats fighting, radios blasting, or people arguing at three in the morning. One night, he was woken by a flashlight shining into his face. It was the police! They searched his pockets, found nothing, and told him he better find somewhere else to live soon.

The next day, Hedley was tired, bored, and miserable.

"You need to clean yourself up!" the dog said to him. "You're getting dirtier than me."

The dog led Hedley to a shelter for homeless people, where he was given a white robe to change into. He put the clothes he had worn for the last week into a washing machine. Then he took a shower.

Afterward, Mutt said, "You smell a lot better now!"

All the time that he slept near the subway station, Hedley kept an eye on his old home. It was difficult for him to observe his family living their orderly lives, and the boy who used to live on the streets enjoying the warmth of Hedley's bedroom, while Hedley froze out there in the cold.

One evening, Hedley noticed his father struggling to pull something large out of the back of his car. It was a shiny new bike! His father wheeled it to the front of the house and called the boy from upstairs to look at it. Then it dawned on Hedley, who was watching all this with interest. It was his birthday! Of course it was! And Hedley's parents had told him they were going to buy him a bike.

Hedley watched as the boy climbed on the bike. He seemed really pleased with the gift.

Hedley was furious.

He ran across the street and shouted at his parents.

"That bike's mine! It's my birthday today, not his! You're my parents!"

"Get out of here!" Hedley's father shouted. Then he told his wife to go indoors and call the police.

Hedley retreated back to his spot outside the boarded-up shop.

"Uh-oh!" the dog said. "You've got us in trouble now!"

Sure enough, later that evening the police arrived.

"You got to move, son!" the policeman said. "You can't sleep here anymore. Find yourself a shelter."

"Can I just sleep here tonight?" Hedley asked. "I'll move in the morning."

"No," the policeman answered. "You have to move now. We've had complaints."

Hedley picked up his sleeping bag. The policeman watched him as he disappeared down the street.

"Where to now?" Hedley wondered.

"I know another good doorway," the dog said. "Follow me! I used to hang out there before you found me."

Hedley followed the dog through the city, turning left, right, then straight, on past City Hall.

The dog led Hedley to a deep doorway that was nicely sheltered from the cold, rain, and wind.

"Thanks, Mutt," Hedley said. "This place will do just fine."

He curled up in the corner nearest the shop door, held Mutt close to him, and thought about the night's events. Eventually, he fell asleep.

It was not long after that, though, when he felt himself being kicked!

"This is my bedroom!" someone was shouting. "You can't sleep here."

Hedley sat up to find a furious man hollering at him. He thought of putting up a fight, but the dog said, "Let's go! I know another place."

He led Hedley to an unoccupied doorway, which wasn't deep enough to keep out the rain. But it would have to do. Hedley covered his sleeping bag with a black trash bag to keep himself and Mutt dry.

The weeks passed. The months passed. In a story, months can pass as quickly as this, but for Hedley, each month was a long, hard month of real time.

Hedley got to know some of the other street people: Farrukh, Donna, Dave the Rave.

Winter turned to spring, spring to summer, summer to autumn. In a story, a year can pass as quickly as this, but for Hedley, the year was a long, hard year of real time. And after autumn, the cold wintry weather returned.

The first snow reminded Hedley of the subway station where he and the dog used to live.

"Let's go check it out, Mutt."

"Good idea," the dog replied.

Hedley and the dog approached the subway station. The shop was still boarded up. Hedley spoke to the toothless newspaperman.

"How you doin'?" Hedley asked.

"Not too bad," the old man answered.

"We're thinking of moving back here for a while," Hedley said. "Think it would be okay?"

"Try it," the old man suggested. "Perhaps they'll make you move again, I don't know."

"We got nothin' to lose," Hedley said.

So they moved back to his old spot.

It was excellent to be back. Hedley kept watch on his old family again. His dad had a new car, he noticed. His little sister, Serena, now had a tricycle of her own that she rode in the yard. The street boy, who had taken Hedley's place, used his fancy bike to ride to school and back every day.

Late one afternoon, Hedley bumped into Dave the Rave. They greeted each other with a tap of the knuckles and stood talking on the sidewalk.

Out of the corner of his eye, Hedley noticed the boy from across the road, the one who lived in Hedley's house, who slept in Hedley's bed, returning from school on the bike that should have been Hedley's.

Suddenly, a car backed out of a side street without looking! An oncoming car had to swerve to avoid it. But now the swerving car was heading straight for the street boy on his bike!

Without hesitation, Hedley dived into the street and pushed the street boy out of the way. The bike and the two boys tumbled onto the pavement. But the car drove past without hitting either of them.

Hedley was lying on the street. His head was aching! He had struck it on the pavement. Blood ran down the side of his face.

"Are you all right?"

Dave the Rave and the street boy were standing over him. They lifted him to his feet.

"Yeah, I'm not too bad."

"Be more careful next time!" the street boy said to him, passing him the bike. Some of the black covering had torn off the seat, but otherwise the bike was in good shape.

Hedley was amazed to have the bike handed over to him!

What's going on? he thought.

The street boy and Dave the Rave walked off. The dog followed behind them. Then the street boy and Dave the Rave parted company. Hedley watched in astonishment as the street boy returned to his spot at the subway station! He got into his green sleeping bag and the dog curled up beside him.

Hedley was dazed!

He thought that if the street boy had gone back to the subway station, perhaps he could try going back home.

So he did.

He wheeled his bike slowly across the road. He walked in through the gate of his house. His mother came running out of the front door.

"Hedley! Are you hurt?"

"No, I'm okay," Hedley answered.

"You've got blood on your face!" Serena said.

Hedley's mother led him indoors and doctored his injury. He went upstairs to wash and change into other clothes. Then he went back into his bedroom. Everything was still the same. It was as if he had never been away!

How warm his bedroom was, and his bed seemed so soft and luxurious with its springy mattress and clean pillows. From the window, he could see snow falling and the street boy huddling up in his green sleeping bag outside the boarded-up shop.

The street boy suddenly noticed Hedley looking at him. For a moment they stared at each other.

It's going to be a cold winter for him, Hedley thought. *I'm going to give him a parka.*

WORD BANK	**luxurious** (lug ZHUR ee us) *adj.*: rich, comfortable, and pleasurable

Studying the Selection

QUICK REVIEW

1. What does Hedley notice one day outside the subway station?

2. How do Hedley's parents react to the street boy?

3. What do Hedley's parents give him for his birthday?

4. Which part of the dog's behavior tells us that this story is a fantasy?

FOCUS

5. Describe how the street boy treats his dog.

6. Why does the street boy share his food with the dog, if he himself has so little?

CREATING & WRITING

7. One of the ideas of this story is that, if we traded places with people, we would understand them much better. Is there someone with whom you would *not* want to trade places? Why not?

8. Write three entries in the street boy's journal. Use the first-person voice.

9. Many of us complain about the slightest inconvenience. We complain if it is a few degrees too hot or too cold, if the choice of foods is not exactly to our liking, and so on. How many of us stop each day to appreciate the many things we have? Write a list of ten things that the street boy did not have and that you do have. On a piece of oak tag or construction paper, draw an attractive border, and write the list of ten things for which you should be thankful. Post the sign in your classroom or in your bedroom at home. Before you complain, read it, and think!

Waking

Lilian Moore

My secret way of waking
is like a place
to hide.
I'm very still,
5   my eyes are shut.
They all think I am sleeping
but
I'm wide awake inside.
They all think I am sleeping
10   but
I'm wiggling my toes.
I feel sun-fingers
on my cheek.
I hear voices whisper-speak.
15   I squeeze my eyes
to keep them shut
so they will think I'm sleeping
BUT
I'm really awake inside
20   —and no one knows!

First Day Back

Yuka Igarashi

My father went to Spain
And came home with
Jet lag
He said he couldn't sleep
5   At night
And that he was awfully tired
All day
And that he felt
Sort of blurry and
10   Sort of bewildered
Almost like he was floating
Somewhere
Well you know
I guess
15   School
And summer
Are in different time zones
Too

TRUTH

BARRIE WADE

Sticks and stones may break my bones,
but words can also hurt me.
Stones and sticks break only skin,
while words are ghosts that haunt me.

5   Slant and curved the word-swords fall
to pierce and stick inside me.
Bats and bricks may ache through bones,
but words can mortify me.

Pain from words has left its scar
10 on mind and heart that's tender.
Cuts and bruises now have healed;
it's words that I remember.

My House

Annette M'baye d'Erneville

I have built my house
Without sand, without water
My mother's heart
Forms a great wall
5   My father's arms
The floor and the roof
My sister's laughter
The doors and the windows
My brother's eyes
10   Light up the house
My home feels good
My home is sweet

ABOUT THE AUTHORS

Born in New York City in 1909, *Lilian Moore* developed a love of reading from the moment she discovered the way to the New York Public Library. When she graduated from college, she took a job teaching children to read, but was frustrated by the lack of good books. She decided to write books that were easy to read and exciting. And she did! She published almost fifty children's books and several volumes of poetry for children. In addition, she worked for many years as a respected editor of children's books. Moore and her husband Sam Reavin lived in Seattle, Washington. She died in 2004.

Annette M'baye d'Erneville was born in Senegal in 1926. After earning her teaching degree in Senegal in 1945, she traveled to Paris to study education. In 1959 she returned to Senegal, where she worked as a reporter. In 1963, she founded a women's magazine—*Aua*. She later became Program Director of Radio Senegal. Throughout her various careers, d'Erneville wrote poetry. She wrote about her love for people, women in African society, and life's challenges. D'Erneville, who writes in French, has published two volumes of poetry.

Studying the Selection   POETRY

Waking

1. What is this poem about? Give a short, simple answer in two or three sentences.

2. The poem has three sentences that use the word *but*. What are they? (Write down each sentence.)

3. Each of the *but* sentences tells us that people think the child is sleeping *but—but* what? What is the child actually doing in each of these instances?

4. What are the two made-up words in the poem?

5. Which one of the made-up words is a metaphor? Which of the made-up words has onomatopoeia?

First Day Back

1. Have you ever experienced jet lag? If you have, describe how it felt in several sentences. If not, describe the difference between feeling sick and feeling well.

2. How many sentences does the poet use?

3. Do you think the comparison of jet lag with summer vacation is a good one? Give your reasons for your answer.

TRUTH

1. This poem borrows its first stanza from a well-known saying. What is that saying?

2. Which three pairs of words (from Lines 2 and 4 in each stanza) *almost* rhyme with each other?

3. Have your words ever bruised someone? What is the best way to apologize for hurtful words you have said?

My House

1. What did the author build her house *without?*

2. What are the four metaphors in the poem?

3. If you were writing a similar poem, to which parts of a house would you compare your father and mother and two of your siblings? Choose different parts from those mentioned in the poem. Be prepared to explain why you chose the parts you did.

UNIT FIVE WRAP-UP

The Memory Box • The Greatest Snowball Fight in History
Founders of the Children's Rain Forest • Jessica Govea
The Street Boy

DON'T JUDGE A BOOK BY ITS COVER!

For *Founders of the Children's Rain Forest,* you chose an organization working to save the rain forest. Then you wrote to them for information. Now is the time for you to use that information.

1. To which organization did you write?

2. Have you received an answer? If not, go to #4.

3. Write about the organization and the work that they do.

4. If you did not receive a response from your organization, write your report from materials supplied by your teacher and from the library.

Think of a good title for your report. Make a cover. Enclose your report in the cover you have made.

CHOOSE YOUR MOTTO

1. A *motto* is a phrase or short sentence that expresses a basic truth. What is a *proverb?* What is an *adage* (ADD idg)? What is a *maxim?* *Motto, proverb, adage,* and *maxim* are four words that are closely related in meaning.

2. Look up the four words in the dictionary and write down their meanings.

3. Below is a list of mottoes, proverbs, and sayings. Pick one that you think describes a character or the circumstances in one of the five stories in this unit.

4. Using any medium you like (paint, pen, crayon, marker), put the motto you have chosen on paper. Oak tag will work best. On the back, note which story or character you think it represents.

- *A candle loses nothing of its light by lighting another candle.*
  — James Keller

- *Injustice anywhere is a threat to justice everywhere.*
  — Martin Luther King, Jr.

- *From small beginnings come great things.* — American Proverb

- *The journey of a thousand miles must begin with a single step.*
  — Chinese Proverb

- *If I am not for myself, who will be for me? If I am not for others, what am I? And if not now, when?* — Hillel

- *Let's treat the world as though we plan to stay!* — Margaret Mead

- *Teachers open the door but you must walk through it yourself.*
  — Chinese Proverb

- *G-d gave burdens, also shoulders.* — Yiddish Proverb

- *There is nothing noble in being superior to some other person.*
  — Indian Proverb

- *All work and no play makes Jack a dull boy.* England, 17th Century

INTERVIEW A CHARACTER, OR BE A CHARACTER THAT IS BEING INTERVIEWED

You will work with one other student.

1. Together, choose a character from one of the stories in Unit Five to be interviewed.

2. One student will be the famous character, and one, the famous radio interviewer.

3. Working together, write a script of the interview, both the questions and the answers.

4. The interview should tell us more about the character than we were able to learn from the story. (You will have to use your imaginations.)

5. You may be funny if you are respectful. If you are exploring serious questions, you may be very serious.

6. Your interview should take about ten minutes.

7. Make sure you practice before presenting your interview to the class.

DRAMATIC PERFORMANCE FROM *JESSICA GOVEA*

This exercise should be done in groups of six.

1. Reread *Jessica Govea.*

2. As a group, decide which part of the story you can act out.

3. Write a script and develop a plan for staging the scene you have written. You may wish to divide the tasks—writing, props, scenery, acting—among the group.

4. Show your teacher your script ahead of time, *with stage directions.*

5. Rehearse at least three times.

6. Make a sign that tells the audience which story you have chosen to act out, and who the characters are. Don't forget about sound effects and props.

unit 6

THE
GRAND
FINALÉ

AUTOBIOGRAPHY

- The prefix *auto-* means *self.* An autobiography is the biography of one's self.

- An autobiography is written in the first-person.

- Autobiography is one type of nonfiction.

- An autobiography can have all of the elements of a fictional story: plot, characterization, dialogue, and theme.

THINK ABOUT IT!

1. Why did the author start running?

2. What does the author mean when he says, "I gave into reality and walked…"?

3. What character trait does the author possess, based on the story?

4. The author writes that he muttered, "'Just keep putting one foot in front of the other.'" Do you think he really said that to himself? If not, what do you think he meant to tell the reader?

Just Jog

In 1999, overweight and out of shape, I began running. The best I could do my first time out was eighteen minutes. In the years since, I have run 5K races and even a 10K, but 18 minutes has remained my benchmark minimum any time I go out. Then, in February, 2001—in the best shape of my life—I was stricken with a blood clot.

Recovery included taking a blood thinner for six weeks, and that meant no running. To make matters worse, even the walking I was doing ended up leading to complications: the blood thinner caused a very painful slow bleed into my left thigh that left me walking with a cane.

I was devastated. All I could do was wait for my body to heal.

Finally, one clear May morning, I decided I'd waited long enough. I laced up my running shoes and headed out for a jog. More of a hop-jog really. My left leg was still weak and quite stiff. I hop-jogged from one telephone pole to the next, then gave in to reality and walked the next segment. Hop-jog. Walk. Hop-jog. Walk. I don't know how long I was out, but I realized I needed a little more time before I'd be running again.

In June, I decided to give it another try, this time on a treadmill. After walking a few minutes to warm up, I increased the pace on the machine and took note of the time. I wasn't going to set any speed records, but I figured I'd shoot for ten minutes steady jogging.

Five minutes passed. No pain. I felt good.

I increased the pace a little.

I was surprised at how easily the ten-minute mark came.

"Don't think." I told myself. "Just jog."

But deep down, as I passed the 12- and 13-minute marks, I knew I was determined to get my 18 minutes.

"Just keep putting one foot in front of the other," I muttered.

16.

16:30.

17.

17:30.

Steady now.

18!

My heart was filled with gratitude as I slowed the treadmill to cool down. I was back!

INTO . . . Small Steps

A young girl becomes ill with a terrible disease—polio. It is like an unseen enemy, striking in the dark, causing injury and death. At the time the story takes place, there is no known way to stop this dread disease. It attacks, and the helpless victim gets sicker and sicker. There are some ways of fighting the illness once it has struck, but they are slow, painful, and often unsuccessful.

Being stricken with polio is like entering a nightmare or a dark tunnel. Where will it lead? How will it end?

EYES ON . . . Autobiography/Author's Purpose

When a writer begins to tell the story of his or her own life, something unexpected may happen. Instead of feeling as though they are writing a personal history, the writer may feel like the story is about somebody else.

As the author writes down some memories, other, forgotten memories may float to the surface. The process of writing may become, for the autobiographer, a journey of discovery.

small STEPS:

The Year I Got Polio

Peg Kehret

Prologue[1]

Before a polio vaccine was developed, polio killed or crippled thousands of people each year. A president of the United States, Franklin Delano Roosevelt, got polio as a young father. He spent the rest of his life in a wheelchair, using hip-high leg braces and a cane when he needed to stand to make a speech.

Children, however, are more likely to get polio than adults are. It is a highly contagious disease, and in 1949 there were 42,033 cases reported in the United States. There was only one case diagnosed that year in Austin, Minnesota: a twelve-year-old girl, Peg Schulze. Me.

The disease's full name is poliomyelitis,[2] or infantile paralysis,[3] but it is usually called polio. The polio virus attacks the nerve cells which control the muscles of the body.

If damage to the nerve cells is slight, the muscle weakness will be temporary. If the virus kills many nerve cells, paralysis will be extensive and possibly permanent.

There is no cure for polio. There are no miracle medicines to stop the damage to nerve cells or repair those already damaged.

When I began to write about my polio days, long-forgotten memories bubbled to the surface. I was astonished by the intense emotions these memories brought with them. Those months, more than any other time of my life, molded my personality.

Since I have no transcript of these events, the dialogue is not strictly accurate, but the people mentioned are all real people. The incidents all happened, and the voices are as close to reality as I can make them.

Although I used fictional techniques[4] to write this book, I can verify my feelings about everything that happened—and feelings are the most important part of any story.

---

1. A *prologue* (PRO log) is an introduction that gives the background for the literary work that follows.
2. *Poliomyelitis* (PO lee O MY uh LY tus)
3. *Infantile paralysis* (IN fun TYL puh RA lih sus)
4. *Fictional techniques* are methods an author uses in writing works of fiction—stories that are not true.

WORD BANK	**accurate** (AK yuh rut) *adj.:* perfectly correct
	verify (VAIR ih fy) *v.:* prove the truth of

The Diagnosis

My ordeal began on a Friday early in September. In school that morning, I glanced at the clock often, eager for the Homecoming parade at four o'clock. As a seventh-grader, it was my first chance to take part in the Homecoming fun. For a week, my friends and I had spent every spare moment working on the seventh-grade float, and we were sure it would win first prize.

My last class before lunch was chorus. I loved to sing, and we were practicing a song whose lyrics are the inscription on the Statue of Liberty. Usually the words "Give me your tired, your poor..." brought goosebumps to my arms, but on Homecoming day, I was distracted by a twitching muscle in my left thigh. As I sang, a section of my blue skirt popped up and down as if jumping beans lived in my leg.

I pressed my hand against my thigh, trying to make the muscle be still, but it leaped and jerked beneath my fingers. I stretched my leg forward and rotated the ankle. Twitch, twitch. Next I tightened my leg muscles for a few seconds and then relaxed them. Nothing helped.

The bell rang. When I started toward my locker, my legs buckled as if I had nothing but cotton inside my skin. I collapsed, scattering my books on the floor.

Someone yelled, "Peg fainted!" but I knew I had not fainted because my eyes stayed open and I was conscious. I sat on the floor for a moment while my classmates collected my books.

"Are you all right?" my friend Karen asked as she helped me stand up.

WORD BANK	**ordeal** (or DEEL) *n.*: any extremely trying or severe test or experience
	lyrics (LIHR iks) *n.*: the words of a song
	buckled (BUK uld) *v.*: collapsed

"Yes. I don't know what happened."

"You look pale."

"I'm fine," I insisted. "Really."

I put my books in my locker and went home for lunch, as I did every day.

Two days earlier, I'd gotten a sore throat and headache. Now I also felt weak, and my back hurt. What rotten timing, I thought, to get sick on Homecoming day.

Although my legs felt wobbly, I walked the twelve blocks home. I didn't tell my mother about the fall or about my headache and other problems because I knew she would make me stay home. I didn't want to miss that parade.

I was glad to sit down to eat lunch. Maybe, I thought, I should not have stayed up so late the night before. Or maybe I'm just hungry. As soon as I eat, I won't feel so weak.

When I reached for my glass of milk, my hand shook so hard I couldn't pick up the glass. I grasped it with both hands; they trembled so badly that milk sloshed over the side.

Mother put her hand on my forehead. "You feel hot," she said. "You're going straight to bed."

It was a relief to lie down. I wondered why my back hurt; I hadn't lifted anything heavy. I couldn't imagine why I was so tired, either. I felt as if I had not slept in days.

I fell asleep right away and woke three hours later with a stiff neck. My back hurt even more than it had earlier, and now my legs ached as well. Several times I had painful muscle spasms in my legs and toes. The muscles tightened until my knees bent and my toes curled, and I was unable to straighten my legs or toes until the spasms gradually passed.

I looked at the clock; the Homecoming parade started in fifteen minutes.

"I want to go to the parade," I said.

Mother stuck a thermometer in my mouth, said, "One

It's a relief to lie down.

Why does my back hurt. I haven't lifted anything heavy.

Why am I so tired. I feel as if I haven't slept in days.

hundred and two," and called the doctor. The seventh-grade float would have to win first place without me. I went back to sleep.

Dr. Wright came, took my temperature, listened to my breathing, and talked with Mother. Mother sponged my forehead with a cold cloth. I dozed, woke, and slept again.

At midnight, I began to vomit. Mother and Dad helped me to the bathroom; we all assumed I had the flu.

Dr. Wright returned before breakfast the next morning and took my temperature again. "Still one hundred and two," he said. He helped me sit up, with my feet dangling over the side of the bed. He tapped my knees with his rubber mallet; this was supposed to make my legs jerk. They didn't. They hung limp and unresponsive. I was too woozy from pain and fever to care.

He ran his fingernail across the bottom of my foot, from the heel to the toes. It felt awful, but I couldn't pull my foot away. He did the same thing on the other foot, with the same effect. I wished he would leave me alone so I could sleep.

"I need to do a spinal tap[5] on her," he told my parents. "Can you take her to the hospital right away?"

Dad helped me out of bed. I was too sick to get dressed.

At the hospital, I lay on my side while Dr. Wright inserted a needle into my spinal column and withdrew some fluid. Although it didn't take long, it was painful.

The laboratory analyzed the fluid immediately. When Dr. Wright got the results, he asked my parents to go to another room. While I dozed again, he told them the diagnosis, and they returned alone to tell me.

Mother held my hand.

"You have polio," Dad said, as he stroked my hair back from my forehead. "You will need to go to a special hospital for polio patients, in Minneapolis."

---

5. A *spinal tap* is a medical test in which fluid is withdrawn from the patient's spine. It can be very painful.

Polio! Panic shot through me, and I began to cry. I had seen Life magazine pictures of polio patients in wheelchairs or wearing heavy iron leg braces. Each year the March of Dimes, which raised money to aid polio patients and fund research, printed a poster featuring a child in a wheelchair or wearing leg braces or using walking sticks. The posters hung in stores, schools, and libraries—frequent reminders of the terrible and lasting effects of polio. Everyone was afraid of polio. Since the epidemics usually happened in warm weather, children were kept away from swimming pools and other crowded public places every summer because their parents didn't want them exposed to the virus.

How could I have polio? I didn't know anyone who had the disease. Where did the virus come from? How did it get in my body?

I didn't want to have polio; I didn't want to leave my family and go to a hospital one hundred miles from home.

I DON'T WANT TO HAVE POLIO!

I don't want to leave my family

and go to a hospital

one hundred miles from home.

As we drove home to pack, I sat slumped in the back seat. "How long will I have to stay in the hospital?" I asked.

"Until you're well," Mother said.

WORD BANK	**fund** *v.*: pay for

I caught the look of dread and uncertainty that passed between my parents. It might be weeks or months or even years before I came home. It might be never; people sometimes died from polio.

That fear, unspoken, settled over us like a blanket, smothering further conversation.

When we got home, I was not allowed to leave the car, not even to say good-bye to Grandpa, who lived with us, or to B.J., my dog. We could not take a chance of spreading the deadly virus. Our orders were strict: I must contaminate no one.

"Karen called," Mother said when she returned with a suitcase. "The seventh-grade float won second prize." I was too sick and frightened to care.

Grandpa waved at me through the car window. Tears glistened on his cheeks. I had never seen my grandfather cry.

Later that morning, I walked into the isolation ward[6] of the Sheltering Arms Hospital in Minneapolis and went to bed in a private room. No one was allowed in except the doctors and nurses, and they wore masks. My parents stood outside on the grass, waving bravely and blowing kisses through the window. Exhausted, feverish, and scared, I fell asleep.

When I woke up, I was paralyzed.

I am paralyzed

6. When a patient has a very contagious disease, he or she is separated, or isolated, from other patients. The section of the hospital where several patients are kept separate from the others is called an *isolation ward.*

Paralyzed from the Neck Down

My mouth felt full of sawdust; my lips stuck together in the corners. As I opened my eyes, I saw a glass of ice water on the table beside my bed. It was exactly what I needed, but when I tried to reach the water, my right arm did not move.

I tried again. Nothing happened. I tried with my left arm. Nothing. I tried to bend my knees so I could roll on my side, but my legs were two logs, stiff and unmoving. I was too weak even to lift my head off the pillow.

"Help!"

A nurse ran in.

"I can't reach the water," I said. "There's something wrong with my hands. I'm thirsty, but when I try to get the glass..."

"Hush," she said. She lifted the glass and slipped a straw between my lips. "There you are. Have your drink."

I took only a sip. "What's wrong with my arms and legs?" I asked. "Why can't I move?"

"You have polio," she said, as if that explained everything.

"But I could move before I fell asleep. I walked in here. I had polio then, and I could still move."

"Don't try to talk. Save your energy." She held the straw to my lips again, and I drank the glass of water. "I'll be right back," she said when I finished.

She returned quickly, with a doctor. While he examined me, the nurse held a clipboard and made notes.

"Move your right hand," the doctor said.

I tried; my hand did not move.

"Try to wiggle your fingers."

My fingers lay like an empty glove.

He put his hand around my wrist and lifted my arm a foot off the bed. "Hold your arm in the air when I let go," he said.

I felt like the Raggedy Ann doll I'd left on my bed at home.

I could feel his hand on my wrist, but when he let go, my arm flopped down. I felt like the Raggedy Ann doll I'd left on my bed at home.

He pulled back the sheet. I wore a hospital gown rather than my own pajamas. I did not remember putting it on, and I wondered who had undressed me.

"Try to lift your left leg."

I closed my eyes and concentrated. My leg remained on the bed.

"Now try to lift your right leg."

My right leg stayed where it was.

"Can you wiggle your toes?"

I could not.

Each time the doctor asked me to move a part of my body and I could not move it, my terror increased. I could talk, I could open and close my eyes, and I could turn my head from side to side on my pillow, but otherwise I could not move at all.

The doctor ran a wooden tongue depressor up the bottoms of my feet. I wanted to kick it away, but my feet wouldn't budge.

He placed his hands on my ribs. "Intercostal expansion is poor," he said.

I felt as if I needed a translator. "What does that mean?" I asked.

"The muscles which expand the rib cage when you breathe are weak," the nurse explained.

The doctor said, "Diagnosis is acute anterior poliomyelitis. The patient is paralyzed from the neck down."

I did not need a translator for his last sentence.

The doctor left, saying he would return in an hour to check me.

"We'll keep you comfortable," the nurse said, "and I'll tell your parents about the paralysis."

"Are they here?" I asked. "I want to see them."

I'm paralyzed from the neck down

paralyzed from
the neck down

ParAlyzed
fRom thE
NeCK DOwN

I AM
PaRALYZED
FROM THE
NECK DOWN

"I'm sorry," she said. "You're in isolation. No visitors are allowed." She started for the door, turned, and added, "We can't risk spreading this disease."

She left me alone with my terror.

Don't think about being paralyzed, I told myself. But how could I think of anything else?

The nurse had forgotten to pull the sheet back up, and the skimpy hospital gown did not even reach my knees. I wanted to cover myself, but I couldn't.

Feeling vulnerable and exposed, I grew more panicky. What if the hospital caught fire? How would I get out?

The doctor's words played over and over in my mind like a broken record. "The patient is paralyzed from the neck down. The patient is paralyzed from the neck down."

I wanted Mother and Dad. I wanted to be well again. I wanted to go home.

When the doctor returned an hour later, I felt short of breath.

"The patient's nostrils are flaring," he said to the nurse. I wondered if he was describing me or a horse.

For two days the fever stayed at one hundred and two, and it became increasingly difficult to breathe. Mostly, I slept, waking often because of muscle spasms or because my back and neck ached so badly. A nurse gently massaged my shoulders, back, and legs, which helped temporarily. I was given aspirin for the pain.

My voice developed a nasal twang. I sounded like a bad tape recording of myself.

The nurses told me that my parents sent their love. They were waiting nearby and wanted to see me, but it was against the hospital rules. Mother and Dad had already been exposed to me at home and in the car when they drove me to the hospital, so why couldn't they visit me now?

WORD BANK	**vulnerable** (VUHL nuh ruh buhl) *adj.*: easily hurt physically or emotionally

Doctors and nurses checked me frequently and urged me to drink something. I drank water, but it became harder and harder to swallow. I wanted only to be left alone so I could sleep. When I slept, I did not hurt.

On my third day at the Sheltering Arms, the doctor said, "The patient may need a respirator."

"University hospital?" the nurse said.

The doctor nodded.

"I'll arrange for an ambulance," the nurse said.

That conversation got my attention, and I roused myself enough to ask, "What's happening?"

The doctor put his hand on my shoulder. "There is more than one kind of polio," he said. "One is spinal polio. It's the most common type and causes paralysis in the patient's arms and legs."

"That's what I have?" I asked. "That's why I can't move?"

"Yes. You have spinal polio. Another kind of polio is respiratory; it causes difficulty in breathing."

I was acutely aware of how hard it was for me to breathe. Was he telling me I had two kinds of polio?

"Because you have respiratory polio, too," he said, "we're transferring you to the University of Minnesota Hospital. We're afraid your lungs may not continue to function on their own."

What was he saying? If my lungs quit working, I would stop breathing, and if I stopped breathing, I would die. Is that what the doctor meant—that I was going to die? I desperately wanted my parents.

The doctor continued: "The Sheltering Arms is a rehabilitation center[7] for polio patients who are trying to regain the use of their muscles. It is not equipped to deal with cases as critical as yours. University Hospital has respirators, and I want you to be near

If my lungs quit working

I WILL STOP BREATHING

IF I STOP BREATHING I will die

Am I GOING TO DIE

I want my parents

---

7. A *rehabilitation center* is a place where sick or injured patients go to recover. They are past the worst stages of their illnesses, and are at the center to receive treatments to help them grow stronger.

one. If your lungs can't function on their own, the respirator will help. It will breathe for you."

I didn't know what a respirator was, but if it would help me breathe, it must be okay. At least it seemed I was not going to die right on the spot.

"You'll be taken by ambulance to University Hospital," he continued. "I hope you'll be back at the Sheltering Arms soon."

I said nothing. I had not wanted to come to the Sheltering Arms in the first place. Why would I be in any hurry to return?

This move was bad news—it meant I was so sick that I needed a hospital with more emergency facilities than the Sheltering Arms had. I could not sit up. I could not move my arms or legs. It was hard to breathe and I was burning with fever and I was far more frightened than I had ever been in my entire life. I not only had polio, I had two kinds of polio—spinal and respiratory.

"I'll call your parents," the doctor said softly, patting my arm. "They can meet you at University Hospital."

I was transferred from the bed to a gurney and wheeled out a door where an ambulance waited. The cool outdoor air brought me out of my feverish stupor. I was surprised to see that it was dark out; I had lost all track of time.

This is backward, I thought. I walked into the hospital by myself and now, three days later, I can't move at all. Hospitals are supposed to make you get better, not worse.

While the attendants opened the ambulance doors and prepared to load me in, I heard a buzzing sound. A mosquito was flying around my head.

Zzzzt. Zzzzt. I turned my face from side to side, hoping to discourage it from landing on me, but the buzzing grew louder

I am too sick for Sheltering Arms

I'm being transferred to University Hospital

WORD BANK gurney (GUR nee) *n.:* a narrow, padded table on wheels used for moving patients

and then abruptly stopped. I could not swat the mosquito or brush it away, and it bit me on the cheek.

As we drove through the streets of Minneapolis, people in cars looked curiously in the ambulance window. I longed to pull the blanket up over my head, but I could not move my hands. Instead, I shut my eyes and pretended I was dead. That seemed a fine joke on those who stared, and gave me great satisfaction.

With my eyes shut, pretending to be dead, I fell asleep. When I woke up, I was in a different hospital bed.

"Where are my parents?" I asked the nurse.

"You're in the isolation ward. No visitors are allowed."

"But the doctor at the Sheltering Arms called them. He told me they would meet me here."

She glanced at my chart. "They were here when you were admitted," she said. "They signed the papers."

"Why didn't someone wake me up?"

Angry tears filled my eyes. I had slept through my chance to see my parents.

No one except the doctors and nurses could come in my room. They wore masks, gowns, and gloves that were sterilized or destroyed after they cared for me.

The next day I had another spinal tap. That afternoon, a new doctor stood beside my bed. "There is more than one kind of polio," he said.

I opened my mouth to interrupt and tell him I already knew all about it, but before I could say anything, he said, "The least common kind is called bulbar polio."

Bulbar? That was a new word. I braced myself for more bad news.

"Bulbar is the most serious form of polio," he continued.

"Worse than spinal or respiratory?" I didn't see how that was

I have bulbar polio
the most serious kind

possible. What could be worse than being paralyzed from the neck down and unable to breathe properly?

"Bulbar polio impairs the patient's ability to talk or swallow."

I whispered my question. "Do I have bulbar polio?" I knew the answer; why else would he be explaining this? But I had to ask.

His answer was simple and direct. "Yes."

I could think of nothing to say. I had three kinds of polio.

"There's a call button next to your hand," he said, indicating the cord with a button at the end that lay on my bed. Then he glanced at my chart. "You can't use it, can you?"

I tried to push the button, just in case I'd had a miraculous cure in the last five minutes, but my fingers remained where they were. "No."

"If you can't swallow and start to choke, yell for a nurse. There's always someone nearby."

His words, intended to reassure me, filled me with panic. If I was choking, how could I call for a nurse?

An Oxygen Tent and a Chocolate Milkshake

Days and nights blurred together.

My parents came in, wearing hospital gowns, gloves, and masks.

As they stood beside my bed, I saw fear in their eyes. I realized they were allowed into the isolation ward now, when they had not been earlier, because I was so sick that the doctors weren't sure if I would live.

I was glad to have them there, though they were not allowed to touch me and could stay only a few minutes. Always, in the past, they had made everything all right for me. I felt safer knowing they were in the room.

I still had a fever. I ached all over, my throat hurt, and I couldn't shift position in bed without help. Periodically a nurse turned me from my side to my back and, later, to the other side. That eased the pain temporarily, but it always came back.

"We're going to put you in an oxygen tent," the doctor said. It was the same doctor who had told me about bulbar polio. Was it the same day? The same week? I didn't know if I had slept five minutes or a month.

"We hope the oxygen will keep you breathing on your own," he continued. "If not, a respirator will help you."

I looked where he pointed, and a wave of horror poured over me as I realized respirator was another name for what was popularly called an iron lung.

I had seen pictures of people in iron lungs. The tube-shaped machine completely enclosed the patient's body. Only the head

If I can't bReAThE, I will bE put IN the iRon LuNg

WORD BANK	**periodically** (PIH ree AH dik lee) *adv.:* every so often

stuck out. Bellows pumped air in and out, causing the patient's lungs to expand and contract.[8] Small doors and portholes on the sides of the iron lung allowed the nurses to put their hands in to bathe the patients and help with toileting. Portions of the doors were clear plastic so the nurses could see what they were doing.

Some patients stayed in iron lungs for the rest of their lives, never again breathing by themselves. I thought it would be like being put in a coffin while you were still alive.

Now an iron lung loomed beside my bed, hoses hanging like tentacles—a gray octopus ready to swallow me at any moment.

As I imagined my future in an iron lung, tears of despair rolled down my cheeks. I could not raise my hand to wipe them away, and they ran into my ears.

iRon LuNg

---

8. *Expand* means to open wider and *contract* means to squeeze together and become smaller. When people breathe, their lungs open wide to admit oxygen, then squeeze closed to force out carbon dioxide.

WORD BANK	**bellows** (BELL oze) *n.:* a device for producing a strong current of air

Until I got polio, I had led a carefree life. My brother, Art, is six years older than I; my parents had longed for a baby girl, and my birth was cause for celebration. Throughout my childhood, I was dearly loved, and I knew it.

My earliest memories are of swinging, with lilacs in bloom on both sides of my swing—flying high past the purple blossoms, surrounded by the scent; of pushing Raggedy Ann and Marilyn, my favorite dolls, in my doll buggy; of sitting on a picnic bench with my mother's relatives around me, all of them singing old folk songs and lullabies.

Nothing in these experiences had prepared me for the words "The patient is paralyzed from the neck down" or the sight of an iron lung standing beside my hospital bed.

The oxygen tent was a sheet of plastic that was draped over me from my waist to the back of my head. Inside the plastic, oxygen was released for me to breathe. A frame kept the plastic three feet above my head and chest while the four sides hung down to touch my bed. Looking through it was like viewing the room through a foggy windshield.

My parents brought me a teddy bear from Art, who was a freshman at Carleton College. They put the little bear inside the oxygen tent.

"This oxygen tent is just what you need," Mother said, her cheerfulness sounding forced. "It will make it easier to breathe, and you'll soon feel better."

The extra oxygen did ease my breathing, but nothing helped the fever and pain.

Once, in the middle of the night, I awoke aching all over. I badly wanted to roll onto my other side.

"Nurse!" I yelled, as loudly as I could. "Nurse!"

The night nurse rushed into my room.

"I need to be turned," I said.

"What?" She said it as if she had never heard of anything so outrageous.

"I need to be turned," I repeated.

"No, you don't!" She stood beside my bed, hands on her hips, and glared at me.

She was a large woman, and seen through the oxygen tent, she looked even bigger.

"I just turned you, not ten minutes ago," she scolded. "I'm not turning you again already. You'll get turned every thirty minutes, the same as every other patient in this ward."

"But my legs hurt."

"They're going to hurt no matter how many times I roll you around, so you might as well get used to it."

"My back hurts, too. I want to lie on my other side." Years of prodding by my mother surfaced; I added the magic word: "Please?"

I need to be turned   I need to be turned   I need to be turned

I need to be turned   I need to be turned   I need to be turned

PLEASE

I am too busy to run in here

just to turn you in that bed.

Don't you call me again

unless it's an emergency.

DO NOT CALL ME UNLESS

YOU CAN'T BREATHE!

"I am too busy to run in here just to turn you in that bed." She shook a finger at me. "Don't you call me again, unless it's an emergency. You hear me? Do not call me unless you can't breathe."

My legs throbbed, my arms ached, my back, neck, and throat hurt. I lay there, helpless, staring at her. She could have turned me in the time it took to tell me no, I thought. And how was I supposed to call for help if I couldn't breathe?

At that moment, I wanted to go home more than I had ever wanted anything, but along with the river of homesickness that flowed through my veins came a trickle of indignation. I was angry at her and angry at my disease. I am not, I decided, going to lie here and be helpless for the rest of my life. I'm going to fight.

I squinted at the nurse through the plastic oxygen tent. Someday, I vowed, she'll be sorry. I'll fight this polio, and I'll beat it. I'll walk out of here, and I'll tell the whole world about the mean nurse who would not help a paralyzed child turn over in bed.

When my parents visited the next day, I told them about the nurse who refused to turn me. They were furious. I don't know what they said, or to whom, but that night, I had a different nurse. The one who wouldn't turn me was never my nurse again.

During those first days in the hospital, I ate almost nothing. Even if food had sounded good, which it didn't, it was now increasingly difficult to swallow. My throat felt swollen shut, and its muscles didn't want to work.

All my life, I had swallowed without any conscious thought. Now I had to think about each step of the process and force my

I'm not going to lie here and be helpless for the rest of my life

I'M GOING TO FIGHT!

WORD BANK	**indignation** (IN dig NAY shun) *n.:* anger at something because it is unfair or insulting

My throat feels swollen
shut, and its muscles
don't want to work

throat muscles to perform what used to be a simple act. It was hard to swallow my own saliva. Food was more than I could manage.

Because of my fever, it was important for me to drink lots of liquid. I tried to drink some ice water each time my parents and the nurses held the glass for me. I was also given apple juice, grape juice, and 7-Up, but they were no easier to swallow than water. I was not offered milk even though I drank milk at home. Because milk creates phlegm, or mucus, in the throat, patients with bulbar polio were not allowed any milk or ice cream for fear it would make them choke.

One evening, a particularly patient nurse coaxed me to drink some 7-Up. She put one hand behind my head and lifted it gently, to make it easier for me to swallow. "Just take little sips," she said.

I wanted to drink the 7-Up, to please her and because I was thirsty. I sucked a mouthful through the straw, but when I tried to swallow, my throat didn't work and all the 7-Up came out my nose. As the fizzy liquid stung the inside of my nose, I sputtered and choked. The choking made it hard to get my breath, and that frightened me. If I couldn't breathe, I would be put in the iron lung.

After that, I didn't want to drink. I was afraid it would come out my nose again; I was afraid of choking. Only the constant urging of my parents and the nurses got enough fluids into me.

Eight days after my polio was diagnosed, my fever still stayed at one hundred two degrees. My breathing was shallow, the painful muscle spasms continued, and every inch of my body hurt. It was like having a bad case of the flu that never ended. My only bits of pleasure in the long hours of pain were the brief visits from my parents and looking at the little teddy bear that Art had sent.

On the afternoon of the eighth day, Mother said, "We can't go on like this. You need more nourishment. You'll never get well if you don't swallow something besides water and juice. Isn't there anything that sounds good? Think hard. If you could have anything you wanted to eat or drink, what would it be?"

"A chocolate milkshake," I said.

NO MILK, my chart stated. NO ICE CREAM.

A chocolate MILKSHAKE!

Mother told a nurse, "Peg would like a chocolate milkshake."

"We can't let her have a milkshake," the nurse replied. "I'm sorry."

"She needs nourishment," Mother declared, "especially liquid. She thinks she can drink a milkshake."

"She could choke on it," the nurse said. "It's absolutely against the doctor's orders." She left the room, muttering about interfering parents.

"You rest for a bit," Mother told me. "We'll be back soon." She and Dad went out.

They returned in less than an hour, carrying a white paper bag. The nurse followed them into my room.

"I won't be responsible for this," she said, as she watched Dad take a milkshake container out of the bag. "Milk and ice cream are the worst things you could give her."

Dad took the lid off the container while Mother unwrapped a paper straw.

"We know you have to follow the rules," Dad said, "but we don't. This is our daughter, and she has had nothing to eat for over a week. If a chocolate milkshake is what she wants, and she thinks she can drink it, then a chocolate milkshake is what she is going to have."

He handed the milkshake to Mother, who put the straw in it.

"What if she chokes to death?" the nurse demanded. "How are you going to feel if you lose her because of a milkshake?"

"If something doesn't change soon," Dad replied, "we're going to lose her anyway. At least this way, we'll know we tried everything we could."

Mother thrust the milkshake under the oxygen tent and guided the straw between my lips.

I sucked the cold, thick chocolate shake into my mouth, held it there for a second, and swallowed. It slipped smoothly down my throat. For the first time since I got sick, something tasted good.

I took another mouthful and swallowed it. I had to work at swallowing, but the milkshake went down. The next mouthful went down, too, and the one after that. I drank the whole milkshake and never choked once, even though I was lying flat on my back the whole time.

When I made a loud slurping sound with my straw because the container was empty, my parents clapped and cheered. The relieved nurse cheered with them.

Within an hour, my temperature dropped. That chocolate milkshake may have saved my life.

That chocolate milkshake may have saved my life!

Studying the Selection

QUICK REVIEW

1. What is the author's name?

2. How old was the author, and where was she living, when she became ill with polio?

3. What does Dr. Wright learn from the spinal tap?

4. When Peg's Grandpa waves goodbye to her through the car window, what does she see that she has never seen before?

FOCUS

5. Why may it be difficult to go back in your mind and relive major life events?

6. What do you think the author means, when she says she has used "fictional techniques"?

CREATING & WRITING

7. Using information from the library and/or materials your teacher supplies, write about one aspect of polio. Choose something you have learned about this disease that interests you.

8. Have you ever been ill? Close your eyes and go back to that time. Then write about it. Write the way you *felt,* from moment to moment.

9. There are many types of get-well cards you can buy. Some are humorous, some are serious, some are friendly, some are formal. Choose the type of get-well card you would send to a friend who was sick, and design a cover. Write a two to four line message inside the card. Save it for a time when someone you know is not feeling well.

At University Hospital Peg found herself under the care of a very sympathetic young doctor named Dr. Bevis. From the moment he removed the oxygen tent and let Peg breathe on her own, Dr. Bevis provided her with the ongoing encouragement she needed to conquer her disease. When Peg began to make progress, Dr. Bevis made her promise that as soon as she could walk again she would visit the hospital and walk for him.

Reaching that great day, however, meant enduring a lot of hard work and pain, starting with a pair of very painful treatments—one involving the placing of hot packs against her skin, the other involving assisted stretching of her muscles, known as the Sister Kenny treatments (named for the Australian nurse who developed them). Once, when Peg was having an especially difficult time with the treatments, Dr. Bevis overheard her screams of pain and reassured her by reminding her that the treatments were necessary if she ever wanted to walk again.

Her roommate at the hospital was a young boy named Tommy, who, unable to breathe on his own because of polio, was confined to an iron lung. After Peg received a radio, she and Tommy enjoyed passing the long hours by listening to it. Their favorite program was a radio show called "The Lone Ranger," the story of a virtuous cowboy who rides around bringing outlaws to justice. In fact, Peg even named her wheelchair after the Lone Ranger's horse, "Silver." Tommy's friendship made Peg's time in the hospital—filled with homesickness, anxiety and painful treatments—more bearable. Furthermore, realizing the seriousness of Tommy's situation helped Peg keep her own struggles in perspective.[9]

---

9. To keep a struggle *in perspective* means to view one's own struggle or problem in comparison to the problems of others. When that is done, the problem usually seems smaller than it did at first.

WORD BANK	**enduring** (in DYOOR ing) *v.:* undergoing suffering with patience and determination
	virtuous (VUR choo us) *adj.:* good; one who has good character and performs good deeds

Star Patient Surprises Everyone

On October First, I lay in bed with my eyes closed, rehearsing a new joke. As I imagined Dr. Bevis's laughter, my leg itched. Without thinking, I scratched the itch. Then, as I realized what I had done, my eyes sprang open.

Had I really used my hand? After three weeks of paralysis, I was almost afraid to believe it, for fear I had dreamed or imagined the movement. Holding my breath, I tried again. The fingers on my left hand moved back and forth.

"I CAN MOVE MY HAND!!" I yelled.

Two nurses rushed into the room.

"Look! I can move my left hand!" I wiggled my fingers jubilantly.

"Get Dr. Bevis," said one of the nurses. She smiled at me as the other nurse hurried out of the room.

"Can she really do it?" asked Tommy. "Can she move her hand?"

"Yes," said the nurse. "Her fingers are moving."

"Hooray!" shrieked Tommy. "The Lone Ranger rides again!"

Dr. Bevis came bounding in. "What is all this shouting about?"

Feeling triumphant, I moved my fingers.

"Try to turn your hand over," he said.

I tried. The hand didn't go all the way, but it moved. It definitely moved. It was my birthday and the Fourth of July all at the same time. I could move my hand!

Dr. Bevis turned my hand palm up. "Try to bend your arm,"

I CAN MOVE MY HAND!!

he said.

My hand lifted an inch or so off the bed before it dropped back down.

"What about the other hand?" he asked. "Is there any movement in your right hand?"

To my complete astonishment, my right hand moved, too. Bending at the elbow, my lower arm raised several inches and I waved my fingers at Dr. Bevis.

By then, I was so excited I felt as if I could jump from that bed and run laps around the hospital.

"This is wonderful," Dr. Bevis said. "This is terrific!"

I agreed.

"When your mother makes her daily phone call," Dr. Bevis said, "she is going to be thrilled."

In the next few days, I improved rapidly. Soon I could use both hands, then my arms. I was able to sit up, starting with two minutes and working up to half an hour. Movement returned to my legs, too. My arms were still extremely weak, but I learned to feed myself again, which did wonders for both my attitude and my appetite. I was no longer totally helpless.

With my bed cranked up, I could balance a book on my stomach and turn the pages myself. I had always liked to read, and now books provided hours of entertainment. The hospital had a small library; day after day, I lost myself in books.

I began reading aloud to Tommy. I quit only when my voice got hoarse, but even then he always begged me to read just one more page. I preferred reading silently because it was faster, but I felt sorry for Tommy who was still stuck in the iron lung, unable to hold a book. I was clearly getting better; he was not. Each day, I read to him until my voice gave out.

Dr. Bevis continued to praise and encourage me. Mrs. Crab bragged about my progress. The nurses called me their star patient. I realized that no one had thought I would ever regain the

I am no longer totally helpless

use of my arms and legs.

A week after I first moved my hand, Dr. Bevis said he wanted to see if I could stand by myself. First, he helped me sit on the edge of the bed. Then, with a nurse on each side, I was eased off the bed until my feet touched the floor. Each nurse had a hand firmly under one of my armpits, holding me up.

"Lock your knees," Dr. Bevis instructed. "Stand up straight."

I tried to do as he said.

"We're going to let go," he said, "but we won't let you fall. When the nurses drop their arms, see if you can stand by yourself."

Tommy, my iron lung cheerleader, hollered, "Do it, kemo sabe! Do it!"

It was wonderful to feel myself in an upright position again. I was sure I would be able to stand alone. I even imagined taking a step or two.

"All right," Dr. Bevis said to the nurses. "Let go."

As soon as they released me, I toppled. Without support, my legs were like cooked spaghetti. The nurses and Dr. Bevis all grabbed me to keep me from crashing to the floor.

Disappointment filled me, and I could tell the others were disappointed, too. The strength had returned so quickly to my arms and hands that everyone expected my legs to be better also.

"I'm sorry," I said. "I tried."

"It will happen," Dr. Bevis said.

They helped me back into bed, and I was grateful to lie down again. Standing for that short time, even with help, had exhausted me and made my back ache.

The twice-daily hot packs and stretching continued, and so did my progress. Each small achievement, such as being able to

can I stand by myself?

WORD BANK	**heralded** (HAIR ul dud) *v.:* publicly welcomed

wiggle the toes on one foot, was heralded with great joy. I had to keep my feet flat against a board at the foot of my bed to prevent them from drooping forward permanently, and I longed to lie in bed without that board.

Why am I getting better and some of the other patients aren't?

Although I was delighted with every small accomplishment, I wondered why I got better and some of the other patients did not. Tommy might spend the rest of his life in the iron lung. It didn't seem fair.

I mentioned this to Dr. Bevis. "Some cases of polio are severe, and some are mild," he said. "When the polio virus completely destroys a nerve center, the muscles controlled by that center are paralyzed forever. If the damage is slight rather than total, the paralysis is temporary. Your muscles were severely weakened, but the nerve damage wasn't total. It's possible for weak muscles to gain back some of their strength."

"So Tommy's polio is worse than mine," I said.

Quick action by my parents helped create my good luck

"That's right. It also helped that your parents took you to the doctor right away. You were already here and diagnosed when you needed oxygen; some people who have respiratory polio are not that fortunate."

I remembered how hard it had been to breathe, and how much the oxygen tent had helped.

Dr. Bevis continued, "Most people think they have the flu and don't get medical help until paralysis sets in. By the time they learn they have polio, and get to a hospital that's equipped to treat them, the respiratory patients often have to go straight into an iron lung. They don't get hot packs or physical therapy until they can breathe on their own again, which might be several months later. The sooner the Sister Kenny treatments are started, the more they help." He smiled at me. "You are one lucky girl."

But it wasn't all luck, I thought; it was quick action by my parents. They helped create my good luck.

"I've been wondering something else, too," I said. "How did I get polio when not one other person in my town got it?"

"Many people have polio and never know it," Dr. Bevis said. "They are highly contagious, but because their symptoms are so slight, they don't see a doctor. There are probably thousands of cases of polio every year that are so mild they are never diagnosed."

"So I caught it from someone who didn't know they had it," I said. It seemed unbelievable to me that anyone could have polio and not realize it.

Mail was delivered every afternoon, and I looked forward to a daily letter from my mother. Most of her letters were signed, "Love, Mother and Dad," but a few were signed with a muddy paw print. Those were from B.J., telling me he had chased a cat or buried a bone. Grandpa depended on Mother to tell me any news, but he sent a gift each week when my parents came to visit.

Art wrote about college life and sent me a new teddy bear just like the one that got burned.

One mail delivery included a brown packet from my school in Austin. When I opened it, dozens of letters from my classmates tumbled out. Karen wrote about a student petition to change the rules so girls could wear casual clothes to school instead of the required dresses. Another girl complained that her new haircut was too short; a third was outraged at the basketball referee.

I had the strange feeling that I was reading about a different lifetime. The other kids were upset about such unimportant things.

Just a few weeks earlier, I, too, had worried about clothes and hair and the basketball team. Now none of this mattered. I had faced death. I had lived with excruciating pain and with loneliness and uncertainty about the future. Bad haircuts and lost ball

Bad haircuts and lost ball games would never bother me again

WORD BANK	**excruciating** (ex KROO shee AYT ing) *adj.:* intensely painful

games would never bother me again.

Even the petition to allow girls to wear whatever they wanted to school, a cause I supported, failed to excite me. I would happily wear a gunnysack, I thought, if I could walk into the school.

"Be glad you aren't here," one boy wrote. "You aren't missing anything but hard tests and too much homework."

He's wrong, I thought. I miss my own room and playing with B.J. and helping Grandpa in the garden. I miss my piano lessons and roller-skating and licking the pan when Mother makes fudge. I miss visiting my aunts and uncles. I miss riding my bike with Karen and playing Monopoly with Richard.

I put the letters aside, knowing I was changed forever. My world was now the hospital. Would I have anything in common with my classmates when I went home? I felt closer now to Tommy, whose head was the only part of him I had ever seen, than I did to the kids who used to be my dearest friends. Tommy understood what it was like to have polio; my school friends could never know.

I miss my own room and playing with B.J. and helping Grandpa in the garden and I miss my piano lessons

Tommy understands what it's like to have polio

My school friends can never understand

By mid-October, Peg no longer needed to be in a hospital, so she moved back to Sheltering Arms to continue her recovery. Aware that he might never leave the confines of the iron lung, she left her radio with Tommy. Upon her return to the Sheltering Arms, Peg met her new roommates—Dorothy, Shirley, Renée and Alice—with whom she would become very close over the next several months.

On the occasion of her parents' first visit to the Sheltering Arms, it became apparent that the other girls did not get regular visits, so Peg's parents "adopted" her roommates, always bringing them special things when they visit. Peg celebrated her 13th birthday with her new friends, hot packs were thankfully replaced by long soaks, and she began therapy sessions with Miss Ballard to relearn how to use her muscles after having lost all her strength for so long.

Dancing the Hula,
Popping a Wheelie

Just before Thanksgiving, Miss Ballard announced, "Tomorrow you're going to stand by yourself."

I knew my physical therapy sessions were helping me. My arms and legs were stronger. My back was stronger, too; I could now sit up for several hours at a time. Still, I worried all evening. I remembered trying to stand alone at University Hospital.

The next morning, Miss Ballard helped me sit with my feet over the side of the bed. She put one arm around my waist and said, "Slide off until your feet hit the floor. Then lock your knees."

"Isn't someone going to help us?" I asked. "What if I fall?"

"I won't let you fall," she said. I didn't see how she could stop me if I collapsed, since I was bigger than she was. Probably, we would both go down.

Alice, whose bed was closest to mine, stared at me but said nothing. I wondered if she hoped I would fall. It had to be hard for her to watch new patients arrive, get better, and leave while she always remained behind with her condition unchanged.

A soft voice from across the room said, "Good luck." Dorothy, who might never stand alone, smiled at me gently.

My fear vanished. I slid forward and put my feet on the floor. With Miss Ballard's hand firmly on my waist, I locked my knees, and stood.

When Miss Ballard let go, I remained standing. I stood straight and steady, with no support, for a full minute, beaming at Dorothy the whole time.

I stood for one full minute without support!

"That's fine," said Miss Ballard.

"Good show," said Dorothy.

"From now on," said Miss Ballard, as she helped me sit on the bed, "you'll stand for awhile every day. Soon you'll be able to get in and out of the wheelchair by yourself."

Each day I stood alone a little longer, and my confidence grew like Jack's beanstalk.

My strength increased daily, and I was measured for a pair of walking sticks. If I could learn to walk with sticks, I wouldn't need the wheelchair any longer.

Walking sticks are similar to crutches except shorter. Instead of going under the armpits, they end just below the elbow. A ring of metal circles the patient's arm at the top of each stick, and there is a wooden crossbar to hold on to.

"Why do I have to wait for new sticks to get here?" I asked. "Dorothy already has a pair, and she only uses them an hour a day. She won't care if I borrow them."

"It is important," Miss Ballard said, "for the walking sticks to be exactly the right height for you. If they are too short, even by only an inch, you would have to lean forward, which would cause back problems. If the sticks are too long, you would not be able to use all of your arm strength for balance."

Willie told me that using sticks strengthened the leg muscles. "If you can walk with sticks," she said, "you may get so strong you won't need them anymore."

I asked Miss Ballard if this was true.

"No two cases are the same," she said. Then she smiled and added, "I hope you'll learn to walk with them and then to walk without them."

As we munched cookies after dinner one Wednesday, Willie came in and said, "Peg, you have a visitor in the lobby."

Quickly, I combed my hair and got into my wheelchair. I couldn't imagine who my visitor was. I wheeled into the elevator, rode to the first floor, and went out to the lobby.

"Hello, Peg."

"Dr. Bevis!" He had a big smile on his face, and I was overjoyed to see him.

"I came to see how my favorite patient is doing," he said. "Believe it or not, I miss your knock, knock jokes."

I told him about my roommates and about the hot baths and about my physical therapy treatments with Miss Ballard.

I hope I'll learn to walk without my sticks

"I've talked with her on the telephone several times," he said. "She tells me you are an exemplary patient and very brave."

I wasn't sure what exemplary meant, but from the way he said it, I figured it was a compliment. I hoped he would report the part about being brave to Mrs. Crab.

"How is Tommy?" I asked.

"When I left, he was listening to the 'Lone Ranger,'" Dr. Bevis said.

"Is he still in the iron lung?"

"Yes. For now."

Dr. Bevis didn't stay long, but his visit left me glowing with pleasure. His parting words were, "Don't forget. You're going to come back to University Hospital and walk for me."

"I'll be there," I said, and this time we both knew it was more than wishful thinking.[10] I just might make it.

In December, Peg was taken home for an overnight visit. She had been terribly excited to go, but after struggling with the difficulty and awkwardness of getting around the house, she returned with a sense of relief and a realization that she was not quite ready to make it outside of the supportive environment of the Sheltering Arms.

Around this time she began attending school at the Sheltering Arms for two hours a day. Informed that if she could pass the year-end tests, she would be promoted along with her friends—and determined not to fall behind her class—Peg studied very hard.

---

10. *Wishful thinking* is thinking something *will* happen when, in reality, one can only *hope* it will happen.

WORD BANK | **exemplary** (egg ZEMP luh ree) *adj.*: perfect; worthy of imitation

[margin note: I'm going to go back to University Hospital and walk for Dr. Bevis]

Good-bye Silver; Hello, Sticks

My walking sticks finally came. As I rubbed my fingers across the smooth wood, I felt as excited as I had when I got my bicycle. I could hardly wait to try them.

"Go slowly," Miss Ballard cautioned after she showed me how to hold the sticks. "Take small steps. Slow and easy."

I listened impatiently, eager to get on with the business of walking. At last the sticks were in my hands, and I was on my feet. Miss Ballard stood beside me, ready to help if I needed her. I was confident that I could stride forward on my own. I was Supergirl, ready to conquer the world.

"On your mark," I said.

"Go slowly," Miss Ballard repeated.

"Get set..."

"Easy," said Miss Ballard. "Slow and easy."

"Go!"

I lurched forward, unsteady and awkward.

"Small steps!" cried Miss Ballard. "Don't try to run."

I wobbled and swayed, barely able to keep my balance. It was not going to be as simple as I had thought.

I have to learn to walk all over again

"It's like learning to walk all over again," Miss Ballard said. "You'll be shaky at first, the way a year-old baby is, but you will do better with practice."

I took her advice about moving slowly—not because I wanted to, but because I wasn't able to move fast. I had to think about the sequence of each step: lift right stick and right foot, move them forward, put them down. Lean on stick for balance. Lift the left stick and the left foot, move them forward, put them down. Slowly, slowly. Small steps. Concentrate.

I felt as if bricks were glued to the soles of my shoes. Trying to lift and move my feet took every ounce of energy I had, and sweat trickled down the back of my neck.

That first day, I took ten small steps, each one slow and deliberate. It was hard to coordinate my arms and my feet, and since my arms were still weak, it took great effort to move and control the wooden sticks. When Miss Ballard said I had gone far enough for the first day, Supergirl slumped with relief back into her wheelchair.

"Good job," said Miss Ballard.

In spite of my weariness, exhilaration filled me, and I felt compelled to pop a wheelie twice as I raced proudly back to my room.

Each day from then on, I went a little farther and a little farther. One small step at a time.

The other girls watched my rapid progress with enthusiasm. There was never any hint of envy over the fact that I, who had arrived at the Sheltering Arms last, was quickly surpassing the rest of them in physical strength and ability. I suppose it didn't hurt to have parents who treated all of my roommates as extra daughters, but I believe it was more than that. Even homemade peanut-butter cookies do not buy true friendship.

We had the kind of camaraderie that I imagine exists between soldiers who have fought together during a long and difficult war. In our case, the enemy was polio. Our battle medals were wheelchairs, back and leg braces, and walking sticks, and we wore them proudly. We were survivors; whatever handicaps we might be left with, polio had not claimed our lives or our spirits.

Our common experiences of pain and paralysis, separation from our loved ones, and an unending struggle to regain the full use of our bodies made us members of an elite sorority[11] that

One small step at a time

---

11. A *sorority* is a club for women attending college. *Elite* means select, exclusive. An *elite sorority* is a club which admits only the best women.

WORD BANK	**exhilaration** (egg ZILL uh RAY shun) *n.:* immense and thrilling joy
	surpassing (sur PASS ing) *v.:* going beyond; exceeding
	camaraderie (KAHM uh RAD uh ree) *n.:* a feeling of close and comfortable friendship

outsiders could never join. The success of one member became the success of all, and Shirley, Renée, Dorothy, and Alice cheered when they learned I had taken ten steps all by myself on my new walking sticks. Even if they would never walk with only sticks to aid them, my progress meant a victory for them, too, against our mutual foe.

Two weeks after I got my sticks, Miss Ballard told me I was strong enough to use them exclusively. I didn't need Silver anymore.

"You gave me a lot of good rides," I whispered as I patted Silver's side for the last time. I blinked back tears, feeling foolish. I had looked forward to this day for months, and now that it was here, I was all weepy about leaving my wheelchair behind.

Silver had carried me to school, distributed countless treats, and taken me safely to O.T.,[12] my sessions with Miss Ballard, visits with other patients, and special events in the sunroom. I'd had many fine times, including my thirteenth birthday, in that wheelchair. As I thought about them, I realized that even if I had never grown strong enough to leave Silver, I still would have been able to lead a happy life.

I took Silver for a farewell trip, which ended with a high-speed dash down the hall, a screech of brakes, and a final shout of "Hi, yo, Silver! Awa-a-ay!" Teetering on the two rear wheels, I tipped farther back than I had ever gone before. It was a terrific last ride.

A terrific last ride!

_____

12. *O.T.* stands for occupational therapy. It is treatment that uses everyday activities to help people relearn physical skills lost through illness or accident.

WORD BANK   **exclusively** (ex KLOO siv lee) *adv.:* only; excluding all others

QUICK REVIEW

1. One of Peg's treatments involves stretching of the muscles. For whom is the treatment named?

2. Who is Peg's roommate at University Hospital?

3. To which radio show do Peg and her roommate listen?

4. Who is Peg's physical therapist at Sheltering Arms?

FOCUS

5. Why does Peg read to Tommy?

6. Why is it hard for Peg to say goodbye to her wheelchair?

CREATING & WRITING

7. Peg and Tommy loved to listen to "The Lone Ranger." They admired this cowboy for his courage, his goodness, and his strength. Talking about him made them feel stronger and more courageous. Is there someone who makes you feel this way? Choose a real person or fictional character and describe his or her traits. Tell how this character makes you feel and explain why thinking about the character helps you.

8. Write about how Peg, Tommy, and Peg's roommates are like soldiers in a war.

9. Some books have illustrations: pictures of scenes from the book. Choose one scene from this section of the story and draw an illustration for it.

A Present for Dr. Bevis

"Stand up straight," Miss Ballard said.

As I practiced with my walking sticks, she kept reminding me of my posture. "Keep your shoulders back. Eyes ahead. Don't look down."

Each week I used my walking sticks more confidently, but I tended to hunch forward and watch the floor. Weak muscles made it difficult to keep my shoulders back, and I looked down all the time because I was afraid I would trip.

One morning, Miss Ballard brought a book to my physical therapy session. I recognized it; it was the bird identification book that was kept near the window in the classroom.

"This is how fashion models learn to stand straight," Miss Ballard told me as she placed the book on my head. "They balance a book on their head and try not to drop it while they walk down the runway."

"It's heavy," I said.

"You're lucky I didn't bring an unabridged dictionary. Let's see how far you can get before it falls."

With Birds of North America perched on my head, I started across the room.

"Good! Good!" exclaimed Miss Ballard. "You look like a fashion model."

It was hard to keep the book from sliding off my head while I walked, especially after I began a running commentary, mimicking the only fashion show I had ever attended, a mother-daughter event at the school.

"Our next model is Peg," I said, "wearing a stunning blue sweatshirt. Note the exquisite stains on her shirt front, done by a special process called spilled spaghetti. The stylish lump in the left sleeve is achieved with a wadded-up Kleenex. Doesn't Peg look gorgeous for a day of physical therapy?"

One memorable morning in late January, Miss Ballard said, "Today you're going to walk a few steps without your sticks."

My heart beat faster.

"Stand here," she said, motioning to a stretch of wall with a sturdy railing, "and hold on to the handrail."

I moved into position, handed her my walking sticks, and grasped the rail. She stood a few feet ahead of me.

"Slowly," she warned. "Heel first, then toe. Don't thump your whole foot down at once."

I nodded.

"If you have trouble, grab the rail."

I nodded again.

She smiled. "Let go of the rail," she said.

I did, too nervous even to tease her by suggesting I might sprint away.

She stretched her hands toward me. "Peg," she said, her voice hushed, "you're going to walk."

I licked my lips and stared at her.

I'm going to walk?

Now," she whispered.

Carefully, I raised one foot and set it down a few inches in front of me. My arms prickled with excitement.

"Heel," Miss Ballard said, "then toe. Small steps."

Wobbling slightly, I moved the other foot. I held my arms a few inches away from my body to help me balance.

"Head up. Don't look down. Shoulders back. Pretend you have the book on your head."

I took another small, unsteady step.

"Heel," she said. "Toe. Heel. Toe." With each word, the excitement in her voice intensified.

Head up, staring at Miss Ballard, I walked. I walked!

Six steps later, my hands grasped hers, and we celebrated our mutual victory with a hug.

I walked!   I walked!

"You still need the walking sticks most of the time," she warned, as she handed them to me. "Don't try to walk alone unless I'm with you."

"Who, me?" I said.

"I mean it, Peg. No walking by yourself." She put her hands on her hips. "And no hula dancing, either."

"How did you know about that?"

I followed her instructions faithfully. I had come too far, at too great a cost, to risk a setback. Besides, I could get around faster with my sticks than I could on my own. Walking unaided slowed me down.

From then on, I practiced walking alone for a short time each day. With Miss Ballard barking directions like an army drill sergeant, I heeled and toed my way around the physical therapy room. Gradually, I gained assurance. I still had to concentrate on each step, but my gait grew smoother and the steps I took became more normal in length.

While I learned to walk by myself, Dorothy struggled to walk using both her new braces and her walking sticks. She tried hard, knowing that if she could not manage, she would always be in a wheelchair.

Renée made more progress than Dorothy did. She needed help getting her leg braces on, but once she was on her feet she could move about with her walking sticks.

On a frigid February morning, Miss Ballard watched me walk alone and said, "How would you like to go home?"

"You mean, for good?"

"Yes. I've done all I can for you. From now on, you only need to continue your exercises and practice walking alone. Go a few

I'M GOING HOME!

steps farther each day without your sticks, the way we've been doing here. I know your parents will help you, and I think you want to help yourself."

I nodded, not trusting myself to speak.

"The doctors have already agreed to your discharge," she went on. "All we have to do is notify your parents that they can come and get you."

Home. I was going home.

"You'll need to come back for checkups," Miss Ballard told me. "Every week at first, and then every month. We have to be sure you continue to make progress."

"It'll be fun to come back; I'll want to see the other kids."

I'm going to miss all of my friends

"They're going to miss you," she said. "We all will."

"I'll miss you, too," I said, and I threw my arms around her.

On my last night at the Sheltering Arms, I passed out all the food from under my bed, declaring I didn't want to haul it home with me. Feeling like my mother's daughter, I gave away my stationery and pen, my hand mirror, my back scratcher, and even my teddy bear, insisting that each of the girls keep something of mine to remember me by.

"We won't miss you," Renée teased, "but we'll sure miss your parents."

"And your food," said Alice.

My emotions were a roller coaster, rocketing to elation that I would soon be home to stay and then plunging to sadness at the thought of leaving my friends.

That night, we sang every song we had ever done. We sang and sang and sang, with the music floating over the five beds and disappearing into our memories.

WORD BANK	**elation** (ee LAY shun) *n.:* extreme happiness

Mother arrived at ten the next morning. I was glad she came early. Once the day of departure had come, I did not want to linger. Even so, the good-byes were hard to say. They were made bearable only by the fact that I had to return for a checkup the following week and I promised to bring a full report from the outside world.

"Never mind the report," said Renée. "Just bring potato chips."

Her humor chased our nostalgia[13] out the door, and I followed.

"Good-bye!" the girls called. "Good-bye! Don't forget to write!"

Miss Ballard saw me to the car, spouting instructions for Mother and reminders for me.

While Mother laid my walking sticks across the back seat, I hugged Miss Ballard. "Thank you," I said. "See you next week."

"No running," Miss Ballard warned as she closed the car door for me. "No funny tricks. No hula."

While Mother got in the driver's side, I rolled down my window.

"Is it okay," I asked Miss Ballard, "if I try out my old roller skates?"

"You'll do nothing of the kind," Mother said.

"I don't want to hear about it," Miss Ballard said, but she smiled at me as she covered her ears.

"We have to stop at University Hospital before we go home," I told Mother. "I promised Dr. Bevis I'd come back and walk for him."

"I know," she said. "I brought him a present."

Somehow, that didn't surprise me.

Once more, I rode from the Sheltering Arms to University Hospital. This time I didn't have to pretend I was dead.

---

13. *Nostalgia* (nuh STAHL juh) is a feeling of longing for something in the past or, as in this case, something that will soon be in the past.

We have to stop at University Hospital before we go home

I promised Dr. Bevis I'd come back and walk for him

"I wasn't sure what to get Dr. Bevis," Mother said, "so I bought him a necktie. I hope he's there today."

He was. We waited in the lobby while he was paged, and he greeted us warmly.

"I see you've graduated to walking sticks," he told me. "No more wheelchair."

"We're on our way home," Mother told him. "Peg was discharged today."

"That's wonderful news."

"We brought you a present," I said. Mother gave him the box.

When he saw the tie, he said, "It's beautiful. I'll think of you whenever I wear it."

"I have something to show you," I said as I handed my walking sticks to Mother.

Then, smiling triumphantly at Dr. Bevis, I walked across the hospital lobby to the information desk, turned, and walked back again. Head up, shoulders back; heel, toe, heel, toe. Small steps.

Dr. Bevis watched closely. "You did it!" he said. "You can walk!"

I stopped in front of him, standing straight. "Thank you for helping me," I said.

"Thank you for coming to show me."

Mother gave me my sticks, and Dr. Bevis went to the door with us. "Good-bye, Peg," he said. "I'm proud of you."

A necktie and two minutes of watching a young girl walk alone. I hope it was adequate payment for all he had given me.

Back to School

When we got home this time, I was no longer a visitor, and we soon settled into a routine. Mornings were exercise time. The first day, Mother opened a paper bag and dumped a pile of marbles on the floor in front of me.

"Miss Ballard said you would know what to do," she told me.

After my exercises, I practiced walking without my sticks. I decided to practice with a book on my head. Twice each day, I walked alone until I grew tired, trying to go one minute longer every session.

The rest of the time, I used my sticks. Because they stuck out on each side, it was harder to walk with them at home than it had been at the Sheltering Arms. Even though Mother and Dad pushed the furniture against the walls, I had less room to maneuver. Still, I was in no hurry to discard my sticks. I felt far more secure with them than I did when I walked alone, and they kept me from becoming too tired.

Every afternoon, I studied. Without the distraction of four roommates, I did my lessons quickly. But I worried that I might be far behind my classmates. What if I didn't pass those final exams?

I was allowed one visitor each day, for fifteen minutes. My friends took turns coming, but the visits seemed strained. Although we were genuinely glad to see each other, they could not help staring at my walking sticks. Instead of giving me news from school, they wanted to hear what it was like to have polio.

"Did it hurt?" they asked. "Were you really paralyzed from the neck down?" "Did you almost die?"

What will it be like, I worried, when I go back to school? Will everyone stare? Will kids I don't even know want to hear the details of my time in the hospital? I felt like a freak in a sideshow, valued only because I was different.

Will everyone stare at me when I go back to school

A week after my discharge, we returned to the Sheltering Arms for my first checkup. Miss Ballard was pleased with my progress. I could hardly wait to see the other girls and catch up on all the hospital news.

When we went up to Room 202, Dorothy, Renée, and Alice were in school, and a new girl was in my bed. I talked awhile with Shirley and left, feeling disappointed and slightly resentful that life at the Sheltering Arms was rolling smoothly along without me.

My second checkup was scheduled at one o'clock, so we went early and visited in Room 202 while the girls ate lunch.

During my first weeks at home, I frequently sat by the window and watched for the mailman, hoping for news from the Sheltering Arms. I wrote regularly to Room 202. Renée and Dorothy wrote back often; Alice wrote occasionally. Shirley could not write by herself, but the letters from the other girls always said, "P.S. Shirley says to tell you hi."

Oddly, I didn't listen to the "Lone Ranger" after I went home. Tonto and Silver now belonged to a different part of my life.

After four checkups, Miss Ballard said I didn't need to come back for a month. When I arrived that time, Dorothy said, "I won't be here the next time you come. I'm going home on Saturday."

"Did the new braces work?" I asked.

Dorothy shook her head, no. "My brothers are building a ramp so I can get in and out of our house."

I'm glad that Dorothy is going home

I was glad that she was going home, and sad that she would always need the wheelchair.

I'm sad that she will always need her wheelchair

When it was time for us to leave, I hugged Dorothy, wondering if I would ever see her again. We promised to write often, and that promise held back my tears.

We had good intentions, but letters between me and my roommates slowed, in both directions. There were two new girls in 202 now.

About two weeks after she was discharged, I got a letter from Dorothy. "I wanted to leave Sheltering Arms more than anything," she wrote, "but now sometimes I wish I could go back. Isn't that silly?"

It wasn't silly to me. We were safe at the Sheltering Arms, cocooned[14] in Room 202, where everyone understood what it was like to have polio. Getting around in the normal world, even in our own homes, was more difficult than hospital life.

In April, I got permission to return to school. I was still on my walking sticks, but I could go up and down stairs if I held the railing with both hands and had someone carry my sticks for me. I was slow because both feet had to touch every step, but I could make it.

Dad bought me a backpack for my books. I was to start by attending only in the mornings. If I could manage that, I would gradually work up to a full day.

On my first day back, I was so nervous my hands began to sweat and I was afraid the sticks would slip out of my grasp. What if people never quit staring? What if no one would carry my sticks up and down stairs for me? What if I couldn't get around in the crowded halls, and fell? Worst of all, what if I discovered that I was hopelessly behind the other kids in every class?

When I walked into my first-period class, which happened to be English, the students whistled and clapped and cheered, welcoming me back. All morning, kids begged for a turn to carry my sticks up or down the stairs. They offered to help me with the backpack. They walked ahead of me in the halls, clearing space.

---

14. *Cocooned* means sheltered and protected from the outer world, like a larva in a cocoon.

I'm going back to school

What if they stare

What if no one will carry my sticks

What if I can't gEt arouNd in the CrowDed halls

WhAt IF I FALL

Without knowing it, I had become a celebrity. Since I was the only person in Austin to get polio that year, the whole town had followed my progress while I was in the hospital. It seems all of Austin had been pulling for me, hoping I would walk again.

Rather than falling behind in my classes, it quickly became clear that I had remained equal or even pulled slightly ahead. By the end of the morning, I felt sure that I would pass the final exams.

My last class of the morning was chorus practice. Thanks to all those songs in the dark, my singing voice was improved, even though I now used my stomach muscles rather than my diaphragm.

As I found my seat and placed my sticks on the floor beside me, I remembered how my skirt had jumped because of my twitching thigh muscle on Homecoming day, and how I had collapsed in the hall when chorus ended.

I had been gone seven months. I had been gone a lifetime. Although I returned on walking sticks, moving slowly and taking small steps, I knew that in many ways, I was stronger than when I left.

I opened my music and began to sing.

I'm sure I will pass the final exams!

I have been gone seven months and in many ways, I am stronger than when I left

WORD BANK	**celebrity** (suh LEB rih tee) *n.*: a famous person

Epilogue

After her recovery from polio, Peg was able to live a rich, full life. She married, raised two children, and has had four grandchildren. She also became a very successful children's author. She sometimes wonders if one reason she writes for the age group she does is that—because of the events described in this book—she remembers that period in her life so vividly. Like Peg, Dorothy, Renée and Alice experienced significant recovery and went on to live active lives—Dorothy and Renée independently, and Alice in a home for people with disabilities. Sadly, Shirley died of polio in 1955, six years after the events described in Small Steps.

About the Author

Peg Kehret was born Margaret Ann Schulze in Wisconsin, on November 11, 1936. At the age of twelve, she contracted polio, a terrible illness which paralyzed her from the neck down. Fortunately, she made a nearly complete recovery. In 1955, she married Carl Kehret; soon after, the couple adopted two children. Peg has always loved to write. She has written radio commercials, plays, magazine stories, and children's books. For many years, Peg and Carl traveled around the U.S. in their motor home with their pets on board. Carl died in 2004. Peg lives in a log house on a ten-acre wildlife sanctuary in Washington State.

FIRST IMPRESSIONS
Many people will have mixed feelings at the end of this story. Do you? What are they?

QUICK REVIEW

1. How do fashion models learn to stand straight?

2. Why does Peg tend to hunch forward and watch the floor, when she is learning to use the walking sticks?

3. What is the name of the book on Peg's head?

4. What does Miss Ballard say, one memorable morning in late January?

FOCUS

5. Why is Miss Ballard's voice hushed, when she says, "Peg, you're going to walk"?

6. What does Peg do on her last night at Sheltering Arms? Why?

CREATING & WRITING

7. If you were Peg, leaving your friends at Sheltering Arms, how would you feel? Write them a group letter describing your mixed feelings.

8. Why doesn't Peg listen to "The Lone Ranger" at home?

9. Make up a good recipe for a chocolate ice cream shake.

NONFICTION

- In nonfiction, all the elements of a story—plot, characterization, setting, and theme—are factual.

- Nonfiction is written to inform, to educate, and to entertain.

- For every type of fiction—mystery, adventure, western, detective, humor, science, and so on—one can find a parallel in nonfiction.

- Remember, even though nonfiction is "true," it is still one person's point of view.

THINK ABOUT IT!

1. Why is Benjamin Franklin called a Founding Father?

2. What are three inventions for which Benjamin Franklin is known?

3. How did Franklin get the idea for the armonica?

4. The author writes that Franklin "was a man whose interests ran wide." Do you think this description is supported by the piece?

Ben Franklin's Not So Famous Instrument

When many people think of Benjamin Franklin (1706-1790), they picture the Founding Father flying a kite in a thunderstorm, waiting for lightning to strike the metal key. In fact, Franklin's contributions to science—indeed to American life—are wide-ranging. In addition to helping to bring our Constitution into being, Franklin invented the lightning rod and bi-focal glasses, designed a new type of fireplace and electric streetlight, and founded America's first fire department and lending library. But few people realize that he also invented a musical instrument, one that was actually quite popular in its day.

Made up of a series of thirty-seven rotating glass bowls, Franklin's instrument was called the "armonica" (not to be confused with the hand-held wind instrument, the "harmonica"). Franklin came up with the idea for the new instrument based on the old dinner table trick of rubbing the rims of water glasses with wet fingertips to produce a unique sound. Franklin had the glass bowls, ranging from three to nine inches in diameter, specially ground so that each produced a separate note.

Strange as it sounds, Franklin's invention became very popular in Europe for a time. Not only were concerts given on the unusual instrument, but legend has it that armonica music was used to accompany a royal wedding in Vienna. Perhaps the greatest testament to the success of the instrument was that both Beethoven and Mozart, two of the world's greatest musical composers, wrote pieces for the new instrument.

In the end, the armonica was doomed to failure. Glass is delicate, making the instrument very difficult to transport and maintain. Furthermore, the armonica's tones were not loud enough to fill great concert halls (remember, this was before amplifiers existed). One other reason has been suggested, however, for the instrument's loss of popularity: it was depressing. In fact, one famous singer and musician, Marianne Davies, suffered from "melancholia" (what we would now call "depression") that many believed was the result of the haunting music produced by the armonica.

Although Franklin's brief contribution to the world of music may be largely unknown, one thing is certain: this was a man whose interests ran as wide as his intellect ran deep.

Blueprint for Reading

INTO . . . *What a Wild Idea*

Have you ever seen a problem and said, "Hey! I could solve that!" or, have you ever seen the solution to some problem and said, "I have a better way to do that!"? Have you ever just let your mind wander and said, "Wow! I have a *wild idea!*"?

Look up the word *wild* in the dictionary. Write down all of its definitions. Think about what Louis Sabin, the author of *What a Wild Idea,* had in mind when he used the word. That's what this piece is about: the odd, silly, crazy, fantastic uses to which human beings put their genius.

EYES ON . . . *Humorous Fiction*

Have you ever heard the expression, "truth is stranger than fiction"? Comic writers and humorists have always been able to make us laugh at the jokes, anecdotes, and tales they have invented. But one day you will discover that the real ideas of real people can often be funnier than *anything* anyone could make up!

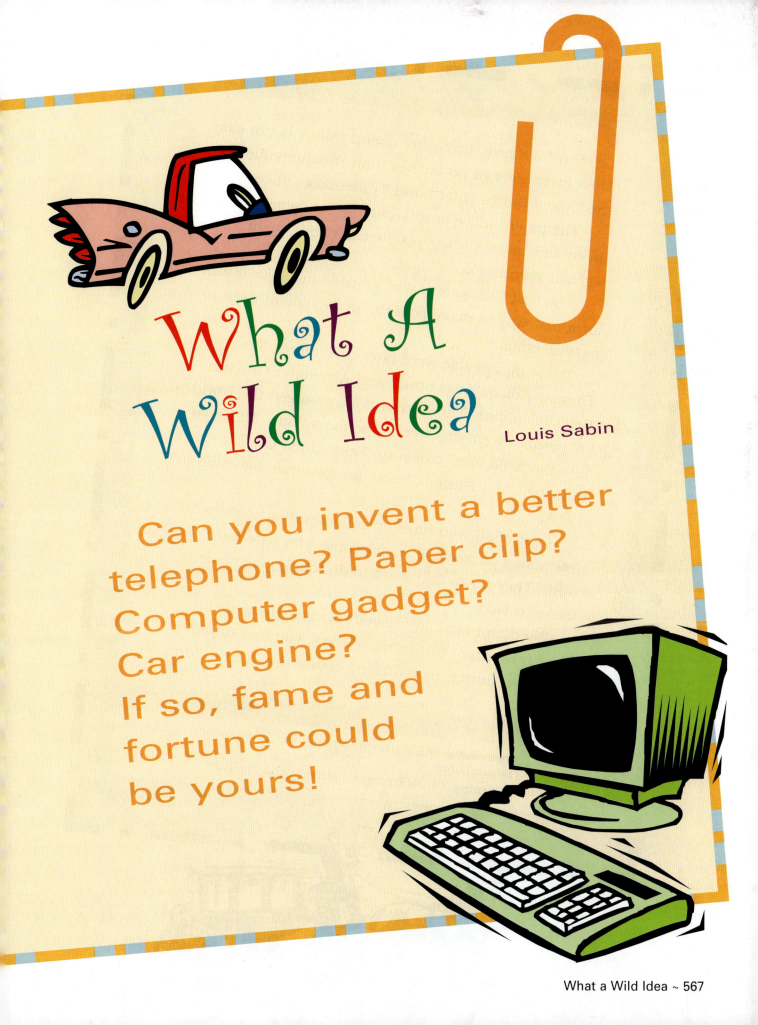

What A Wild Idea

Louis Sabin

Can you invent a better
telephone? Paper clip?
Computer gadget?
Car engine?
If so, fame and
fortune could
be yours!

But take care. Inventing useful things is not easy. Most inventions go no farther than the dusty files of the United States Patent and Trademark Office.

The patent office grants patents, or ownership, for inventions so that other people can't copy them without permission.

The first U.S. patent was granted in 1790. It was for a new way to make potash, an ingredient used to fertilize crops.

More memorable were later inventions, like Thomas Edison's light bulb and Alexander Graham Bell's telephone. Those inventions changed the world.

Other inventions weren't so marvelous. Those go into the "wild idea" category. Take Alfred Clark's Rocking Chair Butter Churn, for example, patented in 1913.

First of all, you have to understand something. Inventions often come from people who hate hard work. They try to find ways to do tough jobs while taking it easy.

No doubt Mr. Clark loved rocking. He probably liked butter too. But in those days, you had to make your own butter, by churning cream. Mr. Clark didn't

| WORD BANK | **memorable** (MEM uh ruh bl) *adj.*: worth remembering; easily remembered |
| | **churning** (CHURR ning) *v.*: stirring and shaking |

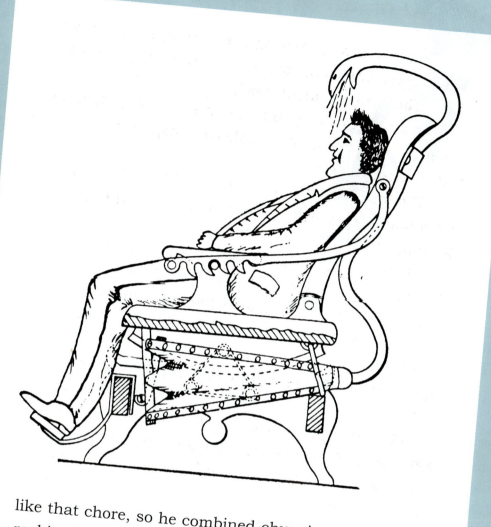

like that chore, so he combined churning and rocking into one activity.

First, you poured cream into a barrel attached to the chair. Then you sat and rocked. After a while—a *long* while—the cream became butter.

There was nothing wrong with the Rocking Chair Butter Churn, or with its cousins: the Rocking Chair Fan (1869) and the Rocking Chair Washing Machine-Bathtub (1890). Nothing except that doing the rocking was actually harder than doing the work the old-fashioned way.

Lucky for everyone, the electric motor was invented and stopped all rocking chair brainstorms forever.

Round about that time, in 1895, another inventor had a wild idea. James Kelly's invention was a hose-and-ring indoor shower. It was a simple invention. You just connected the hose to the bathtub faucet and hung the ring around your neck.

The ring had holes in it. Turn on the water and an instant Niagara covered your body. Sounds like a lot of fun, doesn't it? Unfortunately, the public considered the gadget a washout. It disappeared down the drain of time.

Another snoozer was the alarm bed. There were several versions. The first one (patented in 1882) belonged to Samuel S. Applegate.

Mr. Applegate began with a bed and a clock. Connected to the clock was a lever. At wake-up time, the lever moved a wooden arm that pulled a cord. The

WORD BANK

washout (WASH out) *n.*: (informal) a complete failure or disappointment

lever (LEH ver or LEE ver) *n.*: a bar or rod

cord released a wooden frame with 60 corks attached to it. The frame with corks dropped and hit the sleeper's head. The thing was lightweight so as not to cause head injuries.

Another wake-up wonder was the Ludwig Ederer Alarm Bed of 1900. It worked with steam. The steam built up pressure in pipes. The pressure made the bed tilt up, sending the sleeper sliding slowly to the floor. He landed just hard enough to wake, without being startled by an alarm.

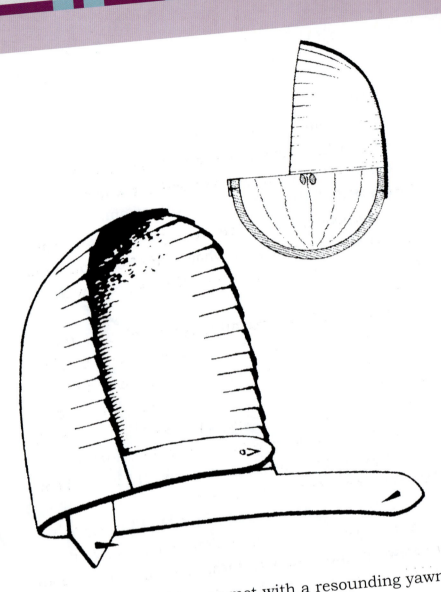

This bold innovation was met with a resounding yawn. Now you're out of bed and ready for breakfast. Look, it's grapefruit! But wait. Those things are dangerous. They squirt juice in people's eyes—but not if you use Joseph Fallek's 1928 grapefruit shield.

WORD BANK

innovation (IN oh VAY shun) *n.*: the introduction of something new or different

resounding (ree ZOWN ding) *adj.*: loud and echoing

This simple waxed-paper hood fit onto a grapefruit half, held in place by little pins. In position, it looked like a baby carriage without wheels. Brilliant!

That would keep juice out of your eye. But say you want to protect your whole body from splatters. For that, try John Maguire's 1883 Raincoat with Drain.

At first, it looks like an ordinary raincoat. But look closer. The rain collects in a cuff at the bottom. Then it drains away from your pants and shoes through a tube that sticks out one side. It worked—but only in a light rain, when you stood perfectly still.

Okay, you've kept your feet dry. But now you need to get them warm. The obvious choice is William Tell Steiger's 1877 Foot Warmer.

Fit the strap around your neck. Breathe into the little rubber cup. Your warm breath travels down tubes worn under your clothes. The tubes end in your shoes, where your breath heats your feet.

In a crazy way, this one makes sense. But who wants to walk around with a cup at his lip and tubes running down his body? Nobody, that's who. True, you could wear the tubes outside your clothes. But then your breath would cool on the way down.

Not all inventions are for human use, of course. Some are for chickens.

Is your poultry too plump? Your fryer too fat? Then try the hen exerciser, invented by William J. Manly in 1906.

It combines a food box and a tilted, spinning platform. When your hen heads for the food, her weight makes the platform turn. To keep eating, she's got to keep moving. Jogging shoes not included.

You can reward your fit fowl with her own goggles, though. In 1903, Andrew Jackson (no, not *that* Andrew Jackson) invented hen sunglasses.

Their purpose? To protect the hen's eyes, of course.

There's an old saying: "Build a better mousetrap and the world will beat a path to your door."

Many have tried. Consider the work of Joseph Barad and Edward E. Markoff, patented in 1908. The trap has a lever in the middle with a bit of cheese on it.

The hungry rodent pokes its head into an opening near the lever. He gets the cheese and trips the lever. This pulls two smaller levers attached to an elastic band with bells on it.

The band snaps around the rodent's neck. It doesn't hurt the animal, just scares him. He rushes back to the nest. The bells scare the other rats. They

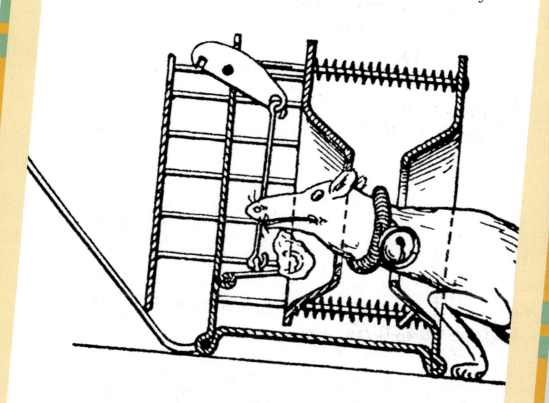

rush out of the nest. Now that they're out in the open, you can catch them.

How? With your own new, improved Better Mousetrap. The world is waiting. Inventors, get to work!

About The Author

Louis Sabin was born in Salt Lake City, Utah in 1930. He served in the U.S. Air Force from 1947 until 1949, then attended Brooklyn College and New York University graduate school. He has edited several magazines including *True Detective* and *Boys' Life.* However, his chief occupation is writing books, most of them about and for young people. In addition to writing over 50 books himself, he has co-authored more than ten books with his wife, Francene. He lives in Milltown, New Jersey.

QUICK REVIEW

1. Who invented the Rocking Chair Butter Churn?

2. What stopped all of the rocking chair brainstorms?

3. Which old saying does the author quote?

4. What activities does William J. Manly's invention combine? For whom is the invention designed?

FOCUS

5. Why do you think Louis Sabin wrote this article?

6. What is the U.S. Patent and Trademark Office?

CREATING & WRITING

7. Write a brief report about an invention and the person who created it.

8. You are an inventor. Describe your invention and the problem it solves.

9. Now draw a picture of your invention. Label the various parts.

DRAMA

- In drama, dialogue replaces narration. We learn everything we need to know from what the characters say and do on stage.

- Other ways that we learn about the plot and characters are through scenery, props, costumes, action, lighting, and sound effects.

- The playwright includes stage directions in the script to instruct the actors and stage managers.

- The same play can be staged in many different ways for different effects.

THINK ABOUT IT!

- How does the reader know which words are the stage directions and which ones are part of the play?

- If your class were performing this little play, how would you transmit the information included in the very first paragraph to the audience?

- Which describes this short drama best: fiction, nonfiction, historical fiction, or science fiction?

- If you were staging this play, what sound effects would you use and where would you put them?

Oh Say Can You See

At one point during the War of 1812, Francis Scott Key, composer of "The Star-Spangled Banner," our national anthem, was stranded in Baltimore Harbor on a British warship, the Tonnant. Key had boarded the ship in an effort to seek the release of an American prisoner-of-war, Dr. William Beanes. Key's request for Beanes' release was granted, but due to the battle about to begin in the harbor, the men were detained for nearly a week.

SCENE ONE. *The deck of the* Tonnant. *Twilight.*

KEY. This is an outrage, Captain! You've acknowledged that Dr. Beanes is innocent. I demand you release us immediately!

CAPTAIN *(smiling).* You are free to go when you choose, Mr. Key. But with a battle raging, I can't get you any closer to shore. It might be a long swim. Sit. Enjoy the fireworks. *(Exits.)*

BEANES. Patience, Key. All things in time. *(A flash of light, then a loud burst.)* It seems they've barely waited for nightfall to get the bombardment underway. We'll be lucky if Fort McHenry stands tomorrow.

BEANES. *(Another bomb burst.)* Look at the size of the Stars and Stripes they've got flying. It'll be torn to shreds.

KEY. Never underestimate the determination of men fighting for their own land, Beanes. Old Glory's what'll keep the men fighting. *(To a cabin boy.)* You there, be kind enough to fetch me a quill, paper, and ink.

KEY. "...what so proudly we hailed, at the twilight's last gleaming..."

SCENE TWO. *Key's cabin. The next morning.*

(Key sits at desk, quill pen in hand. A loud knock at the door.)

BEANE'S VOICE. Key! Come quickly! The Fort stands! And you'll never believe it—Old Glory—she's waving in the wind like a proud mother!

KEY *(shouting).* Be right there! *(He rushes to a porthole and looks out. Hurries back to his desk, dipping his pen and writing. To himself as he writes.)* "Oh say can you see, by the dawn's, early light." *(He holds the poem out in front of him for a look.)* There, that's it.

(Key folds the paper, tucks it into his back pocket, and exits cabin.)

Blueprint for Reading

INTO . . . *Flight Into Danger*

George Spencer is a passenger on a DC-4 airplane flying from Winnipeg to Vancouver. The night is clear, the flight is routine, the plane is full of calm, sleepy passengers. Dinner is served and all is well. Then—first one, then two, then three passengers take sick. What has happened? What will happen if the pilot takes sick, too? Will the people panic, or will they work together? Will those who are not sick have the courage to do what must be done? Is there a doctor on board? More importantly, is there another pilot on board?

EYES ON . . . *Theater*

What is more exciting than a play? Watching a good one is entertaining, but staging one is even more fun. A play has something for everyone—writers, artists, actors, technical people— whatever you like to do, your talents can be used in staging a play.

Flight Into Danger is full of suspense; in fact, the plot is so strong that it can easily be performed as a radio play. Even without seeing any actors or scenery, the audience sits spellbound until the play's very last scene.

The play's theme is a powerful one: courage in the face of danger. As we read the play, we wonder: what would I have done if I'd been there?

Flight into Danger
CHARACTERS

ABOARD FLIGHT 714

The passengers:
GEORGE SPENCER
DR. FRANK BAIRD
EIGHT MALE PASSENGERS
TWO WOMEN PASSENGERS

The crew:
CAPTAIN
FIRST OFFICER
STEWARDESS

AT VANCOUVER AIRPORT
CAPTAIN MARTIN TRELEAVEN
AIRPORT CONTROLLER
HARRY BURDICK
SWITCHBOARD OPERATOR
RADIO OPERATOR
TOWER CONTROLLER
TELETYPE OPERATOR

AT WINNIPEG AIRPORT
FIRST PASSENGER AGENT
SECOND PASSENGER AGENT

ARTHUR HAILEY

ACT I

(Fade in. *The passenger lobby of Winnipeg Air Terminal at night. At the departure counter of Cross-Canada Airlines, a male passenger agent in uniform (first agent) is checking a manifest. He reaches for P.A. mike.)*

FIRST AGENT. Flight 98, direct fleetliner service to Vancouver, with connections for Victoria, Seattle, and Honolulu, leaving immediately through gate four. No smoking. All aboard, please.

(*During the announcement* GEORGE SPENCER *enters through the main lobby doorway. About thirty-five, he is a senior factory salesman for a motor-truck manufacturer.* SPENCER *pauses to look for the Cross-Canada counter, then hastens toward it, arriving as the announcement concludes.)*

SPENCER. Is there space on Flight 98 for Vancouver?

FIRST AGENT. Sorry, sir, that flight is full. Did you check with reservations?

SPENCER. Didn't have time. I came straight out on the chance you might have a "no show" seat.

FIRST AGENT. With the big football game on tomorrow in Vancouver, I don't think you'll have much chance of getting out before tomorrow afternoon.

SPENCER. That's no good. I've got to be in Vancouver tomorrow by midday.

FIRST AGENT (*hesitates*). Look, I'm not supposed to tell you this, but there's a charter flight in from Toronto. They're going out to the coast for the game. I did hear they were a few seats light.

> WORD BANK
>
> **manifest** (MAN ih fest) *n.:* a list of the cargo or passengers carried by a ship, plane, truck, or train
> **hastens** (HAYS ens) *v.:* hurries

SPENCER. Who's in charge? Where do I find him?

FIRST AGENT. Ask at the desk over there. They call themselves Maple Leaf Air Charter. But mind, I didn't send you.

SPENCER *(smiles)*. Okay, thanks.

(SPENCER *crosses to another departure counter which has a cardboard sign hanging behind it—Maple Leaf Air Charter. Behind the desk is a casually dressed agent. He is checking a manifest.)*

SPENCER. Excuse me.

SECOND AGENT. Yes?

SPENCER. I was told you might have space on a flight to Vancouver.

SECOND AGENT. Yes, there's one seat left. The flight's leaving right away, though.

SPENCER. That's what I want.

SECOND AGENT. Very well, sir. Your name, please?

SPENCER. Spencer—George Spencer.

SECOND AGENT. That'll be fifty-five dollars for the one-way trip.

SPENCER. Will you take my air travel card?

SECOND AGENT. No, sir. Just old-fashioned cash.

SPENCER. All right. *(Produces wallet and counts out bills.)*

SECOND AGENT *(handing over ticket)*. Do you have any bags?

SPENCER. One. Right here.

SECOND AGENT. All the baggage is aboard. Would you mind keeping that with you?

SPENCER. Be glad to.

SECOND AGENT. Okay, Mr. Spencer. Your ticket is your boarding pass. Go through gate three and ask the gate agent for Flight 714. Better hurry.

SPENCER. Thanks a lot. Good night.

SECOND AGENT. Good night.

(Exit SPENCER. *Enter* STEWARDESS.*)*

SECOND AGENT. Hi, Janet. Did the meals get aboard?

STEWARDESS. Yes, they've just put them on. What was the trouble?

SECOND AGENT. Couldn't get service from the regular caterers here. We had to go to some outfit the other side of town. That's what held us up.

STEWARDESS. Are we all clear now?

SECOND AGENT. Yes, here's everything you'll need. *(Hands over papers)* There's one more passenger. He's just gone aboard. So that's fifty-six souls in your hands.

STEWARDESS. I'll try not to drop any.

SECOND AGENT *(reaching for coat).* Well, I'm off for home.

STEWARDESS *(as she leaves).* Good-night.

SECOND AGENT *(pulling on coat).* Good-night. *(Calls after her)* Don't forget to cheer for the Blue Bombers tomorrow.

(The STEWARDESS *waves and smiles.)*

(Dissolve to. The passenger cabin of a DC-4 airliner. There is one empty aisle seat. Seated next to it is DR. FRANK BAIRD, *55.* GEORGE SPENCER *enters, sees the unoccupied seat, and comes toward it.)*

SPENCER. Pardon me, is this anyone's seat?

BAIRD. No.

SPENCER. Thanks.

*(*SPENCER *sheds his topcoat and puts it on the rack above the seats. Meanwhile the plane's motors can be heard starting.)*

(Cut to. Film insert of four-engined airplane exterior. Night, the motors starting.)

(Cut to. The passenger cabin.)

BAIRD. I presume you're going to the big game like the rest of us.

SPENCER. I'm ashamed to admit it, but I'd forgotten about the game.

BAIRD. I wouldn't say that too loudly if I were you. Some of the more exuberant fans might tear you limb from limb.

SPENCER. I'll keep my voice down. *(Pleasantly)* Matter of fact, I'm making a sales trip to the coast.

BAIRD. What do you sell?

SPENCER. Trucks.

BAIRD. Trucks?

SPENCER. That's right. I'm what the local salesmen call the guy from head office with the special prices…Need any trucks? How about forty? Give you a real good discount today.

BAIRD *(laughs)*. I couldn't use that many, I'm afraid. Not in my line.

SPENCER. Which is?

BAIRD. Medicine.

SPENCER. You mean you're a doctor?

BAIRD. That's right. Can't buy one truck, leave alone forty. Football is the one extravagance I allow myself.

SPENCER. Delighted to hear it, Doctor. Now I can relax.

(As he speaks, the run-up of the aircraft engines begins, increasing to a heavy roar.)

BAIRD *(raising his voice)*. Do you think you can in this racket? I never can figure out why they make all this noise before take-off.

SPENCER *(shouting, as noise increases)*. It's the normal run-up of the engines. Airplane engines don't use battery ignition like

WORD BANK	**exuberant** (ex OO ber ent) *adj.*: full of high spirits and enthusiasm

you have in your car. They run on magneto ignition, and each of the magnetos is tested separately. If they're okay and the motors are giving all the power they should—away you go!

BAIRD. You sound as if you know something about it.

SPENCER. I'm pretty rusty now. I used to fly fighters in the air force. But that was ten years ago. Reckon I've forgotten most of it...Well, there we go.

(The tempo of the motors increases. BAIRD *and* SPENCER *lean toward the window to watch the take off, although it is dark outside.)*

(Cut to. Film insert of airplane taking off, night.)

(Cut to. The passenger cabin. The noise of the motors is reduced slightly, and the two men relax in their seats.)

SPENCER. Gum?

BAIRD. Thank you.

(The STEWARDESS *enters from aft of airplane and reaches for two pillows from the rack above.)*

STEWARDESS. We were held up at Winnipeg, sir, and we haven't served dinner yet. Would you care for some?

SPENCER. Yes, please.

(The STEWARDESS *puts a pillow on his lap.)*

STEWARDESS *(to* BAIRD*).* And you, sir?

BAIRD. Thank you, yes. *(To* SPENCER*)* It's a bit late for dinner, but it'll pass the time away.

STEWARDESS. There's lamb chop or grilled halibut.

BAIRD. I'll take the lamb.

SPENCER. Yes, I'll have that, too.

STEWARDESS. Thank you, sir.

BAIRD *(to* SPENCER*)*. Tell me...By the way, my name is Baird.

SPENCER. Spencer, George Spencer.

(They shake hands.)

BAIRD. How'd 'do. Tell me, when you make a sales trip like this, do you...

(Fade voices and pan with the STEWARDESS, *returning aft. Entering the airplane's tiny galley, she picks up a telephone and presses a call button.)*

VOICE OF FIRST OFFICER. Flight deck.

STEWARDESS. I'm finally serving the dinners. What'll "you all" have—lamb chops or grilled halibut?

VOICE OF FIRST OFFICER. Just a minute. *(Pause)* Skipper says he'll have the lamb...Oh, hold it!...No, he's changed his mind. Says he'll take the halibut. Make it two fish, Janet.

STEWARDESS. Okay. *(The* STEWARDESS *hangs up the phone and begins to arrange meal trays.)*

(Cut to. SPENCER *and* BAIRD.)

SPENCER. No, I hadn't expected to go west again this quickly.

BAIRD. You have my sympathy. I prescribe my travel in small doses.

(The STEWARDESS *enters and puts meal tray on pillow.)*

BAIRD. Oh, thank you.

STEWARDESS. Will you have coffee, tea, or milk, sir?

BAIRD. Coffee, please.

STEWARDESS. I'll bring it later.

WORD BANK   **galley** (GAL ee) *n.:* the kitchen area of a ship, plane, or camper

BAIRD. That'll be fine. *(To* SPENCER.) Tell me, do you follow football at all?

SPENCER. A little. Hockey's my game, though. Who are you for tomorrow?

BAIRD. The Argos, naturally. *(As the* STEWARDESS *brings second tray)* Thank you.

STEWARDESS. Will you have coffee, tea, or—

SPENCER. I'll have coffee, too. No cream.

(The STEWARDESS *nods and exits.)*

SPENCER *(to* BAIRD). Must be a calm night outside. No trouble in keeping the dinner steady.

BAIRD *(looking out of window)*. It is calm. Not a cloud in sight. Must be a monotonous business flying these things, once they're off the ground.

SPENCER. It varies, I guess.

(Audio. *Fade up the roar of motors.*)

(Dissolve to. *Film insert of airplane in level flight, night.*)

(Dissolve to. *The aircraft flight deck. The* CAPTAIN *is seated on left, the* FIRST OFFICER *on right. Neither is touching the controls.*)

FIRST OFFICER *(into radio mike)*. Height 16,000 feet. Course 285 true. ETA Vancouver 0505 Pacific Standard. Over.

VOICE ON RADIO. Flight 714. This is Winnipeg Control. Roger. Out.

(The FIRST OFFICER *reaches for a log sheet and makes a notation, then relaxes in his seat.)*

FIRST OFFICER. Got any plans for Vancouver?

CAPTAIN. Yes, I'm going to sleep for two whole days.

(The STEWARDESS *enters with a meal tray.)*

STEWARDESS. Who's first?

CAPTAIN. You take yours, Harry.

(The STEWARDESS *produces a pillow and the* FIRST OFFICER *slides back his seat, well clear of the control column. He places the pillow on his knees and accepts the tray.)*

FIRST OFFICER. Thanks.

CAPTAIN. Everything all right at the back, Janet? How are the football fans?

STEWARDESS. They tired themselves out on the way from Toronto. Looks like a peaceful, placid night.

FIRST OFFICER *(with mouth full of food, raising fork for emphasis).* Aha! Those are the sort of nights to beware of. It's in the quiet times that trouble brews. I'll bet you right now that somebody's getting ready to be sick.

STEWARDESS. That'll be when you're doing the flying. Or have you finally learned how to hold this thing steady? *(To* CAPTAIN*)* How's the weather?

CAPTAIN. General fog east of the mountains, extending pretty well as far as Manitoba. But it's clear to the west. Should be rockabye smooth the whole way.

STEWARDESS. Good. Well, keep junior here off the controls while I serve coffee. *(Exits)*

FIRST OFFICER *(calling after her).* Mark my words! Stay close to that mop and pail.

CAPTAIN. How's the fish?

FIRST OFFICER *(hungrily).* Not bad. Not bad at all. If there were about three times as much it might be a square meal.

(Audio. *Fade voices into roar of motors.*)

(Dissolve to. *The passenger cabin.* SPENCER *and* BAIRD *are concluding their meal.* BAIRD *puts down a coffee cup and wipes his mouth with a napkin. Then he reaches up and presses a call button above his head. There is a soft "ping," and the* STEWARDESS *enters.*)

STEWARDESS. Yes, sir?

BAIRD. That was very enjoyable. Now, if you'll take the tray I think I'll try to sleep.

STEWARDESS. Surely. *(To* SPENCER*)* Will you have more coffee, sir?

SPENCER. No, thanks.

(*The* STEWARDESS *picks up the second tray and goes aft.* SPENCER *yawns.*)

SPENCER. Let me know if the noise keeps you awake. If it does, I'll have the engines stopped.

BAIRD *(chuckles).* Well, at least there won't be any night calls—I hope.

(BAIRD *reaches up and switches off the overhead reading lights so that both seats are in semi-darkness. The two men prepare to sleep.*)

(Dissolve to. *Film insert of airplane in level flight, night.*)

(Dissolve to. *The passenger cabin. The* CAPTAIN *emerges from the flight deck and strolls aft, saying "Good evening" to one or two people who glance up as he goes by. He passes* SPENCER *and* BAIRD, *who are sleeping. As the* CAPTAIN *progresses, the* STEWARDESS *can be seen at the rear of the cabin. She is bending solicitously over a woman passenger, her hand on the woman's forehead. The* CAPTAIN *approaches.*)

CAPTAIN. Something wrong, Miss Burns?

STEWARDESS. This lady is feeling a little unwell. I was going to get her some aspirin. *(To the* WOMAN PASSENGER*)* I'll be back in a moment.

CAPTAIN. Sorry to hear that. What seems to be the trouble?

(The WOMAN PASSENGER *has her head back and her mouth open. A strand of hair has fallen across her face, and she is obviously in pain.)*

FIRST WOMAN PASSENGER *(speaking with an effort).* I'm sorry to be such a nuisance, but it hit me all of a sudden…just a few minutes ago…dizziness and nausea and a sharp pain…*(indicating abdomen)* down here.

CAPTAIN. Well, I think the Stewardess will be able to help you.

*(*STEWARDESS *returns.)*

STEWARDESS. Now, here you are; try these. *(She hands over two aspirins and a cup of water. The passenger takes them, then puts her head back on the seat rest.)*

FIRST WOMAN PASSENGER. Thank you very much. *(She smiles faintly at the* CAPTAIN.*)*

CAPTAIN *(quietly, taking the* STEWARDESS *aside).* If she gets any worse you'd better let me know and I'll radio ahead. But we've still five hours' flying to the coast. Is there a doctor on board, do you know?

STEWARDESS. There was no one listed as a doctor on the manifest. But I can go round and ask.

CAPTAIN *(looks around).* Well, most everybody's sleeping now. We'd better not disturb them unless we have to. See how she is in the next half hour or so. *(He bends down to show concern.)* Try to rest, madam, if you can. Miss Burns will take good care of you.

(The CAPTAIN *nods to the* STEWARDESS *and begins his return to the flight deck. The* STEWARDESS *arranges a blanket around the* WOMAN PASSENGER. SPENCER *and* BAIRD *are still sleeping as the* CAPTAIN *passes.)*

(Dissolve to. *Film insert of airplane in level flight, night.*)

(Dissolve to. *The passenger cabin.* SPENCER *stirs and wakes. Then he glances forward to where the* STEWARDESS *is leaning over another section of seats, and her voice can be heard softly.*)

STEWARDESS. I'm sorry to disturb you, but we're trying to find out if there's a doctor on board.

FIRST MALE PASSENGER. Not me, I'm afraid. Is something wrong?

STEWARDESS. One of the passengers is feeling unwell. It's nothing too serious. *(Moving on to the next pair of seats)* I'm sorry to disturb you, but we're trying to find out if there's a doctor on board.

(*There is an indistinct answer from the two people just questioned, then* SPENCER *sits forward and calls the* STEWARDESS.)

SPENCER. Stewardess! *(indicating* BAIRD, *who is still sleeping)* This gentleman is a doctor.

STEWARDESS. Thank you. I think we'd better wake him. I have two passengers who are quite sick.

SPENCER. All right. *(Shaking* BAIRD'S *arm)* Doctor! Doctor! Wake up!

BAIRD. Um…Um…What is it?

STEWARDESS. Doctor. I'm sorry to disturb you. But we have two passengers who seem quite sick. I wonder if you'd take a look at them.

BAIRD *(sleepily).* Yes…yes…of course.

(SPENCER *moves out of the seat to permit* BAIRD *to reach the aisle.* BAIRD *then follows the* STEWARDESS *aft to the* FIRST WOMAN PASSENGER. *Although a blanket is around her, the woman is shivering and gasping, with her head back and eyes closed. The doctor places a hand on her forehead, and she opens her eyes.*)

STEWARDESS. This gentleman is a doctor. He's going to help us.

FIRST WOMAN PASSENGER. Oh, Doctor!...

BAIRD. Now, just relax.

(He makes a quick external examination, first checking pulse, then taking a small pen-type flashlight from his pocket and looking into her eyes. He then loosens the blanket and the woman's coat beneath the blanket. As he examines her, she gasps with pain.)

BAIRD. Hurt you there? *(With an effort she nods.)* There?

FIRST WOMAN PASSENGER. Oh, yes! Yes!

(BAIRD replaces the coat and blanket, then turns to the STEWARDESS.)

BAIRD *(with authority)*. Please tell the captain we must land at once. This woman has to be gotten to a hospital immediately.

STEWARDESS. Do you know what's wrong, Doctor?

BAIRD. I can't tell. I've no means of making a proper diagnosis. But it's serious enough to land at the nearest city with hospital facilities. You can tell your captain that.

STEWARDESS. Very well, Doctor. *(Moving across the aisle and forward)* While I'm gone will you take a look at this gentleman here? He's also complained of sickness and stomach pains.

(BAIRD goes to a male passenger indicated by the STEWARDESS. The man is sitting forward and resting his head on the back of the seat ahead of him. He is retching.)

BAIRD. I'm a doctor. Will you put your head back, please?

(The man groans, but follows the doctor's instruction. He is obviously weak. BAIRD makes another quick examination, then pauses thoughtfully.)

BAIRD. What have you had to eat in the last twenty-four hours?

SECOND MALE PASSENGER *(with effort).* Just the usual meals...breakfast...toast and eggs...salad for lunch...couple of sandwiches at the airport...then dinner here.

(The STEWARDESS *enters, followed by the* CAPTAIN.)*

BAIRD *(to the* STEWARDESS*).* Keep him warm. Get blankets around him. *(To the* CAPTAIN*)* How quickly can we land, Captain?

CAPTAIN. That's the trouble. I've just been talking to Calgary. There was a light fog over the prairies earlier, but now it's thickened and everything is closed in this side of the mountains. It's clear at the coast, and we'll have to go through.

BAIRD. Is that faster than turning back?

CAPTAIN. It would take us longer to go back now than to go on.

BAIRD. Then, how soon do you expect to land?

CAPTAIN. At about 5 A.M. Pacific time. *(As* BAIRD *glances at his watch)* You need to put your watch ahead two hours because of the change of time. We'll be landing in three hours forty-five minutes from now.

BAIRD. Then, I'll have to do what I can for these people. Can my bag be reached? I checked it at Toronto.

CAPTAIN. We can get it. Let me have your tags, Doctor.

*(*BAIRD *takes out a wallet and selects two baggage tags which he hands to the* CAPTAIN.)*

BAIRD. There are two tags. It's the small overnight case I want.

(As he finishes speaking, the airplane lurches violently. BAIRD *and the* STEWARDESS *and the* CAPTAIN *are thrown sharply to one side. Simultaneously the telephone in the galley buzzes several times. As the three recover their balance the* STEWARDESS *answers the phone quickly.)*

STEWARDESS. Yes?

FIRST OFFICER'S VOICE *(under strain)*. Come forward quickly. I'm sick!

STEWARDESS. The First Officer is sick. He says come forward quickly.

CAPTAIN *(to* BAIRD*)*. You'd better come too.

(The CAPTAIN *and* BAIRD *move quickly forward, passing through the flight deck door.)*

(Cut to. The flight deck. The FIRST OFFICER *is at the controls on the right-hand side. He is retching and shuddering, flying the airplane by will power and nothing else. The* CAPTAIN *promptly slides into the left-hand seat and takes the controls.)*

CAPTAIN. Get him out of there!

(Together BAIRD *and the* STEWARDESS *lift the* FIRST OFFICER *from his seat, and as they do, he collapses. They lower him to the floor, and the* STEWARDESS *reaches for a pillow and blankets.* BAIRD *makes the same quick examination he used in the two previous cases. Meanwhile the* CAPTAIN *has steadied the aircraft, and now he snaps over a button to engage the automatic pilot. He releases the controls and turns to the others, though without leaving his seat.)*

CAPTAIN. He must have been changing course when it happened. We're back on auto pilot now. Now, Doctor; what is it? What's happening?

BAIRD. There's a common denominator in these attacks. There has to be. And the most likely thing is food. *(To the* STEWARDESS*)* How long is it since we had dinner?

STEWARDESS. Two and a half to three hours.

BAIRD. Now, then, what did you serve?

STEWARDESS. Well, the main course was a choice of fish or meat.

BAIRD. I remember that; I ate meat. *(Indicating the* FIRST OFFICER*)* What did he have?

STEWARDESS *(faintly, with dawning alarm)*. Fish.

BAIRD. Do you remember what the other two passengers had?

STEWARDESS. No.

BAIRD. Then, go back quickly, and find out, please.

(As the STEWARDESS *exits,* BAIRD *kneels beside the* FIRST OFFICER, *who is moaning.)*

BAIRD. Try to relax. I'll give you something in a few minutes to help the pain. You'll feel better if you stay warm.

*(*BAIRD *arranges the blanket around the* FIRST OFFICER. *Now the* STEWARDESS *reappears.)*

STEWARDESS *(alarmed).* Doctor, both those passengers had fish. And there are three more cases now. And they ate fish too. Can you come?

BAIRD. Yes, but I need that bag of mine.

CAPTAIN. Janet, take these tags and get one of the passengers to help you. *(Hands over* BAIRD*'s luggage tags)* Doctor, I'm going to get on the radio and report what's happening to Vancouver. Is there anything you want to add?

BAIRD. Yes. Tell them we have three serious cases of suspected food poisoning, and there appear to be others. When we land, we'll want ambulances and medical help waiting, and the hospitals should be warned. Tell them we're not sure, but we suspect the poisoning may have been caused by fish served on board. You'd better suggest they put a ban on serving all food that originated wherever ours came from until we've established the source for sure.

CAPTAIN. Right. *(He reaches for the radio mike, and* BAIRD *turns to go aft. But suddenly a thought strikes the* CAPTAIN.) Doctor, I've just remembered....

BAIRD. Yes.

CAPTAIN *(quietly)*. I ate fish.

BAIRD. When?

CAPTAIN. I'd say about half an hour after he did. *(Pointing to the* FIRST OFFICER*)* Maybe a little longer. Is there anything I can do?

BAIRD. It doesn't follow that everyone will be affected. There's often no logic to these things. You feel all right now?

CAPTAIN. Yes.

BAIRD. You'd better not take any chances. Your food can't be completely digested yet. As soon as I get my bag I'll give you something to help you get rid of it.

CAPTAIN. Then, hurry, Doctor. Hurry! *(Into mike)* Vancouver control. This is Maple Leaf Charter Flight 714. I have an emergency message. Do you read? Over.

VOICE ON RADIO *(Vancouver* OPERATOR*)*. Go ahead, 714.

CAPTAIN. We have serious food poisoning on board. Several passengers and the First Officer are seriously ill...

(Dissolve to. *The luggage compartment below the flight deck. A passenger is hurriedly passing up bags to the* STEWARDESS. BAIRD *is looking down from above.)*

BAIRD. That's it! That's it down there! Let me have it!

(Fade out.)

Studying the Selection

FIRST IMPRESSIONS
What do you think will happen on board within the next hour?

QUICK REVIEW

1. From what city did the plane depart and where was it scheduled to land?

2. What is Baird's profession?

3. Where had Spencer learned to fly a plane?

4. Which meals caused the passengers to be sick and which proved safe to eat?

FOCUS

5. In the first part of a suspense story, the author lays out many details that will be important later in the story. An example from a different story of such a detail is the pocketknife given to the boy at the beginning of *The Black Stallion;* the knife turns out to be very important later on in the story. Look through Act One of *Flight Into Danger,* and find three or more characters, lines, or objects that you think will be important in the story later on. Explain the reason for your choices.

CREATING & WRITING

6. The setting of a play adds atmosphere to the story. If, for example, a play is set in a desert, an atmosphere of extreme heat, loneliness, and thirst is created. What sort of feeling does the setting of an airplane contribute to the play's suspense? In a paragraph or two, write about how the airplane setting made you feel as you read Act One.

7. Do you think *Flight Into Danger* could be made into a radio play? Explain why or why not. Remember that in a radio play, the audience only hears the actors but does not see them or the scenery.

8. As one of the props for the play, a stage manager would surely want to include a Blue Bombers pennant to be carried by some of the passengers. Design the pennant and draw a picture of it in the Blue Bombers colors of your own choosing.

ACT II

(Fade in. *The control room, Vancouver Airport. At a radio panel an* OPERATOR, *wearing headphones, is transcribing a message on a typewriter. Partway through the message he presses a button on the panel and a bell rings stridently, signaling an emergency. At once an* AIRPORT CONTROLLER *appears behind the* OPERATOR *and reads the message as it continues to come in. Nearby a telephone switchboard manned by an* OPERATOR, *and a battery of teletypes clattering noisily.)*

CONTROLLER *(over his shoulder, to the* SWITCHBOARD OPERATOR*)*. Get me Area Traffic Control, then clear the teletype circuit to Winnipeg. Priority message. *(Stepping back to take phone)* Vancouver controller here. I've an emergency report from Maple Leaf Charter Flight 714, ex-Winnipeg for Vancouver. There's serious food poisoning among the passengers and the First Officer is down too. They're asking for all levels below them to be cleared, and priority approach and landing. ETA is 0505...Roger. We'll keep you posted. *(To a* TELETYPE OPERATOR *who has appeared)* Got Winnipeg? *(As the* TELETYPE OPERATOR *nods)* Send this message. Controller Winnipeg. Urgent. Maple Leaf Charter Flight 714 reports serious food poisoning among passengers believed due to fish dinner served on flight. Imperative check source and suspend all other food service originating same place. That's all. *(To the* SWITCHBOARD OPERATOR*)* Get me the local agent for Maple Leaf Charter. Burdick's his name—call his home. And after that, I want the city police—the senior officer on duty. *(*CONTROLLER *crosses to radio control panel and reads message which is just being completed. To the* RADIO OPERATOR*)* Acknowledge. Say that all altitudes below them are being cleared, and they'll be advised of landing instructions here. Ask them to keep us posted on condition of the passengers.

SWITCHBOARD OPERATOR. Mr. Burdick is here at the airport. I have him on the line now.

CONTROLLER. Good. Controller here. Burdick, we've got an emergency on one of your flights—714, ex-Toronto and Winnipeg. *(Pause)* No, the aircraft is all right. There's food poisoning among the passengers, and the First Officer has it too. You'd better come over. *(Replaces phone. Then to the* SWITCHBOARD OPERATOR*)* Have you got the police yet? *(As the* OPERATOR *nods)* Right, put it on this line. Hullo, this is the Controller, Vancouver Airport. Who am I speaking to, please? *(Pause)* Inspector, we have an emergency on an incoming flight. Several of the passengers are seriously ill, and we need ambulances and doctors out here at the airport. *(Pause)* Six people for sure, maybe more. The flight will be landing at five minutes past five local time—that's about three and a half hours. Now, will you get the ambulances, set up traffic control, and alert the hospitals? Right. We'll call you again as soon as there's anything definite.

(During the above, HARRY BURDICK, *local manager of Maple Leaf Air Charter, has entered.)*

BURDICK. Where's the message?

(The RADIO OPERATOR *hands him a copy which* BURDICK *reads.)*

BURDICK *(to* RADIO OPERATOR*).* How's the weather at Calgary? It might be quicker to go in there.

CONTROLLER. No dice! There's fog down to the deck everywhere east of the Rockies. They'll have to come through.

BURDICK. Let me see the last position report. *(As* CONTROLLER *passes a clipboard)* You say that you've got medical help coming?

CONTROLLER. The city police are working on it now.

BURDICK. That message! They say the First Officer is down. What about the Captain? Ask if he's affected, and ask if there's a doctor on board. Tell them we're getting medical advice here in case they need it.

CONTROLLER. I'll take care of that.

BURDICK *(to the* SWITCHBOARD OPERATOR*).* Will you get me Doctor Knudsen, please? You'll find his home number on the emergency list.

CONTROLLER *(into radio mike).* Flight 714, this is Vancouver.

(Dissolve to. The airplane passenger cabin. BAIRD *is leaning over another prostrate passenger. The main lighting is on in the cabin, and other passengers, so far not affected, are watching, with varying degrees of concern and anxiety. Some have remained in their seats; others have clustered in the aisle. The doctor has obtained his bag and it is open beside him. The* STEWARDESS *is attending to another passenger nearby.)*

BAIRD *(to the* STEWARDESS*).* I think I'd better talk to everyone and tell them the story. *(Moving to center of cabin, he raises his voice.)* Ladies and gentlemen, may I have your attention, please? If you can't hear me, perhaps you would come a little closer. *(Pause, as passengers move in)* My name is Baird, and I am a doctor. I think it's time that everyone knows what is happening. So far as I can tell, we have several cases of food poisoning, and we believe that the cause of it was fish which was served for dinner.

SECOND WOMAN PASSENGER *(with alarm, to man beside her).* Hector! We both had fish!

BAIRD. Now, there is no immediate cause for alarm or panic, and even if you did eat fish for dinner, it doesn't follow that you are going to be affected too. There's seldom any logic to these things. However, we are going to take some precautions, and the Stewardess and I are coming around to everyone, and I want you to tell us if you ate fish. If you did we'll tell you what to do to help yourselves. Now, if you'll go back to your seats we'll begin right away. *(To the* STEWARDESS, *as passengers move back to their seats)* All we can do now is to give immediate first aid.

STEWARDESS. What should that be, Doctor?

BAIRD. Two things. First, everyone who ate fish must drink several glasses of water. That will help dilute the poison. After that we'll give an emetic. I have some emetic pills in my bag, and if there aren't enough we'll have to rely on salt. Do you have salt in the galley?

STEWARDESS. A few small packets which go with the lunches, but we can break them open.

BAIRD. All right. We'll see how far the pills will go first. I'll start at the back here. Meanwhile you begin giving drinking water to the passengers already affected and get some to the First Officer too. I'll ask someone to help you.

FIRST MALE PASSENGER. Can I help, Doc?

BAIRD. What did you eat for dinner—fish or meat?

FIRST MALE PASSENGER. Meat.

BAIRD. All right. Will you help the Stewardess bring glasses of water to the people who are sick? I want them to drink at least three glasses each—more if they can.

STEWARDESS *(going to galley)*. We'll use these cups. There's drinking water here and at the rear.

FIRST MALE PASSENGER. All right, let's get started.

BAIRD *(to the* STEWARDESS*)*. The Captain! Before you do anything else you'd better get him on to drinking water, and give him two emetic pills. Here. *(Takes bottle from his bag and shakes out the pills)* Tell him they'll make him feel sick, and the sooner he is, the better.

STEWARDESS. Very well, Doctor.

WORD BANK	**emetic** (ee MET ik) *n.:* a medicine to make a person vomit

SECOND WOMAN PASSENGER *(frightened)*. Doctor! Doctor! I heard you say the pilots are ill. What will happen to us if they can't fly the plane? *(To husband)* Hector, I'm frightened.

THIRD MALE PASSENGER. Take it easy, my dear. Nothing has happened so far, and the doctor is doing all he can.

BAIRD. I don't think you'll have any reason to worry, madam. It's quite true that both of the pilots had the fish which we believe may have caused the trouble. But only the First Officer is affected. Now, did you and your husband eat fish or meat?

THIRD MALE PASSENGER. Fish. We both ate fish.

BAIRD. Then, will you both drink at least three—better make it four—of those cups of water which the other gentleman is bringing around. After that, take one of these pills each. *(Smiling)* I think you'll find there are little containers under your seat. Use those. *(Goes to rear of plane)*

FOURTH MALE PASSENGER *(in broad English Yorkshire accent)*. How's it commin', Doc? Everything under control?

BAIRD. I think we're holding our own. What did you have for dinner?

FOURTH MALE PASSENGER. Ah had the bloomin' fish. Didn't like it neither. Fine how d'you do this is. Coom all this way t'see our team win, and now it looks like ah'm headed for a mortuary slab.

BAIRD. It really isn't as bad as that, you know. But just as a precaution, drink four cups of water—it's being brought around now—and after that take this pill. It'll make you feel sick.

FOURTH MALE PASSENGER *(pulls carton from under seat and holds it up)*. It's the last time I ride on a bloomin' airplane! What service! They give you your dinner and then coom round and ask for it back.

BAIRD. What did you have for dinner, please—meat or fish?

FIFTH MALE PASSENGER. Meat, Doctor.

SIXTH MALE PASSENGER. Yes, I had meat too.

BAIRD. All right, we won't worry about you.

SEVENTH MALE PASSENGER. I had meat, Doctor.

EIGHTH MALE PASSENGER. I had fish.

DOCTOR. Very well, will you drink at least four cups of water please? It'll be brought round to you. Then take this pill.

SIXTH MALE PASSENGER (*slow speaking*). What's caused this food poisoning, Doctor?

BAIRD. Well, it can either be caused through spoilage of the food, or some kind of bacteria—the medical word is staphylococcus poisoning.

SIXTH MALE PASSENGER (*nodding knowledgeably*). Oh yes...staphylo...I see.

BAIRD. Either that, or some toxic substance may have gotten into the food during its preparation.

SEVENTH MALE PASSENGER. What kind do you think this is, Doctor?

BAIRD. From the effect, I suspect a toxic substance.

SEVENTH MALE PASSENGER. And you don't know what it is?

BAIRD. We won't know until we make laboratory tests. Actually, with modern food-handling methods—the chances of this happening are probably a million to one against.

STEWARDESS (*entering*). I couldn't get the First Officer to take more than a little water, Doctor. He seems pretty bad.

BAIRD. I'll go to him now. Have you checked all the passengers in the front portion?

STEWARDESS. Yes, and there are two more new cases—the same symptoms as the other passengers.

WORD BANK   **toxic** (TOX ik) *adj.*: poisonous

BAIRD. I'll attend to them—after I've looked at the First Officer.

STEWARDESS. Do you think....

(Before the sentence is completed the galley telephone buzzes insistently. BAIRD and the STEWARDESS exchange glances quickly; then, without waiting to answer the phone, race to the flight deck door.)

(Cut to. The flight deck. The CAPTAIN is in the left-hand seat. Sweat pouring down his face, he is racked by retching, and his right hand is on his stomach. Yet he is fighting against the pain and attempting to reach the radio transmitter mike. But he doesn't make it, and as BAIRD and the STEWARDESS reach him, he falls back in his seat.)

CAPTAIN *(weakly).* I did what you said...guess it was too late....You've got to give me something, Doctor...so I can hold out...till I get this airplane on the ground....You understand?...It'll fly itself on this course...but I've got to take it in...Get on the radio...Tell control...

(During the above BAIRD and the STEWARDESS have been helping the CAPTAIN from his seat. Now he collapses into unconsciousness, and BAIRD goes down beside him. The doctor has a stethoscope now and uses it.)

BAIRD. Get blankets over him. Keep him warm. There's probably a reaction because he tried to fight it off so long.

STEWARDESS *(alarmed).* Can you do what he said? Can you bring him round long enough to land?

BAIRD *(bluntly).* You're part of this crew, so I'll tell you how things are. Unless I can get him to a hospital quickly, I'm not even sure I can save his life. And that goes for the others too.

STEWARDESS. But—

BAIRD. I know what you're thinking, and I've thought of it too. How many passengers are there on board?

STEWARDESS. Fifty-six.

BAIRD. And how many fish dinners did you serve?

STEWARDESS (*composing herself*)**.** Probably about fifteen. More people ate meat than fish, and some didn't eat at all because it was so late.

BAIRD. And you?

STEWARDESS. I had meat.

BAIRD (*quietly*)**.** Did you ever hear the term "long odds"?

STEWARDESS. Yes, but I'm not sure what it means.

BAIRD. I'll give you an example. Out of a total field of fifty-five, our chances of safety depend on there being one person back there who not only is qualified to land this airplane, but who didn't choose fish for dinner tonight.

(*After her initial alarm the* STEWARDESS *is calm now, and competent. She looks* BAIRD *in the eye and even manages a slight smile.*)

STEWARDESS. Then, I suppose I should begin asking.

BAIRD (*thoughtfully*)**.** Yes, but there's no sense in starting a panic. (*Decisively*) You'd better do it this way. Say that the First Officer is sick and the Captain wondered if there's someone with flying experience who could help him with the radio.

STEWARDESS. Very well, Doctor. (*She turns to go.*)

BAIRD. Wait! The man who was sitting beside me! He said something about flying in the war. And we both ate meat. Get him first! But still go round to the others. There may be someone else with more experience.

(*The* STEWARDESS *exits and* BAIRD *busies himself with the* FIRST OFFICER *and the* CAPTAIN. *After a moment,* GEORGE SPENCER *enters.*)

SPENCER. The Stewardess said—(*then, as he sees the two pilots*)...No! Not both pilots!

BAIRD. Can *you* fly this airplane—and land it?

SPENCER. No! No! Not a chance! Of course not!

BAIRD. But you told me you flew in the war.

SPENCER. So I did. But that was fighters—little combat airplanes, not a great ship like this. I flew airplanes which had one engine. This has four. Flying characteristics are different. Controls don't react the same way. It's another kind of flying altogether. And besides that, I haven't touched an airplane for over ten years.

BAIRD *(grimly)*. Then, let's hope there's someone else on board who can do the job...because neither of these men can.

(The STEWARDESS *enters and pauses.)*

STEWARDESS *(quietly)*. There's no one else.

BAIRD. Mr. Spencer, I know nothing of flying. I have no means of evaluating what you tell me. All I know is this: that among the people on this airplane who are physically able to fly it, you are the only one with any kind of qualification to do so. What do you suggest?

SPENCER *(desperately)*. Isn't there a chance—of either pilot recovering?

BAIRD. I'll tell you what I just told the Stewardess here. Unless I can get them to a hospital quickly, I can't even be sure of saving their lives.

(There is a pause.)

SPENCER. Well—I guess I just got drafted. If either of you are any good at praying, you can start any time. *(He slips into the left-hand seat.)* Let's take a look. Altitude 16,000. Course 290. The ship's on automatic pilot—we can be thankful for that. Air speed 210 knots. *(Touching the various controls)* Throttles, pitch, mixture, landing gear, flaps, and the flap

indicator. We'll need a check list for landing, but we'll get that on the radio....Well, maybe we'd better tell the world about our problems. *(To the* STEWARDESS*)* Do you know how to work this radio? They've added a lot of gismos[1] since my flying days.

STEWARDESS *(pointing).* It's this panel up here they use to talk to the ground, but I'm not sure which switches you have to set.

SPENCER. Ah, yes, here's the channel selector. Maybe we'd better leave it where it is. Oh, and here we are—"transmit." *(He flicks a switch, and a small light glows on the radio control panel.)* Now we're in business. *(He picks up the mike and headset beside him, then turns to the other two.)* Look, whatever happens I'm going to need another pair of hands here. Doc, I guess you'll be needed back with the others, so I think the best choice is the stewardess here. How about it?

STEWARDESS. But I know nothing about all this!

SPENCER. Then that'll make us a real good pair. I'll tell you what to do ahead of time. Better get in that other seat and strap yourself in. That all right with you, Doc?

BAIRD. Yes, do that. I'll take care of things in the back. And I'd better go there now. Good luck!

SPENCER. Good luck to *you.* We're all going to need it.

(BAIRD *exits.)*

SPENCER. What's your first name?

STEWARDESS. Janet.

SPENCER. Okay, Janet. Let's see if I can remember how to send out a distress message....Better put on that headset beside you. *(Into mike)* May Day! May Day! May Day! *(To the* STEWARDESS*)* What's our flight number?

---

1. The word *gismo* is an old-fashioned, informal word for "gadget."

STEWARDESS. 714.

SPENCER *(into mike).* This is Flight 714, Maple Leaf Air Charter, in distress. Come in anyone. Over.

VOICE ON RADIO *(immediately, crisply).* This is Calgary, 714. Go ahead!

VOICE ON RADIO *(Vancouver* OPERATOR*).* Vancouver here, 714. All other aircraft stay off the air. Over.

SPENCER. Thank you, Calgary and Vancouver. This message is for Vancouver. This aircraft is in distress. Both pilots and some passengers—*(To the* STEWARDESS*)* How many passengers?

STEWARDESS. It was seven a few minutes ago. It may be more now.

SPENCER. Correction. At least seven passengers are suffering from food poisoning. Both pilots are unconscious and in serious condition. We have a doctor on board who says that neither pilot can be revived. Did you get that, Vancouver? *(Pause)* Now we come to the interesting bit. My name is Spencer, George Spencer. I am a passenger on this airplane. Correction: I was a passenger. I have about a thousand hours' total flying time, but all of it was on single-engine fighters. And also, I haven't flown an airplane for ten years. Now, then, Vancouver, you'd better get someone on this radio who can give me some instructions about flying this machine. Our altitude is 16,000, course 290 magnetic, air speed 210 knots. We are on automatic pilot. Your move, Vancouver. Over. *(To the* STEWARDESS*)* You want to make a bet that that stirred up a little flurry down below?

(The STEWARDESS *shakes her head, but does not reply.)*

(Dissolve to. The control room, Vancouver. The CONTROLLER *is putting down a phone as the* RADIO OPERATOR *brings a message to him. He reads the message.)*

CONTROLLER. Oh, no! *(To the* RADIO OPERATOR*)* Ask if—No, let me talk to them.

(The CONTROLLER *goes to panel and takes the transmitter mike. The* RADIO OPERATOR *turns a switch and nods.)*

CONTROLLER *(tensely).* Flight 714. This is Vancouver control. Please check with your doctor on board for any possibility of either pilot recovering. Ask him to do everything possible to revive one of the pilots, even if it means neglecting other people. Over.

SPENCER'S VOICE ON RADIO. Vancouver, this is 714, Spencer speaking. I understand your message. But the doctor says there is no possibility whatever of either pilot recovering to make the landing. He says they are critically ill and may die unless they get hospital treatment soon. Over.

CONTROLLER. All right, 714. Stand by, please. *(He pauses momentarily to consider the next course of action. Then briskly to the* SWITCHBOARD*)* Get me Area Traffic Control— fast. *(Into phone)* Vancouver controller. The emergency we had!...Right now it looks like it's shaping up for a disaster.

(Fade out.)

Studying the Selection

FIRST IMPRESSIONS

Who do you think is the hero of this act—Baird or Spencer? Why?

QUICK REVIEW

1. What is Harry Burdick's job?

2. Why can't the plane land at Calgary?

3. What two things can those who ate fish do to help themselves?

4. What does Dr. Baird think is the cause of the food poisoning?

FOCUS

5. What does Baird say to Spencer to convince him that he must fly the plane? Do you think his words are convincing?

6. What could you learn from Baird about how best to behave in a stressful situation?

7. What is the turning point of this act?

CREATING & WRITING

8. Have you ever heard of Murphy's Law? It goes like this: whatever can go wrong *will* go wrong. Most people say this with a smile, because it is meant to be humorous. In *Flight Into Danger,* it proves to be true in a very terrible way. Write a list of all the things that *could go* wrong that did go wrong.

9. On the other hand, a few things went right! Write a (much shorter) list of those things.

10. If your class were staging this play, they might design programs to hand out to the audience. The cover of the program might feature a menu of the meals that were served on board flight 714, with a picture of a plane on top. Make up a menu that includes an appetizer, main course, side dishes, and dessert. Then, create your menu/program cover. Make sure the title of the play is somewhere on the cover.

ACT III

(Fade in. *The control room, Vancouver. The atmosphere is one of restrained pandemonium. The* RADIO OPERATOR *is typing a message. The teletypes are busy. The controller is on one telephone, and* HARRY BURDICK *on another. During what follows, cut back and forth from one to the other.)*

CONTROLLER *(into phone).* As of right now, hold everything taking off for the East. You've got forty-five minutes to clear any traffic for South, West, or North. After that, hold everything that's scheduled outward. On incoming traffic, accept anything you can get on the deck within the next forty-five minutes. Anything you can't get down by then for sure, divert away from the area. Hold it. *(A messenger hands him a message which he scans. Then to messenger)* Tell the security officer. *(Into phone)* If you've any flights coming in from the Pacific, divert them to Seattle. And any traffic inland is to stay well away from the east-west lane between Calgary and Vancouver. Got that? Right.

BURDICK *(into phone).* Is that Cross-Canada Airlines?...Who's on duty in operations?...Let me talk to him. *(Pause)* Mr. Gardner, it's Harry Burdick of Maple Leaf Charter. We have an incoming flight that's in bad trouble, and we need an experienced pilot to talk on the radio. Someone who's flown DC-4's. Can you help us? *(Pause)* Captain Treleaven? Yes, I know him well. *(Pause)* You mean he's with you now? *(Pause)* Can he come over to control right away? *(Pause)* Thank you. Thank you very much. *(To the* SWITCHBOARD

OPERATOR) Get me Montreal. I want to talk with Mr. Barney Whitmore. You may have to try Maple Leaf Air Charter office first, and someone there'll have his home number. Tell them the call is urgent.

SWITCHBOARD OPERATOR. Right. *(To the* CONTROLLER*)* I've got the fire chief.

CONTROLLER *(into phone).* Chief, we have an emergency. It's Flight 714, due here at 0505. It may be a crash landing. Have everything you've got stand by. If you have men off duty, call them in. Take your instructions from the tower. They'll tell you which runway we're using. And notify the city fire department. They may want to move equipment into this area. Right. *(To the* SWITCHBOARD OPERATOR*)* Now get me the city police again—Inspector Moyse.

SWITCHBOARD OPERATOR. I have Seattle and Calgary waiting. They both received the message from Flight 714 and want to know if we got it clearly.

CONTROLLER. Tell them thank you, yes, and we're working the aircraft direct. But ask them to keep a listening watch in case we run into any reception trouble. *(Another message is handed him. After reading, he passes it to* BURDICK.*)* There's bad weather moving in. That's all we need. *(To the* SWITCHBOARD OPERATOR*)* Have you got the police? Right! *(into phone)* It's the airport Controller again, Inspector. We're in bad trouble, and we may have a crash landing. We'll need every spare ambulance in the city out here—and doctors and nurses too. Will you arrange it? *(Pause)* Yes, we do— fifty-six passengers and a crew of three. *(Pause)* Yes, the same time—0505. That's less than three hours.

BURDICK *(to the* SWITCHBOARD OPERATOR*).* Is Montreal on the line yet?...Yes, give it to me...Hullo. Hullo. Is that you, Barney?...It's Harry Burdick in Vancouver. I'll give you this fast, Barney. Our flight from Toronto is in bad trouble. They have food poisoning on board, and both pilots and a lot of

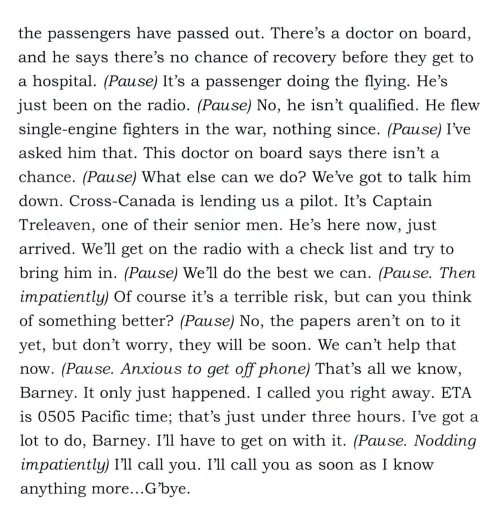

the passengers have passed out. There's a doctor on board, and he says there's no chance of recovery before they get to a hospital. *(Pause)* It's a passenger doing the flying. He's just been on the radio. *(Pause)* No, he isn't qualified. He flew single-engine fighters in the war, nothing since. *(Pause)* I've asked him that. This doctor on board says there isn't a chance. *(Pause)* What else can we do? We've got to talk him down. Cross-Canada is lending us a pilot. It's Captain Treleaven, one of their senior men. He's here now, just arrived. We'll get on the radio with a check list and try to bring him in. *(Pause)* We'll do the best we can. *(Pause. Then impatiently)* Of course it's a terrible risk, but can you think of something better? *(Pause)* No, the papers aren't on to it yet, but don't worry, they will be soon. We can't help that now. *(Pause. Anxious to get off phone)* That's all we know, Barney. It only just happened. I called you right away. ETA is 0505 Pacific time; that's just under three hours. I've got a lot to do, Barney. I'll have to get on with it. *(Pause. Nodding impatiently)* I'll call you. I'll call you as soon as I know anything more...G'bye.

(During the foregoing CAPTAIN MARTIN TRELEAVEN, *forty-five, has entered. He is wearing an airline uniform. As* BURDICK *sees* TRELEAVEN, *he beckons him, indicating that he should listen.)*

BURDICK *(to* TRELEAVEN). Did you get that?

TRELEAVEN *(calmly).* Is that the whole story?

BURDICK. That's everything we know. Now, what I want you to do is get on the horn and talk this pilot down. You'll have to help him get the feel of the airplane on the way. You'll have to talk him round the circuit. You'll have to give him the cockpit check for landing, and—so help me—you'll have to talk him onto the ground.

(CAPTAIN TRELEAVEN *is a calm man, not easily perturbed. While* BURDICK *has been talking, the* CAPTAIN *has been filling his pipe. Now, with methodical movements, he puts away his tobacco pouch and begins to light the pipe.)*

TRELEAVEN *(quietly).* You realize, of course, that the chances of a man who has only flown fighter airplanes, landing a four-engine passenger ship safely are about nine to one against.

BURDICK *(rattled).* Of course I know it! You heard what I told Whitmore. But do you have any other ideas?

TRELEAVEN. No. I just wanted to be sure you knew what we were getting into, Harry....All right. Let's get started. Where do I go?

CONTROLLER. Over here.

(They cross to the radio panel, and the OPERATOR *hands him the last message from the aircraft. When he has read it, he takes the transmitter mike.)*

TRELEAVEN. How does this thing work?

RADIO OPERATOR *(turning a switch).* You're on the air now.

TRELEAVEN *(calmly).* Hullo, Flight 714. This is Vancouver, and my name is Martin Treleaven. I am a Cross-Canada Airlines captain, and my job right now is to help fly this airplane in. First of all, are you hearing me okay? Over.

VOICE OF SPENCER. Yes, Captain, loud and clear. Go ahead, please.

TRELEAVEN. Where's that message? *(As* OPERATOR *passes it, into mike)* I see that I'm talking to George Spencer. Well, George, I don't think you're going to have much trouble. These DC-4's handle easily, and we'll give you the drill for landing.

| WORD BANK | **perturbed** (pur TURBD) *v.:* disturbed; troubled |
| | **methodical** (meth AH dih kul) *adj.:* systematic; slow and careful |

But first of all, please tell me what your flying experience is. The message says you have flown single-engine fighters. What kind of airplanes were these, and did you fly multi-engine airplanes at all? Let's hear from you, George. Over.

(Cut to. *The flight deck.*)

SPENCER *(into mike).* Hullo, Vancouver, this is 714. Glad to have you along, Captain. But let's not kid each other, please. We both know we need a lot of luck. About my flying. It was mostly Spitfires and Mustangs. And I have around a thousand hours' total. And all of that was ten years ago. Over.

(Cut to. *The control room.*)

TRELEAVEN *(into mike).* Don't worry about that, George. It's like riding a bicycle. You never forget it. Stand by.

CONTROLLER *(to* TRELEAVEN*).* The air force has picked up the airplane on radar, and they'll be giving us courses to bring him in. Here's the first one. See if you can get him on that heading.

TRELEAVEN *(nods. Then into mike).* 714, are you still on automatic pilot? If so, look for the auto pilot release switch. It's a push button on the control yoke and is plainly marked. Over.

(Cut to. *The flight deck.*)

SPENCER *(into mike).* Yes, Vancouver. I see the auto pilot switch. Over.

(Cut to. *The control room.*)

TRELEAVEN *(into mike).* Now, George, in a minute you can unlock the automatic pilot and get the feel of the controls, and we're going to change your course a little. But first, listen carefully. When you use the controls they will seem very heavy and sluggish compared with a fighter airplane. But don't worry; that's quite normal. You must take care, though, to watch your air speed carefully, and do not let it fall below 120 knots while your wheels and flaps are up. Otherwise you will stall. Now, do you have someone up there who can work the radio to leave you free for flying? Over.

(Cut to. *The flight deck.*)

SPENCER *(into mike)*. Yes, Vancouver. I have the Stewardess here with me, and she will take over the radio now. I am now going to unlock the automatic pilot. Over. *(To the* STEWARDESS *as he depresses the auto pilot release)* Well, here we go. *(Feeling the controls,* SPENCER *eases into a left turn. Then, straightening out, he eases the control column slightly forward and back.)*

(Cut to. *The control room.*)

TRELEAVEN'S VOICE. Hullo, 714. How are you making out, George? Have you got the feel of her yet?

(Cut to. *The flight deck.*)

SPENCER. Tell him I'm on manual[2] now and trying out some gentle turns.

STEWARDESS *(into mike)*. Hullo, Vancouver. We are on manual now and trying out some gentle turns.

(Cut to. *The control room.*)

---

2. The word *manual* means "by hand" and is the opposite of "automatic." When Spencer says he's "on manual," he means he's turned off the "automatic pilot" and is handling all the controls himself.

WORD BANK   **depresses** (de PRESS iz) *v.:* presses down

TRELEAVEN *(into mike).* Hullo, George Spencer. Try the effect on fore-and-aft control on your air speed. To begin with, close your throttles slightly and bring your air speed back to 160. Adjust the trim as you go along. But watch that air speed closely. Remember to keep it well above 120. Over.

(Cut to. *The flight deck.*)

SPENCER *(tensely. Still feeling out the controls).* Tell him okay.

STEWARDESS *(into mike).* Okay, Vancouver. We are doing as you say.

TRELEAVEN'S VOICE *(after a pause).* Hullo, 714. How does she handle, George?

SPENCER *(disgustedly).* Tell him sluggish, like a wet sponge.

STEWARDESS. Sluggish, like a wet sponge, Vancouver.

(Cut to. *The control room. There is a momentary relaxing of tension as* CAPTAIN TRELEAVEN *and the group around him exchange grins.*)

TRELEAVEN *(into mike).* Hullo, George Spencer. That would be a natural feeling, because you were used to handling smaller airplanes. The thing you have got to remember is that there is a bigger lag in the effect of control movements on air speed, compared with what you were used to before. Do you understand that? Over.

(Cut to. *The flight deck.*)

SPENCER. Tell him I understand.

STEWARDESS *(into mike).* Hullo, Vancouver. Yes, he understands. Over.

(Cut to. *The control room.*)

TRELEAVEN *(into mike).* Hullo, George Spencer. Because of that lag in air speed you must avoid any violent movements of the controls, such as you used to make in your fighter airplanes. If you *do* move the controls violently, you will over-correct and be in trouble. Is that understood?

(Cut to. *The flight deck.*)

SPENCER *(nodding, beginning to perspire)*. Tell him—yes, I understand.

STEWARDESS *(into mike)*. Yes, Vancouver. Your message is understood. Over.

(Cut to. *The control room.*)

TRELEAVEN *(into mike)*. Hullo, George Spencer. Now I want you to feel how the ship handles at lower speeds when the flaps and wheels are down. But don't do anything until I give you the instructions. Is that clear? Over.

(Cut to. *The flight deck.*)

SPENCER. Tell him okay; let's have the instructions.

STEWARDESS *(into mike)*. Hullo, Vancouver. Yes, we understand. Go ahead with the instructions. Over.

TRELEAVEN'S VOICE. First of all, throttle back slightly, get your air speed at 160 knots, and adjust your trim to maintain level flight. Then tell me when you're ready. Over.

SPENCER. Watch that air speed, Janet. You'll have to call it off to me when we land, so you may as well start practicing.

STEWARDESS. It's 200 now…190…185…180…175…175…165… 155…150… *(Alarmed)* That's too low! He said 160!

SPENCER *(tensely)*. I know. I know. Watch it! It's that lag on the air speed I can't get used to.

STEWARDESS. 150…150…155…160…160…It's steady on 160.

SPENCER. Tell them.

STEWARDESS *(into mike).* Hullo, Vancouver. This is 714. Our speed is steady at 160. Over.

(Cut to. *The control room.*)

TRELEAVEN *(into mike).* Okay, 714. Now, George, I want you to put down twenty degrees of flap. But be careful not to make it any more. The flap lever is at the base of the control pedestal and is plainly marked. Twenty degrees will mean moving the lever down to the second notch. Over.

(Cut to. *The flight deck.*)

SPENCER. Janet, *you'll* have to put the flaps down. *(Pointing)* There's the lever.

TRELEAVEN'S VOICE. Can you see the flap indicator, George? It's near the center of the main panel.

SPENCER. Here's the indicator he's talking about. When I tell you, push the lever down to the second notch and watch the dial. Okay?

STEWARDESS. Okay. *(Then with alarm)* Oh, look at the air speed! It's down to 125!

(SPENCER *grimaces and pushes the control column forward.*)

SPENCER *(urgently).* Call off the speed! Call off the speed!

STEWARDESS. 140...150...160...170...175...Can't you get it back to 160?

SPENCER *(straining).* I'm trying! I'm trying! *(Pause)* There it is.

(Cut to. *The passenger cabin.*)

SECOND WOMAN PASSENGER *(frightened).* Hector! We're going to crash! I know it! Oh, do something! Do something!

BAIRD *(appears at her elbow).* Have her take this. It'll help calm her down. *(Gives pill and cup to the* THIRD MALE PASSENGER*)* Try not to worry. That young man at the front is a very experienced pilot. He's just what they call "getting the feel" of the airplane. *(He moves aft in the cabin.)*

FIRST MALE PASSENGER. Doctor!

BAIRD. Yes.

FIRST MALE PASSENGER. Tell us the truth, Doctor. Have we got a chance? Does this fellow know how to fly this thing?

BAIRD. We've got all kinds of chances. He's a very experienced pilot; but it's just that he's not used to flying this particular type, and he's getting the feel of it.

FOURTH MALE PASSENGER. You didn't need none of them pills to make me sick. Never mind me dinner. Now ah'm workin' on yesterday's breakfast.

(Cut to. *The flight deck.)*

STEWARDESS *(into mike).* Hullo, Vancouver. Air speed is 160, and we are ready to put down the flaps. Over.

(Cut to. *The control room.)*

TRELEAVEN *(into mike).* Okay, 714. Go ahead with your flaps. But be careful—only twenty degrees. Then, when you have twenty degrees down, bring back the air speed to 140, adjust your trim, and call me again. Over.

(Cut to. *The flight deck.)*

SPENCER. Okay, Janet—flaps down! Twenty degrees.

(The STEWARDESS *pushes down the flap lever to its second notch.)*

SPENCER. Tell them we've got the flaps down, and the air speed's coming to 140.

STEWARDESS *(into mike).* Hullo, Vancouver. This is 714. The flaps are down, and our air speed is 140.

(Cut to. *The control room.)*

TRELEAVEN. All right, 714. Now, the next thing is to put the wheels down. Are you still maintaining level flight?

(Cut to. *The flight deck.)*

SPENCER. Tell him—more or less.

STEWARDESS *(into mike).* Hullo, Vancouver. More or less.

(Cut to. *The control room.)*

RADIO OPERATOR. This guy's got a sense of humor.

BURDICK. That's a *real* help.

TRELEAVEN *(into mike).* Okay, 714. Try to keep your altitude steady and your speed at 140. Then, when you *are* ready, put down the landing gear and let your speed come back to 120. You will have to advance your throttle setting to maintain that air speed, and also adjust your trim. Is that understood? Over.

(Cut to. *The flight deck.)*

SPENCER. Ask him—what about the propeller controls and mixture?

STEWARDESS *(into mike).* Hullo, Vancouver. What about the propeller controls and mixture? Over.

(Cut to. *The control room.)*

CONTROLLER. He's thinking, anyway.

TRELEAVEN (*into mike*). Leave them alone for the time being. Just concentrate on holding that air speed steady with the wheels and flaps down. Over.

(Cut to. *The flight deck.*)

SPENCER. Wheels down, Janet, and call off the air speed.

STEWARDESS (*selects landing gear down*). 140...140...140...135...130...125...120...115...The speed's too low!

SPENCER. Keep calling it!

STEWARDESS. 115...120...120...Steady on 120.

(Cut to. *The control room.*)

TRELEAVEN (*into mike*). Hullo, George Spencer. Your wheels should be down by now, and look for three green lights to show that they're locked. Over.

(Cut to. *The flight deck.*)

SPENCER. Are they on?

STEWARDESS. Yes—all three lights are green.

SPENCER. Tell them.

STEWARDESS (*into mike*). Hullo, Vancouver. Yes, there are three green lights.

(Cut to. *The control room.*)

TRELEAVEN. Okay, 714, now let's put down full flaps so that you can feel how the airplane will handle when you're landing. As soon as full flap is down, bring your air speed back to 110 knots and trim to hold it steady. Adjust your throttle setting to hold your altitude. Is that understood? Over.

(Cut to. *The flight deck.*)

SPENCER. Tell him yes.

STEWARDESS *(into mike).* Yes, Vancouver. That is understood.

SPENCER. Full flap, Janet! Push the lever all the way down, and call off the air speed.

STEWARDESS. 120...115...115...110...110...

SPENCER. Okay, tell 'em we've got full flap and air speed 110, and she still handles like a sponge, only more so.

STEWARDESS *(into mike).* Hullo, Vancouver. We have full flap, and air speed is 110. And the pilot says she still handles like a sponge, only more so.

(Cut to. *The control room. Again there is a momentary sense of relief.*)

TRELEAVEN *(into mike).* That's nice going, George. Now I'm going to give you instructions for holding your height and air speed while you raise the flaps and landing gear. Then we'll run through the whole procedure again.

(Cut to. *The flight deck.*)

SPENCER. Again! I don't know if my nerves'll stand it. *(Pause)* All right. Tell him okay.

(Dissolve to. *Control room clock showing 2:55.*)

(Dissolve to. *Control room clock showing 5:20.*)

(Dissolve to. *The control room.* CAPTAIN TRELEAVEN *is still seated in front of the transmitter, but has obviously been under strain. He now has his coat off and his tie loosened, and there is an empty carton of coffee beside him.* BURDICK *and the* CONTROLLER *are in the background, watching tensely. A phone rings and the* CONTROLLER *answers it. He makes a note and passes it to* TRELEAVEN.)

TRELEAVEN (*into mike*). Hullo, Flight 714. Our flying practice has slowed you down, and you are later than we expected. You are now twelve minutes flying time from Vancouver Airport, but it's getting light, so your landing will be in daylight. You should be able to see us at any minute. Do you see the airport beacon? Over.

STEWARDESS'S VOICE. Yes, we see the airport beacon. Over.

TRELEAVEN. Okay, George, now you've practiced everything we need for a landing. You've flown the ship with wheels and flaps down, and you know how she handles. Your fuel feeds are checked, and you're all set to come in. You won't hear from me again for a few minutes because I'm moving to the control tower so I'll be able to see you on the circuit and approach. Is that clear? Over.

STEWARDESS'S VOICE. Yes, Vancouver, that is understood. Over.

TRELEAVEN. All right, George. Continue to approach at two thousand feet on your present heading and wait for instructions. We'll let you know the runway to use at the last minute, because the wind is shifting. Don't forget, we want you to do at least one dummy run, and then go round again so you'll have practice in making the landing approach. Over. (*He mops his forehead with a crumpled handkerchief.*)

(Cut to. *The flight deck.* SPENCER, *too, has his coat off and tie loosened. His hair is ruffled, and the strain is plainly beginning to tell on him. The* STEWARDESS *is still in the co-pilot's seat, and* BAIRD *is standing behind them both. The* STEWARDESS *is about to acknowledge the last radio message, but* SPENCER *stops her.*)

SPENCER. I'll take it, Janet. (*Into mike*) No dice, Vancouver. We're coming straight in, and the first time is "it." Dr. Baird is here beside me. He reports two of the passengers and the

First Officer are in critical condition, and we must land in the next few minutes. The doctor asks that you have stomach pumps and oxygen equipment ready. Over.

(Cut to. *The control room.*)

BURDICK. He mustn't! We need time!

TRELEAVEN. It's his decision. By all the rules he's in command of the airplane. *(Into mike)* 714, your message is understood. Good luck to us all. Listening out. *(To* BURDICK *and the* CONTROLLER*)* Let's go.

(Dissolve to. *The flight deck.*)

SPENCER. This is it, Doctor. You'd better go back now and make sure everybody's strapped in tight. Are both the pilots in seats?

BAIRD. Yes.

SPENCER. How about the passengers who aren't sick? Are they worried?

BAIRD. A little, but there's no panic. I exaggerated your qualifications. I'd better go. Good luck.

SPENCER *(with ironic grin).* Thanks.

(Dissolve to. *The control tower, Vancouver Airport. It is a glass-enclosed area, with radio panels and other equipment, and access is by a stairway from below. It is now daylight and the* TOWER CONTROLLER *is looking skyward, using binoculars. There is the sound of hurried feet on the stairway and* TRELEAVEN, *the* CONTROLLER, *and* BURDICK *emerge in that order.*)

TOWER CONTROLLER. There he is!

(TRELEAVEN *picks up a second pair of binoculars, looks through them quickly, then puts them down.*)

TRELEAVEN. All right—let's make our decision on the runway. What's it to be?

TOWER CONTROLLER. Zero eight. It's pretty well into wind now, though there'll be a slight crosswind from the left. It's also the longest.

TRELEAVEN (*into mike*). Hullo, Flight 714. This is Martin Treleaven in Vancouver Tower. Do you read me? Over.

(Cut to. *The flight deck.*)

STEWARDESS (*into mike*). Yes, Vancouver Tower. Loud and clear. Over.

(Cut to. *The tower.*)

TRELEAVEN (*crisply, authoritatively, yet calmly*). From here on, do not acknowledge any further transmissions unless you wish to ask a question. You are now ready to join the airport circuit. The runway for landing is zero eight. That means you are now cross-wind and will shortly make a left turn on to the downwind leg. Begin now to lose height to one thousand feet. Throttle back slightly and make your descent at 400 feet a minute. Let your air speed come back to 160 knots and hold it steady there...Air speed 160.

CONTROLLER (*reaching for phone*). Runway is zero eight. All vehicles stand by near the extreme south end. Do not, repeat not, go down the runway until the aircraft has passed by you, because it may swing off. Is that clear? (*Pause*) Right.

(Cut to. *Film insert of fire trucks and ambulances. They are manned and move away with sirens wailing.*)

(Cut to. *The flight deck.* SPENCER *is pushing the throttles forward, and the tempo of the motors increases.*)

SPENCER. Tell them we're at one thousand feet and leveling off.

STEWARDESS *(into mike).* Vancouver Tower. We are now at one thousand feet and leveling off. Over.

TRELEAVEN'S VOICE. Now let's have twenty degrees of flap. Do not acknowledge this message.

SPENCER. Twenty degrees of flap, Janet.

(The STEWARDESS *reaches for flap lever and pushes it down while she watches the flap indicator.)*

TRELEAVEN'S VOICE. When you have your flaps down, bring your air speed back slowly to 140 knots, adjust your trim, and begin to make a left turn onto the downwind leg. When you have turned, fly parallel with the runway you see on your left. I repeat—air speed 140 and begin a left turn.

(Cut to. Close-up of an instrument panel showing artificial horizon and air-speed indicator. The air speed first comes to 130, goes slightly below it, then returns to 130. The artificial horizon tilts so that the airplane symbol is banked to the left.)

(Cut to. The flight deck. SPENCER *has control yoke turned to the left and is adjusting the throttles.)*

(Cut to. The tower.)

TRELEAVEN. Watch your height! Don't make that turn so steep! Watch your height! More throttle! Keep the air speed on 140 and the nose up! Get back that height! You need a thousand feet!

(Cut to. The flight deck. SPENCER *eases the throttle open, and the tempo of the motors increases. He eases the control column forward, then pulls back again.)*

(Cut to. Close-up of climb and descent indicator. The instrument first shows a descent of 500 feet per minute, then a climb of 600 feet, and then gradually begins to level off.)

(Cut to. *The control tower.* CAPTAIN TRELEAVEN *is looking out through binoculars, the others anxiously behind him.*)

TRELEAVEN *(angrily)*. He can't fly the bloody thing! Of course he can't fly it! You're watching fifty people going to their deaths!

BURDICK *(shouting)*. Keep talking to him! Keep talking! Tell him what to do!

TRELEAVEN *(urgently, into mike)*. Spencer, you can't come straight in! You've got to do some circuits, and practice that approach. You've enough fuel left for three hours' flying. Stay up, man! Stay up!

(Cut to. *The flight deck.*)

SPENCER. Give it to me! *(Taking the mike. Then tensely)* Listen, down there! I'm coming in! Do you hear me?...I'm coming in. There are people up here who'll die in less than an hour, never mind three. I may bend your precious airplane a bit, but I'll get it down. Now, get on with the landing check. I'm putting the gear down now. *(To the* STEWARDESS*)* Wheels down, Janet!

(*The* STEWARDESS *selects landing gear "down," and* SPENCER *reaches for the throttles.*)
(Cut to. *Film insert of airplane in flight, day. Its landing wheels come down.*)
(Cut to. *The flight deck.*)

STEWARDESS *(looks out of window, then back to* SPENCER*)*. Wheels down and three green lights.

(Cut to. *The tower.*)

BURDICK. He may not be able to fly, but he's sure got guts.

TRELEAVEN *(into mike).* Increase your throttle slightly to hold your air speed now that the wheels are down. Adjust your trim and keep that height at a thousand feet. Now check your propeller setting and your mixture—propellers to fully fine; mixture to full rich. I'll repeat that. Propellers to fully fine; mixture to full rich.

(Cut to. *The flight deck.)*

SPENCER *(to himself, as he moves controls).* Propellers fully fine. Mixture full rich. *(To the* STEWARDESS) Janet, let me hear the air speed.

STEWARDESS. 130...125...120...125...130...

(Cut to. *The tower.)*

TRELEAVEN *(into mike).* You are well downwind now. You can begin to make a left turn on the crosswind leg. As you turn, begin losing height to 800 feet and let your air speed come back to 120. I'll repeat that. Start a left turn. Lose height to 800. Air speed 120. *(He picks up binoculars, then puts them down hurriedly, and takes mike again.)* You are losing height too fast! You are losing height too fast! Open up! Open! Hold your height, now! Keep your air speed at 120.

(Cut to. *The flight deck.)*

STEWARDESS. 110...110...105...110...110...120...120...Steady at 120.

SPENCER. What an insensitive wagon this is! It doesn't respond! It doesn't respond at all!

STEWARDESS. 125...130...130...Steady on 130.

(Cut to. *The tower.)*

TRELEAVEN. Start your turn into wind now to line up with the runway. Make it a gentle turn—you've plenty of time. As you turn, begin losing height, about 400 feet a minute. But be ready to correct if you lose height too fast. Adjust your trim as you go...That's right!...Keep turning! As soon as you've completed the turn, put down full flap and bring your air speed to 115. I'll repeat that. Let down 400 feet a minute. Full flap. Then air speed 115. *(To the others)* Is everything ready on the field?

CONTROLLER. As ready as we'll ever be.

TRELEAVEN. Then, this is it. In sixty seconds we'll know.

(Cut to. *The flight deck.)*

SPENCER *(muttering)*. Not quite yet...a little more...that should do it. *(As he straightens out of the turn)* Janet, give me full flap!

(The STEWARDESS *reaches for the flap control, pushes it down, and leaves it down.)*

SPENCER. Height and air speed!

STEWARDESS. 700 feet, speed 130...600 feet, speed 120...500 feet, speed 105...We're going down too quickly!

SPENCER. I know! I know! *(He pushes throttles forward, and tempo of the motors increases.)* Keep watching it!

STEWARDESS. 450 feet, speed 100...400 feet, speed 100...

(Cut to. *Film insert of airplane (DC-4) with wheels and flaps down, on a landing approach.)*

(Cut to. *The tower.)*

TRELEAVEN *(urgently into mike)*. Open up! Open up! You're losing height too fast! *(Pause)* Watch the air speed! Your nose is too high! Open up quickly or she'll stall! Open up, man! Open up!

BURDICK. He heard you. He's recovering.

TRELEAVEN *(into mike).* Maintain that height until you get closer into the runway. But be ready to ease off gently...You can start now...Let down again...That looks about right...But watch the air speed. Your nose is creeping up... *(More steadily)* Now, listen carefully, George. There's a slight crosswind on the runway, and your drift is to the right. Straighten up just before you touch down, and be ready with your right rudder as soon as you are down. And remember to cut the switches if you land too fast. *(Pause)* All right, your approach is good...Get ready to round out— now! *(Pause. Then urgently)* You're coming in too fast! Lift the nose up!

(Cut to. *The flight deck.)*

TRELEAVEN'S VOICE. Lift the nose up! Back on the throttles! Throttles right back! Hold her off! Not too much! Not too much! Be ready for that crosswind! Ease her down, *now!* Ease her down!

(Cut to. *Film insert of a landing wheel skimming over a runway and about to touch down. As it makes contact, rock picture to show instability.)*

(Cut to. *The flight deck. There is a heavy thud, and* SPENCER *and the* STEWARDESS *are jolted in their seats. There is another, another, and another. Everything shakes.)*

SPENCER *(shouting).* Cut the switches! Cut the switches!

(The STEWARDESS *reaches upward and pulls down the cage of the master switches. Instantly the heavy roar of motor stops, but there is still a whistling because the airplane is traveling fast.* SPENCER *stretches out his legs as he puts his full strength into applying the airplane toe brakes, at the same time pulling back on the control column. There is a screaming of rubber on pavement, and* SPENCER *and the* STEWARDESS *are thrown violently to the left. Then, except for the hum of the radio and gyros, there is a silence as the airplane stops.)*

SPENCER *(disgustedly).* I ground looped! I did a miserable ground loop! We're turned right around the way we came!

STEWARDESS. But we're all right! We're all right! You did it! You did it!

(She leans over and gives him a thumbs up sign. SPENCER *pulls off his radio headset. Outside there is a rising note of approaching sirens. Then, from the headset we hear* CAPTAIN TRELEAVEN*'s voice.)*

TRELEAVEN'S VOICE *(exuberantly).* Hullo, George Spencer. That was probably the worst landing in the history of this airport. So don't ever ask us for a job as a pilot. But there are some people here who'd like to shake you by the hand, and later on we'll buy you a real supper—no fish! Stay right where you are, George! We're coming over.

(Fade out.)

ABOUT THE AUTHOR

Arthur Hailey was born in Luton, England in 1920. He joined the Royal Air Force in 1939, and served as a pilot until 1947, when he moved to Canada. His career as a writer began in 1955 when, on a flight across Canada, he began to fantasize about what might happen if both the pilot and co-pilot took sick, leaving him to fly the plane. As soon as he got home, he wrote *Flight Into Danger,* a play based on these imaginings. It was a hit! Hailey went on to write many extremely popular books and plays. Mr. And Mrs. Hailey have six children and live in Nassau, Bahamas.

Studying the Selection

FIRST IMPRESSIONS
As you read the story, did you think the plane would land safely, or did you fear it would crash? Did the author keep you in suspense throughout the play?

QUICK REVIEW

1. What does Burdick ask Captain Treleaven to do?

2. What chances does Treleaven think Spencer has of landing the plane safely?

3. What does Spencer mean when he tells Janet to "call off the air speed"?

4. Why does Spencer refuse to do any practice approaches before landing the plane?

FOCUS

5. Contrast Spencer's confidence in Act Two to his confidence in Act Three.

CREATING & WRITING

6. Have you ever needed to behave in a courageous way, even if you were unprepared or frightened inside? Tell the story in a few paragraphs. Courage may be needed for something as small as overcoming shyness, or as great as saving someone's life. Every one of us has had to draw upon our courage at one time or another.

7. *Flight Into Danger* has four different settings. What are they? Leaf through the play and write a brief description of each setting. Imagine that your class is staging the play. You would need scenery, props, and costumes for the four settings. What props and costumes could you provide for each of the settings? Write a list of several items that you could contribute to the scenery, props, and/or costumes of each setting.

8. A few weeks after the DC-4's successful landing, the crew of the plane had a dinner in honor of George Spencer. At the end of the dinner, they gave him a plaque that was engraved with words that honored and thanked him for his courage. Design a plaque and draw a picture of it on a full piece of paper. Make sure to include the message that the crew engraved on the plaque.

LESSON IN LITERATURE . . .

A NONSENSE POEM

- Nonsense poems are to be enjoyed for their rhythm, rhyme, and humor.

- A poem may be "nonsense" because the **words** sound real but are not.

- A poem may be "nonsense" because the **people, creatures,** or **objects** are funny inventions with unusual characteristics.

- A poem may be "nonsense" because the **situation** described is impossible and ridiculous.

THINK ABOUT IT!

1. There are three reasons listed for why a poem is considered "nonsense." Which one describes "The Better Letter"?

2. The poem has lots of words that rhyme with "better." Which two real words rhyme with "better"?

3. The poem has some other words that are not completely made up, but are changed a little to rhyme with "better." What are three examples of single words that have been changed?

4. The poem has several two-word combinations that have been humorously changed to rhyme with 'better." What are the four two-word combinations?

The Better Letter Shoshana Henig

Wouldn't it be better
If you'd received this letter –
Although somewhat squashed and wetter –
In the mouth of a giraffe?

I'll bet you wouldn't forget 'er
And you'd no doubt try to pet 'er
Though you'd never reach her head-er
And she'd just look down and laugh.

Then, while you'd frown and fret-er
She just may chew up the letter
(That you hadn't even read-er)
With a loud, resounding crunch!

Or even better yetter,
If someone hadn't fed 'er
You may wish you'd never met 'er
When she nibbles you for lunch!

Blueprint for Reading

INTO . . . *The Quangle Wangle's Hat*

Almost everyone has read a Dr. Seuss book or the poems in *Alice in Wonderland* and wondered: could these nonsense rhymes have some hidden meaning? Read *The Quangle Wangle's Hat* and enjoy it for what it is: a funny nonsense poem. But think about this: Edward Lear was a very shy person. He was often ill and had poor eyesight. Could Edward Lear have been writing about *himself* in this poem? Could Quangle Wangle Quee *be* Edward Lear in disguise? Don't forget, Quangle Wangle's face is completely hidden by his one hundred and two-foot-wide hat! The Crumpetty Tree where he lives is a lonely place, just like Edward Lear's home. Is that just a coincidence— or does this poem have a hidden message?

EYES ON . . . *Nonsense*

What is nonsense? We all know what it is, but might find it difficult to express. Simply put, nonsense is something that *doesn't make sense.*

Is a poem nonsense because of its silly **words?** Sometimes. The Quangle Wangle's hat has "ribbons and bibbons." Is it nonsense because of the **creatures** or **objects** in it? Sometimes. Have you ever seen "a Crumpetty tree"? Is it nonsense because the **situations** are ridiculous? Sometimes. What animal lives on top of a tree and wears a wide beaver hat?

The wonderful thing about nonsense is that, for a split second, it sounds real—until you laugh and say, "no—that's nonsense!"

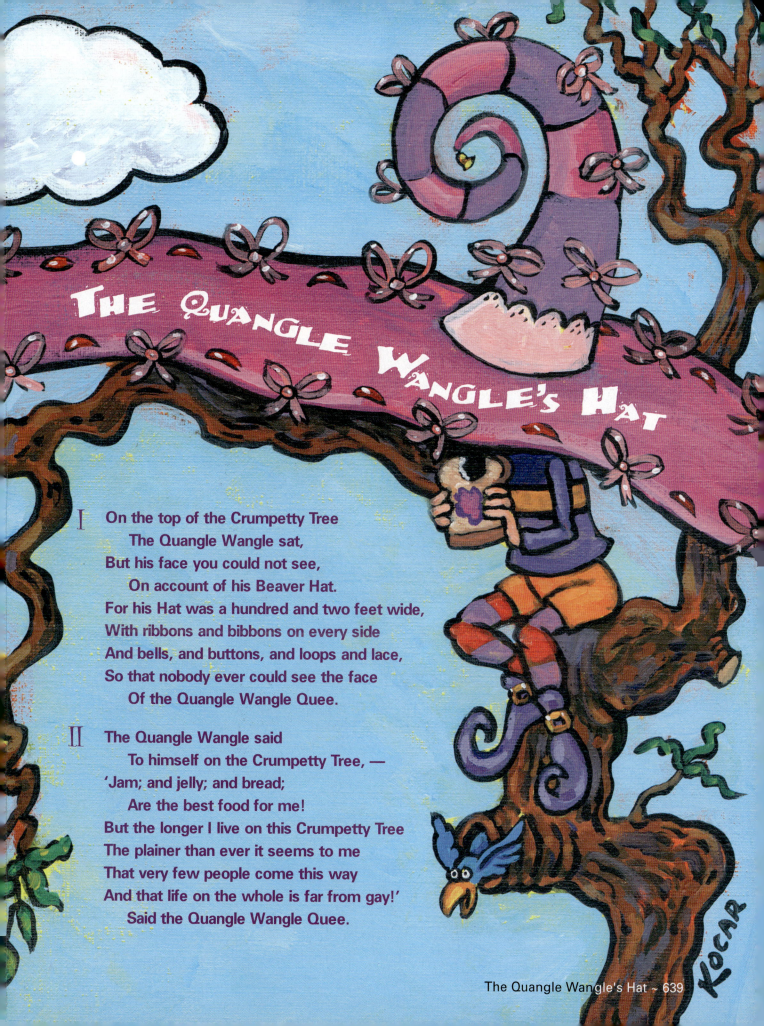

THE QUANGLE WANGLE'S HAT

I   On the top of the Crumpetty Tree
      The Quangle Wangle sat,
But his face you could not see,
      On account of his Beaver Hat.
For his Hat was a hundred and two feet wide,
With ribbons and bibbons on every side
And bells, and buttons, and loops and lace,
So that nobody ever could see the face
      Of the Quangle Wangle Quee.

II   The Quangle Wangle said
      To himself on the Crumpetty Tree, —
'Jam; and jelly; and bread;
      Are the best food for me!
But the longer I live on this Crumpetty Tree
The plainer than ever it seems to me
That very few people come this way
And that life on the whole is far from gay!'
      Said the Quangle Wangle Quee.

III   But there came to the Crumpetty Tree,
       Mr and Mrs Canary;
And they said, — 'Did you ever see
       Any spot so charmingly airy?
May we build a nest on your lovely Hat?
Mr Quangle Wangle, grant us that!
O please let us come and build a nest
Of whatever material suits you best,
       Mr Quangle Wangle Quee!'

IV   And besides, to the Crumpetty Tree
       Came the Stork, the Duck, and the Owl;
The Snail, and the Bumble-Bee,
       The Frog, and the Fimble Fowl;
(The Fimble Fowl, with a Corkscrew leg;)
And all of them said, — 'We humbly beg,
We may build our homes on your lovely Hat, —
Mr Quangle Wangle, grant us that!
       Mr Quangle Wangle Quee!'

V And the Golden Grouse came there,
　　　And the Pobble who has no toes, —
And the small Olympian bear, —
　　　And the Dong with a luminous nose.
And the Blue Baboon, who played the flute, —
And the Orient Calf from the Land of Tute, —
And the Attery Squash, and the Bisky Bat, —
All came and built on the lovely Hat
　　　Of the Quangle Wangle Quee.

VI And the Quangle Wangle said
　　　To himself on the Crumpetty Tree, —
'When all these creatures move
　　　What a wonderful noise there'll be!'
And at night by the light of the Mulberry moon
They danced to the Flute of the Blue Baboon,
On the broad green leaves of the Crumpetty Tree,
And all were as happy as happy could be,
　　　With the Quangle Wangle Quee.

ABOUT THE AUTHOR

Although he is best known for his nonsense rhymes, **Edward Lear** actually spent most of his life as an artist and traveler. Edward Lear was born in 1812, the twentieth child in his family. As a teenager, Edward supported his impoverished parents by selling his drawings. Later, because of ill health, Lear traveled to one country after another, seeking a warm climate and new sights to paint. While visiting friends, he wrote his most famous nonsense poem, *The Owl and the Pussycat*, to amuse their three-year-old daughter. Edward Lear died in Italy in 1888.

Studying the Selection

FIRST IMPRESSIONS

What is this poem about?

QUICK REVIEW

1. What is the setting of the poem?

2. What does the Quangle Wangle Quee look like?

3. What does the Quangle Wangle like to eat?

4. In the poem, what do we learn about the Pobble?

FOCUS

5. What makes the Quangle Wangle Quee sad? What makes him happy?

6. Your teacher will assign you one stanza from the poem. (1) Make a list of the pairs or sets of words that begin with the same letter. (2) List the pairs or sets of words that rhyme. (3) List the words that have similar consonant combinations inside but don't rhyme, for example, *Bumble* and *Fimble*.

CREATING & WRITING

7. Take one character from the poem. Describe its physical appearance, as you imagine the character to look.

8. Do some research on Edward Lear. Write a short biography. Make sure you mention some of his other works. For your final paragraph write what kind of person you think he was.

9. Choose one of the animals in *The Quangle Wangle's Hat* and make a mask to wear for the class performance (which comes later, in the Unit Six Wrap-Up).

LESSON IN LITERATURE . . .

AUTHOR'S VIEWPOINT

- The author's viewpoint will depend on many things, among them the author's age, gender, and nationality.

- Two people (for example, a young child and an old person) might tell the same story from two completely different viewpoints.

- In fiction, the story will sometimes be told from the viewpoint of one of the characters.

- Sometimes a story is told from the point of view of an anonymous narrator.

THINK ABOUT IT!

1. What do the letters DWB stand for?

2. Describe what DWB do.

3. How would you describe this piece: fiction, nonfiction, autobiography, or historical fiction?

4. How does the narrator define a "hero"?

Not Everyday Heroes, But Heroes Every Day

In the next selection you will read about a man who became a hero, not because he sought to, but because life presented him with the opportunity, and he rose to the challenge. Most heroes are like this. They are not people whose job it is to be a hero, but rather people who rise to the challenges life presents in sometimes heroic ways. However, there are some people whose line of work puts them in the hero's shoes day in and day out. Firefighters and police officers come to mind. There's another group of heroes you may not know about: Doctors Without Borders (DWB).

DWB is an organization that provides medical supplies and services to people in approximately eighty countries worldwide, who might not otherwise receive any medical care. DWB got started in the early 1970s during a civil war in Nigeria, a country in West Africa. Every year, the group mobilizes nearly 2,000 brave doctors and other volunteers from countries all over the world to respond to wars, disasters, and refugee crises around the globe. In 1999, the organization won the Nobel Peace Prize in recognition of its efforts.

But winning the Nobel Peace prize doesn't guarantee a peaceful life, and the doctors at DWB spend their days helping people in some of the scariest situations. For example, the organization has provided medical aid in Afghanistan for the past 24 years, through a long war between that country and the former Soviet Union, the reign of the Taliban, and then through the U.S.-led invasion and occupation of the country. During this time, volunteers have worked in the presence of land mines and flying bullets. They have also had to diagnose and treat unfamiliar diseases, diseases like diphtheria, which, thanks to vaccinations, no longer exist in Western countries.

Many religions and cultures the world over emphasize the importance of charity, of sharing one's own gifts with others. Through their heroic actions day in and day out, the volunteers of Doctors Without Borders offer a shining example to the world of this value.

Blueprint for Reading

INTO . . . Passage to Freedom

In Nazi-occupied Europe, the Jewish people were rounded up. Those who fled were hunted down. The Jews of Germany, Poland, Austria, the Czech Republic, Slovakia, Hungary, Romania, Belarus, Lithuania, Latvia, the Ukraine, Italy, Belgium, Holland, France, Spain, and Portugal were doomed. Switzerland even made it illegal for Jews to cross its borders. Wherever they fought back, they were crushed. Wherever they set sail, no port would admit them.

The non-Jews who rescued Jewish people were so few in number that they were like a teardrop in a storm. But, as it has been written, the rescuers' deeds are "too great to be measured." This is the true story of Chiune Sempo Sugihara, rescuer.

EYES ON . . . Fictionalized Nonfiction

When you start reading, ask yourself: who *wrote* this story? Remember, this is nonfiction. The story describes the heroic actions of a man who actually lived and did these things.

The narrator calls this man his *father.* Since this is nonfiction, can we assume that the narrator is the author? One would certainly think so, especially since the Afterword, which appears on the last page, is signed by Hiroki Sugihara, Sempo Sugihara's son.

However, the author is not the younger Sugihara. The author is Ken Mochizuki. As Mr. Mochizuki worked on the story, he felt he had to write in the first person—as if he had been Sempo Sugihara's young son at the time of the events.

This is an interesting device for you to think about, when it comes to doing your own writing.

PASSAGE TO FREEDOM

(THE SUGIHARA STORY)   BY KEN MOCHIZUKI

There is a saying that the eyes tell everything about a person.

At a store, my father saw a young Jewish boy who didn't have enough money to buy what he wanted. So my father gave the boy some of his. That boy looked into my father's eyes and, to thank him, invited my father to his home. That is when my family and I went to a Hanukkah[1] celebration for the first time. I was five years old.

---

1. *Hanukkah* (HAH nuh kuh)

WORD BANK

diplomat (DIP luh MAT) *n.:* a person who has been appointed by the government of his or her country to deal with the governments of other countries on matters that concern them both

In 1940, my father was a diplomat, representing the country of Japan. Our family lived in a small country called Lithuania. There was my father and mother, my Aunt Setsuko, my younger brother Chiaki, and my three-month-old baby brother, Haruki. My father worked in his office downstairs.

In the mornings, birds sang in the trees. We played with girls and boys from the neighborhood at a huge park near our home. Houses around us were hundreds of years old. In our room, Chiaki and I played with toy German soldiers, tanks, and planes. Little did we know that the real soldiers were coming our way.

Then one early morning in late July, my life changed forever.

My mother and Aunt Setsuko woke Chiaki and me up, telling us to get dressed quickly. My father ran upstairs from his office.

"There are a lot of people outside," my mother said. "We don't know what is going to happen."

In the living room, my parents told my brother and me not to let anybody see us looking through the window. So, I parted the curtains a tiny bit. Outside, I saw hundreds of people crowded around the gate in front of our house.

The grown-ups shouted in Polish, a language I did not understand. Then I saw the children. They stared at our house through the iron bars of the gate. Some of them were my age. Like the grown-ups, their eyes were red from not having slept for days. They wore heavy winter coats—some wore more than one coat, even though it was warm outside. These children looked as though they had dressed in a hurry. But if they came from somewhere else, where were their suitcases?

"What do they want?" I asked my mother.

"They have come to ask for your father's help," she replied. "Unless we help, they may be killed or taken away by some bad men."

Some of the children held on tightly to the hands of their fathers, some clung to their mothers. One little girl sat on the ground, crying.

I felt like crying too. "Father," I said, "please help them."

My father stood quietly next to me, but I knew he saw the children. Then some of the men in the crowd began climbing over the fence. Borislav and Gudje, two young men who worked for my father, tried to keep the crowd calm.

My father walked outside. Peering through the curtains, I saw him standing on the steps. Borislav translated what my father said: He asked the crowd to choose five people to come inside and talk.

My father met downstairs with the five men. My father could speak Japanese, Chinese, Russian, German, French, and English. At this meeting, everyone spoke Russian.

WORD
BANK

peering (PEER ing) *v.:* looking intensely, in the attempt to see something clearly

I couldn't help but stare out the window and watch the crowd, while downstairs, for two hours, my father listened to frightening stories. These people were refugees—people who ran away from their homes because, if they stayed, they would be killed. They were Jews from Poland, escaping from the Nazi[2] soldiers who had taken over their country.

The five men had heard my father could give them visas—official written permission to travel through another country. The hundreds of Jewish refugees outside hoped to travel east through the Soviet Union[3] and end up in Japan. Once in Japan, they could go to another country. Was it true? the men asked. Could my father issue these visas? If he did not, the Nazis would soon catch up with them.

My father answered that he could issue a few, but not hundreds. To do that, he would have to ask permission from his government in Japan.

That night, the crowd stayed outside our house. Exhausted from the day's excitement, I slept soundly. But it was one of the worst nights of my father's life. He had to make a decision. If he helped these people, would he put our family in danger? If the Nazis found out, what would they do?

But if he did not help these people, they could all die.

My mother listened to the bed squeak as my father tossed and turned all night.

The next day, my father said he was going to ask the government about the visas. My mother agreed it was the right

---

2. A *Nazi* was a member of the political party that controlled Germany from 1933 to 1945. This party, headed by the dictator, Adolf Hitler, set out to dominate the world and murder all of the Jews. These policies were the cause of World War II, fought from 1939-1945.

3. The *Soviet Union* was a government that existed from 1918-1991. It was made up of 15 small countries that had once been part of the Russian Empire.

WORD BANK

visas (VEE zuhz) *n.:* official papers indicating that the bearer has permission to enter a particular country

issue (ISH oo) *v.:* put forth; write out an official document

thing to do. My father sent his message by cable.[4] Gudje took my father's written message down to the telegraph office.[5]

I watched the crowd as they waited for the Japanese government's reply. The five representatives came into our house several times that day to ask if an answer had been received. Any time the gate opened, the crowd tried to charge inside.

Finally, an answer came from the Japanese government. It was "no." My father could not issue that many visas to Japan. For the next two days, he thought about what to do.

---

4. A *cable* is a telegram sent through heavy wires, called cables, that are placed under water. At the time this story takes place, cables were the fastest means of communication.

5. A person who wished to send a cable had to submit the message to a clerk at the *telegraph office*. The clerk would then cable or telegraph the message.

WORD BANK **representatives** (REP ree ZEN tuh TIVZ) *n.:* individuals who speak for and act on behalf of a group

Hundreds more Jewish refugees joined the crowd. My father sent a second message to his government, and again the answer was "no." We still couldn't go outside. My little brother Haruki cried often because we were running out of milk.

I grew tired of staying indoors. I asked my father constantly, "Why are these people here? What do they want? Why do they have to be here? Who are they?"

My father always took the time to explain everything to me. He said the refugees needed his help, that they needed permission from him to go to another part of the world where they would be safe.

"I cannot help these people yet," he calmly told me. "But when the time comes, I will help them all that I can."

My father cabled his superiors yet a third time, and I knew the answer by the look in his eyes. That night, he said to my

mother, "I have to do something. I may have to disobey my government, but if I don't, I will be disobeying my conscience."

The next morning, he brought the family together and asked what he should do. This was the first time he ever asked all of us to help him with anything.

My mother and Aunt Setsuko had already made up their minds. They said we had to think about the people outside before we thought about ourselves. And that is what my parents had always told me—that I must think as if I were in someone else's place. If I were one of those children out there, what would I want someone to do for me?

I said to my father, "If we don't help them, won't they die?"

With the entire family in agreement, I could tell a huge weight had been lifted off my father's shoulders. His voice was firm as he told us, "I will start helping these people."

Outside, the crowd went quiet as my father spoke, with Borislav translating.

"I will issue visas to each and every one of you to the last. So, please wait patiently."

The crowd stood frozen for a second. Then the refugees burst into cheers. Grown-ups embraced each other, and some reached to the sky. Fathers and mothers hugged their children.

My father opened the garage door and the crowd tried to rush in. To keep order, Borislav handed out cards with numbers. My father wrote out each visa by hand. After he finished each one, he looked into the eyes of the person receiving the visa and said, "Good luck."

Refugees camped out at our favorite park, waiting to see my father. I was finally able to go outside.

Chiaki and I played with the other children in our toy car. They pushed as we rode, and they rode as we pushed. We chased

WORD BANK   **conscience** (KAHN shuntz) *n.*: the inner sense that directs a person to choose right over wrong
embraced (em BRAYST) *v.*: hugged

each other around the big trees. We did not speak the same language, but that didn't stop us.

For about a month, there was always a line leading to the garage. Every day, from early in the morning till late at night, my father tried to write three hundred visas. He watered down the ink to make it last. Gudje and a young Jewish man helped out by stamping my father's name on the visas.

My mother offered to help write the visas, but my father insisted that he be the only one, so no one else could get into trouble. So my mother watched the crowd and told my father how many were still in line.

One day, my father pressed down so hard on his fountain pen, the tip broke off. During that month, I only saw him late at night. His eyes were always red and he could hardly talk. While he slept, my mother massaged his arm, stiff and cramped from writing all day.

Soon my father grew so tired, he wanted to quit writing the visas. But my mother encouraged him to continue. "Many people are still waiting," she said. "Let's issue more visas and save as many lives as we can."

While the Germans approached from the west, the Soviets came from the east and took over Lithuania. They ordered my father to leave. So did the Japanese government, which reassigned him to Germany. Still, my father wrote the visas until we absolutely had to move out of our home. We stayed at a hotel for two days, where my father still wrote visas for the many refugees who followed him there.

Then it was time to leave Lithuania. Refugees who had slept at the train station crowded around my father. Some refugee men surrounded my father to protect him. He now just issued permission papers—blank pieces of paper with his signature.

As the train pulled away, refugees ran alongside. My father still handed permission papers out the window. As the train picked up speed, he threw them out to waiting hands. The people in front of the crowd looked into my father's eyes and cried, "We will never forget you! We will see you again!"

I gazed out the train window, watching Lithuania and the crowd of refugees fade away. I wondered if we would ever see them again.

"Where are we going?" I asked my father.

"We are going to Berlin," he replied.

Chiaki and I became excited about going to the big city. I had so many questions for my father. But he fell asleep as soon as he settled into his seat. My mother and Aunt Setsuko looked really tired too.

Back then, I did not fully understand what the three of them had done, or why it was so important.

I do now.

AFTERWORD

Each time that I think about what my father did at Kaunas, Lithuania, in 1940, my appreciation and understanding of the incident continues to grow. In fact, it makes me very emotional to realize that his deed saved thousands of lives, and that I had the opportunity to be a part of it.

I am proud that my father had the courage to do the right thing. Yet, his superiors in the Japanese government did not agree. The years after we left Kaunas were difficult ones. We were imprisoned for eighteen months in a Soviet internment camp;[6] and when we finally returned to Japan, my father was asked to resign from diplomatic service. After holding several different jobs, my father joined an export company, where he worked until his retirement in 1976.

My father remained concerned about the fate of the refugees, and at one point left his address at the Israeli Embassy in Japan.

---

6. During a war, enemies, prisoners of war, and those suspected of disloyalty, are imprisoned. Another word for imprisonment is *internment*. The prison in which such people are interned is called an *internment camp*.

WORD
BANK

gazed (GAYZD) *v.:* looked intently
incident (IN sih dent) *n.:* event, happening
resign (ree ZYN) *v.:* give up a position or job

Finally, in the 1960s, he started hearing from "Sugihara survivors," many of whom had kept their visas, and considered the worn pieces of paper to be family treasures.

In 1969, my father was invited to Israel, where he was taken to the famous Holocaust memorial,[7] Yad Vashem. In 1985, he was chosen to receive the "Righteous Among Nations" Award from Yad Vashem. He was the first and only Asian to have been given this great honor.

In 1992, six years after his death, a monument to my father was dedicated in his birthplace of Yaotsu, Japan, on a hill that is now known as the Hill of Humanity. In 1994, a group of Sugihara survivors traveled to Japan to rededicate the monument in a ceremony that was attended by several high officials of the Japanese government.

The story of what my father and my family experienced in 1940 is an important one for young people today. It is a story that I believe will inspire you to care for all people and to respect life. It is a story that proves that one person can make a difference.

Thank you.
Hiroki Sugihara

---

7. During World War II, the Nazis, and those who helped them, caused the deaths of over six million Jews. This systematic destruction of the Jewish people became known as *the Holocaust*. After the war, many museums, buildings, and monuments were erected in memory of the six million. These are called *Holocaust memorials*.

WORD BANK **inspire** (in SPY uhr) *v.:* fill one with a certain feeling, usually, the desire to do good

ABOUT THE AUTHOR

Ken Mochizuki was born in 1954 in Seattle, Washington. His grandparents were from Japan, but his parents and siblings were born in America. His first book told the (fictional) story of a Japanese American family's experience during WWII. Although *Passage to Freedom* is nonfiction, Mochizuki wrote it in the first person, as though he were the young boy in the story. The story's main character, Chiune Sugihara, remains one of Mochizuki's personal heroes.

Studying the Selection

FIRST IMPRESSIONS
Which of Mr. Sugihara's many good qualities do you admire the most?

QUICK REVIEW

1. Who is the author?

2. Who is the narrator?

3. Where does the story take place?

4. What are the names of the people in this heroic family?

FOCUS

5. How many times did Chiune Sugihara cable the Japanese government? Why do you think he kept going back, after the first *No?* What was his conflict?

6. What fictional technique has the author used?

CREATING & WRITING

7. Why did the Sugiharas do what they did, when it could mean death, imprisonment, disgrace, or loss of career? What were the consequences of their actions?

8. This is an opportunity for you to do what Ken Mochizuki has done here. (1) Pick an event or particular period: a war, a journey—forced or voluntary, a natural disaster, the first use of a new medicine (you could even be the patient!), and so forth. (2) Learn as much as you can about the setting, the people, and their actions. (3) You are a ten-year-old family member living the day-to-day details of the event. (4) Write what you experience and what you see on a given day. As the author has done, you will use the first person. Write in the present tense.

9. Use crayons or paint, and a large sheet of paper. Give your piece of paper a title. Then show how the Jews waiting at the gate felt.

The Butterfly
AND THE
Caterpillar

A FABLE OLD IS HERE RETOLD

Joseph Lauren

Leah Neustadter

A BUTTERFLY, ONE SUMMER MORN,
SAT ON A SPRAY OF BLOSSOMING THORN
AND, AS HE SIPPED AND DRANK HIS SHARE
OF HONEY FROM THE FLOWERED AIR,
5 BELOW, UPON THE GARDEN WALL,
A CATERPILLAR CHANCED TO CRAWL.
"HORRORS!" THE BUTTERFLY EXCLAIMED,
"THIS MUST BE STOPPED! I AM ASHAMED
THAT SUCH AS I SHOULD HAVE TO BE
10 IN THE SAME WORLD WITH SUCH AS HE.
PROTECT ME FROM SUCH UGLY THINGS!
DISGUSTING SHAPE! WHERE ARE HIS WINGS!
FUZZY AND GRAY! EATER OF CLAY!
WON'T SOMEONE TAKE THE WORM AWAY!"
15 THE CATERPILLAR CRAWLED AHEAD,
BUT, AS HE MUNCHED A LEAF, HE SAID,
"EIGHT DAYS AGO, YOUNG BUTTERFLY,
YOU WORMED ABOUT THE SAME AS I.
JUST WAIT—A FEW WEEKS FROM TODAY
20 TWO WINGS WILL BEAR ME FAR AWAY
TO BRIGHTER BLOOMS AND LOVELIER LURES,
WITH COLORS THAT OUTRIVAL YOURS.
SO, FLUTTER-FLIT, BE NOT SO PROUD;
EACH CATERPILLAR IS ENDOWED
25 WITH POWER TO MAKE IT BY AND BY
A BRIGHT AND MERRY BUTTERFLY.
REMEMBER, YOU WHO SCORN ME SO,
YES YOU WHO MAKE SO LOUD A SHOW,
THAT YOU AND OTHER MOTHS AND MILLERS
30 ARE ONLY DRESSED UP CATERPILLARS."

THE EAGLE

ALFRED LORD TENNYSON

He clasps the crag with crooked hands;
Close to the sun in lonely lands,
Ringed with the azure world, he stands.

The wrinkled sea beneath him crawls;
5   He watches from his mountain walls,
And like a thunderbolt he falls.

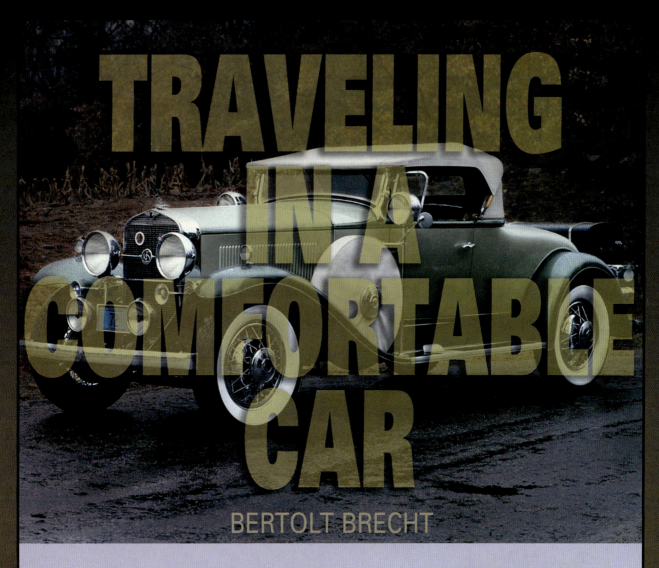

TRAVELING IN A COMFORTABLE CAR

BERTOLT BRECHT

Traveling in a comfortable car
Down a rainy road in the country
We saw a ragged fellow at nightfall
Signal to us for a ride, with a low bow.
5   We had a roof and we had room and we drove on
And we heard me say, in a peevish voice: No
We can't take anyone with us.
We had gone on a long way, perhaps a day's march
When suddenly I was shocked by this voice of mine
10   This behavior of mine and this
Whole world.

Alfred Lord Tennyson was born in 1809 in Lincolnshire, England. One of twelve children, Tennyson rose from an impoverished childhood to fame and noble title. Before he was eighteen, his first volume of poetry was published. At college, he began a warm and close friendship with another student, Arthur Hallam. The two became inseparable, and it was on a trip to Spain that Tennyson wrote *The Eagle.* Tennyson continued to write and publish poetry, but it was the long, mournful poem he wrote upon the death of Hallam that skyrocketed him to fame. Soon after, he was chosen poet laureate of England. He died in 1892.

Born in Augsburg, Germany in 1898, **Bertolt Brecht,** one of the greatest playwrights of the 20th century, was surrounded by controversy for most of his life. In the 1930s, his strong anti-war and communist beliefs made him an enemy of the Nazi government. Forced to leave Germany, he went first to Scandinavia, then to Russia, and finally to the United States. Brecht's communist beliefs made him unpopular with the U.S. government and, in 1948, he returned to Germany, settling in communist East Berlin, where he remained until his death in 1956.

Studying the Selection — POETRY

The Butterfly and the Caterpillar

1. Why is this poem *not* free verse?

2. Please use a dictionary, and write down the definitions of the following ten words from the poem: *morn, spray, chance* (as in *chanced to crawl*), *worm* (noun), *worm* (verb), *lure, outrival, endow, loud, miller.*

3. How is this poem a fable?

4. Why does the butterfly have such a horror of the caterpillar?

5. Think of an insect that makes you uncomfortable. Write down what it is. Now, think of some insulting name for it—similar to the butterfly's calling the caterpillar, *Eater of clay!*

The Eagle

1. How many lines, stanzas, sentences, and beats-per-line does *The Eagle* have? What is the rhyme scheme?

2. What is the metaphor in the first line?

3. Which consonants are repeated often in the words of the poem?

4. What is the simile in the last line of the poem?

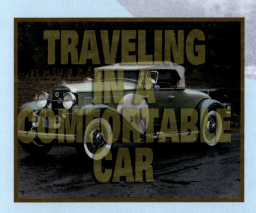

1. The poem could have been called, *Traveling in a Car*. How does Bertolt Brecht's use of the word *comfortable* contribute to the poem?

2. Where does the poet repeat the letter *r?*
   - Where does the poet repeat the letters *f* and *ll?*
   - Where does the poet repeat the letter *g?*

3. What is the effect of the repeated words in Line 5?

4. What is this poem really about?

MY NAME IS AESOP

1. You are Aesop. You are working on your book of fables. Make a cover for your book that hints at the stories inside.

2. Think of a saying that you could use as the moral of a fable. If it is helpful to you, write down several sayings, and give it some thought.

3. You are going to write a fable that uses your saying as the moral of the story. The title of your fable should be drawn from the animals that you use for your characters. Decide which two animals you want to use. Your fable can be poetry or prose. Don't forget to describe the setting. Don't forget to use dialogue. You want your animals to disagree with each other about something important. You will show this in the dialogue. When you have finished writing your fable, look it over to make sure you haven't left anything out. Now recopy it for your book.

4. The second fable for your book will be your prose translation of the poem, *The Butterfly and the Caterpillar.* Remember to make your sentences short. When you write a prose translation, you can have many more sentences than the poem does. You can use simpler words, too.

5. Make a Table of Contents and put your book of fables together. If you wish, add some pictures. Remember to number the pages.

GETTING THE ANGLE ON THE QUANGLE WANGLE

The Cast of Characters:

The Quangle Wangle Quee

Mr. and Mrs. Canary

The Stork

The Duck

The Owl

The Snail

The Bumble-Bee

The Frog

The Fimble Fowl (with the Corkscrew leg)

The Golden Grouse

The Pobble (who has no toes)

The small Olympian bear

The Dong (with a luminous nose)

The Blue Baboon (who plays the flute)

The Orient Calf (from the Land of Tute)

The Attery Squash

The Bisky Bat

Remember the masks you made? Now it's time to use them. Your teacher will divide the class into groups of three to six students. Has your class made masks for every character? Group 1 will make masks for the missing characters (if there are any) and create the props such as the Flute and the Mulberry moon. Group 2 will make the hat. (Make it huge, but not too huge. Don't forget about the ribbons and bibbons on every side and the bells and buttons and loops and lace.) Group 3 will write the script. Group 4 will make the Crumpetty Tree. Your teacher will assign parts. This should be a splendid production!

PERFORMANCE & MEMORY

This is it. Your big day is here.

1. Which is your favorite poem in the book? You will pick a poem, or part of a long poem, from any one of the poems in the book.

2. Write out the poem. It will probably help, in fact, if you write it out a few times.

3. Read the poem aloud several times.

4. Now it is time to memorize the poem.

5. Practice, practice, practice.

6. Practice before an audience of family members or friends.

7. Recite the poem for your class, and don't forget: Do not look down. Do not speak too quickly—say each word slowly and clearly. Speak up—loudly. Use expression in your voice. Good luck!

Mosdos Press Literature

- GLOSSARY
- INDEX OF AUTHORS AND TITLES

glossary

A

abound (uh BOWND) *v.:* are filled or supplied with

accommodation (uh KOM uh DAY shun) *n.:* place for housing and feeding

accurate (AK yuh rut) *adj.:* perfectly correct

achievement (uh CHEEV ment) *n.:* something accomplished through great effort or skill

activist (AK tih vist) *n.:* one who is very involved in groups and organizations, whose goals are to change existing policies

adamantly (ADD uh munt LEE) *adv.:* firmly and insistently; strongly and definitely

adapted (uh DAPP ted) *v.:* suited by nature or design to a particular use or situation

affidavit (AH fih DAY vit) *n.:* a written statement made with the promise to tell the truth

aide (AYD) *n.:* an assistant or helper

alarmed (uh LARMD) *adj.:* suddenly frightened or worried

altered (ALT urd) *v.:* changed

amateur (AM uh CHOOR) *n.:* not professional or expert; a person who is unskilled or inexperienced in a particular activity

ambition (am BIH shun) *n.:* a strong desire for success, fame, wealth, or the like, and the willingness to work for it

ambled (AM buld) *v.:* walked slowly and casually

analyze (AN uh LYZE) *v.:* to examine each part of something in a careful, logical way

apathy (A puh THEE) *n.:* a complete lack of interest; indifference

aristocratic (uh RISS tuh KRATT ik) *adj.:* belonging to a class of people who are educated, wealthy, and"well-born"

array (uh RAY) *n.:* an orderly grouping or arrangement, especially for troops

B

bandit *n.:* an outlaw, a robber

bank *n.:* the slope or high ground next to a river

banner *n.:* a large sign painted on cloth

barges (BAR juz) *n.:* flat-bottomed vessels, usually pushed or towed through the water, for carrying freight or passengers

barrage (buh RAZH) *n.:* a heavy, prolonged attack

bayonets (BAY uh NETS) *n.:* a long-pointed steel weapon attached to the open end of a gun

glossary

beachcomber (BEECH kohm er) *n.:* one who looks carefully (combs) along the beach for objects of interest

beckoning (BEK uh ning) *v.:* motioning to someone to come closer

belligerent (buh LIJ urr int) *adj.:* argumentative; displaying an eagerness to fight

bellows (BELL oze) *n.:* a device for producing a strong current of air

bias (BY us) *n.:* prejudice; a positive or negative feeling towards something that is not based on logic or sense of fairness

billowing (BIL oh ing) *v.:* swelling and puffing out

blazed (BLAYZD) *v.:* gleamed or glowed brightly

bluffs *n.:* cliffs

bolted (BOLT ed) *v.:* suddenly tried to break free

bombarded (bahm BAR ded) *v.:* pelted; threw objects at a target repeatedly

bounding (BOWND ing) *v.:* leaping in great steps and jumps

boycott (BOY kot) *v.:* refuse to buy, sell, or use a product

brigade (brih GAYD) *n.:* a unit of an army having two or more regiments; several brigades make up a division

broad (BRAWD) *adj.:* wide

broadside (BROAD side) *n.:* the whole side of a ship above the water line

brocades (broe KAYDZ) *n.:* expensive fabrics with raised designs, often woven with gold or silver threads

brooded (BROO did) *v.:* worried about; thought about moodily

buckled (BUK uld) *v.:* collapsed

buffeting (BUFF ih ting) *n.:* repeated hitting and pushing

buoys (BOYS) *n.:* a floating object, fastened or anchored so that it remains in one place, used as a marker for sailors

burrowing (BURR oh ing) *v.:* digging down

burrows (BURR ohz) *n.:* holes or tunnels in the ground made by an animal

C

cajole (kuh JOLE) *v.:* persuade; coax

camaraderie (KAHM uh RAD uh ree) *n.:* a feeling of close and comfortable friendship

canopy (KAN uh pee) *n.:* the cover formed by the leafy upper branches of the trees in a forest

canter (KAN ter) *n.:* an easy gallop

glossary

captivity (kap TIV ih TEE) *n.:* being held as a prisoner

cargo (KAR go) *n.:* freight carried by a ship or airplane

cavorting (kuh VORT ing) *v.:* jumping and prancing merrily about

celebrity (suh LEB rih tee) *n.:* a famous person

chap *n.:* fellow, guy

chink (CHEENK) *n.:* crack; narrow opening

churning (CHURR ning) *v.:* stirring and shaking

clasped *v.:* gripped; firmly grasped

commemoration (kuh MEM uh RAY shun) *n.:* in memory of some person or event

commuters (kum YOO ters) *n.:* people who travel to and from work

complex (kuhm PLEX) *adj.:* complicated and difficult to understand or deal with

concocted (kun KAHK ted) *v.:* made up; put together many ingredients resulting in something new and different

conflagration (KAHN fluh GRAY shun) *n.:* a huge, destructive fire

confront (kun FRONT) *v.:* meet face to face, often with a demand or accusation

congenial (kuhn JEE nee uhl) *adj.:* agreeable; pleasant

congregating (KAHNG ruh gay ting) *v.:* meeting; assembling

conscience (KAHN shuntz) *n.:* the inner sense that directs a person to choose right over wrong

conspicuous (kun SPIK yoo us) *adj.:* noticeable; standing out

constructive (kun STRUK tiv) *adj.:* helping to improve and build (the opposite of destructive)

countered (KOWN terd) *v.:* answered a question with a question

credentials (kruh DENN shulz) *n.:* documents showing that a person has privileges

crevices (KREH viss iz) *n.:* long, deep cracks

cross *adj.:* angry

curtly (KURT lee) *adv.:* briefly and a bit rudely

customary (KUSS tuh MAIR ee) *adj.:* usual

D

dart *v.:* move swiftly and suddenly

debris (duh BREE) *n.:* the remains of anything destroyed; bits of old waste matter lying about

glossary

deliberately (de LIB uh rut LEE) *adv.:* carefully and knowingly

delirious (dih LEER ee us) *adj.:* a state of illness in which a person is unconscious but has strange, dreamlike visions

deluges (DELL yooj iz) *n.:* huge rainstorms

depresses (de PRESS iz) *v.:* presses down

descended (dee SEND ed) *v.:* came down

desolate (DEH suh lut) *adj.:* empty, deserted, and lonely

desperation (DESS puh RAY shun) *n.:* a feeling of hopelessness

despondent (dih SPOND ent) *adj.:* extremely discouraged; feeling hopeless

deteriorating (dee TEER ee uh RAYT ing) *v.:* becoming worse in some or many ways

dictate (DIK tayt) *v.:* say or read aloud words so that they can be written down, typed, or recorded

diminished (dih MIN ished) *v.:* lessened

diplomat (DIP luh MAT) *n.:* a person who has been appointed by the government of their country to deal with the governments of other countries on matters concerning both

discriminated (dis KRIM ih NAY ted) *v.:* were treated unfairly because of prejudice

distinctive (diss TINK tiv) *adj.:* unusual; having a special quality or style

distract (diss TRAKT) *v.:* draw someone's attention away

divert (dy VURT) *v.:* turn aside from its intended goal

dominates (DAHM ih nayts) *v.:* rules over; controls

drifted (DRIFF ted) *v.:* slowly moved away

driftwood (DRIFT wood) *n.:* wood floating or cast ashore by a body of water

dunes (DOONZ) *n.:* sand hills

E

earnestly (UR nust lee) *adv.:* seriously, sincerely

edging (EDJ ing) *v.:* moving slowly and cautiously

eerie (EER ee) *adj.:* strange, mysterious, and somewhat frightening

elated (ee LAY ted) *adj.:* immensely happy

elation (ee LAY shun) *n.:* extreme happiness

glossary

embankment (em BANK ment) *n.:* a long mound of raised earth next to a stream or river

embraced (em BRAYST) *v.:* hugged

emerged (ee MURJD) *v.:* came out from

emetic (ee MET ik) *n.:* a medicine to make a person vomit

enduring (in DYOOR ing) *v.:* undergoing suffering with patience and determination

enigma (uh NIG muh) *n.:* a puzzling occurrence; a mystery that seems unsolvable

evacuate (ee VAK yoo AYT) *v.:* leave

excesses (EX sess iz) *n.:* extremes; unusually large amounts or degrees of something

exclusively (ex KLOO siv lee) *adv.:* only; excluding all others

excruciating (ex KROO shee AYT ing) *adj.:* intensely painful

exemplary (egg ZEMP luh ree) *adj.:* perfect; worthy of imitation

exhilaration (egg ZILL uh RAY shun) *n.:* immense and thrilling joy

exploit (ex PLOIT) *v.:* use selfishly for one's own ends

extinguished (ex TING wishd) *v.:* put out (a light or a fire)

exuberant (ex OO ber ent) *adj.:* full of high spirits and enthusiasm

F

facade (fuh SOD) *n.:* the front of a building, especially a decorative one

feeble (FEE bul) *adj.:* weak

filet knife (fih LAY NYF) *n.:* a knife used to remove the bones of meat or fish

fitful (FIT full) *adj.:* stopping and starting

flitted (FLITT ed) *v.:* flew swiftly from one place to another, settling only for a moment

forager (FOR uh jer) *n.:* one who wanders about looking for food, provisions, or some unexpected find

foreman (FOR mun) *n.:* a person in charge of a department or group of workers, as in a factory

forlorn (for LORN) *adj.:* lonely and sad

fragments (FRAG ments) *n.:* bits and pieces of something

frantically (FRAN tik lee) *adv.:* wildly and desperately

fruitlessly (FROOT luss lee) *adv.:* unsuccessfully; with no useful outcome

fund *v.:* pay for

furrow (FUR oh) *n.:* a narrow groove made in the ground by a plow

glossary

futile (FEW tuhl) *adj.:* useless, ineffective

G

gale (GAYL) *n.:* a strong wind

galley (GAL ee) *n.:* the kitchen area of a ship, plane, or camper

gap *n.:* a break or opening in a row of objects or in a wall

gaped (GAYPT) *v.:* to open or part widely

gazed (GAYZD) *v.:* looked intently

genteel (jen TEEL) *adj.:* well-bred; polite (today, used to mean overly polite)

gig (GIG) *n.:* a light boat rowed with four, six, or eight long oars

glass *n.:* mirror

glimpsed (GLIMPST) *v.:* saw for a brief moment

graffiti (gruh FEE tee) *n.:* words or pictures painted illegally on public property

grampus (GRAMP us) *n.:* a large dolphin

grizzled (GRIZ uhld) *adj.:* having gray hair

gurney (GUR nee) *n.:* a narrow, padded table on wheels used for moving patients

gutted *v.:* removed the inner parts, such as the stomach and intestines

H

hastens (HAYS ens) *v.:* hurries

hauled (HAWLD) *v.:* pulled or tugged with force

hazards (HAZZ erds) *n.:* dangers

hectic (HEK tik) *adj.:* rushed and confused

heirloom (AIR loom) *n.:* a family possession handed down from one generation to another

heist *n.:* a robbery or holdup

heralded (HAIR ul dud) *v.:* publicly welcomed

hitched *v.:* fastened, tied

hoarded (HOHRD ed) *v.:* something hidden and guarded–often, money or food

hoist (HOYST) *v.:* raise; lift

horizon (huh RI zun) *n.:* the place in the distance where the sky and earth appear to meet

hutch *n.:* a pen or enclosed coop for animals

I

idealist (i DEEL ist) *n.:* a person who is guided more by spiritual goals than practical ones

glossary

illuminated (ill LOO mih NAY ted) *v.:* lit up

imminent (IM ih nent) *adj.:* about to occur

incident (IN sih dent) *n.:* event, happening

incubating (IN kyew BAY ting) *v.:* sitting on (eggs) for the purpose of hatching

indignation (IN dig NAY shun) *n.:* anger at something because it is unfair or insulting

inert (in URT) *adj.:* still; unmoving

ingenious (in JEEN yuss) *adj.:* clever and original

ingenuity (IN juh NOO ih TEE) *n.:* creativity in solving problems or overcoming obstacles

inhabitants (in HAB ih tunts) *n.:* people or animals who live in a place

injustice (in JUST iss) *n.:* an unfair act

innovation (IN oh VAY shun) *n.:* the introduction of something new or different

inscription (in SKRIP shun) *n.:* a word or words carved on stone or other hard surface; a brief dedication or note written by hand in a book, on a photograph, or on a similar item

inspire (in SPY uhr) *v.:* fill one with a certain feeling, usually, the desire to do good

intercede (IN ter SEED) *v.:* help or defend someone by pleading or arguing on his behalf with another person

intercepted (IN ter SEP ted) *v.:* stopped someone or something on the way to its destination

issue (ISH oo) *v.:* put forth; write out an official document

L

laboriously (luh BORR ee us LEE) *adv.:* with much difficulty and effort

labyrinth (LAB uh rinth) *n.:* a complicated and confusing set of paths, through which it is difficult to find one's way

laden (LAY dun) *adj.:* very full of something

legislators (LEH jiss LAY torz) *n.:* lawmakers

level (LEH vul) *adj.:* sensible; spoken in a calm, even voice

lever (LEH ver or LEE ver) *n.:* a bar or rod

linger (LING er) *v.:* stay longer than usual

litany (LITT uh nee) *n.:* a long prayer in which many of the lines are repeated

lobby (LAH bee) *v.:* to work at influencing lawmakers to vote a certain way

glossary

loner (LO ner) *n.:* a person who has little to do with other people

lull *n.:* a temporary calm or quiet

lurched *v.:* swayed or tipped suddenly

luxurious (lug ZHUR ee us) *adj.:* rich, comfortable, and pleasurable

lyrics (LIHR iks) *n.:* the words of a song

M

makeshift (MAYK shift) *adj.:* temporary

manifest (MAN ih fest) *n.:* a list of the cargo or passengers carried by a ship, plane, truck, or train

marshes (MAR shiz) *n.:* areas of waterlogged soil, having no trees and covered with rushes, cattails, and other grasses

meditative (MEH dih TAY tiv) *adj.:* thoughtful

melodically (muh LODD ih klee) *adv.:* tunefully; with a beautiful melody

melodious (muh LOE dee us) *adj.:* tuneful; sweet-sounding

memorable (MEM uh ruh bl) *adj.:* worth remembering; easily remembered

mercilessly (MURR suh luss lee) *adv.:* without pity

methodical (meth AH dih kul) *adj.:* systematic; slow and careful

milling (MILL ing) *v.:* moving aimlessly

miserly (MY zer lee) *adv.:* stingy

momentum (mo MENT um) *n.:* a feeling or energy that increases once the action is underway

monarch (MAHN ark) *n.:* king; ruler

monotonously (muh NOT uh nuss lee) *adv.:* dully and boringly

monument (MAHN yoo ment) *n.:* any lasting evidence or outstanding example of something

motionless (MO shun luss) *adj.:* not moving, still

mottled (MOTT uld) *adj.:* marked with spots or blotches of different colors or shades

mourned (MORND) *v.:* said in a sad, sorrowful tone

mufflers *n.:* scarves

musket (MUSS kit) *n.:* an old-fashioned gun used by foot soldiers (later replaced by the rifle)

N

naive (NAH eve) *adj.:* lacking in experience, judgment, or information

glossary

naturalist (NACH ruh list) *n.:* a person who is an expert in natural history, especially a zoologist or botanist

negotiate (nuh GO she ATE) *v.:* work towards an agreement through discussion and bargaining

novelty (NAH vul tee) *n.:* new experience

O

occasional (uh KAY zhun ul) *adj.:* occurring or appearing only once in a while

omen (OH mun) *n.:* a sign that something will happen; an omen can be "good" or "evil"

optimist (AHP tuh mist) *n.:* one who generally expects things to turn out well; a person with a positive, upbeat attitude

optimistic (OPP tuh MISS tik) *adj.:* hopeful; positive; having a feeling that all will turn out well

ordeal (or DEEL) *n.:* any extremely trying or severe test or experience

P

panic (PAN ik) *n.:* a sudden, overwhelming fear

peaked (PEEKD) *adj.:* having a pointed top

peddle (PED dl) *v.:* sell

peering (PEER ing) *v.:* looking intensely, in the attempt to see something clearly

perch *n.:* a high position or resting place

periodically (PIH ree AH dik lee) *adv.:* every so often

perish (PAIR ish) *v.:* die

persisted (pur SIS ted) *v.:* continued to make a point in spite of opposition

persistence (pur SISS tuntz) *n.:* firmly keeping to a particular course of action in spite of opposition

perturbed (pur TURBD) *v.:* disturbed; troubled

pesticides (PEST ih SYDS) *n.:* chemicals used for killing insects

petition (puh TISH un) *n.:* a document, signed by many people, that makes a request or demand

piercingly (PEER sing lee) *adv.:* sharply and knowingly

plaque (PLACK) *n.:* a metal plate engraved with the name of a person being honored

plunged (PLUNJD) *v.:* threw himself about

poacher (POE cher) *n.:* one who hunts illegally on property belonging to someone else

pottering (usually puttering, PUTT er ing) *v.:* doing "odds and ends" of small jobs

pouted (POW ted) *v.:* showed discontent or ill humor in a gloomy and silent way

preened *v.:* trimmed or smoothed feathers with the beak or tongue

prejudice (PREH juh diss) *n.:* an already formed opinion not based on actual experience; an unreasoning like or dislike

premises (PREH mi suz) *n.:* a building and its grounds

proclamation (PRAHK luh MAY shun) *n.:* an official announcement

prominent (PRAHM ih nent) *adj.:* leading, important, or well-known

puckered *v.:* drew together tightly, forming wrinkles

purling (PURR ling) *adj.:* flowing with a curling or rippling motion, as a shallow stream over stones

purposefully (PUR puss full lee) *adv.:* seriously, with a goal in mind; determinedly

Q

quivering (KWIV er ing) *v.:* trembling; shaking

quizzically (KWIZ ik lee) *adv.:* questioningly

R

radiance (RAY dee unts) *n.:* shining brightness

rallied (RA leed) *v.:* brought together for a common purpose

rarely (RAIR lee) *adv.:* hardly ever

raspy (RASP ee) *adj.:* not smooth; rough and grating

raucous (RAW kus) *adj.:* loud and harsh

receding (ree SEE ding) *adj.:* returning to a lower level; moving back and further away

recruits (rih KROOTS) *n.:* new members of the army

reel *v.:* to pull out of the water by winding a fishing line around a small wheel or spool

regiments (REJ ih ments) *n.:* a unit of soldiers in an army; several regiments make up a brigade

relish (RELL ish) *n.:* great enjoyment

renovated (REN uh VAY tuhd) *v.:* restored to good condition as by repairing or remodeling

representatives (REP ree ZEN tuh TIVZ) *n.:* individuals who speak for and act on behalf of a group

reservoir (REZ urv WAHR) *n.:* a place where water is stored

glossary

resign (ree ZYN) *v.:* give up a position or job

resolved (re ZAHLVD) *v.:* firmly decided on a course of action

resounded (ree ZOWND ed) *v.:* echoed

resounding (ree ZOWN ding) *adj.:* loud and echoing

resourceful (rih SORSS ful) *adj.:* able to deal skillfully and promptly with new situations

responded (ree SPOND ed) *v.:* answered

restraint (ree STRAINT) *n.:* control, holding back

retreat (rih TREET) *v.:* move back, away from the enemy

ridicule (RID ih KYOOL) *v.:* make fun of

rigmarole (RIG muh rohl) *n.:* confused or meaningless talk

riot (RY itt) *n.:* a noisy, violent public disorder caused by a crowd of people

ruckus (RUCK iss) *n.:* uproar; a noisy commotion

rugged (RUG ged) *adj.:* rough; rocky and hilly

rural (RUH rul) *adj.:* characteristic of or having to do with the country (compare to urban: characteristic of or having to do with the city)

ruthless (ROOTH luss) *adj.:* without pity; cruel

S

salvage (SAL vuj) *v.:* to save from being destroyed or thrown out

sapling (SAPP ling) *n.:* a young tree

savage (SA vudg) *adj.:* wild; fierce

scarlet (SKAHR lut) *adj.:* of a deep red color

scorched (SKORCHD) *adj.:* slightly burned

serenely (suh REEN lee) *adv.:* calmly; peacefully

shaft *n.:* a passageway leading deep into the ground

sheath (SHEETH) *n.:* a close-fitting case for the blade of a knife or sword

shimmered *v.:* glowed and softly shone with a flickering light

shrewdly (SHROOD lee) *adv.:* sharply and cleverly

shrubs *n.:* woody plants with many separate stems, smaller than a tree

sibling (SIBB ling) *n.:* a brother or sister

sinister (SIN iss ter) *adj.:* looking a bit frightening or threatening

site (SYT) *n.:* area or exact place where something is to be located or built

sleuth (SLOOTH) *n.:* detective

spar (SPAHR) *n.:* a strong pole to which a boat's sail is attached

staggering (STAG er ing) *v.:* walking unsteadily; tottering

steadying (STED ee ing) *adj.:* calming

stealthily (STELL thuh lee) *adv.:* quietly, carefully, and secretly so as not to be discovered

stewed (STOOD) *v.:* fretted; worried; fussed

struggle (STRUH gul) *n.:* a fight

superiors (suh PIH ree urz) *n.:* higher in position; those who have greater power

surpassing (sur PASS ing) *v.:* going beyond; exceeding

surveyed (sur VAYD) *v.:* looked at; inspected

sympathetic (SIM puh THEH tik) *adj.:* to have a positive or favorable feeling about something

T

tackle (TAH kuhl) *n.:* equipment for fishing, such as lines and hooks

team (TEEM) *n.:* two or more horses, oxen, or other animals harnessed together to draw a vehicle

tersely (TURSS lee) *adv.:* briefly

thicket (THIK et) *n.:* a dense growth of bushes or small trees

thrashed *v.:* beat soundly; hit repeatedly

threaded (THRED ed) *v.:* made its way past or around obstacles

thriving (THRY ving) *adj.:* doing very well; prospering

timber (TIM ber) *n.:* trees; an area of woodland or forest

torrent (TAW rent) *n.:* a huge, rushing stream of water

toxic (TOX ik) *adj.:* poisonous

traipsing (TRAYPS ing) *v.:* tramping through

trespassing (TRESS pass ing) *v.:* entering someone's property without the owner's permission

trifle (TRY fl) *adj.:* a bit

triumphant (try UMF unt) *adj.:* expressing joy over a success or victory

triumphed (TRY umft) *v.:* rejoiced over a victory

glossary

truce (TROOSS) *n.:* a temporary peace agreement

U

undeniable (un dee NY uh bul) *adj.:* clearly real and true

union (YOON yun) *n.:* an association of workers formed to protect the rights of its members

urban (URR bun) *adj.:* having to do with a city

V

vandalized (VAN duh LYZD) *v.:* deliberately destroyed or damaged

verify (VAIR ih fy) *v.:* prove the truth of

vigorously (VIG uh russ LEE) *adv.:* energetically; forcefully

virtuous (VUR choo us) *adj.:* good; one who has good character and performs good deeds

visas (VEE zuhz) *n.:* official papers indicating that the bearer has permission to enter a particular country

vise (VYZ) *n.:* a tool with two jaws that can be adjusted to hold an object firmly

void (VOYD) *n.:* emptiness

vulnerable (VUHL nuh ruh buhl) *adj.:* easily hurt physically or emotionally

W

washout (WASH out) *n.:* (informal) a complete failure or disappointment

weaned (WEEND) *v.:* ended the period of time when a baby was fed only milk; introduced the baby to solid food

wharf (HWARF) *n.:* a pier; a wooden walkway built next to or jutting into the water so that boats can come alongside it to load or unload

wizened (WEE zund) *adj.:* withered; shriveled

wounded (WOON ded) *adj.:* injured

wrath (RATH) *n.:* fierce anger

writhed (RYTHD) *v.:* twisted and turned in pain

index of authors and titles